MORPHEME ORDER AND SEMANTIC SCOPE

Athapaskan languages are well known for their intricate morphology, in particular the complexity of their verbs. The significance of these languages for linguistic theory is widely acknowledged. In this book Keren Rice offers a rich typological survey of morpheme ordering in Athapaskan verbs, with implications for both synchronic grammar and language change. Arguing against a view that sees morpheme order in Athapaskan languages as templatic and essentially without principle, she shows that verb structure is in fact widely predictable across languages if appropriate syntactic factors and an overarching principle of semantic scope are taken into account. The presentation also includes a detailed study of argument and aspectual systems. This landmark volume is the first major comparative study of its type for the Athapaskan language family, combining descriptive depth with a contemporary theoretical perspective. Clear and insightful, it will be welcomed by Athapaskanists, typologists, and historical and theoretical linguists alike.

Keren Rice is professor of linguistics at the University of Toronto, where she also coordinates the university's Aboriginal Studies Program. She has previously written a grammar of Slave, an Athapaskan language of Canada. This book was awarded the Leonard Bloomfield Book Award. She has also written numerous articles and co-edited several books on Athapaskan languages and linguistics.

CAMBRIDGE STUDIES IN LINGUISTICS

General editors: S. R. ANDERSON, J. BRESNAN, B. COMRIE,
W. DRESSLER, C. EWEN, R. HUDDLESTON, R. LASS,
D. LIGHTFOOT, J. LYONS, P. H. MATTHEWS, R. POSNER,
S. ROMAINE, N. V. SMITH, N. VINCENT

Morpheme Order and Semantic Scope

CAMBRIDGE STUDIES IN LINGUISTICS
In this series

68 LJILJANA PROGOVAC: *Negative and positive polarity: A binding approach*
69 R. M. W. DIXON: *Ergativity*
70 YAN HUANG: *The syntax and pragmatics of anaphora*
71 KNUD LAMBRECHT: *Information structure and sentence form: Topic, focus, and the mental representations of discourse referents*
72 LUIGI BURZIO: *Principles of English stress*
73 JOHN A. HAWKINS: *A performance theory of order and constituency*
74 ALICE C. HARRIS and LYLE CAMPBELL: *Historical syntax in cross-linguistic perspective*
75 LILIANE HAEGEMAN: *The syntax of negation*
76 PAUL GORRELL: *Syntax and parsing*
77 GUIGLIELMO CINQUE: *Italian syntax and Universal Grammar*
78 HENRY SMITH: *Restrictiveness in case theory*
79 D. ROBERT LADD: *Intonational phonology*
80 ANDREA MORO: *The raising of predicates: Predicative noun phrases and the theory of clause structure*
81 ROGER LASS: *Historical linguistics and language change*
82 JOHN M. ANDERSON: *A notional theory of syntactic categories*
83 BERND HEINE: *Possession: Cognitive sources, forces and grammaticalization*
84 NOMI ERTESCHIK-SHIR: *The dynamics of focus structure*
85 JOHN COLEMAN: *Phonological representations: Their names, forms and powers*
86 CHRISTINA Y. BETHIN: *Slavic prosody: Language change and phonological theory*
87 BARBARA DANCYGIER: *Conditionals and prediction: Time, knowledge and causation in English*
88 CLAIRE LEFEBVRE: *Creole genesis and the acquisition of grammar: The case for Haitian Creole*
89 HEINZ GIEGERICH, *Lexical strata in English: Morphological causes, phonological effects*

Supplementary volumes

LILIANE HAEGEMAN: *Theory and description in generative syntax: A case study in West Flemish*
A. E. BACKHOUSE: *The lexical field of taste: A semantic study of Japanese taste terms*
NICKOLAUS RITT: *Quantity adjustment: Vowel lengthening and shortening in early Middle English*

Morpheme Order and Semantic Scope

WORD FORMATION IN THE
ATHAPASKAN VERB

KEREN RICE
University of Toronto

CAMBRIDGE
UNIVERSITY PRESS

PUBLISHED BY THE PRESS SYNDICATE OF THE UNIVERSITY OF CAMBRIDGE
The Pitt Building, Trumpington Street, Cambridge, United Kingdom

CAMBRIDGE UNIVERSITY PRESS
The Edinburgh Building, Cambridge CB2 2RU, UK   http://www.cup.cam.ac.uk
40 West 20th Street, New York, NY 10011-4211, USA   http://www.cup.org
10 Stamford Road, Oakleigh, Melbourne 3166, Australia
Ruiz de Alarcón 13, 28014 Madrid, Spain

© Keren Rice 2000

This book is in copyright. Subject to statutory exception
and to the provisions of relevant collective licensing agreements,
no reproduction of any part may take place without
the written permission of Cambridge University Press.

First published 2000

Printed in the United States of America

Typeface Times Roman 10.25/13 pt.   *System* LaTeX 2_ε [TB]

A catalog record for this book is available from the British Library.

Library of Congress Cataloging in Publication Data
Rice, Keren, 1949–
Morpheme order and semantic scope: word formation in the
Athapaskan verb / Keren Rice.
p.   cm. – (Cambridge studies in linguistics)
Includes bibliographical references.
ISBN 0-521-58354-3 (hardback)
1. Athapascan languages – Verb phrase.   2. Athapascan languages –
Word order.   3. Athapascan languages – Morphemics.   I. Title.
II. Series.
PM641.R53   1999
497'.2 – dc21   99-20442
                                                                                    CIP

ISBN 0 521 58354 3 hardback

Contents

Preface *page* xi

1 Introduction: Beginning the Journey   1

PART I. FIRST STEPS

2 Introducing the Problem   9
    2.1 The Templatic Nature of the Athapaskan Verb   9
    2.2 Templatic Properties of the Verb   10
    2.3 The Verb and Word Formation   15

3 Global Uniformity and Local Variability:
A Possible Account   20
    3.1 Two Hypotheses   20
    3.2 Defining Scope   24
    3.3 Theoretical Preliminaries   26

PART II. THE LEXICAL ITEMS

4 First Stop: Introducing the Lexical Items   33
    4.1 Definitions   33
    4.2 Preverbs   35
    4.3 Quantificational Elements   41
    4.4 Incorporates   68
    4.5 Other Lexical Material   71
    4.6 Summary   73

5 A Brief Side Trip: The Position of the Verb Stem   74

6 Ordering of the Lexical Items   79
    6.1 On the Ordering of the Lexical Items   79
    6.2 Principles of Ordering   82

	6.3	Ordering within the Preverbs	84
	6.4	Ordering within the Quantificational Elements	101
	6.5	Ordering within the Incorporates	106
	6.6	Summary	107
	6.7	Ordering among Constituents	107
	6.8	The Other Lexical Items (Negative, Inceptive)	121
	6.9	Summary	124
7	Voice/Valence		126
	7.1	Background Assumptions	127
	7.2	Productive Uses	128
	7.3	Middles and Causatives	158
	7.4	Idiosyncratic Nature	165
	7.5	The Lexical Entry	168
	7.6	Summary	169
8	Summary: Lexical Items		171

PART III. THE FUNCTIONAL ITEMS

9	An Introduction to the Functional Elements		175
10	Pronominals		180
	10.1	Subject Form Pronominals	180
	10.2	The Status of Object Inflection	203
	10.3	On Noncanonical Subjects	210
	10.4	A Return to the Ordering Questions	222
	10.5	Problems for Object-Subject Inflection Ordering	224
	10.6	Summary: The Pronominal Inflection System	244
11	The Aspect System		246
	11.1	Aspect 1: Viewpoint Aspect	246
	11.2	Aspect 2: Situation Type Aspect	251
	11.3	Ordering within Aspect	281
	11.4	On the Role of the Suffixes	283
	11.5	On the Position of the Suffixes	295
	11.6	Beyond Slave	303
	11.7	Ordering and Combinatorics	310
	11.8	Summary	320
	11.9	Appendix: A Comparative Look: Situation Aspect and Aspectually Determining Morphemes	321
12	Qualifiers and Their Ordering		324
	12.1	The Qualifiers: Content	324

Contents

12.2	The Ordering of Qualifiers	332
12.3	Summary	341

13 On the Ordering of Functional Items — 342
- 13.1 The Ordering of Objects and Situation Aspect — 342
- 13.2 The Ordering of First/Second Person Subjects and Aspect — 346
- 13.3 The Ordering of Subject Number and Aspect — 348
- 13.4 The Ordering of Subject Number and Qualifiers — 350
- 13.5 The Ordering of Noun Class Markers — 353
- 13.6 The Ordering of Pronouns and the Middle Voice Qualifier: Semipassives in Navajo — 355
- 13.7 Situation Aspect and *d/n* Qualifiers in Navajo — 356
- 13.8 A Navajo 'Floating' Qualifier — 357
- 13.9 Interacting Systems — 359

PART IV. A VIEW OF THE LEXICON

14 The Scope Hypothesis and Simplifying the Lexicon — 369

15 Evidence from the Lexicon — 373
- 15.1 Predictions — 373
- 15.2 Summary — 383

PART V. THE END OF THE JOURNEY

16 Looking Back, Looking Ahead — 387
- 16.1 On the Nature of the Lexical Entry — 387
- 16.2 On the Distinction between Inflection and Derivation — 391
- 16.3 On the Domain of Word Formation — 393
- 16.4 On the Role of Scope in Determining Morpheme Order — 394
- 16.5 On Consequences for a Template Model — 395
- 16.6 On Consequences for Historical Change — 396
- 16.7 For the Future — 398

PART VI. APPENDIXES

1 Templates and Affix Ordering — 401
- 1.1 The Template — 401
- 1.2 Pan-Athapaskan Templates — 404

2 The Languages — 406
- 2.1 Language Classification — 406
- 2.2 Why These Languages? — 408

3 Summary of Constraints and Language Differences — 409
    3.1 Ordering Principles — 409
    3.2 Interfaces — 412
    3.3 Differences Not Related to Scope — 412
    3.4 Idiosyncrasies — 414

Notes — 415
References — 431
Name Index — 443
Languages Index — 447
Subject Index — 449

Preface

Whenever linguists discover that I work on Athapaskan languages, I can anticipate the first question that they will ask – however could a child come to learn the order of morphemes in the verb of one of these languages? The order of morphemes seems to be completely without rhyme or reason. Morpheme order is thus a question that is everpresent in one's mind when studying languages of this family. I first began to tackle this problem in 1991, with work on the so-called disjunct prefixes of the Athapaskan verb. A crosslinguistic survey revealed something very striking – little variation existed across the family in terms of the ordering of these elements. I began to feel that I was on the road to an explanation of the ordering of this part of the verb, but the so-called conjunct portion of the verb still left me baffled. One day in the early 1990s Chomsky gave a talk here at the University of Toronto, and I began to get some glimmerings; at least the ordering began to look somewhat less random than it had hitherto seemed. It was after this that I decided that this was a research question that I had to pursue. The quest to come to some personal understanding of morpheme order took me several years, as there was much I had to learn in many different arenas. I still have many questions about morpheme ordering, probably at least as many as I began with, but I feel that I am on a road to understanding what makes the morpheme ordering learnable. It is this journey that I take the reader on in this book.

The thanks due in writing a book like this are especially numerous. First, thank you to the Killam Foundation for providing me with the very valued release from teaching responsibilities that gave me the time that I needed to undertake this project. I could not have done the basic research required for this book without that time. Second, thank you to the 1995 organizers of the Linguistic Institute for inviting me to teach a course in the structure of Athapaskan languages. That course too gave me the opportunity to do the basic research for this book. Many thanks to the students and visitors in that class for their interest, enthusiasm, and support.

My greatest debt of thanks goes to Leslie Saxon. Much of the work on pronominals arises out of joint work, as does much of the discussion of the iterative in chapter 4. I have tried many ideas out on her, and she has read much of this manuscript, but she is not responsible for any misinterpretations on my part. Her support has been invaluable to me in finishing this book.

Sharon Hargus has also been of invaluable help, in both listening and helping with Babine-Witsuwit'en data. Many thanks to her for her support.

The community of Athapaskan linguists has heard many of the ideas in this book. The details and precision of the excellent work by Athapaskan linguists have allowed for the kind of research that I have done in this book; without this research to build on, this book would have been impossible. Many, many thanks to Ed Cook, Aryeh Faltz, Ted Fernald, Victor Golla, Eloise Jelinek, Dagmar Jung, Jim Kari, Andrej Kibrik, Michael Krauss, Sally Midgette, Bill Poser, Brian Potter, Chad Thompson, Siri Tuttle, MaryAnn Willie, and Bob Young. I hope that I have not forgotten anyone, and I apologize if I have. This book could not have been conceived without Jim Kari's work to build on.

Thanks are also due to many other linguists, listed here in alphabetical order, for discussion of various issues in this book: Sasha Aikenvald, Mark Baker, Susana Béjar, Joan Bybee, Elizabeth Cowper, Scott Delancey, Bob Dixon, Tom Givón, Ken Hale, Alana Johns, Diane Massam, Marianne Mithun, David Perlmutter, Betsy Ritter, Carlota Smith, Peggy Speas, Sally Thomason, Lisa Travis, and Barbara Unterbeck. None of these people are responsible for misinterpretations on my part, and I thank each one of them.

Thanks too to audiences at various colloquia and conferences where work that is part of this book was presented. These include the University of Calgary, the University of Essex, the University of Cologne, the University of Toronto, the University of Oregon, the 1997 Workshop in Challenges in Inflection and Derivation at the University of Sussex, the 1994 Conference on Configurations at the University of Québec at Montréal, and the 1997 Workshop on Voice and Valency at Australia National University, sponsored by the Centre for Research on Linguistic Typology. Many thanks to the people at the Alaska Native Language Center, University of Alaska, Fairbanks, for their enormous hospitality when I visited for a week in April 1996.

This book could not have been done without the numerous speakers of the languages. The Slave speakers are thanked individually in Rice 1989; here I would like to again thank Lucy Ann Yakeleya for her help in recent years. See the sources for direct acknowledgment of the work of other individuals.

I also owe a debt of thanks to the wonderful people at Cambridge University Press – Judith Ayling for encouraging me to take on this project and Steve Anderson, Christine Bartels, Beatrice Santorini, and Helen Wheeler for seeing it through.

Finally, my family, Arthur Jacobs, Rachel Jacobs, and Hannah Jacobs, have shown great forbearance with my long hours in front of the computer, my books spread out over the floor, my sometimes inability to respond appropriately when I have been otherwise preoccupied. I don't know if they really understand what this project is about, but they have demonstrated extreme patience with its long gestation.

1

Introduction: Beginning the Journey

Athapaskan languages are often thought of as the ultimate challenge by linguists interested in issues of morphosyntax, and linguists working on these languages are alternately admired and pitied. The languages have notoriously complex verb morphology, with the verb typically described as consisting of a stem and a number of prefixes, both inflectional and derivational, whose ordering is unpredictable and must be stipulated through the use of position class morphology, or a template. In addition, phonological patterning in the verb is typically also considered to be unpredictable, and some type of boundary information is built into the template. It often appears as if any generalization that one draws about morphosyntax is falsified by the verb of some Athapaskan language. As a result, the bulk of work on Athapaskan languages has taken as its primary concern aspects of verb morphology. This book represents yet another contribution to that area. It concerns a topic that has garnered much attention in Athapaskan languages, the ordering of morphemes within the verb. My contribution, as I discuss in this chapter, is to question the notion of a template as a word formation device. Instead, I propose that morpheme ordering is to a large degree regulated by principles of scope.

Consider first some of the oddities exhibited by a verb of the description in the last paragraph. First, template morphology is highly marked in languages of the world (see, for example, Myers 1987, Rice 1991, 1993, Speas 1984, 1987, 1990, 1991a,b, and, from a somewhat different perspective, Baker 1988, 1996). As pointed out by Myers 1987, if template morphology is required, then three types of morphological systems exist — concatenative systems, nonconcatenative systems, and templatic systems — with the last restricted to only a very few language families.

Second, Athapaskan languages have been claimed to exhibit particularly extreme templates. For example, it is generally observed that inflection stands outside of derivation rather than inside of or interspersed with derivation (e.g., Anderson 1982, 1988, Beard 1995, Bybee 1985a). In the verb of Athapaskan languages, however, inflectional morphemes are, on the surface, interleaved with derivational morphemes.

Third, it is generally claimed that within morphological systems dependencies are strictly local (e.g., Allen 1978, Lieber 1980, Siegel 1978), with morphological subcategorization frames referring only to adjacent elements. Athapaskan languages are rife with discontinuous dependencies between morphemes within the verb.

Fourth, languages tend to exhibit some functional unity in positioning morphemes with respect to each other. Athapaskan languages do not appear to exhibit such unity. For instance, subjects can be marked in more than one position in the verb, aspect is indicated in more than one position of the verb, and a position can house material of disparate functions.

The Athapaskan verb thus appears to counterexemplify many claims that have been made about universal properties of language. It is therefore a worthy, and formidable, object of study. In this book I examine the verb of Athapaskan languages anew, trying to show that the deeper understanding of the Athapaskan verb that has been achieved over the past few years through detailed studies of several of the languages leads us to a very different conception of the verb than that traditionally held.

Before turning to the verb, I would like to justify some of the decisions that underlie the focus of this book. First is the decision to look beyond a template as a mechanism for accounting for word formation in Athapaskan languages. A template, as discussed in the Athapaskan literature (see Kari 1989 for the most complete and in-depth justification of templates; see chapter 2 for discussion), is a surface mechanism that orders the morphemes of the verb. In Kari's view, the template is independent of word formation; he argues that word formation follows principles of universal grammar, but that word formation is not reflected in the surface ordering of morphemes. Rather, the morphemes are slotted into a template in an order that obscures the word formation processes.

Here I examine briefly a few of the predictions of template morphology. Suppose that morphemes within a word are ordered in a random way, specified by a template. What properties might one expect to find in looking at languages of this morphological type? One potential property is that languages within a family might differ with respect to morpheme order. Since morpheme order is not a consequence of principles but rather of stipulation, one might expect that individual languages would have changed in different ways from their common ancestor. This is in fact a property of some systems.

For example, in studies of clitic ordering in Romance dialects, Auger 1994, Bonet 1991, 1995, Cummins and Roberge 1994, Perlmutter 1971, and others have found that preverbal clitics may occur in different orders in the different languages and across dialects within a language. They argue that the ordering of clitics is not a consequence of syntactic or semantic factors but simply given by a postsyntactic template. The ordering of the clitics provides no clue to structure. Thus, if the ordering of elements within the verb differs randomly from one language to the next, the template analysis is supported. If, on the other hand, regular patterns that crosscut the languages are found, one must question whether the theoretical device of a template is appropriate.

Another property that one might expect to find in a template system is that, for any given language, morpheme ordering is completely fixed, modulo any systematic phonological processes that modify the order. This too is a property of the Romance clitics. While different orderings exist when the language group is examined as a whole, when any individual dialect is studied, ordering is fixed within it. If this kind of ordering is found across the languages within the Athapaskan family, templates would appear to be an appropriate device for accounting for the structure of the verb. If, on the other hand, some variations in ordering are found within an individual language that cannot be attributed to phonological processes, the use of templates must again be questioned.

Languages that exhibit template morphology thus have a set of morphological properties that are distinct from properties of languages that are not best described in such a way. A return to this issue within the Athapaskan language family is in order to see if the languages really are best accounted for by the device of a template.

A second decision is to study a number of Athapaskan languages rather than to focus on a single one. This decision has both positive and negative consequences. The negative ones are obvious – it is hard to do in-depth crosslanguage studies of this sort and do justice to every language examined. However, I believe that the positive consequences outweigh this. It is often difficult to tell from the study of a single language whether a pattern in language is something odd and unusual about that language, or whether it is part of a syndrome. It is only by examining related languages that we can sort out the language-particular idiosyncrasies and the systematic patterns; see, for example, Croft 1990, Hale 1998, and Hale and Platero 1996 for similar arguments. For instance, the fact that all Athapaskan languages show the odd pattern of intermingling what are traditionally considered to be inflectional and derivational morphology leads one to wonder just what it is about these languages that makes this a persistent pattern.

The goal of this book is to examine the Athapaskan language family from two perspectives that I term 'global uniformity' and 'local variability'. Global uniformity refers to the properties that are common across the language family; local variability concerns the ways in which the languages differ. I argue that the languages show a tremendous amount of global uniformity that is due to general principles of grammar. Athapaskan languages also show local variability – the ordering of morphemes within the verb in different languages can differ, and in fact even within a single language some variability is possible. I argue that this variability is principled rather than the random type of variability predicted by the template model. In particular, I argue that there is an overarching principle of scope, or semantic compositionality, that determines the ordering of morphemes within the verb of Athapaskan languages, and that requires morphemes of greater scope to occur in a fixed position with respect to morphemes within their scope. Specifically, in Athapaskan languages morphemes of greater scope appear to the right of morphemes within their scope. Such a principle is not a surprising one – the relationship between morpheme order and scope is one that has often been noted in various theoretical approaches (e.g., Baker 1988, Bybee 1985a, Cherchia and McConnell-Ginet 1990, Foley and van Valin 1984, Frawley 1992, Greenberg 1966, van Valin 1993). This principle accounts for global uniformity: given a universal scope relationship, the morphemes could not be ordered any other way. It also accounts for a certain amount of local variability: in some cases, given two morphemes A and B, either A may occur in the scope of B or, on a different reading, B may occur in the scope of A. In this case too scope is relevant, with variability related to the possibility of differing scopal relations. There are also times when this principle is irrelevant – morphemes may have no scopal relationship to each other. In this case we again find variability across the family and, at times, within a language. Finally, when the scopal principle is examined more carefully, it turns out to encompass a number of different subprinciples that may interact in different ways in different languages, again creating some variability across the family.

The argument that morpheme order in the Athapaskan verb is to a large degree predictable from a principle of scope forms the major thrust of this book. A second, and subsidiary, goal of the book also involves taking a different perspective on the verb, this time with respect to structure. In discussions of the morphology of the verb of Athapaskan languages, it is generally assumed that the verb is formed lexically (e.g., Hargus 1988, Kari 1989, 1992, Randoja 1990) – this is apparent in the very choice of the term 'morphology' to describe the structure of the verb word. But recent work has suggested that this standard assumption may be wrong, and that the verb 'word' is a clause formed in the syntax (see, for example, Rice 1993, 1998 and Speas 1990). The second goal of the book is therefore to argue for the hypothesis that the Athapaskan verb is a word from a phonological perspective but a phrase from a morphosyntactic perspective. This conception of the verb offers a new way of addressing a number of problems that have occupied Athapaskanists but for which no clear solution has been forthcoming – for instance, the problem of what counts as inflection and what as derivation.

To meet these two goals, I undertake an examination of much of what is assumed about the Athapaskan verb. Major sections are devoted to reanalyses of the position classes posited for the verb. In particular, the functional material in the verb is the object of detailed study.

Before closing this chapter, a brief discussion of the object of study, the Athapaskan language family, is in order. Athapaskan languages are spoken in three geographically discontinuous regions of North America. Northern languages are located in parts of the U.S. state of Alaska, the Canadian Yukon and Northwest Territories, and the Canadian provinces of British Columbia, Alberta, Saskatchewan, and Manitoba. Apachean languages are spoken in the Southwest of the United States, including Arizona, Colorado, New Mexico, and Utah. The Pacific Coast languages are located in the United States in northern California and Oregon. A time depth of 2,000 years separation is posited, with the Pacific Coast group having split off first. See appendix 2 for a list of languages. The languages are similar in verb morphology, with a morphologically rich verb, as will become clear in this book.

This book is organized in four parts as follows. The first part provides a setting. The goals of chapter 2 are twofold. I define template morphology and examine the properties that Athapaskan languages exhibit that have led to the claim that they have template morphology, and I review accounts in the Athapaskan literature of word formation. Chapter 3 sets out the principle of scope. The second part of the book tests the hypothesis that ordering is fixed in the presence of scopal relations and variable in the absence of scopal relations among the lexical morphemes of the verb. The third part extends this hypothesis to the functional items and includes a study of two major functional systems of the verb, the aspectual system and the pronominal system. Each of these parts begins with an overview of the content of the morphemes belonging to the category discussed. The fourth part examines the lexicon and unites the ideas introduced throughout.

We are now ready to begin our journey into the mysteries of the Athapaskan verb. I hope that readers find this journey as exciting, tantalizing, stimulating, sometimes frustrating, but always provocative, as I have.

PART I

FIRST STEPS

2

Introducing the Problem

Athapaskan languages have verbs that are extraordinarily complex, and that pose a challenge to theories of morphosyntactic structure (see, for example, Aronoff 1994, Hargus 1988, Rice 1993, 1998, Speas 1984, 1987, 1990, 1991a,b, Spencer 1991, Travis 1992, for discussion). The verb word is complex in many ways: it is morphologically rich, the surface ordering of morphemes is apparently without reason, discontinuous dependencies are frequent, and blocking effects between morphemes of identical shape but different meaning are abundant.

The goal of this chapter is to outline the structure of an Athapaskan verb as traditionally described and to examine the claim that a template is required to define the ordering of morphemes within the verb.

2.1 The Templatic Nature of the Athapaskan Verb

As discussed in chapter 1, the verb in Athapaskan languages is typically described as consisting of a template, or string of fixed order positional classes. The template orders the morphemes, and each morpheme is marked lexically for the position in the template that it occurs in. In addition, phonological boundary types are lexically associated with the different morphemes in order to account for their phonological properties.

A template for Slave ([slevi]), adapted from Rice 1989, is given in (1). See appendix 1 for a list of templates proposed in the literature for a number of languages of the family. Terminology will be clarified throughout the book; I do not attempt to define terms here.

(1) preverb # quantificational elements # incorporate # object % third person subject % qualifier + subsituation aspect + situation aspect + viewpoint aspect + 1/2 person subject = voice/valence + root + aspect suffix

Kari 1989 proposes the template in (2) for Ahtna ([atnə]). (This is slightly modified to reflect terminology used in this book; see appendix 1 for Kari's original template.)

(2) preverb + iterative + distributive + incorporate + thematic # third person plural plus y + direct object + first person plural + indefinite object-subject + y-thematic + third person plural subject = areal qualifier + conative + inceptive + d qualifier + n qualifier + z + gh qualifier % transitional + s perfective-negative + situation aspect + viewpoint aspect + subject [voice/valence + root + suffixes

The template includes morphological information (basic role of morphemes in a position), ordering information, and phonological information (represented by boundary symbols #, %, +, [, and =). Details of the morphology are developed throughout the book.

2.2 Templatic Properties of the Verb

In the rest of this chapter, I examine the properties of templates from two perspectives. First is a study of how the term 'template' has been used in the morphology literature, and second is an examination of the use of the template within the Athapaskan literature.

Spencer 1991 provides a detailed discussion of the properties of languages with verbs characterized by template or position class morphology. As he says, "What is striking about such languages is that it is difficult or impossible to analyze the formation of such complex words as the addition of affixes one by one to a stem. Rather, we seem to find that each affix has its position in the string and optional affixes are slotted into this string, at the appropriate point in the sequence, as required" (Spencer 1991:208). Spencer takes Navajo as his primary exemplar of template morphology.

The general notion of a template is well captured by Inkelas 1993. She argues that languages exist "in which morphemes or morpheme classes are organized into a total linear ordering that has no apparent connection to syntactic, semantic, or even phonological representation" (Inkelas 1993:560).

Simpson and Withgott 1986, in a detailed discussion of the definition of template morphology, distinguish template morphology from layered morphology, or morphology exhibiting constituent structure, on the basis of several criteria. The ones in the following list are summarized from Spencer 1991:212–213; see also Stump 1998:33–35 for discussion.

2.2 Templatic Properties of the Verb

i. Zero morphemes are prevalent in template morphology but not in layered morphology.
ii. Layered morphology gives rise to headed structures, template morphology doesn't.
iii. Layered morphology is constrained by some principle of adjacency, template morphology isn't.
iv. Layered morphology doesn't permit an 'inner' morpheme to be chosen on the basis of what an 'outer' morpheme will be, template morphology permits this kind of 'lookahead.'

In general, Athapaskan languages can be said, at least superficially, to exhibit all of the properties of template morphology languages, as discussed in what follows. One of the goals of this book is to argue that, at least in the Athapaskan language family, these are superficial properties only, and that when the languages are understood in greater depth there is reason to think that they actually share properties with layered morphology languages.

2.2.1 Zero Morphemes

Simpson and Withgott 1986 argue that zero morphemes are prevalent in template morphology but not in layered morphology. A number of the positions in the templates in (1) and (2) are often argued to contain zero morphemes. Among these are a null voice/valence, a null viewpoint aspect (imperfective), a null situation aspect, and, in some analyses, a null subject (non-first/second person).

2.2.2 Discontinuous Dependencies

Simpson and Withgott 1986 also argue that template morphology may exhibit discontinuous dependencies. Within the string defined in (1), many discontinuous dependencies are argued to exist. For instance, many verb roots must occur with a particular qualifier; some Slave examples are given in (3). The verb 'be afraid, scared' has a prefix *n* and the stem *ji* (3a).[1] The verbs 'lie' and 'talk' always occur with the areal marker *go*. These can be separated by a number of different morphemes; the examples show situation aspect, viewpoint aspect, and subject intervening between the first and second elements of these complex verbs. The lexical entry is shown on the first line, a verb word on the second line, and the internal morphology of this word on the third line.

(3) a. n-ji   'be afraid, be scared'
 nehji   'I am afraid, scared.'
 ne qualifier + h 1sg Subject + ji stem
 b. go-ts'i   'lie'
 guíts'i   'We laugh.'
 go areal Object + í 1pl Subject + ts'i 'lie'
 c. go-de   'talk'
 goyide   'I talked.'
 go areal Object + y situation aspect + i viewpoint aspect/1sg Subject + de 'talk'

Some adverbial-type items are treated as complex; for example, some preverbs obligatorily occur with a particular qualifier. Slave examples are given in (4), where the preverb *ná* and the qualifier *n* both occur. In this semantic class of verbs, these are inseparable – one does not occur without the other, and they are assumed to constitute a single lexical entry (see, for instance, Hargus 1988 and Rice 1989).

(4) a. **ná**kiney$\underset{\sim}{\text{i}}$ht'u
 ná preverb + ki 3pl acting on 3sg + ne qualifier + y situation aspect + $\underset{\sim}{\text{i}}$ viewpoint aspect + h voice/valence + t'u 'action with fist, uncontrolled'
 'They punched him/her/it.'
 b. **ná**seney$\underset{\sim}{\text{i}}$ta
 ná preverb + se 1sg Object + ne qualifier + y situation aspect + $\underset{\sim}{\text{i}}$ viewpoint aspect + ta 'action with foot, uncontrolled'
 'S/he kicked me.'

Discontinuous dependencies can also be found between certain pronominals and voice/valence morphemes. For instance, the presence of a reflexive or reciprocal direct object requires the presence of the middle voice marker. In addition, the *d* self-benefactive (for oneself) also requires this voice marker.

2.2.3 Metathesis

Spencer 1991:209–210 suggests that template languages may exhibit unusual phonological properties such as metathesis. In this section I briefly discuss this process, which displaces morphemes from where the template would have them.

2.2 Templatic Properties of the Verb

Many Athapaskan verbs exhibit some metathesis effects within the verb. As Hargus 1995a points out, metathesis effects may be triggered by syllable structure and other phonological constraints. Thus affix order may be affected by phonological processes. For example, in Navajo the unspecified object /'/ (glottal stop) generally precedes the unspecified human subject [zh], as in (5a).[2] However, if a vowel precedes, then the object and subject metathesize, as in (5b), according to the rule in (5c). In these data, I do not provide full morpheme-by-morpheme breakdowns, but boldface the portion of the verb relevant to the metathesis process and separate morphemes with hyphens.

(5) Navajo (Young and Morgan 1987)
 a. **'-a-zh**-d-oo-yį́į́ł
  ' a unspecified Object + zh unspecified human Subject
  'He'll eat something.' (67)
 b. ni-**zh-'**-nd-oo- ł-bąs
  zh unspecified human person Subject + ' unspecified Object
  'He'll park (an unspecified wheeled object).' (68)
 c. V ' zh C → V zh ' C
  1 2 3 4   1 3 2 4

This metathesis occurs in a well-defined phonological environment, a type of metathesis that is not confined to template morphology. See chapters 12 and 13 for additional discussion.

In the Navajo example in (5), there is a phonological condition for metathesis. In addition, metathesis may involve the interchange of two affixes with no apparent phonological conditioning. One such Navajo case is cited by Spencer. In (6), the unspecified object /'/ and the qualifier /d/ appear in an unusual order. The unspecified object generally precedes the qualifier (not illustrated), but in this case, it follows.

(6) Navajo (Spencer 1991:211)
 b-a-**di-'**-n-í-'ą
 b 3 oblique Object + a postposition + d qualifier + ' unspecified Object + n situation aspect + í viewpoint aspect/1sg Subject +'ą
 'handle compact object, perfective'
 'I loaned small round object to him.'

It is this type of unconditioned metathesis that Spencer notes as an unusual property of template morphology. This property would be unexpected in a language with layered morphology where compositionality is argued to be a primary factor in determining morpheme order.

Hargus 1988 discusses several cases of metathesis in Sekani. I give a single example here; see chapter 12 for additional illustration.

(7) a. Qualifier ɬ + inceptive *d*:
ɬə-d-a-jìh-e
ɬə qualifier + d inceptive + a future + jìh 'be sweet' + e suffix
'S/he will be sweet.' (Hargus 1988:111)
b. Inceptive *d* + qualifier ɬ:
də-ɬ-a-jìh-e
də inceptive + ɬ qualifier + a future + jìh 'be sweet' + e suffix
'S/he will be sweet.'

Here, two different orders of the morphemes *d* inceptive and ɬ qualifier are possible.

The unconditioned morphological metatheses are rather odd and should be kept in mind as the reader continues through this book. If a template defines a rigid ordering of elements, then it is an important issue why metathesis can break up the rigid ordering demanded by the template in the absence of conditioning phonological factors.

2.2.4 Other Templatic Properties

Simpson and Withgott 1986 identify two further properties of templates, namely that template morphology does not involve headed structures and that it allows lookahead, where an inner morpheme can be chosen on the basis of an outer morpheme. I will not discuss headedness here, but examine choice of one morpheme by another.

Whether an inner morpheme can be chosen by an outer morpheme depends on what one defines as inner and outer. Different models of word formation have been proposed in the Athapaskan literature; some of these are discussed in section 2.3. If one assumes a strictly linear model of word formation, where affixes closer to the stem are added before affixes further from the stem, then Athapaskan languages indeed demonstrate inner morphemes being chosen by outer morphemes. For instance, the reflexive, a direct object, requires the presence of the nonadjacent middle voice marker, a morpheme that is closer to the stem. In addition, as discussed in chapter 11, preverbs and quantificational elements are generally said to be involved in the choice of situation aspect markers, which are closer to the stem.

To conclude, Athapaskan languages have surface prototypical properties of languages that are considered to have template morphology.

2.3 The Verb and Word Formation

Given the complex nature of the Athapaskan verb, word formation has long been a topic of interest in the Athapaskan literature. While the Athapaskan verb is generally described by a template, the template itself is not always thought to provide insight into the formation of the verb. This is because in the Athapaskan literature the template is often treated as a surface constraint that describes morpheme order rather than as a dynamic model that describes word formation.

Three basic views regarding word formation can be identified in the Athapaskan literature. First is the view best exemplified by Kari 1989, 1990, 1992, based on Hoijer 1946a, 1946b, Sapir and Hoijer 1967, Young and Morgan 1987, and others; a closely related model is developed in Randoja 1990. According to this perspective, word formation is a complex series of processes involving several layerings, with derivational affixation preceding inflectional affixation. The starting point in the model of word formation is called the verb theme in the Athapaskan literature. The theme is equivalent to the basic lexical entry – it includes all the material that must be present, no matter what derivational and inflectional morphology is performed. A root is a necessary component of the verb theme. A verb theme often also includes a lexicalized voice/valence marker. In addition, qualifiers, certain object pronouns, and preverbs may be part of the verb theme, meaning that they can be assigned no independent meaning but are simply listed as part of the basic lexical entry. Verb themes can be viewed as similar to idiomatic expressions; see chapter 16. The next layer of word formation is generally termed 'verb base'. This level is defined as the level at which derivational elements are added to the verb theme, yielding the verb word minus inflection. In forming the base, Kari proposes a number of derivational stages. The final stage of word formation (apart from what Kari terms syntactic word formation, which I will not consider here) involves the formation of the verb word through the addition of inflectional elements. Word formation in Kari's model thus involves a process of 'interrupted synthesis' (Kari 1989, 1992, Whorf 1932, 1956), with discontinuous strings of prefixes, a root, and a suffix. The actual surface ordering of morphemes bears no necessary resemblance to how word formation takes place, but rather is fixed by a template that serves to linearize the morphemes. More specifically, Kari 1992 proposes the model outlined in (8). The details of this model may not be clear at this point, but the overall scheme is, I hope, apparent. I have added to Kari's flow chart the positions involved at each level of word formation (in italics, taken from (2)), to show that linear ordering is not relevant to word formation.

(8) **Lexicon**
(*root, preverb, qualifier, thematic, voice/valence*)
   Verb theme (transitivity + thematic prefixes + root + theme category)
   secondary theme formation (e.g., causative, gender, incorporation)
Derivation
   aspectual derivation (derivation + conjugation + aspect)
      (*situation aspect, suffixes, preverbs*)
   postaspectual derivations (inceptive, errative)
      (*inceptive, qualifier*)
   superaspectual derivations (customary, distributive)
      (*iterative, distributive, suffixes*)
   nonaspectual derivations (iterative, passive, benefactive, gender, incorporation, etc.)
      (*voice/valence, iterative, incorporate, qualifiers, preverbs*)
Base (verb word minus inflection)
inflection
   mode-negative insertion
   pronominal insertion
      (*viewpoint aspect, negative, suffixes, object, subject*)
Underlying form
postinflectional level (relativization, nominalization)
Phonetic form
(Phonology begins at the level of inflection and applies through the rest of the levels.)

This model of word formation is similar to the one proposed by Bonet 1991, 1995 and Cummins and Roberge 1994 for Romance, where word formation is principled and a template provides for actual morpheme ordering. The model meets an important criterion that is often identified as universal: derivation precedes inflection. The approach also allows for a morpheme to function either as part of a lexical entry or derivationally, accounting for one and the same form being used both idiosyncratically and systematically. Discontinuous dependencies are accounted for: the discontinuities are present in the surface string, but from the point of view of word formation, they are not discontinuous. Metathesis receives a phonological account – it operates after word formation is completed (Kari 1989). This perspective on word formation eliminates the template as a type of word formation device; it is, rather, simply a device for ordering morphemes. This is both the virtue and, for me, the downfall of this model. Notice that the word formation process

2.3 The Verb and Word Formation

is rendered completely opaque by the surface order of morphemes, which is determined solely by the template. The levels of word formation do not follow from anything that is visible in the linear string. Thus it is difficult to find empirical evidence bearing on the model, as any possible surface ordering is congruent with the hypothesis that word formation proceeds from the most lexicalized material through regular derivation through inflection. The model is theoretically driven and impermeable to empirical argument.

The second major model of word formation in the Athapaskan literature is that argued for by Hargus 1988. Hargus adopts a Lexical Phonology model of word formation, arguing that word formation mirrors the ordering in the template. This position is taken up by Halpern 1992. Basically, Hargus argues that word formation and phonology go hand in hand (in Kari's model, phonology follows all word formation). It is striking, when one refers to the template in (1), repeated as (9), that the phonological boundary types are ordered in the way they are. The voice/valence and stem (root plus suffixes) form the first level of word formation. Following this, the next set of prefixes is added in two steps, as evidenced by the two phonological boundary types, + and %. Finally, the outer prefixes, marked by #, are added to the verb.

(9) preverb # quantificational elements # incorporate # object % third person subject % qualifier + subsituation aspect + situation aspect + viewpoint aspect + 1/2 person subject = voice/valence + root + tense/mode/aspect suffix

As Hargus 1988:74 points out, the model that she proposes provides a straightforward characterization of the domains of phonological rules in Sekani, and word formation and phonological processes proceed hand in hand. Just as in Kari's model, for a complex lexical entry it is necessary to indicate positional information for the components of the entry. The primary difference between the two models is not in the lexical entries themselves but rather in the way that words are built up. In Hargus's model the constituents of morphologically complex words need not be arranged in lexical entries in a way that resembles their surface forms (1988:51). Word formation is related to phonological rather than to morphological levels. In this model, discontinuities are captured through the existence of complex lexical entries, metatheses can occur at the word level, and blocking, which I have not discussed, can occur on word formation as, interestingly, blocking occurs only between morphemes on the same level or with the same boundary type. See chapter 13.

A more recent development of this second model is found in Hargus and Tuttle 1997 and Potter 1996. Adopting Optimality Theory (e.g., Archangeli and Langendoen 1997, Prince and Smolensky 1993), these authors propose, following Anderson 1996, that morpheme order is determined in large part by a series of alignment constraints that order morphemes before the stem, and that the ranking of the constraints determines the optimal order. For instance, the highest-ranked alignment constraint requires that subject agreement prefixes be closest to the stem; the next highest-ranked constraint requires that aspect be closest to the stem, and so on. This model is similar to the template model in stipulating the ordering of morphemes (although it differs in interesting ways; see Hargus and Tuttle 1997). Potter's model differs in that he argues that morpheme order is further controlled by a principle similar to the Mirror Principle (Baker 1985, 1988), adapted from work by Rice 1993 and Speas 1990. Basically, Potter claims that a verb enters the syntax as a full word consisting of a stem and an unordered bundle of inflectional elements (lexical items within the verb are ignored, as they are in many other accounts, including McDonough 1990 and Speas 1990). The inflectional elements are ordered by alignment constraints, which in turn are regulated by a syntactic functional hierarchy.

Each of these models has certain advantages and disadvantages. Kari's model captures the well-supported generalization that inflection is external to derivation, but at a very abstract level. Although Anderson 1982 cautions that the generalization that derivation precedes inflection must be evaluated with respect to word formation and not with respect to linear ordering, linear ordering itself in Athapaskan languages provides no clue at all to the operation of word formation. This model is thus theoretically driven, and, as noted earlier, the surface forms provide little or no empirical support for Kari's claim. From a perspective of learnability, it is difficult to imagine what would enable a child to learn the relationship between word formation and morpheme order. The Hargus model and the Optimality Theory models deriving from it, on the other hand, are well supported by the surface ordering. These models suffer from a different problem – a claim inherent to the model is that the fixed ordering of inflection and derivation as reflected in Kari's model simply represents a common pattern, and that the linguist need not be particularly concerned on encountering a language that looks very different. See Potter 1996, however, for discussion of how to limit possible orderings within an Optimality Theory model.

The third model, which I develop in this book, is exemplified by Rice 1993, 1998 and Speas 1990. In these models, word formation is argued to be syntactic, and, for Rice 1993, 1998, morpheme ordering follows largely from scopal relations.

2.3 The Verb and Word Formation

I leave this chapter with a conundrum then, one that will be examined in the remainder of the book. The ordering of morphemes in the verb of Athapaskan languages is, at least on the surface, unusual. Based on characteristics such as the intermingling of inflection and derivation, the use of zero morphemes, morphologically controlled metathesis, nonlocal dependencies, and the selection of inner morphemes by outer morphemes, these languages appear to be quite distinct from languages that Simpson and Withgott 1986 argue to have layered morphology. The dilemma is that such an analysis requires a new class of languages, languages with template morphology, or, at best, a class of languages with abstract layered morphology with little relationship between the process of word formation and the actual linear ordering.

In the remainder of this book, I hope to provide a model that meets two goals – an account of morpheme order and an account of word formation – and that yields insight into both the global uniformity and local variability found in the family. I argue that the templatic characteristics of Athapaskan languages require careful re-examination and that, with deeper analysis, these languages can be seen to share many properties with languages with layered morphology. The next chapter sets out the basic hypothesis that I will pursue in the remainder of this book: that morpheme ordering is by and large controlled by scope.

3

Global Uniformity and Local Variability: A Possible Account

As this book unfolds, we will see that the verbs of the Athapaskan family exhibit two attributes, outlined in chapter 1. First, global uniformity exists – morpheme order is similar across the family. Second, so does local variability – some variability in morpheme order occurs both within a language and across the family. In this chapter I examine some possible hypotheses to account for both of these properties.

3.1 Two Hypotheses

One can imagine different ways of accounting for the fact that the Athapaskan language family as a whole exhibits both global uniformity and local variability. I outline two here. Under both hypotheses, global uniformity has its origins in the languages having a common source, but they differ as follows. Under one hypothesis, it is the common source and history of the languages that accounts for the global uniformity. It is an accident of history that certain properties remained stable across the language family while others were subject to change within individual languages. I call this the template hypothesis. Under a second hypothesis, global uniformity finds its origins in the languages having a common source, but results additionally from principles of universal grammar, which might be either diachronic or synchronic. I call this the universal or scope hypothesis.

In this chapter I examine why certain aspects of verb morphology are invariant while others have been susceptible to change, both across languages and within a particular language. I argue for the second hypothesis, that principles of universal grammar play a role in determining what remains stable. I assume further that the principles involved in determining morpheme ordering are synchronic, rather than being principles of diachronic change. Specifically, I argue that the stable aspects of morpheme order result from

3.1 Two Hypotheses

properties of universal grammar while the unstable ones are not controlled by universal grammar. Thus, universal principles act as a regulator on both synchronic morpheme order and language change: certain kinds of variability in morpheme order are not found because they would violate universal principles.

I come at this issue through the side door, so to speak. Taking a comparative perspective, one can view the languages from two extremes. One is to wonder at how similar the languages are despite the years of separation. From this perspective, it is the global uniformity that is striking. The alternative is to wonder at how different the languages are despite the common ancestor. From this perspective, the focus of attention is the considerable amount of local variability in the language family. My goal is to reconcile these two extremes. I do so by first outlining ways in which the languages differ from each other. We will see that they vary in many respects: there have been major phonological, morphosyntactic, and syntactic developments that differentiate the languages. Nevertheless, certain aspects have remained absolutely invariant. I believe that this requires an explanation, and it is this explanation that I will seek in the next chapters.

I begin then by examining some ways in which the languages differ, starting with phonological differences. Proto-Athapaskan is reconstructed as having both plain and glottalized stops in stem-final position (e.g., Leer 1979). These developed in several ways across the family. In some languages (e.g., Ahtna) both plain and glottalized stops are maintained stem-finally. In other languages (e.g., Koyukon) final stops are maintained, but the laryngeal distinction between plain and glottalized is neutralized. In still other languages, all nondental stops develop into their homorganic fricative counterpart (e.g., Navajo). Finally, in some languages, stem-final consonants lose their place of articulation phonetically, and are realized on the surface as either Ø or [h] (e.g., Slave).

Another phonological difference concerns the development of what is reconstructed as glottal constriction on a vowel (Krauss 1978). In some languages, this is maintained as a glottal stop (e.g., Ahtna), in some it is realized as high tone (e.g., Slave), in others it is realized as low tone (e.g., Dogrib), and in still others it is realized as low tone in heavy syllables (and all light syllables also surface as low tone; e.g., Navajo). Vowels develop differently in terms of quality and quantity. Some languages do not allow clusters of more than two consonants (e.g., Navajo, Sekani, Slave); others allow longer clusters (e.g., Galice). Some have severe restrictions on the first consonant of a cluster (e.g., Beaver, Navajo, Sekani, Slave); others are less restrictive (e.g., Ahtna, Carrier). The languages thus differ phonologically in a number of ways.

Morphophonemic differences exist as well. In some languages, fricatives beginning verb stems are always voiced (e.g., Ahtna, Carrier, Koyukon); in others, such fricatives alternate between voiced and voiceless depending on phonological environment (e.g., Apache, Beaver, Chipewyan, Sekani, Slave). Languages also differ in the intricate morphophonemics of the aspect-first/second person subject-voice/valence span of the verb.

The languages also differ in morphosyntactic ways. In some, for example, transitive verbs with third person subjects virtually require an object pronoun, which thus patterns as agreement (e.g., Apache, Navajo). In others an object pronoun is absent if the object is nominal (e.g., Koyukon, Slave). In still others a pronominal occurs with an overt object if the object is specific, but not if it is nonspecific (Babine-Witsuwit'en; Gunlagson 1995). Some languages have a verbal negative in addition to a syntactic negative (e.g., Ahtna, Carrier, Koyukon, Minto); in others the verbal negative paradigm is absent (e.g., Hupa, Navajo, Sekani, Slave). Some languages have a robust future paradigm (e.g., Ahtna, Babine-Witsuwit'en, Carrier, Koyukon, Navajo); in others the future is largely subsumed under the optative (e.g., Chipewyan, Dogrib, Slave). Some languages have a full optative paradigm (e.g., Ahtna, Navajo, Slave), others restrict the optative to certain persons (see Golla 1970:67 on Hupa), and still others have no reflex of the optative (see Cook 1984:212 on Tsuut'ina). In some languages, stative verbs appear in a single viewpoint aspect (e.g., Navajo); in others they take all viewpoints (northern languages). Some languages use the noun classifier system (see chapter 12) very productively (e.g., Ahtna, Dena'ina, Carrier, Koyukon); in others it is of limited productivity (e.g., Slave).

Finally, the languages differ in syntactic ways. Some have head-internal and head-final relative clauses (see Platero 1978 on Navajo); others have head-internal and head-initial relative clauses (see Rice 1989 on Slave). Some languages have a class of verbs that require what are generally called direct discourse complements. In these languages verbs such as 'say' and 'want' require pronouns in the complement that are interpreted from the point of view of the main clause subject (see Rice 1989 on Slave, Saxon 1998 on Dogrib, Schauber 1975 on Navajo). In a second language group, such a class of verbs is missing, and all complement verbs have pronouns that are interpreted from the point of view of the speaker (see Denham 1995 on Babine-Witsuwit'en). Some languages allow free formation of causatives, with causatives based on forms with either agent or patient subjects (e.g., Ahtna), while others freely allow causatives based only on forms with patient subjects (e.g., Slave). Noun incorporation follows a similar pattern (see Rice, forthcoming a, on causatives

3.1 Two Hypotheses

and noun incorporation). The languages differ in the formation of questions (see Denham 1997 on Babine-Witsuwit'en, Potter 1997 on Apache, Rice 1989 on Slave).

Many more such differences among the languages will come up in the course of this book. That there are so many differences makes it all the more surprising that verbal morpheme order exhibits so little variation across the family.

One might wonder why I have digressed so far from the verb itself. The reason is as follows. Given that Athapaskan languages have changed from their common ancestor in many ways and at all levels of grammar, the fact of stability is surprising: Why haven't all areas been susceptible to change? In other words, why, given the amount of change found in the languages, have certain aspects remained stable?

Focusing on the lexicon, the template and scope hypotheses make different predictions. These are stated here and discussed in detail in chapter 15, after I have examined a fuller range of similarities and differences among the languages. A template, as conceived in the Athapaskan literature, is a list of positional restrictions associated with the lexical entry of each relevant morpheme; for example, a morpheme is listed as occupying position 6. Suppose that a new morpheme evolves. The template view makes no predictions as to where this morpheme might appear in the verb – it would simply be marked for its own restrictions. One might therefore expect the template to change as old morphemes disappear and new morphemes enter the language. The scopal perspective, on the other hand, leads one to expect that the template would basically be maintained as morphemes are lost and introduced in different form. If one morpheme is lost and another develops with the same function, the new morpheme, all others things being equal, should occupy the same position as the old one.

Another difference between the hypotheses can be seen by examining elements whose function has shifted over time. Under the template perspective, one might expect a functional change to occur without any positional change; under the scopal perspective, such a change might well yield a change in position.

Finally, the hypotheses differ in their predictions concerning items whose meaningful content has eroded. Again, under the template hypothesis, there is no reason to expect the position of such elements to change. Under the scope hypothesis, one might expect such elements to vary more in position than ones with a robust meaning. I return to these issues in chapter 15.

3.2 Defining Scope

In the remainder of this book I argue for the following hypothesis.

(1) Global uniformity is due to the presence of scopal relationships, or semantic compositionality, between the morphemes involved. Variability arises when (i) no scopal relationship exists between morphemes, or (ii) the scopal relations of the morphemes in question can be varied.

The term scope is used in two senses in linguistics. In the first sense, in which I use the term, it concerns semantic compositionality. In particular, given three items X, Y, and Z, items X and Y combine with each other and then combine as a unit with Z. The semantics of Z is added to that of X and Y as a unit. For instance, a direct object combines with a verb before a subject does, as the verb and direct object enter into a closer semantic relationship with each other than either does with the subject. The ordering of inflection outside of derivation provides another example: this can be understood as the surface realization of a scopal relationship. For instance, a plural affix pluralizes a noun with a derivational affix, not just the noun on its own. This notion is similar to Bybee's 1985 relevance to the verb for functional items or to Baker's 1985, 1988 Mirror Principle for lexical items, according to which ordering of morphemes mirrors the order of syntactic operations, with the consequence that "one can deduce from them [the ordering of morphemes – KR] the semantic relationships among the elements of the clause" (Baker 1988:422). The term scope is often used in this way; see, for instance, Baker 1992, 1996, Brunson 1989, 1992, Foley and van Valin 1984, Jackendoff 1972, Jelinek and Willie 1996, McCawley 1988, and Speas 1984, among others. This notion is also familiar from discussions of word formation and bracketing paradoxes, which are said to arise in a word like *ungrammaticality* because semantically *un* must be added to *grammatical* before *ity* is, but phonologically *ity* must be added first (see Sproat 1998:342–346 for an overview of the literature on bracketing paradoxes). The first ordering reflects the semantics of the word while the second reflects its phonology. Baker 1992:102, in a discussion of Quechua, provides examples in which either the morpheme meaning 'want' precedes the one meaning 'cause' or vice versa, and comments that "morpheme order correlates with semantic scope in a simple and predictable way: the morpheme farther from the verb stem is interpreted as having scope over the morpheme closer to the verb stem ... This is no coincidence; on the contrary, it is a universal property of languages as far as I know (see Baker 1988 for references) ... the scopal relationships that hold between those clauses [the clauses headed by the main verb, the affix *want*, and the affix *cause* – KR]

3.2 Defining Scope

are represented by syntactic embedding in the usual way." In the most general sense, semantic compositionality guards against the kind of 'morpheme salad' allowed by a template. As I will show, morphemes in Athapaskan languages do not occur in some random order within a word, but their ordering is a reflection of their meaning relationships.

The second sense of scope in the literature concerns quantifiers and Quantifier Raising and provides motivation for a Logical Form component of the grammar. In my use of the term scope, I refer only to the notion of semantic compositionality.

Although the scope principle accounts for structural relationship among morphemes, it is not in itself sufficient to determine their left-to-right ordering and requires supplementing with a language-particular setting for directionality. I assume that scopal relationships are structurally represented, with a morpheme of greater scope c-commanding (Langacker 1969, Reinhart 1976) a morpheme within its scope (e.g., Baker 1985, 1988, Foley and Van Valin 1984, Marantz 1984). I will further assume that the Athapaskan languages require that the c-commanding morpheme occur to the right of an element in its scope, yielding a head-final structure. This setting follows from the general setting for headedness in the languages, which are typically head-final – the verb is sentence-final, the languages are postpositional.[1] Given that the languages are head-final overall, the functional heads are expected to be final as well, with the more rightward ones c-commanding the more leftward ones. As I will argue, the ordering in which one would expect the functional heads to occur is exactly that predicted by the scope principle. The sole discrepancy is that the verb stem and voice/valence are in an unexpected spot, to the right of the functional heads.

Two kinds of evidence bearing on the scope hypothesis must be examined. The first comes from a study of scopal relations in cases of fixed morpheme ordering, the prediction being that the morphemes bear some fixed meaning relationship to each other in such cases. The second comes from an examination of scopal relations in cases of variability, the prediction being that the morphemes in question bear no relationship to each other or that they have a relationship but that it is not fixed. Both of these are examined in the following chapters. In addition, a third factor can underlie variability. While I have stated the scope principle as a single principle, in fact, scope is an overarching principle that subsumes several subprinciples. These may sometimes conflict with each other. For instance, I propose one subprinciple requiring that arguments with specific reference have scope over those with nonspecific reference and another demanding that subjects have scope over objects. Suppose that a subject is nonspecific in reference and an object specific. Depending on which subprinciple takes precedence within a language, either ordering may occur. Thus, two possible orderings are predicted across languages by universal principles depending upon which is more important in the language at hand.

Assuming that support is found for this hypothesis, we find a rather different model of the Athapaskan verb than has previously been proposed. In Kari's model (e.g., Kari 1989, 1990, 1992), discussed in chapter 2, word formation proceeds according to universal principles but the word formation process cannot be reconstructed from the actual surface linear ordering. In the model proposed by Hargus 1988, the template essentially provides the mechanism for word formation. In the model argued for in this book, there is a direct relationship between morpheme order and word formation.

3.3 Theoretical Preliminaries

In this section I outline a number of theoretical assumptions. The first assumption is that the verb word in Athapaskan languages should not be considered to be a word lexically, but rather is simply a phonological word; it is syntactically a phrase. This idea is not a new one – as early as 1915, Sapir recognized that the Athapaskan verb differs in many ways from the verb of a typical polysynthetic language. Sapir wrote, "most of the elements [of the Na-Dene verb complex] *preserve* a considerable share of individuality, while many can, indeed, be shown to be identical in origin with, or specialized forms of, independent stems... [In an example of a Chipewyan verb complex] the first three elements... have all *lost* their absolute independence and all four... have *settled down* to a rigidly prescribed order relatively to each other" (quoted in Krauss 1965:27). In 1929 Sapir wrote, "The Na-Dene languages... while presenting a *superficially* polysynthetic aspect are built up *fundamentally* of monosyllabic elements of prevailingly nominal significance which have fixed order with reference to each other and combine into morphologically 'loose' words..." (quoted in Krauss 1965:27). The idea that the verbal word need not necessarily be lexically formed has been taken up recently in work by Jelinek and Willie 1996, Rice 1993, 1998, Speas 1990, and others.

A second assumption is that the morphemes of the verb divide into two categories, lexical items and functional items. Lexical items include the morphemes of what is termed in the Athapaskan literature the disjunct part of the verb (preverb, quantifiers, incorporates) and stems; the functional items include the material that indicates person, number, noun class, and aspect.

Napoli 1993:169 provides the following definitions of lexical and functional categories: "Lexical categories would be A, N, P, and V, the categories that dominate lexical items and are semantically 'whole.' But functional

3.3 Theoretical Preliminaries

categories would be quite different in at least the following ways:

(a) They would not be semantically 'whole' or rich, but instead would serve to functionally introduce their complement.
(b) In accordance with (a), they would not assign a theta-role to their complement.
(c) In accordance with (a), they would be limited to taking only a single complement, since they are not semantically rich or complex enough to introduce multiple elements.
(d) In accordance with (a), they would be stressless under most circumstances.
(e) In accordance with (a), they would be a closed set.
(f) In accordance with (a), their maximal projection would function to 'close off' the phrase, giving it an integrity or wholeness."

I will argue in more detail for this characterization of the verb in the following chapters.

A third assumption is that complex lexical entries (discontinuous dependencies) are parallel to phrasal idioms such as *strike out*. Both pieces of the idiom are listed separately with their own meanings and, additionally, the idiom is listed in the lexicon with its idiosyncratic meaning. I do not treat these as discontinuous morphs but as phrasal units with lexicalized meaning; see chapter 16.

A fourth assumption also concerns lexical entries. I assume that lexical entries are less than fully specified semantically; see, for example, Bouchard 1995, Carter 1988, Cowper 1995, and Cummins 1996 for recent discussion. This has consequences for the lexicon (chapter 14), and many of these are discussed throughout the book. In such a case, the detailed meaning that the item takes on is determined by the construction in which it appears. For instance, a particular quantificational adverb is sometimes translated as 'again', sometimes as 'back', and sometimes as 'customarily'. I argue in chapter 5 that this is a single lexical entry, with the specific meaning determined by aspectual properties of the verb with which it occurs. A second example is a morpheme identified in the Athapaskan literature as a discontinuous constituent with the reflexive and reciprocal, among others. I argue in chapter 7 that the morpheme in question has the general meaning 'middle voice'; its particular contribution depends on other material in the construction.

Fifth, I assume the following basic model for the verb word. As mentioned earlier, I assume that the verb word is not a lexical construct, but a phrase. The phrase consists of a verb phrase, which contains the lexical prefixes and the stem. Arrayed above the verb phrase are functional categories, indicating agreement, number, aspect, and the like; details of this structure will be refined as I proceed; see Rice 1993, 1998, Rice and Saxon 1994, and Speas 1990 for discussion and justification of this type of model. Finally, verb suffixes indicate aspect and are category assigners; see chapter 11. Part of this assumption is that the structure of the verb word is hierarchical rather than flat, or fanlike, in nature; I present no evidence for this. I assume that the verb has the (simplified) structure in (2).[2]

(2)

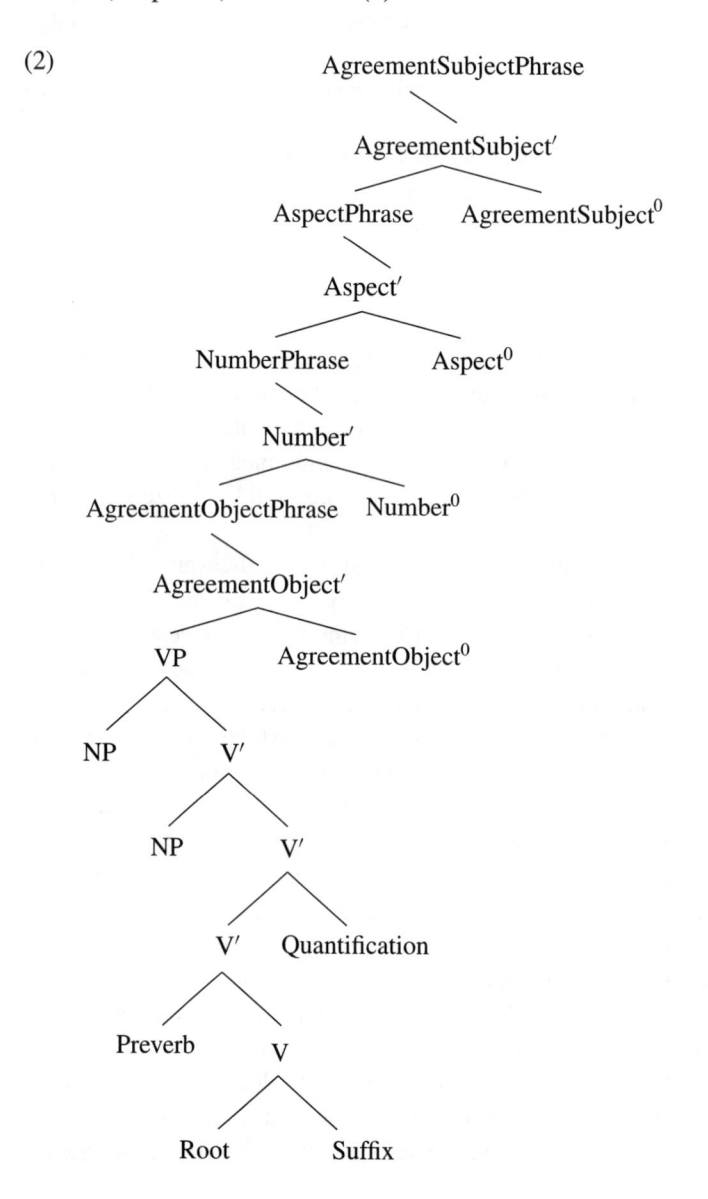

```
                    AgreementSubjectPhrase
                           /    \
                        AgreementSubject'
                         /           \
                  AspectPhrase    AgreementSubject⁰
                   /      \
                Aspect'
                /     \
        NumberPhrase   Aspect⁰
          /     \
        Number'
        /     \
AgreementObjectPhrase  Number⁰
     /      \
  AgreementObject'
    /       \
   VP    AgreementObject⁰
  /  \
 NP   V'
     / \
    NP  V'
       / \
      V'  Quantification
     / \
 Preverb  V
         / \
      Root  Suffix
```

3.3 Theoretical Preliminaries

Sixth, a note on terminology is in order. I use the term 'morpheme' without taking a stand on the issue of whether morphology is actually better regarded as morpheme-based or lexeme-based (see, for example, Aronoff 1994 and Beard 1995 for discussion). See chapter 16 for brief discussion.

Finally, I follow Baker 1985, 1988, Marantz 1984 and others in assuming that semantic scope relations are structurally represented. In particular, if a morpheme X has scope over a morpheme Y, then X must c-command Y. I argue that Athapaskan languages are characterizable overall as a class of languages where semantic structure is directly represented syntactically, or by overt morpheme order, and not obscured by syntactic or phonological operations.

With this background and these assumptions, I now undertake an examination of the structure of the verb in Athapaskan languages, beginning with the lexical items.

PART II

THE LEXICAL ITEMS

4

First Stop: Introducing the Lexical Items

The chapters in this part of the book examine the lexical items that form part of the verb in an Athapaskan language (chapter 6). In addition, this part includes discussion of the position of the verb stem with respect to other lexical items (chapter 5) and the status of the voice/valence markers (chapter 7). It is in this domain of the verb, I argue, that we see the greatest discrepancy between surface ordering and what I claim the underlying ordering to be; semantic factors are a primary determinant in the ordering, but syntactic factors enter in as well. I argue in chapter 7 that the voice/valence elements, like the verb stems, are predicative in nature. I further argue in chapters 5 and 7 that the predicative elements of the verb originate outside of their surface positions and move to them. Finally, I argue in chapter 6 that the ordering of the preverbs, quantificational elements, and incorporates is not unexpected, but is a direct consequence of scopal ordering, with elements of greater scope appearing to the right of those within their scope. In the rest of this chapter, I introduce the reader to the lexical elements of the verb.

4.1 Definitions

Recall from chapter 2 that the surface ordering of elements within the verb word of an Athapaskan language is often expressed as a template. The Slave template is repeated in (1); see appendix 1 for templates in a number of languages.

(1) preverb # quantificational elements # incorporate # object % third person subject % qualifier + subsituation aspect + situation aspect + viewpoint aspect + 1/2 person subject = voice/valence + root + tense/mode/aspect suffix

4.1.1 The Traditional Groupings

The preverbs, quantificational elements, and incorporates form a set of items that are traditionally called disjunct prefixes in the Athapaskan literature. The disjunct prefixes, which I will treat as lexical items, are distinguished from the other prefixes of the verb in two main ways. First, they form a group semantically: they generally have well-defined lexical meanings. Second, they differ from the other prefixes phonologically. These prefixes can be of the shape CV, CVC, CVV (long vowel), CVVC, and, occasionally, C. The full range of consonants occurs in initial position, and they occur with almost the full range of vowels. They have full tonal possibilities in tone languages. The remainder of the prefixes, 'conjunct prefixes' in the Athapaskan literature, are, with rare exceptions, of the surface shape C or CV (depending on language), where V is the unmarked vowel of the language (a reflex of Proto-Athapaskan schwa); a few prefixes have the shape V or VC (these vowels include i, a, u as well as the schwa reflex). The set of consonants in these prefixes is limited, largely to plain coronals. In tone languages, a small number of these prefixes have lexically marked tone, but in general they are lexically toneless, with predictable tone.

The lexical items pattern phonologically similarly to independent words: they only rarely enter into phonological processes with functional prefixes, while functional prefixes are often affected by phonological processes. The lexical prefixes also only rarely enter into phonological processes with each other. In other words, their surface forms are largely identical to their lexical entries. The lexical prefixes are considered to be part of the verb word for phonological reasons – they phrase with the rest of the verb word phonologically, and some phonological processes distinguish their patterning from the patterning of separate words. See, for instance, Cook 1984, Hargus 1988, 1991, 1997, forthcoming, Kari 1975, 1976, Randoja 1990, and Rice 1989, 1992, 1993 for detailed discussion.

4.1.2 Terminology

In considering the lexical items, I begin by defining a framework within which to examine them. A useful distinction in discussing these items is that between entities and events; see, for instance, Frawley 1992. Entities and events enter into predication, or the way that individuals (entities) instantiate, embody, carry out, take on, or are linked to properties, actions, attributes, and states (events). Entities are individuals that are independent and can stand alone; events do not stand alone.

4.2 Preverbs

Entities and events form the primitives of predication. In addition to these basic distinctions, an individual lexical entry may contain different types of information. Three types of information are often argued to contribute to the semantics of a particular lexical item: event structure, argument structure, and qualia structure (see, for example, Foley and Van Valin 1984, Frawley 1992, Grimshaw 1990, Pustejovsky 1995, Smith 1996b, Tenny 1994 for discussion of models using these kinds of systems; for qualia see Pustejovsky 1995, Smith 1996b, Talmy 1987). Event structure contributes information about the type of situations involved, including processes, transitions, and states. Argument structure provides information about the number and type of thematic roles involved, including agent, theme, instrument, and location. In addition, I include under the rubric argument structure the types of aspectual roles required by verbs – an argument may provide, for instance, an initiator to an event or may delimit an event. These two types of structures receive consideration in this chapter, chapter 7, and Part III. Finally qualia structure, as defined by Pustejovsky 1995:61, provides particulars of the event, yielding information about figure, motion, path, ground, manner, cause, and state (Smith 1996b, based on Pustejovsky 1995 and Talmy 1987). The lexical items in the verb contribute to these systems: incorporated nouns meet requirements of argument structure, quantificational elements serve to modify the event structure or the argument structure, and all have a contribution to make to qualia structure.

While entity and event are concepts related to meaning, they bear a general relationship to lexical categories – entities tend to equate with nouns and events with verbs. Entities can be realized as syntactic arguments or adjuncts; events as verbs.

4.2 Preverbs

Preverbs in Athapaskan languages are elements that modify predicates, and are composed largely of qualia information.[1] They often occupy two positions in the Athapaskan literature, incorporated postposition and adverb. Both represent manner and oblique relations such as direction, location, and benefaction. Relational preverbs express concepts such as illative (e.g., Slave *zhuná* 'in', *´zhi* 'into'), elative (e.g., Slave *ká* 'out'), inessive (in), adessive (on, at), ablative (from), allative (to), supraessive (on), and so on.[2]

Preverbs indicating manner are sampled in (2) and (3). The data is organized as follows. The first line shows a preverb with its general meaning. Some entries contain more than a preverb; see below for discussion. The boundary symbol '#' is used with preverbs; *D* represents middle voice. The second line shows a verb containing this preverb, the third line gives a translation, and the fourth line provides a rough morphological breakdown for this verb. I use the terminology developed in this book in the glosses, as Athapaskanists will quickly recognize. The fourth line is a form of the verb without the particular preverb; the fifth line shows the morphology of this form. The preverb under discussion is in boldface.

(2) Slave manner preverbs
    a. **ts'e#** 'in half'
       ts'e-ne-h-ch'i
       ts'e 'in half' # ne 2sg Subject + h valence = ch'i 'tear, imperfective'
       'You sg. split it in half.'
       cf. ne-h-ch'i
       ne 2sg Subject + h valence = ch'i 'tear, perfective'
       'You sg. split, tore.'
    b. **te#** d 'too much'
       te-de-y-į-se
       te 'too much' # de qualifier + y situation aspect + į perfective viewpoint = se 'cry, perfective'
       'S/he cried too much.'
       cf. y-į-se
       y situation aspect + į perfective viewpoint = se 'cry, perfective'
       'S/he cried.'
       te-'e-**d**-a-dlo
       te 'too much' # 'e unspecified Object + d qualifier + a situation aspect = dlo 'laugh, perfective'
       'S/he laughed too much.'
       cf. rá-'e-y-į-dlo
       rá preverb # 'e unspecified Object + y situation aspect + į perfective viewpoint = dlo 'laugh, perfective'
       'S/he laughed.'
    c. **'eshíh#** 'pretend'
       'eshí-į-tsé
       'eshíh 'pretend' # į situation aspect/perfective viewpoint = tsé 'cry, perfective'
       'S/he almost cried.'
       cf. į-tsé
       į situation aspect/perfective viewpoint = tsé 'cry, perfective'
       'S/he cried.'

4.2 Preverbs

    'eshí-i̯-'á
    'eshíh# 'pretend' #i̯ situation aspect/perfective viewpoint = 'á 'chew, eat perfective'
    'S/he made a chewing action.'
    cf. i̯-'á
    i̯ situation aspect/perfective viewpoint = 'á 'eat, chew, perfective'
    'S/he ate, chewed.'

(3) Ahtna manner preverbs (Kari 1990)
    a. **ka#**d(+D) 'randomly, completely, into pieces'
    ka-y-d-ghi-tsaetl'
    ka preverb # y disjoint anaphor + d qualifier + ghi situation aspect = tsaetl 'chop, split, perfective'
    'He chopped it up, split it up' (377)
    cf. i-ghi-tsaetl'
    i disjoint anaphor + ghi situation aspect = tsaetl' 'chop, split, perfective'
    'He was chopping it.' (377)
    ka-d-ghi-c'el
    ka preverb # d qualifier + ghi situation aspect = c'el 'tear, perfective'
    'It got torn up.' (124)
    cf. z-c'eł
    z situation aspect/perfective viewpoint = c'eł 'tear'
    'It tore.' (124)

    b. **su#** 'sufficiently, enough'
    su-di-ghi-ł-caax
    su 'enough' # + di qualifier + ghi situation aspect + ł valence = caax 'big, imperfective'
    'It (board) is big enough.' (466)
    cf. d-ghi-ł-caax, ghi-ł-caax
    d qualifier + ghi situation aspect + ł valence = caax 'big, imperfective'
    'He, it is big.' (466)
    su-ghi-ł-des
    su 'enough' # ghi situation aspect + ł valence = des 'heavy, imperfective'
    'It is heavy enough.' (152)
    cf. d-ghi-ł-des
    d qualifier + ghi situation aspect + ł valence = des 'heavy, imperfective'
    'It is heavy.' (152)

c. **cin'**# 'pretending'
cin'-de-l-tsagh
cin' 'pretend' # de qualifier + l voice/valence = tsagh 'cry, imperfective'
'S/he is pretending to cry.' (374)
cf. tsagh
'S/he is crying.' (374)
da-**cin'**-de-l-tsaan
da part of lexical entry 'die' # **cin'** 'pretend'# de qualifier + l voice/valence = tsaan 'go, being exhausted, sick, tired, perfective'
'S/he pretended to die.' (367)
cf. da-z-tsaan
da # z situation aspect = tsaan 'go being exhausted, sick, tired, perfective'
'S/he died.' (367)

I begin discussion with a justification of my choice of a single category that I call preverb rather than the two categories of incorporated postposition and adverb. A more standard display of disjunct prefixes, the positions marked by #, is presented in (4). This particular example is taken from Slave, based on Rice 1989, although the general form of the template is reported widely elsewhere. See Rice 1991b for additional discussion.

(4)   object of postposition = **postposition** # **adverb** # distributive # iterative # incorporate #

Other treatments of the disjunct complex range from three positions (e.g., Golla 1970 on Hupa) to six positions with subpositions, for a total of nine positions (e.g., Kari 1989, 1990, 1992 on Ahtna); see appendix 1. The disjunct complexes in the verbs of the different languages are very similar, however, involving postposition, adverb, iterative, and plural elements in all languages and an incorporate position in some languages.

Starting at the extreme left in (4), the term 'object of postposition' is self-explanatory: these morphemes are pronominal markers that indicate agreement with the object of the postposition that follows.[3] 'Postposition' refers to a postpositional stem that is phonologically incorporated into the verb word; they mark relations.[4] 'Adverbs' are of two major types, expressing relations (spatial, temporal) and manner.

Various kinds of evidence are generally offered for assigning a morpheme to a particular category. Prime among these is distributional evidence: a category is a set of morphemes showing the same privileges of occurrence. Categories can also be established on the basis of inflection, syntactic patterning,

4.2 Preverbs

phonological characteristics, and function. In establishing the category of particular morphemes within the lexical items of the verb of an Athapaskan language, I assume that distributional evidence and functional similarity are primary. The lexical items generally show no inflection, syntactic patterning, or phonological characteristics that provide positive evidence for category membership, and indeed these criteria may provide no evidence as to status. Based on the criteria of distribution and function, the lexical items can be viewed as falling in the three major categories in (1): preverb, quantificational element, and incorporate. More than one preverb, quantificational element, and incorporate may be present at the same time; based on this type of evidence I suggest that these categories define three major constituent types within which a certain amount of iteration is possible. See chapter 6 for details. The presence of two morphemes of a particular category does not require two distinct positions for that category (as proposed by Kari 1989), but is a result of adjunction within a constituent.

A move toward reducing the two positions of postposition and at least some adverbs to a single category is discussed by Kari 1989. He treats these positions as a single 'zone,' or group of morphemes, that are adjacent and share similar phonological properties.

The evidence for a single category of postpositions and the relational adverbs is threefold. First, postpositions and relational adverbs are functionally similar, marking oblique relations. Morphemes in these two positions express similar concepts. Some are postpositions (e.g., Slave *ʼzhi* 'into'), while others are adverbs (e.g., Slave *zhuná* 'in,' *ká* 'out'). A particular relation may thus be expressed by either a postposition or an adverb.

Second, postpositions and relational adverbs belong to the same substitution class, as illustrated for Slave in (5). (5a) shows a morpheme traditionally called an adverb, while (5b) shows a morpheme normally called a postposition.

(5)   a. **ts'í-e-tɬah**
      ts'í 'lost' # e situation aspect = tɬah 'singular, dual go by land, perfective'
      'S/he got lost.'
  b. O **wą-e-tɬah**
      wą 'to' # e situation aspect = tɬah 'singular, dual go by land, perfective'
      'S/he was transported to O.'

Postpositions and relational adverbs thus show similar privileges of occurrence, differing from each other in that the postposition has an object, while the adverb does not.

Finally, one and the same morpheme can occur either with or without an object. A morpheme that is commonly labeled adverb can occur with an object, as in (6b), in which case it is called a postposition.

(6) Ahtna (Kari 1990)
    a. Adverb
        ts'i   'from, off from, out from'
        ts'i-i-ni-'aan
        ts'i from # i disjoint anaphor + ni situation aspect = 'aan 'handle default object, perfective'
        'He brought it out.' (414)
    b. Postposition
        O-ts'i   'out from, away from O'
        hw-**ts'i**-ni-yaa
        hw area = **ts'i** from # ni situation aspect = yaa 'singular go by land, perfective'
        'He came from a place.' (414)

In (6a) *ts'i* has no object, and for this reason is classed as an adverb; in (6b) *ts'i* has an object, [hw] 'place', and so it is classified as a postposition. Conversely, a morpheme that is generally called a postposition can occur without an object. This is shown in (7) for the morpheme *ghá*.[5]

(7) Slave
    a. Postposition
        'e-**ghá**-la-ye-da
        'e- unspecified Object = **ghá** postposition # la 'work' # ye qualifier= da stem, imperfective
        'S/he works.'
    b. Adverb
        xá-la-ye-de-da
        xá adverb # la 'work' # ye qualifier+ de self-benefactive = da stem
        'S/he works for him/herself.'

In (7a) the morpheme *ghá* functions as a postposition with an unspecified object. In (7b), on the other hand, it is found without an object, thus appearing to be an adverb.

Evidence thus is strong that the postpositions and the relational adverbs are of a single category type. Kari 1989, 1990 too proposes a single constituent for which he adopts the term 'derivational/thematic zone.' I will use a grammatical term for these morphemes, and adopt the term 'preverb.' Craig and Hale 1988:312 introduce the term 'preverb' for morphemes "whose semantic content falls within the range generally attributed to so-called oblique relations that are typically expressed by means of adpositions or semantic cases." The Athapaskan preverbs fall under this definition, as discussed earlier, making the use of this term appropriate.

As discussed earlier, one difference between postpositions and adverbs in the traditional sense of these words is that postpositions require a complement while adverbs do not. In order to capture this distinction, I assume that the primary difference between traditional postpositions and adverbs is in their argument structure: preverbs may be obligatorily transitive, obligatorily intransitive, or optionally transitive. A preverb that is obligatorily transitive is what is traditionally termed a postposition and must occur with a complement,[6] while one that is intransitive is what is traditionally called an adverb and cannot occur with an object. The optionally transitive preverbs are those that can occur with or without an object. These preverbs are similar in nature to the particles in English verb-particle constructions; for instance, *up* in *clean up*, *out* in *go out*, and *around* in *run around*.

4.3 Quantificational Elements

Returning now to (1), following the preverbs comes a position that I have called quantificational elements. Two major types of quantifiers can be identified in all languages, an adverbial quantifier and a nominal quantifier.

In this section I provide an overview of the functions of the quantificational elements found in the verb of Athapaskan languages. Before turning in detail to the individual quantifiers, I provide some brief background on quantification.

Quantifiers are often divided into two types depending on their function. Basically, one type of quantifier is involved with the nominal system, quantifying over individuals or entities, and the second type is involved in the verbal system, quantifying over events. The details of the classification differ slightly from author to author, but the overall distinction holds. I follow Jelinek 1995, Matthewson 1996, Partee 1991, and Partee et al. 1987, among others, in using the terms D-quantifier and A-quantifier. D-quantifiers function as determiners and enter into a relationship with entities, or arguments; A-quantifiers function as adverbs and enter into a relationship with events. Typical D-quantifiers in English include *most*, *all*, *every*, and *many*, while typical A-quantifiers include *always* and *usually*. I will argue that the distributive and multiple quantifiers in Athapaskan languages quantify over entities, while the iterative is part of the event system. In order to do this, it is necessary to define more specifically what is meant by an entity as opposed to an event.

In section 4.1.2 I defined entity as an individual that is independent and can stand alone. This is a broad, and vague, definition, and does not tell us exactly what an entity is. Entity can be more specifically defined by enumerating the types of elements that enter into entity systems. One way of doing this is to examine the roles that entities play in events, or the semantic or thematic relations that connect entities to events or arguments to predicates. Frawley 1992:224 divides these relationships into two major types depending on the relationship between the argument and the event. The first type of relationship, participant roles, is entailed by the predication. These required arguments include, typically, a logical actor (agent, author, instrument), theme (or patient), experiencer, goal, and source. The second type, which Frawley calls nonparticipant or circumstantial roles, derives from the semantic context of the predication (Frawley 1992:202) and includes locative, reason, purpose, manner, path, and time. Participant roles answer questions of 'who' and 'what' while nonparticipant roles answer questions of 'where, why, when, how' (Frawley 1992:202). Syntactically, participant roles often are coded as arguments and nonparticipant roles as adjuncts. In the following discussion, I use the terms 'entity' and 'argument' interchangeably, with the term 'argument' referring to both syntactic arguments and adjuncts.

I summarize here the major components of a lexical entry that are relevant to this book. First are semantic categories of entity and event; these correlate to a high degree with the categories noun and verb. Second are the relationships between entities and events. Entities enter into thematic relations (e.g., agent, theme, goal) and aspectual relations (e.g., initiator, delimiter) with events; these are part of argument structure, which defines the number of arguments required by a verb and the thematic and aspectual relations these bear to the verb. Third are the aspectual categories that define the event itself, or event structure; these include processes, transitions, and states. A final component is qualia structure; I pay little attention to this. Thematic relations are important to this chapter, aspectual relations are discussed in chapter 7, and event structure is a major topic of chapter 11.

4.3.1 Distributive Quantifier

In the following sections I survey the use of the form that is called the distributive in different languages of the family and then present arguments that it functions as a D-quantifier.

4.3.1.1 On the Use of the Distributive in Different Languages

Navajo

In Navajo, the distributive quantifier has the shape *da*. Young and Morgan 1987:62 define the distributive as "a prefix that serves to denote plurality, usually in a distributive rather than a collective sense – i.e. each of 3+ subjects or objects in contradistinction to a group of 3+." Young and Morgan 1987 note that in Navajo, the distributive occurs with nouns, pronouns, postpositional objects, and some particles as well as with verbs.

The distributive can combine with both intransitive and transitive verbs. With intransitive verbs, it indicates that the subject refers to three or more individuals. The distributive is in boldface in the following forms, and stems are separated by a hyphen. The morpheme-by-morpheme glosses are quite general. I do not attempt to convey underlying representations, but only distinguish morphology that is visible on the surface.

(8) a. tsin   b-ąąh   ha-**da**-s-ii-'-na'
        tree   3-on   up-**distributive**-situation aspect-1nonsg Subject-
                middle voice-stem, perfective
        'We (3+ each) climbed the tree.' (Young and Morgan 1987:62)
    b. **de**-í-n-íi-kááh
        distributive-?-qualifier-1nonsg Subject-stem, imperfective
        'We (3+) are walking along (as individual members of a line of people, or of a scattered group).' (Young and Morgan 1987:62)
        cf. y-ii-kah
            situation aspect-1nonsg Subject-stem, progressive
            'We (3+) are walking along (in a compact group).'
    c. ńdíshchíí-yaa-gi   n-**da**-az-tį́
        pine tree-under   preverb-**distributive**-situation aspect-stem,
                perfective
        'They (3+) are lying (each) under a (separate) pine tree.' (Young and Morgan 1987:63)
        cf. ndíshchíí-yaa-gi   si-tį́
            pine tree-under   situation aspect-stem, perfective
            'He's lying under the pine tree.' (Young and Morgan 1987:63)

(8c) contains a verb stem that requires a singular subject; the form with *da* necessarily involves distributivity rather than collectivity of the plural subject.

With transitive verbs, the facts are more complex: *da* may pluralize the subject, object, or both (Young and Morgan 1987:63). If the subject is singular, *da* must pluralize the object; if the object is singular, *da* must pluralize the subject; if the subject and object are not clearly singular, *da* can be construed as referring to the subject, object, or both (Young and Morgan 1987:63). The first and third cases are illustrated in (9).

(9) a. tsin   'ahá-**da**-sé-ti'
       stick   apart-**distributive**-situation aspect/viewpoint aspect/1sg Subject-stem, perfective
       'I broke the stick into (3+) pieces.'
    b. kin   'á-**da**-yii-laa
       house thus-**distributive**-situation aspect/perfective viewpoint-stem, perfective
       'They (3+) built the house, he built the (3+) houses, they (3+) built the (3+) houses.'

The distributive has the role of indicating an individualized plural. It can be used in a second way in Navajo: it can simply indicate that a verb has a plural as opposed to a dual subject. In Navajo, the distributive functions as a modifier of an argument (subject of a verb, object of a verb, complement of a postposition). Whether it indicates a simple plural (as opposed to dual) subject or functions as a true distributive quantifier, it relates to arguments.

Jicarilla Apache

Jicarilla Apache is similar to Navajo in terms of the function of its distributive, *daa*. It can be a marker of a plural as opposed to a dual subject, as in (10).

(10) a. naa-go-sh-t'i
        preverb-areal-1sg Subject-stem, imperfective
        'I joke.' (Jung 1995)
     b. naa-gǫǫ-ł-t'i
        preverb-areal/1nonsg Subject-valence-stem, imperfective
        'We (dual) joke.'
     c. naa-**daa**-gǫǫ-ł-t'i
        preverb-**distributive**-areal/1nonsg Subject-valence-stem, imperfective
        'We (plural) joke.'

Jung 1995 hypothesizes that the lexical item called distributive expresses simple plurality with stems that are lexically unmarked for number. With stems that are lexically marked for number, as in the Navajo examples in (8c) and (9b), the distributive expresses distributive number.

As in Navajo, the distributive reading is not limited to the subject.

(11) **daa**-nah-z-áa-ł-ts'iį
distributive-1/2nonsg Object-situation aspect-2nonsg Subject-valence-stem, perfective
'You two hit us (3+)/you (3+) hit us two.' (Jung 1995)

Again as in Navajo, the distributive in Jicarilla Apache modifies the reading of participant roles.

Chipewyan

The distributive in Chipewyan bears a similarity to that of Navajo and Jicarilla Apache: it indicates plural number as opposed to dual number, and it marks distributivity of subjects or objects. This is shown in (12). The distributive has the form *dá*.

(12) a. h-u-ł-tsi
        epenthetic-2nonsg Subject-valence-stem, imperfective
        'You dual/plural make it.' (Li 1946:414)
    b. **dá**-h-u-ł-tsi
        distributive-epenthetic-2nonsg Subject-valence-stem, imperfective
        'You pl. all make it.' (Li 1946:414)

The distributive can also modify objects.

(13) bɛ-yέ   xá-**dá**-na-'ɛ-s-dzis
      3.out of   out-**distributive**-iterative-unspecified Object-1sg Subject-stem, imperfective
      'I sip out of several vessels customarily.' (Li 1946:417)

In the three languages discussed so far, the distributive pluralizes, and may also individuate, the argument to which it relates. The distributive in these languages relates to entities and does not affect the view of the event, but rather modifies the thematic relations involved in the event.

Other Languages

In some other Athapaskan languages, the function of the distributive is more complex. The distributive in these languages does not distinguish a general plural versus dual as in Navajo, Jicarilla Apache, and Chipewyan; it serves only to individuate. It can relate to subjects and objects, but also distributes over locations.

The distributive in languages including Ahtna, Beaver, Carrier, Koyukon, Sekani, Slave, and Tsuut'ina can modify subjects. Several examples, taken from a range of languages, are given in (14)–(24). The distributive morpheme is in boldface.

The Distributive and Arguments

Cook 1984 provides examples of the Tsuut'ina distributive *dà* as an argument.

(14) Tsuut'ina (Cook 1984:220)
    a. **dà**-dí-záy
       distributive-qualifier-stem
       'Each is crumply.'
       cf. dí-záy
       qualifier-stem
       'It is crumply.'
    b. **dà**-yí-tɬ'ùw
       'Each is moldy.'
       cf. yí-tɬ'ùw
       'It is moldy.'
    c. **dà**-ghā-sùɬ
       distributive-2pl Subject-stem
       'Each of ye are dragging it along.'
       cf. yī-sùɬ
       epenthetic/1sg Subject-stem
       'I am dragging some of it.'

Hargus 1988:166 states that the distributive plural prefixes in Sekani (*dà* and *yàdà*) can relate to separate subjects or separate objects. An example of each is given in (15).

(15) Sekani (Hargus 1988:166–167)
    a. **yà-dà**-yə-ts'ə-z-'ās
       distributive-distributive-qualifier-unspecified human Subject-situation aspect-stem
       'We sneezed separately.'
    b. che-**dà**-n-į-h-bets
       incorporate-**distributive**-situation aspect-2sg Subject-valence-stem
       'You sg. boil separate objects.'

Beaver too is similar. The distributive has the form *dà* or *dànà*.

4.3 Quantificational Elements

(16) Beaver (Randoja 1990:124)
    a. **dà**-ghə-d-ì-ze
       distributive-human plural Subject-qualifier-qualifier-stem
       'They each shout.'
    b. ga   **dà-nà**-d-èe-ch'il
       rabbit **distributive-distributive**-qualifier-situation aspect/1sg
                Subject-stem
       'I skinned many rabbits.'

In Dena'ina (Tenenbaum 1978:160–161), the distributive *n* is used to indicate plurality of the subject, as in (17a–c) or of the object, as in (17d).

(17) Dena'ina (Tenenbaum 1978)
    a. de-**n**-qe-shin
       preverb-**distributive**-human plural Subject-stem
       'They pl. are pretty.' (160)
    b. ch'a-**n**-da-s-tuk'
       preverb-**distributive**-qualifier-situation aspect-stem
       'They (his paws) were worn out (plural hand things worn away).' (161)
    c. kadałtin   ve-ch'a-**n**-'i-łin
       blood   3-from-**distributive**-epenthetic-stem
       'He was bleeding all over (plural streams of blood were flowing from him).' (161)
    d. ye-ghu   se-**n**-de-n-gis
       disjoint anaphor-from preverb-**distributive**-qualifer-qualifier-
                                    stem
       'He skinned plural small animals one at a time (he tore fur from plural small objects).' (161)

In Slave too the distributive *yá* can modify subjects or objects, as illustrated in (18).

(18) Slave (Rice 1989)
    a. ke-n-é-yǫ
       human plural Subject-qualifier-situation aspect/perfective viewpoint stem
       'They grew.'
       yá-ke-n-į́-yǫ
       distributive-human plural Subject-qualifier-qualifier/perfective viewpoint aspect-stem
       'They each grew.'

b. ná-ne-y-i-h-kwa
preverb-qualifier-situation aspect-perfective viewpoint/1sg Subject-valence-stem
'I whipped it.'
ná-**yá**-ne-h-kwa
preverb-**distributive**-qualifier/situation aspect/perfective viewpoint/ 1sg Subject-valence-stem
'I whipped each separately.'

Ambiguities arise, as in the Slave examples in (19).

(19) Slave (Rice 1989)
    a. tę   chǫ-'e-n-í-ka
       ice preverb-unspecified Object-situation aspect-1pl Subject-stem
       'We made a hole in the ice.'
    b. tę   chǫ-**yá**-'e-wh-í-ka
       ice preverb-**distributive**-unspecified Object-situation aspect-1pl Subject-stem
       'We each made a hole in the ice (subject), we each made lots of holes in the ice (subject, object), we made lots of holes in the ice (object).'

Morice 1932:370 uses the term 'pluralitive' in Carrier for what is elsewhere termed distributive and identifies the element *ne* as, above all, denoting "some sort of partitive or localitive intent in addition to the idea of plurality." Some examples are given in (20). In (20a,b) the distributive relates to the object, and in (20c,d) to the subject.

(20) Carrier (Morice 1932)
    a. eḵě-es-krěs
       preverb-1sg Subject-stem
       'to write down, draw, trace one word, letter or figure' (II:370)
       eḵe-**nê**-es-krez
       preverb-**distributive**-1sg Subject-stem
       'to write down many words'
    b. na-ne-s-něh
       preverb-qualifier-1sg Subject-stem
       'to put out, extinguish' (II:372)
       na-**ne**-ne-s-no
       preverb-**distributive**-qualifier-1sg Subject-stem
       'to put out several fires'

4.3 Quantificational Elements

    c. ɬ-teɬ-ra-ɬ-kres
    reciprocal-preverb-preverb-valence-stem
    'to be crossed together (two lines, etc. in shape of cross)' (II:371)
    ɬ-teɬ-ra-**ne**-ɬ-kres
    reciprocal-preverb-preverb-**distributive**-valence-stem
    'several pairs be crossed'

    d. the-t-qas
    situation aspect-valence-stem
    'It spawns.' (II:370)
    ne-the-t-qas
    distributive-situation aspect-valence-stem
    'They spawn.' (involves place since each fish deposits eggs separately)

Morice implies a close relationship between the plurality and the locational nature of this item. If the distributive is an individuated plural, as discussed so far, then translations involving different spaces are not surprising, as these translations reinforce the individuated nature of the quantifier; see the next section.

In Ahtna (Kari 1979, 1990), the distributive *n* does not quantify over agentive subjects, but does relate to objects and to subjects of some descriptive verbs (see chapter 11).

(21) Ahtna (Kari 1990)
    a. de-**n**-ɬ-des
    preverb-**distributive**-valence-stem
    'They (nonhuman) are heavy.' (285)
    b. da-na-**n**-ku-gh-ii-ɬ-tl'u'
    preverb-iterative-**distributive**-human plural Object-situation aspect-perfective viewpoint-1sg Subject/valence-stem
    'I tied them up again.' (40)
    c. ben   ɬ-ke-ni-baen
    lake   preverb-preverb-situation aspect/perfective viewpoint-stem
    'He swam across the lake.' (101)
    ben   ɬ-ke-**n**-n-ez-baen
    lake   preverb-preverb-**distributive**-qualifier-situation aspect/
        perfective viewpoint-stem
    'He swam across pl. lakes.' (101)

Koyukon and Babine-Witsuwit'en are the last languages that I discuss here. In these languages, plurality can be indicated by the distributive or by another item that has been termed the multiple. I postpone discussion of the multiple until section 4.4.

In Koyukon, the distributive *n* can relate to objects.

(22) Koyukon (Axelrod 1993)
    a. ye-ghʉ-nee-ɬ-tsot
       disjoint anaphor-through-situation aspect-valence-stem
       'S/he quickly cut a hole through it.' (89)
    b. ye-ghʉ-**n**-'etl-tsot
       disjoint anaphor-through-**distributive**-situation aspect/perfective viewpoint/valence-stem
       'S/he cut several holes in it (hide, while skinning it hastily).'

In Babine-Witsuwit'en, the distributive *n* modifies subjects of intransitives and objects of transitives.

(23) Babine-Witsuwit'en (Hargus 1997)
    a. bə-ɣe-**n**-ts'ə-Gəz
       3 object-incorporate (skin)-**distributive**-1pl Subject-stem
       'We are skinning several.' (389)
    b. ne-**n**-c'ə-n-iz-əc-ɬ-'ɛl
       preverb-**distributive**-unspecified object-qualifier-situation aspect-1sg Subject-valence-stem
       'I felled several trees.' (390)

The distributive can quantify over oblique objects, as in the Slave examples in (24).

(24) Slave (Rice 1989)
    a. ye-yi-**yá**-we-ta
       disjoint anaphor-preverb-**distributive**-situation aspect-stem
       'S/he kicked at each.' (695)
    b. be-k'e-**ya**-'é-de-h-se
       3-on-**distributive**-unspecified Object-qualifier/situation aspect/perfective viewpoint/1sg Subject-valence-stem
       'I planed each.' (handled unspecified object on each) (695)

Locations and Times

In the examples discussed in the previous section, the distributive is related to participant roles of agent, patient, theme, and the like – it modifies entities.[7] It can therefore be thought of as a determiner, or D-quantifier. In this section,

4.3 Quantificational Elements

I continue with the same group of languages and show an additional function of the distributive, one that appears to relate to events rather than to entities.

It is often stated in the Athapaskan literature that the distributive can relate to events as well as to arguments. For instance, in Koyukon, the distributive expresses a repeated or 'here and there' quality about the state or activity or plurality of the patient (Axelrod 1993:89). Cook 1984:219–220, while not defining the distribution of the distributive in Tsuut'ina, discusses it in a chapter entitled 'Aspect Prefixes.' Hargus 1988:166 states that the distributive plural prefix marks actions in Sekani; Randoja 1990:124 says that the distributive in Beaver can mark actions performed separately or sequentially and events occurring in a number of locations, and Tenenbaum 1978:160 says that the distributive plural prefix indicates plurality of the subject of the verb or of the action itself in Dena'ina. Kari 1990:285 notes that the Ahtna distributive can indicate separate intervals and places. Finally, Rice 1989:677 indicates that the Slave distributive quantifies over both entities and events. These statements thus must make one question the status of the distributive as a D-quantifier alone. Could it be an adverbial quantifier, or A-quantifier, as well? I begin this section by providing examples where the distributive is said to modify events rather than entities. I then argue that the distributive is a D-quantifier rather than an A-quantifier in all of its uses.

In Koyukon, the distributive is often translated as referring to an activity that takes place here and there or to a state that is located here and there.

(25) Koyukon (Axelrod 1993)
   a. no-hoo-nee-ł-tseen'
      preverb-areal-situation aspect/perfective viewpoint-valence-stem
      'It (beaver) built (a dam) across (the stream).' (90)
      nʉ'ʉ-n-hoo-tl-tsee'
      preverb-**distributive**-areal-situation aspect/perfective viewpoint/valence-stem
      'It built (dams) across (the stream) at several places.'
   b. łaats   daa-łe-nokk
      sand   qualifier-situation aspect/voice-stem
      'There is some sand there.' (90)
      yeh   **ne**-daa-łe-nokk
      house **distributive**-qualifier-situation aspect/voice-stem
      'It (dust) is in piles here and there in the house.'
   c. k'e-l-dzes
      unspecified Object-voice/valence-stem
      'S/he is dancing.' (92)

nʉ'-ʉ-n-k'e-l-dzes
preverb-**distributive**-unspecified Object-voice/valence-stem
'S/he danced across (the creek) here and there (i.e., s/he danced across the creek and then came to another one and danced across it, and so on).' (92)

d. kkun'   ghee-tlaatl
   wood   situation aspect-stem
   'S/he chopped wood.' (92)
   kkun'   **ne**-hʉ-tlaaɬ
   wood   **distributive**-human plural Subject-stem
   'They were chopping wood here and there.'

In (25a), the distributive has a twofold function. It pluralizes the theme (dams) and indicates that the dams were not all built at the same place but in different places, stressing individuation of the theme. In (25c,d), the distributive translates as 'here and there', stressing that the event took place at a number of individual locations.

Similar translations are found for Slave distributives.

(26) Slave (Rice 1989)
a. ná-ne-y-i-h-kwa
   preverb-qualifier-situation aspect-perfective viewpoint/1sg Subject-valence-stem
   'I whipped it.' (679)
   ná-**yá**-ne-h-kwa
   preverb-**distributive**-qualifier/situation aspect/perfective viewpoint/1sg Subject-valence-stem
   'I whipped it here and there, whipped each separately, whipped it over and over.'

b. dé-ta
   qualifier/situation aspect/perfective viewpoint-stem
   'It kicked.' (678)
   yá-d-į́-ta
   distributive-qualifier-qualifier/perfective viewpoint-stem
   'It kicked many times.'

c. go-y-i-h-gé
   areal-situation aspect-perfective viewpoint/1sg Subject-valence-stem
   'I set posts.' (679)

4.3 Quantificational Elements

    go-**yá**-th-i-h-gé
    areal-**distributive**-situation aspect-perfective viewpoint/1sg Subject-valence-stem
    'I set one post after another.'
  d. tę chǫ-'e-n-í-ka
    ice preverb-unspecified Object-situation aspect-1pl Subject-stem
    'We made a hole in the ice.' (180)
    tę chǫ-**yá**-'e-wh-í-ka
    ice preverb-**distributive**-unspecified Object-situation aspect-1pl Subject-stem
    'We made one hole after another in the ice.'

Ahtna too is similar.

(27) Ahtna
  a. tene   ł-ke-t-a-ya:ł
    trail   preverb-preverb-inceptive-situation aspect-stem
    'He'll cross the trail.' (Kari 1979:95)
    tene   ł-ke-**n**-t-a-ya'
    trail   preverb-preverb-**distributive**-inceptive-situation aspect-stem
    'He'll cross the trail at several points; he'll cross plural travels.' (Kari 1979:95)
  b. na-**n**-n-ez-t'ak
    preverb-**distributive**-qualifier-situation aspect/perfective viewpoint-stem
    'It flew down several times.' (Kari 1990:343)
  c. di-t-xa-ł-tl'eł
    preverb-inceptive-situation aspect-1sg Subject/valence-stem
    'I'll pour it into it.' (Kari 1979:95)
    di-**n**-tx-a-ł-tl'iit
    preverb-**distributive**-inceptive-situation aspect-1sg Subject/valence-stem
    'I'll pour it into them (several containers).' (Kari 1979:95)

Dena'ina too has similar readings.

(28) Dena'ina (Tenenbaum 1978)
    nił-teh   ch'a-**n**-h-gha-ni-la
    reciprocal-postposition preverb-**distributive**-areal-qualifier-situation aspect-stem
    'untangle it (take pl. things apart spatially from each other in a series of actions)' (161)

Some Beaver examples with close readings are given in (29).

(29) Beaver (Randoja 1990)
    a. **dà**-də-ze
       distributive-qualifier-stem
       'They yelled over and over.' (124)
    b. ya-**dà**-gh-əs-twən
       distributive-distributive-qualifier-1sg Subject-stem
       'I put objects here and there.' (124)

Finally, in Carrier, as mentioned earlier, Morice 1932:II370 states that the distributive "often denotes some sort of a partitive or localitive intent in addition to the idea of plurality"; he suggests the term 'localitivo-pluralitive' for this item.[8]

(30) Carrier (Morice 1932)
    a. ta-·-dî-s-ˈaih
       'keep a door shut' (II:370)
       ta-**nê**-·-dî-s-ˈaih
       'keep doors shut in several places'
    b. hwo-de-the-s-qût
       'to disinfect (to spread essences, odors, smoke)' (II:372)
       n-o-de-the-s-qet
       'to disinfect in several places' (*no = nehwo*)

In all of these languages then, the distributive appears to indicate individuated plurality of events in addition to that of entities.

4.3.1.2 Cross-Language Comparison

While the languages differ in several ways, there are similarities. The table in (31) provides a comparison.

(31)
Languages	Subject	Object	Locations	Times
Chipewyan, Jicarilla Apache, Navajo	√	√		
Slave, Sekani, Beaver, Carrier	√	√	√	√
Ahtna, Dena'ina, Koyukon	√ (limited)	√	√	√

The columns Subject and Object represent entities; Locations and Times are treated in the literature as instances in which the distributivity is over the event.

4.3 Quantificational Elements

The question that I raise is whether the distributive is solely a D-quantifier or a general quantifier, serving as both a D-quantifier and an A-quantifier, as suggested in the Athapaskan literature? I will argue that it is a D-quantifier only. To do this, I establish two points. First, locations are treated as entities in the Athapaskan languages for purposes of agreement, and second, alternative means exist in the languages to quantify the number of events.

In examples where the distributive might relate to events, it pluralizes and individuates the number of locations in space or time in which an event takes place. As discussed in section 4.3, locations represent a type of entity, although a nonparticipant rather than a participant in the event (Frawley 1992:224).

Locations in space and time play an interesting role in Athapaskan languages. In general, locations in space or time are best viewed as part of the entity, or nominal, system in the family. The way to see this is to examine the use of the prefixes called areal or spatial and the indefinite or unspecified pronoun in the Athapaskan literature. The areal is viewed as a gender (noun class) marker (e.g., Kari 1990) or an agreement marker (e.g., Thompson 1993); which specific grammatical function it has is not relevant here. Notice that what the noun class system and the agreement system have in common with each other is that they relate to entities rather than to events. The following examples show that when the subject or object of a verb or the object of a postposition is a location in either space or time, as in (32) and (34)–(36), or an expletive element, as in (33), the areal element, in boldface, occurs. Areal entities include weather, rivers, mountains, houses, holes, cities, and other locations in space and time; see the grammars for details.

(32) Subject
    a. Slave
       go-wele
       area-hot
       'It (weather) is hot.'
    b. Sekani
       sahghè'   **gh**ǫ-chà'
       river   **area**/perfective viewpoint-big
       'The river is big.' (Hargus 1988:195)
    c. Witsuwit'en
       dzin **ho**-n-yiz
       day   **area**-perfective viewpoint-long
       'The day is long.' (Hargus 1995b)
       ne-**o**-ł-tan
       preverb-**area**-valence-stem
       'It rained.'

d. Koyukon
hu-dee-zoonh
area-qualifier-good
'The weather is good.' (Thompson 1989a:114)

(33) Dummy subject
Koyukon
Santa Claus   **h**oo-laanh
                  area-be
'There is a Santa Claus.' (Thompson 1989a:120)

(34) Object
a. Beaver
kwǫ   s-à -**wə̀**-nį-'ǫ
house 1sg Oblique-postposition-area-situation aspect/
      perfective viewpoint/2sg Subject-stem
'You sg. gave a house to me.' (Randoja 1990:114)
tlęza   kà-**wə**-ts'ets
dog   preverb-area-stem
'dog digs a hole' (Randoja 1990:114)

b. Witsuwit'en
wə-ɬ-dzixw
area-valence-stem
'He, she rakes an area.' (Hargus 1995b)

c. Ahtna
ku-ɬ-tsiin
area-valence-stem
'He built it (structure).' (Kari 1990:243)

d. Sekani
mə-t'adzę̀'   **w**ə̀-s-ch'ǫ
3possessor-back   **area**-situation aspect-stem
'He was shot in the back.' (Hargus 1988:195)

(35) Object of a postposition
a. Ahtna
hw-k'eze
area-alongside
'alongside the area' (Kari 1990:243)

b. Koyukon
Fairbanks   **hu**-ts'a   t-aal-yo
              area-to   inceptive-situation aspect/perfective
                      viewpoint-stem
'S/he went to Fairbanks.' (Thompson 1993:318)

4.3 Quantificational Elements

    c. Slave
       sǫbak'e   **go**-ts'ę́
       Yellowknife   **area**-to
       'to Yellowknife'

(36) Agreement
    a. Slave
       dzine   **go**-cho
       day   **area**-big
       'big day, holiday'
    b. Sekani
       mįghe   ta-**wə**-də-ch'e
       lake   preverb (three)-**area**-qualifier-stem
       'three lakes' (Hargus 1988:195)

Thus, when an areal noun is a direct argument of a verb or postposition or when an areal noun is modified, agreement is found in the form of the areal element. In addition, the areal occurs as an expletive, as in (33), an element generally considered to be pronominal.

When an areal noun is an adjunct instead of an argument, areal agreement is absent.

(37) Slave (Rice 1989)
    a. Argument
       hįdi dziné   **go**-ts'ę
       last day   **area**-to
       'until yesterday'
    b. Adjunct
       hįdi   dziné   ná-de-ya
       last   day   preverb-inceptive/situation aspect/perfective
                                  viewpoint/1sg Subject-stem
       'I returned yesterday.'

When the areal word 'yesterday' is a complement of a postposition, as in (37a), the areal marker *go* is present. When it is an adjunct, however, as in (37b), the areal marker is not found. Thus the areal marker only appears when an areal noun is an argument of a verb or postposition or is modified, but it is not found when an areal noun is an adjunct.

Just as the areal agreement marker can be used to mark locations in time and space, the unspecified pronoun can also be used in this way. In Navajo, the unspecified pronoun can be used with time reference or with reference to an event (Young 1997).

(38) Navajo (Young 1997)
    a. y-ee   'i-'-íí-ł-'ą́
       disjoint   preverb-**unspecified Object**-qualifier-valence-stem
       anaphor-with
       'He declared the pawn or loan period expired.' (literally: 'He caused indefinite object to move away out of sight.') (15)
    b. 'adą́ą́dą́ą́   Késhmish   'a-z-lį́į́'
       yesterday   Christmas   **unspecified Object**-situation aspect/
                                                 perfective viewpoint-stem
       'Yesterday was Christmas.' (18)

In these examples, the unspecified pronoun refers to a location in time. That location is an argument of the verb rather than an adjunct; it surfaces in a pronominal form. Again, the entitylike nature of locations in time and space is evident. Slave has similar examples.

(39) na-ła-'e-de-h-ndih gha
     preverb-preverb-**unspecified Object**-qualifier-1sg Subject-stem future
     'I will pour it out anytime, later.' (Rice 1989:631)

Koyukon too has instances of the unspecified pronoun having spatial reference. Thompson 1991:71 provides examples of its use together with a time word to indicate that an event occupies the entire period of time specified by the time word.

(40) Koyukon
    a. dzaan   k'o-hoł
       day   **unspecified Object**-sg walk
       'He walked all day.'
    cf. dzaan   tuh   gha-hoł
       day   during situation aspect-sg walk
       'He walked during the day.'

How does the distribution of the areal marker relate to the function of the distributive? The distributive clearly quantifies over an entity when that entity is an argument of a verb or postposition, as can be seen in the examples where it relates to a subject or an object. What if the distributive quantifies over an adjunct such as a location in space or time? We have seen that areal agreement is never found in this environment. However, there is no reason to believe that the status of an element changes from that of an entity to something else – there is simply no way of marking agreement. If this is the case, then the

4.3 Quantificational Elements

distributive can be viewed as relating to entities, where locations in time and place are entities, as suggested by the use of areal agreement.

The distributive thus appears to be a D-quantifier, or a quantifier over entities. It can quantify over both syntactic arguments and adjuncts in many of the languages (e.g., Slave), whereas it is limited to syntactic arguments in others (e.g., Navajo). What syntactic arguments and adjuncts have in common with each other is that they are both entities. The distributive contributes then to the interpretation of the type of plurality assigned to an entity.

Another slightly different perspective on the distributive is possible. Assume that the distributive is a determiner that modifies the meaning of an entity. It designates plural number and further indicates individuation. One way of reinforcing individuation in translation is by indicating different locations in either space or time. Thus, it is possible that the distributive never relates to adjuncts; this could in many cases be an accident of translation rather than a true fact about the languages.

Two further points are worthy of brief attention. First, Athapaskan languages have a rich system of marking plurality of events; this is discussed in chapter 11. Event plurality is generally marked through the aspect system rather than by quantifiers. In Navajo, for instance, as noted by Faltz 1995:300, event plurality without argument plurality is not marked by the distributive, but through other means. Plurality is an important concept in Athapaskan languages, with plurality of events and plurality of entities marked in different ways.

Second, while I have argued that the distributive modifies only entities, it interacts with the event system in that it is often accompanied by a situation aspect marker indicating an accomplishment. As discussed in chapter 11, the presence of this situation aspect marker reinforces the semantics of the distributive as requiring individuated rather than collective readings. This patterning may suggest that the distributive relates to the event system rather than, or in addition to, the entity system. However, it is not uncommon crosslinguistically to find that uncontroversial determiners carry aspectual information. For instance, in Bella Coola (Davis and Saunders 1975:14, Matthewson 1996:29), a Salishan language, there is a primary distinction on a proximal/nonproximal dimension, which encodes both spatial and temporal proximity. Frawley 1992:289 cites Denny 1978 as recognizing that deictic systems may mark semantic features such as verticality and boundedness. The situation aspect system in Athapaskan languages involves boundedness. This feature is marked in the aspect system, but can be a property of determiner systems as well. It is not surprising then to find the distributive, a type of determiner, interacting with the aspect system, though still part of the entity system.

4.3.2 Multiple

A second type of D-quantifier, the so-called multiple, is identified in two of the Athapaskan languages. It is illustrated in (41) and (42).

(41) Babine-Witsuwit'en: *ye* 'all, all over' (Hargus 1997)
    a. kwən   ne-**ye**-n-is-t-nəq
       fire   preverb-**multiple**-distributive-qualifier-situation aspect-voice-stem
       'All of the fires went out.' (389)
    b. **ye**-n-hə-ɬ-qət
       multiple-distributive-human plural Subject-valence-stem
       'They're each swollen up all over.' (390)

(42) Koyukon multiple: *yen* (Axelrod 1993)
    a. k'e-l-dzes
       unspecified Object-voice/valence-stem
       'S/he is dancing.' (92)
       yen-k'e-hee-l-dzees
       multiple-unspecified Object-human plural Subject-voice/valence-stem
       'They (many) are dancing.' (multiple)
    b. yee-l-dzaakk
       disjoint anaphor-situation aspect-stem
       'S/he put pitch on it (canoe); buttered it (bread).' (93)
       beedoy **yen**-'ee-dzaakk
       canoe **multiple**-epenthetic-stem
       'S/he put pitch on many canoes.'

Axelrod 1993:91 indicates that the multiple in Koyukon marks that one of the arguments of the verb (subject or object) is unusually numerous (in contrast, the distributive indicates the spatial distribution of such a quantity). The Koyukon multiple appears to be cognate with the Carrier numerositive discussed in note 8. Based on Axelrod's discussion of the multiple, it appears to be a D-quantifier in Koyukon, and the Babine-Witsuwit'en and Carrier translations are consistent with this analysis. The distributive and multiple differ in two major respects. Although both are D-quantifiers marking plurality, the distributive is a universal quantifier, indicating total quantity and also individuation, whereas the multiple may indicate either total quantity (translation as 'all') or partial quantity (translations as 'many, some'). The two quantifiers differ in that the distributive is truly distributive in meaning,

4.3 Quantificational Elements

referring to the individuals that make up the totality. The multiple, on the other hand, appears to refer to the collective totality ('all' translations) or to some number that exceeds the expected norm for the context ('many' translations). That is, it is the aggregate amount of individuals, not the individuals themselves that the speaker considers to be significant. Its use differs somewhat from language to language, and further work on its meaning is in order. The difference between the distributive and multiple D-quantifiers is summarized in (43); the analysis of the multiple must be treated as tentative in the absence of more data.[9]

(43)

	Distributive	Multiple	Totalative (Hupa)
Plural	+	+	+
Totality	+	+/−	+
Individuated	+	−	−
Collective	−	+	+

See Frawley 1992:468–469 for discussion of these various types of quantification.

4.3.3 Iterative

The third element that I have identified as a quantifier is generally termed the iterative in the Athapaskan literature. The iterative indicates phasal quantification and has as its core meaning that essentially the same event is repeated. I will first look at its use and then turn to its function, arguing that it too is a quantifier. But instead of being a quantifier that relates to the entity system, it is a quantifier that relates to the event system, or an A-quantifier.

The iterative can have one of several translations into English, depending on what it combines with: it can mean 'back', 'again', 'another', or, when combined with a customary stem (see chapter 11), a habitual, customary event or state. Just which readings are found depends on aspectual characteristics of the verb and on whether the argument of the verb can be affected in the same way more than once.

I begin by looking at the range of meanings of the iterative in several of the languages. In Hupa, the iterative has the form *na*. It indicates that an action is repeated or that a motion is reversed (Golla 1970:118). Golla indicates that when the iterative co-occurs with a verb of directional motion, it reverses the verb's meaning, as in (44a), while with other verbs, it signals repetition, as in (44b).

(44) a. Hupa: directional motion theme
yeh-**na**-'-win-di-yay
preverb-**iterative**-3 human Subject-situation aspect-voice-stem
'He went back inside.' (119)
na-'-Wi-wi-ł-di-te:l
iterative-3 human Subject-1sg Object-situation aspect-valence-voice-stem
'He was taking me along back.' (119)
b. Hupa: nonmotion verb
na:-k'yi-da:ye'
iterative-unspecified Subject-stem
'(The flower) blooms again.' (118)
na:-**na**-'-wa
preverb-**iterative**-3 human Subject-stem
'He moves about again.' (119)

In Slave, a slightly wider range of translations is found. Nevertheless, I argue, following Rice and Saxon 1997, that the iterative is a single morpheme, just as it is in Hupa. The different readings are determined by what it combines with.

First, the iterative *na* can co-occur with a customary stem form (see chapter 11); in this case, the verb has a customary reading.

(45) Slave iterative *na*: customary (Rice 1989)
a. ni-d-į́-dhah
preverb-qualifier-situation aspect/perfective viewpoint-stem
'S/he picked up plural objects.' (672)
ni-**na**-d-į́-dheh
preverb-**iterative**-qualifier-situation aspect/perfective viewpoint-stem, customary
'S/he picked up plural objects repeatedly.'
b. ná-de-wé
preverb-qualifier-stem
'It is broken.' (672)
ná-**na**-de-we
preverb-**iterative**-qualifier-stem, customary
'It is always broken.'

A common translation for the iterative is 'again'. The repeated event can either be identical to the original event or essentially the same, differing by one or more participants.

4.3 Quantificational Elements

(46) Slave iterative *na*: 'again' (Rice 1989)
    a. shé-tį
       incorporate-stem
       'S/he is dining.' (732)
       na-shé-tį
       iterative-incorporate-stem
       'S/he is dining again.'
    b. ná-ne-y-i-ta
       preverb-qualifier-situation aspect-viewpoint aspect/1sg Subject-stem
       'I kicked him/her.' (732)
       nǫ-ne-y-i-ta
       preverb/**iterative**-qualifier-situation aspect-viewpoint aspect/1sg Subject-stem
       'I kicked him/her again.' (iterative is nasalization on [o])

With verbs involving motion and transfer, the iterative is translated as 'return to a previous location' or 'back'.

(47) Slave iterative *na*: 'return to previous location, back'
    a. k-a-'ó
       human plural Subject-situation aspect-stem
       'They are going by water.' (731)
       ra-k-a-t-'ó
       iterative-human plural Subject-situation aspect-middle voice-stem
       'They are returning by water.'
    b. te-ye-d-é-h-xa
       preverb-disjoint anaphor-qualifier-situation aspect/perfective viewpoint-valence-stem
       'S/he threw (wood) in the water.' (732)
       te-**na**-ye-d-é-h-xa
       preverb-**iterative**-disjoint anaphor-qualifier-situation aspect/perfective viewpoint-valence-stem
       'S/he threw (wood) back in the water.'

The iterative is sometimes translated as 'another', where the event is repeated, but the subject or object involved in the event is substituted for.

(48) Slave iterative *na*: 'another'
    a. gohfįtí **ra**-h-sį
       ax   **iterative**-valence-stem
       'S/he made another ax handle.'

b. se   fí-la-d-į-tł'i
   log   preverb-preverb-qualifier-2sg Subject-stem
   'Throw a log on the fire.' (733)
   se   fí-la-**ra**-d-į-tł'i
   log   preverb-preverb-**iterative**-qualifier-2sg Subject-stem
   'Throw another log on the fire.'

Finally, the iterative is part of the basic lexical entry of a verb involving inherent repetition or the return to an earlier state; this use is called the reversative in the Athapaskan literature.

(49) Slave iterative *na*: part of lexical entry
   a. **ra**-ye-y-į-k'á
      iterative preverb-disjoint anaphor-situation aspect-perfective viewpoint-stem
      'S/he sharpened it.'
   b. **na**-e-ghį
      iterative preverb-situation aspect-stem
      'It thawed.'
   c. **na**-ts'e-jé
      iterative preverb-unspecified human Subject-stem
      'become well, heal'
   d. **na**-ts'e-geh
      iterative preverb-unspecified human Subject-stem
      'unlace, untie'

An iterative form is often ambiguous between two readings. In particular with a verb whose object or subject need not be interpreted as wholly affected and can potentially either be acted on again in the same way or return to its original state or location, the event may be totally repeated along with its arguments, or an argument may be substituted for.

(50) Slave ambiguities
   a. **na**-ts'e-d-í-h-tɬa
      iterative-unspecified human Subject-qualifier-qualifier-valence-stem
      'One starts the fire again, starts another fire.'
   b. **na**-y-é-h-k'é
      iterative-disjoint anaphor-situation aspect/perfective viewpoint-valence-stem
      'S/he shot it again, shot another one.'

4.3 Quantificational Elements

c. me-**na**-hú-d-le
3 Object-**iterative**-qualifier-middle voice-stem
'S/he is deceased again, another person is deceased.'

With verbs involving a location or point of transfer, the iterative can entail either a return to the original location or a single repetition of an event.

(51) Slave ambiguities
a. ni-**na**-ts'e-d-í-'a
preverb-**iterative**-unspecified human Subject-qualifier-qualifier-stem
'One takes back clothlike object, picks up clothlike object again.'
b. ke-**na**-go-ts'e-d-i̧-h-sho̧
areal-**iterative**-areal-unspecified human Subject-qualifier-perfective viewpoint-valence-stem
'One regains consciousness, finds out again.'

Based on the distribution of the iterative, Rice and Saxon 1997 argue that there is a single lexical entry for the iterative element, as in (52).

(52) The iterative is an operator on events, specifying a repetition.
- In addition to simple repetition: With verbs of motion, a reading glossed as '(returning) back (to a previous location)' is always possible.
- With other verbs implying a location (for example, verbs of handling) a reading indicating '(returning) back (to a previous location)' is possible.
- With verbs whose argument is affected, two readings are possible. In the first the action is repeated on the same object, or the repetition involves the same event and the same participants as the original event (Evans 1995:239, in a discussion of the iterative in the Australian language Mayali, calls this 'exact replay'). In the second a different object is affected in the same way, or the event is the same although one or more participants are substituted for (Evans 1995:239 identifies this as 'replays with token-replacement(s)'). With verbs whose argument cannot be affected in the same way twice, only the latter reading is possible.

The core function of the iterative then is to contribute to event structure, indicating a single repetition of an event. The exact reading is determinable from the construction, with the semantics of the verb making a major contribution to the semantics of the construction. The iterative affects the view of the event – it is repeated. While arguments can be involved, as either the same object or a different object can be affected, these are not involved in a primary way. Rather, the particular way in which an argument is affected follows the semantics of the verb. The iterative on its own contributes only to event structure.

The examination of other languages reveals quite similar facts. Some examples of the different readings in a few languages are given in (53).

(53) 'again'
- a. Tsuut'ina[10]
  xā-**ná**-yì-s-tó
  preverb-**iterative**-situation aspect-1sg Subject-stem
  'I pulled it out again.' (Cook 1984:220)
- b. Dena'ina
  nu-yi-ł-jeh
  iterative-disjoint anaphor-valence-stem
  'He hit her again.' (Tenenbaum 1978:172)
- c. Sekani
  chu-**na**-ts'ə-n-ès-dǫ
  preverb-**iterative**-unspecified human Subject-qualifier-situation aspect-stem
  'We are drunk again.' (Hargus 1988:164)
- d. Beaver
  dəgwòt   k'è-**na**-s-da
  knee   preverb-**iterative**-situation aspect-stem
  'S/he squatted again.' (Randoja 1990:128)
- e. Ahtna
  na-h-ni-daes
  iterative-area-2sg Subject-stem
  'Speak again!' (Kari 1990:291)
  na-łi-si-z-'ał
  iterative-incorporate-1sg Object-situation aspect/perfective viewpoint-stem
  'A dog (*łi*) bit me again.' (Kari 1990:79)
- f. Carrier
  na-de-s-ni
  iterative-qualifier-1sg Subject-stem
  'I say again.' (Morice 1932, II:343)

4.3 Quantificational Elements

(54) 'return to a previous location, back'
    a. Dena'ina
       nu-ghe-d-yuł
       iterative-situation aspect-middle voice-stem
       'He's walking back.' (Tenenbaum 1978:172)
    b. Sekani
       na-dè-s-ja
       iterative-inceptive-situation aspect-voice/stem
       'S/he went back.' (Hargus 1988:164)
    c. Beaver
       na-nə-s-chush
       iterative-situation aspect-1sg Subject-stem
       'I give back clothlike object.' (Randoja 1990:128)
    d. Ahtna
       na-ki-daetl'
       iterative-human plural Subject-stem
       'They returned.' (Kari 1990:144)
       na-xay-de-l-nen
       iterative-incorporate-qualifier-voice/valence-stem
       'Winter (*xay*) returned.' (Kari 1990:212)
    e. Carrier
       na-rhe-s-na
       iterative-qualifier-1sg Subject-stem
       'I revive.' (cf. *rhesna* 'I live.') (Morice 1932, II:343)
       hwo-sa-**na**-s-ˈaih
       area-preverb-**iterative**-1sg Subject-stem
       'I bring back.' (Morice 1932, II:344)

(55) 'another'
    a. Dena'ina
       nu-ven-da-l-tin
       iterative-incorporate-qualifier-voice/valence-stem
       'another lake (*ven*) lying' (Tenenbaum 1978:172)
    b. Ahtna
       ghadi   **na**-ł-tsin
       another **iterative**-valence-stem
       'He made another one.' (Kari 1990:212)

(56) Reversative
    Ahtna
    na-t-a-d-yaex
    iterative preverb-inceptive-situation aspect-voice-stem
    'It will heal.' (Kari 1990:433)

The same type of ambiguities arise as are found in Slave.

(57) Carrier (Morice 1932, II:343)
   a. es-tcût
      'to take'
   b. **na**-z-tcût
      iterative-situation aspect-stem
      'take again, take back, retake'

The iterative and the distributive thus contrast in terms of the kind of contribution they make to a predication: the iterative contributes to the understanding of the event and the distributive to the understanding of the arguments. This will be important in chapter 5, where I examine the ordering relationship between the iterative and the distributive.

The semantics of the iterative is especially interesting in Navajo. Young and Morgan 1987 propose three lexical items, one for each of the meanings associated with the iterative (return to previous state, single repetition, customary). I return to this in chapter 6.

4.4 Incorporates

The incorporates are of two basic types. First are entity incorporates. These are nouns that represent participant roles (agents, themes) or nonparticipant roles (locations, instruments). Second are event incorporates, or stems that introduce a second event.

Consider first entity incorporates. Examples of incorporated themes are given in (58). In all languages that allow incorporation of arguments, this type is found.

(58) Incorporated themes – objects
   a. Slave
      ní-**yati**-dé-ni̧-'ǫ
      preverb-**incorporate**-qualifier-situation aspect/perfective
      viewpoint-stem
      yati 'word'
      'S/he blamed (placed words).'
      ra-**xe**-ye-h-'a
      iterative-**incorporate**-situation aspect-1sg Subject-stem
      xe 'pack'
      'I am packing it back.' (literally: I handle pack back)

4.4 Incorporates

    b. Beaver (Randoja 1990)
    je-**gwòt**-s-i-'ǫ
    preverb-**incorporate**-situation aspect-perfective viewpoint/1sg
    Subject-stem
    gwòt 'knee'
    'I bumped my knee.' (132)

    c. Koyukon (Axelrod 1990)
    nelaan   e-no-**hʉghʉɬ**-ghe-'oɬ
    meat   preverb-iterative-**incorporate**-situation aspect-stem
    hʉghʉɬ 'raft'
    'S/he is bringing home a raft loaded with meat.'(181)
    to-k'e-**ggoyh**-hʉ-de-ghee-lo
    preverb-unspecified possessor-**incorporate**-area-qualifier-situation
    aspect-stem
    ggoyh 'young'
    'It (duck) put its young into the water.' (183)

Theme subjects are also able to incorporate.

(59) Incorporated themes – subjects
    a. Slave
    te-**she**-n-i̧-'a
    preverb-**incorporate**-situation aspect-perfective viewpoint-stem
    she 'tail'
    'tail extends into water' (place name)

    b. Ahtna (Kari 1990)
    ka-**hwnes**-ne-ɬ-'aa
    preverb-**incorporate**-situation aspect-valence-stem
    hwnes 'raft'
    'Ridges (like raft logs) extend in ascending lines.' (302)

    c. Koyukon (Axelrod 1990)
    do-**haaɬ**-le-'onh
    preverb-**incorporate**-situation aspect-stem
    haaɬ 'trap'
    'A trap is set up there.' (191)

In some languages, agent incorporation is found as well.

(60) Incorporated agents
    a. Koyukon (Axelrod 1990)
    kk'o-**'eɬts'eeyh**-yee-dzoyh
    preverb-**incorporate**-situation aspect-stem
    eɬts'eeyh 'wind'
    'The wind is moving them around.' (185)

to-hebe-t-aatl-taanh
incorporate-human plural Object-inceptive-situation aspect/
perfective viewpoint/valence-stem
to 'water'
'They floated away [water carried them off].' (186)
nee-**to**-nee-yo
preverb-**incorporate**-situation aspect/perfective viewpoint-stem
to 'water'
'The water stopped rising.' (187)
nee-**ts'eeyh**-nee-gheł
preverb-**incorporate**-situation aspect/perfective viewpoint-stem
ts'eeyh 'boat'
'The boat came to a stop.' (189)
b. Ahtna (Kari 1990)
ka-na-**ł**-de-l-ghos
preverb-iterative-**incorporate**-qualifier-voice/valence-stem
łi 'dog'
'The dogs are howling now and then.' (207)

Incorporated entities also indicate location, instrument, and other nonparticipant roles.

(61) a. Slave
ne-ts'ę   ná-**da**-de-h-di
2sg Object-postposition   preverb-**incorporate**-qualifier-1sg
                  Subject-stem
da 'mouth'
'I defend you sg. (help with words).'
k'e-**ke**-e-h-dzoh
preverb-**incorporate**-situation aspect-1sg Subject-voice/stem
ke 'foot'
'I skated, slid on feet.'
ká-**įze**-ts'e-d-a-mį
preverb-**incorporate**-unspecified human Subject-qualifier-situation
aspect-stem
įze 'slush snow'
'One walked (swam) through slush snow.'

b. Beaver
k'è-**ke**-e-s-dzos
preverb-**incorporate**-situation aspect-1sg Subject-voice/stem
ke 'foot'
'I slid around on feet.' (Randoja 1990:133)

Incorporation in which the incorporate specifies a second event contemporaneous with the first is found in many languages.

(62) a. Slave
k'ína-**shin-e**-de-da
preverb-**incorporate-suffix**-qualifier-voice/stem
shin 'sing, song' + e adverbial suffix
da 'sg. go'
'S/he walks around singing.'
b. Beaver (Randoja 1990)
k'è-**bə̀d-e**-də-s-dà
preverb-**incorporate-suffix**-qualifier-1sg Subject-voice/stem
bə̀d 'be hungry' + e adverbial suffix
dà 'sg. go'
'I walk around eating.' (134)
c. Ahtna (Kari 1990)
s-ta-**bes**-ghi-ni-l-cuut
preverb-preverb-**incorporate**-qualifier-situation aspect-voice/valence-stem
bes 'drag'
cuut 'take'
'Drag it away!' (107)
d. Koyukon (Axelrod 1990)
b-e-no-**tseł**-'ee-de-tlaakk
3 Object-postposition-iterative-**incorporate**-situation aspect/viewpoint aspect-voice-stem
tseł 'wet'
tlaakk 'go'
'S/he came home soaking wet.' (184)

The semantics of incorporation is discussed in chapter 6.

4.5 Other Lexical Material

All of the languages have preverbs and quantifiers, and some have incorporates. Some have additional elements. Two other types of lexical items have been identified, a negative in Carrier (Morice 1932) and Babine-Witsuwit'en (Hargus 1997) and an inceptive (see Morice 1932 for Carrier, Hargus 1997 for Babine-Witsuwit'en, and Hargus 1988 for Sekani).

A negative lexical item is reported in a few languages. It is illustrated in (63).

(63) Negative
    a. Carrier (Morice 1932)
       des-ni
       'I say.' (II:248)
       ł-dezes-nih
       'I do not say.'
       a˙-des-khaih
       'I mend.' (II:249)
       a-łê˙-dezes-khai
       'I do not mend.'
    b. Babine-Witsuwit'en (Hargus 1997)
       nə-**we**-s-ye'
       preverb-**negative**-negative-stem
       'S/he can't walk.' (389)
       ye-ne-**we**-yə-d-i-l-ɣəs
       preverb-iterative-**negative**-disjoint anaphor-qualifier-situation aspect-voice/valence-stem
       'S/he didn't chew it to pieces again.' (389)

The function of the negative will be discussed in greater detail in chapter 6.

The final lexical item that I discuss is a marker of inceptivity.

(64) Inceptive
    a. Carrier (Morice 1932)
       hwê-nez-qĕ
       'I commenced to get mad.' (II:163)
       ha-thè-**hwê**-u-nes-tłĕ
       'I commence digging up the soft bottom.' (II:163)
    b. Babine-Witsuwit'en (Hargus 1997)
       kwən ne-**o**-n-i-t-nəq
       fire iterative-**inceptive**-qualifier-situation aspect-voice-stem
       'The fire started to go out.' (389)
       ye-**o**-n-i-gə-l-q'ət
       multiple-**inceptive**-qualifier-aspect-1sg Subject-voice/valence-stem
       'I started to swell up all over.' (390)

c. Sekani (Hargus 1988)
   whè-n-i-tsègh
   inceptive-qualifier-qualifier/perfective viewpoint/1sg Subject-stem
   'I started to cry.' (162)
   ts'e-**whè**-sə-n-i̧-h-sət
   preverb-**inceptive**-1sg Object-qualifier-qualifier/perfective viewpoint/1sg Subject-stem
   'S/he started to wake me up.' (163)

The inceptive is verbal in nature; see chapter 6 for more detail.

4.6 Summary

Three major categories, preverb, quantifier, and incorporate, make up the nonstem lexical items of Athapaskan languages, or what are traditionally called the disjunct prefixes. More than one of each of these is possible within a verb word. In the following chapters, after a brief aside on the position of verb stems, I turn to the primary question of this study: What orders do the lexical items appear in, and is this ordering principled?

5

A Brief Side Trip: The Position of the Verb Stem

A preliminary task, prior to an investigation of ordering relationships among the lexical elements in the verb, is the establishment of the position of the verb stem in Athapaskan languages. Abstracting away from details of the verb, we find that across the language family, the morphemes in the verb come in the order in (1).

(1)   lexical items – functional items – voice/valence – verb stem

The positioning of the verb stem at the right edge of the verb word is surprising for several reasons. First, it has long been observed that inflection tends to fall outside of derivation (see Anderson 1982, 1988 for detailed discussion). Although the definition of what is inflectional and derivational (for which I use the terms functional and lexical, respectively) in Athapaskan languages is not completely clear (see Kibrik 1995, Rice 1993, Speas 1990 and chapter 16), the Athapaskan verb nevertheless is a striking counterexample to this generalization. Recall the template for Slave provided in chapter 2, repeated here as (2).

(2)   preverb # quantificational elements # incorporate # object % third person subject % qualifier + subsituation aspect + situation aspect + viewpoint aspect + 1/2 person subject = voice/valence + root + tense/mode/aspect suffix

The items in (2) that are separated by the # boundary symbol are known in the Athapaskan literature as disjunct prefixes. These are generally considered to be derivational (see chapter 4 for details); I treat them as lexical items. The items separated by % and + boundary symbols are known in the Athapaskan literature as conjunct prefixes. This category is a rather mixed bag in terms

The Position of the Verb Stem

of inflectional/derivational status. Some of the prefixes are generally agreed to be inflectional (e.g., viewpoint aspect; pronominals, but see Sandoval and Jelinek 1989 and Willie 1991 on pronominals as arguments), whereas others are regarded as derivational (e.g., noun class markers, situation aspect, subsituation aspect). I argue in Part III that these are all functional items. At least on the surface, then, we see a massive violation of the generalization about inflection and derivation, with derivation appearing to the left of inflection, rather than adjacent to the stem, as expected if the model that derivation precedes inflection is directly mirrored in morpheme order. If the verb stem were, say, at the left edge of the verb word rather than at the right edge, the ordering would instantiate an expected and common ordering among languages (e.g., Bybee 1985a, Speas 1991b).

In addition, when just the ordering of functional items in relation to the verb stem is considered, the ordering does not follow patterns observed in crosslinguistic studies. The basic ordering among the functional items is as in (3); see chapters 8 through 13 for details.

(3) object – subject number – qualifier – subsituation aspect – situation aspect – viewpoint aspect – subject agreement – voice/valence – stem

Bybee 1985a, in a study of the ordering of a number of morphological categories in a wide range of languages, observes that agreement marking for subject tends to be ordered further from the verb than does aspect. In addition, aspectual affixes marking categories such as perfective and imperfective (viewpoint) tend to be ordered further from the verb than do affixes marking aspects like inceptive (subsituation aspect). Foley and Van Valin 1984, working from a different database, find evidence for this same ordering; see also Van Valin 1993. But exactly the reverse ordering is found in Athapaskan languages – first and second person subject pronominals are closer to the verb stem than is aspect in general, and viewpoint aspect is in turn closer to the verb stem than is subsituation aspect. If the verb stem were to the left of the functional items rather than to their right, the ordering of morphemes would again be as expected from other languages.

An additional factor suggests that the verb stem is in an odd position in the Athapaskan verb. This has to do with the semantic relationship of the lexical material within the verb to the verb stem. Recall that the lexical material includes preverbs, quantificational elements, and, in some languages, incorporates. A traditional assumption in the Athapaskan literature is that the preverbs are often listed as part of the lexical entry of the verb or concatenated with the verb stem at an early level of word formation; see, for example,

Kari 1979, 1990, 1992, Randoja 1990, Rice 1993, and Speas 1984 for recent explicit statements of this assumption. The reason for the assumption is that the preverbs and the stem combine to yield the main meaning of the verb word. The concatenation may be idiosyncratic, or the meaning of the whole may be predictable from the meaning of the parts, but in either case it is this unit that forms the base for later word formation.

The closeknit relationship between a preverb and the verb stem can be seen by examining preverbs like those in (4) and (5).

(4) Slave (Rice 1989)
   ká-d-i̧-tɬa
   ká 'out' # d inceptive + i̧ 2sg Subject = tɬa 'singular, dual go on land'
   'You sg. go out.'
(5) Ahtna (Kari 1990)
   ka-ghi-yaa
   ka 'up and out, up from below' # ghi situation aspect/perfective viewpoint = yaa 'singular, dual go on land, perfective'
   'He came up and out, up from below.' (234)

In these examples, the preverb (ká in Slave, ka in Ahtna) restricts the meaning of the verb stem, expressing something about the direction of going.

The assumption that the ordering of word formation reflects semantic compositionality directly is not unusual. As discussed in chapter 3, it is a common assumption in the Athapaskan literature, and it is a driving force behind works that argue that morpheme order is not a reflection of word formation. It is a common assumption within the theoretical literature as well; see chapter 3.

Assuming that semantic compositionality is represented structurally, further evidence that the verb stem and preverbs form a close constituent is provided by the relationship of quantificational elements to the preverb-verb stem unit. There is evidence that the preverb-verb stem unit falls within the scope of the iterative even though the preverb-verb stem do not form a surface constituent – the iterative modifies the preverb-stem complex, not the stem or the prefixes alone. This is argued for explicitly in Kari 1979, 1990, Randoja 1990, and Speas 1984 (who assumes that the Navajo iterative and distributive have scope over the preverbs), and it is widely assumed in the Athapaskan literature. For instance, consider the iterative form of the Slave example in (4), shown in (6). The iterative is realized here as nasalization of the vowel of the preverb.

(6) kǫdi̧tɬa
    ká 'out' # na iterative # d inceptive + i̧ 2sg Subject = tɬa '1, 2 go on land'
    'You sg. go back out.'

In this example, the iterative indicates that it is the going out that is repeated, suggesting that the iterative has scope over the event as a whole, not just over the going. This can be seen more dramatically in a verb like the Slave example in (7).

(7) téhkǫyetɬa
    teh 'water' # ká 'out' # na iterative # ye situation aspect = tɬa '1, 2, go on land'
    'S/he went out of the water again.'

This verb is grammatical on the gloss given – s/he had gone out of the water once and then went out again (entailing that s/he had reentered water). It cannot mean, for instance, that s/he went into the water, out of the water and then into the water again and is, at the reference point, in the water; rather s/he must be out of the water at the reference time.

The iterative thus has scope over the preverb-stem in that it modifies the meaning of the complex, not just of the stem or the preverb. Again, assuming that this type of scope relationship is represented structurally, the verb stem belongs in a constituent with the preverbs, and this entire unit must be in a position lower than that of the iterative element. This suggests a remote syntactic structure along the lines of (8).

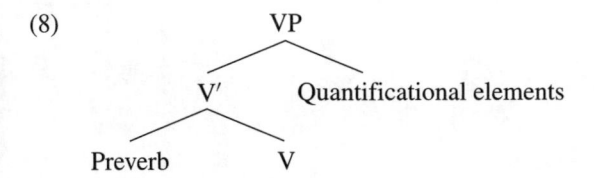

(8)
```
            VP
           /  \
         V'    Quantificational elements
        /  \
   Preverb   V
```

Considerations of the sort just discussed are found in the literature as arguments for underlying ordering and constituency. For instance, Larson 1988 argues that oblique objects are structurally closer to the verb in English than are direct objects based in part on the semantics of idioms. A fundamental assumption underlying movement rules in syntax is that semantic relationships between a verb and its arguments are directly reflected at some deep level of structure; if an argument is removed from a verb, it must have originated in a position that reflects its semantic relationship with the verb. Thus the structural representation of semantic compositionality has precedent in linguistic theory in general.

Facts such as those discussed in this chapter (ordering of inflection and derivation, ordering among functional items, relationship of verb stem to preverbs, relationship of preverb-verb stem complex to quantificational adverbs) lead to the hypothesis that a primary idiosyncrasy of the Athapaskan verb is that the verb stem is located in the 'wrong' place in the surface string.

In the remainder of this book, I assume a movement-based account along the lines proposed in Speas 1990, 1991b and Rice 1993, 1998. I elaborate on this structure in the chapters to come, but the basic conceptual idea is captured in (8). The verb stem originates as a sister to the preverbs, both of which are within the scope of, and therefore enter into semantic composition as a unit with, quantificational elements. Given this position, the Athapaskan verb is, at a deep level, not a counterexample to the generalization that inflection is outside derivation. Rather, it fits the observations made by Bybee about the position of functional morphemes with respect to the verb and with respect to each other, and it reflects semantic compositionality. What is unusual about the verb is the surface position of the stem – it moves from its position within the verb phrase to the right of the functional morphemes.

6

Ordering of the Lexical Items

In this chapter I examine the ordering of the lexical items discussed in chapter 4. I argue that evidence exists, both within individual languages and across the family, for the following generalizations:

(i) Elements in a fixed scopal relationship occur in a fixed order with respect to each other.
(ii) Elements in which the scopal relationship can be reversed occur in variable order, with interpretation related to order.
(iii) Elements that do not enter into a scopal relationship with each other may occur in different orders, both within a particular language and across the family.

As a result, elements that are related by scope have a predictable ordering, whereas ones that do not enter into a scopal relationship must have their ordering stipulated for the particular language.

6.1 On the Ordering of the Lexical Items

In the Athapaskan literature, statements are often made to the effect that ordering is relatively fixed within the functional (conjunct) complex across the family, but that when the lexical (disjunct) complex is examined, ordering varies. For instance, Cook 1989:194–195, in a discussion of the numbering of verb prefix positions, states that "pan-Athapaskan prefix order may be established at least for the conjunct prefixes where the differences in prefix categories are primarily in the disjunct prefixes." Kari 1989:449 makes this point explicitly: "the innermost prefixes [functional – KR] are more directly comparable across the languages than are the outermost prefixes [lexical – KR]." Hargus 1988:162 takes a similar position, observing that "there is greater cross-linguistic diversity in the inventory and positions of the Athabaskan disjunct prefixes than there is in the conjunct prefixes." The general sense one gets then in reading the Athapaskan literature is that the languages exhibit variability in the ordering of the lexical items. If the order of lexical items is truly variable, this supports the prediction of the template analysis that morpheme order can vary across a language family. In this section, then, I examine ordering of the items across the family to see just how much the languages differ.

Recall from chapter 4 that the lexical items include preverbs, quantificational elements, and, in some languages, incorporates and indicators of negation and inception. Appendix 1 gives detailed information on the ordering of affixes for a number of languages. The languages overall show fewer differences in the order of categories than might be expected if no principles underlie the ordering. When all the languages are taken into account, generalizations about both global uniformity and local variability can be drawn. Abstracting away from the incorporates, the generalization in (1) is apparent.

(1)   Preverbs precede quantificational elements.

Taking the incorporates into account, another generalization is available:[1]

(2)   In languages with incorporates, preverbs precede incorporates.

These two statements capture the global uniformity found in the verb across the family. As shown in (3), local variability is also found. Ignoring the preverbs, the ordering of quantificational material and incorporates is not identical across the languages. Some languages appear on more than one line since they permit variable ordering.

(3)   **Ordering of non-preverb lexical items**   **Sample languages**
      iterative-distributive-*incorporate*   Ahtna, Koyukon
      distributive-iterative-*incorporate*   Ahtna, Chipewyan, Slave
      iterative-*incorporate*-**distributive**   Dena'ina, Tsuut'ina,
                                                       Beaver, Dogrib

      incorporate-**distributive-iterative**   Slave
      incorporate-**iterative-distributive**   Beaver, Koyukon
      (distributive)-*incorporate*-**iterative-** Sekani
         distributive-(iterative)-inceptive
      (distributive)-iterative-*incorporate*-   Sekani
         distributive-(iterative)-inceptive

6.1 On the Ordering of the Lexical Items

    iterative-multiple-negative-*incorporate*-   Babine-Witsuwit'en
        inceptive-**distributive**
    iterative-distributive // iterative-   Navajo, Apache // Hupa
        plural (Hupa)
    distributive-iterative-inceptive-   Carrier
        incorporate-negative

Before turning to discussion of local variability, an additional type of global uniformity is apparent in (3). In languages with an inceptive lexical item (Sekani, Babine-Witsuwit'en, Carrier), this occurs to the right of the preverbs and the iterative.

(4)   The inceptive appears to the right of preverbs and the iterative.

Focusing now on local variability, the table in (3) shows that in addition to global uniformity, local variability, both within languages and across the family, occurs. I detail some types of local variability in the following discussion. One type of variation involves the ordering of incorporates with respect to quantifiers.

(5)   The ordering of incorporates and quantificational elements varies both across the family and within individual languages.

A second type of variability concerns the ordering of the iterative and distributive, which is not fixed in Ahtna, Koyukon, and Sekani. In Slave and Chipewyan, the iterative is reported to appear to the right of the distributive, while in other languages, the ordering is reversed. This is summarized in (6).

(6)   The ordering of the iterative and the distributive quantificational elements varies both across the family and within individual languages.

A cross-language study thus reveals both global uniformity and local variability within the lexical portion of the Athapaskan verb. The kinds of local variability suggest that perhaps the statements quoted at the beginning of this chapter are correct – the order of elements seems random across the languages. However, the strict placement of preverbs, combined with fixed ordering within the preverbs, as we will see in section 6.3, suggests that the ordering is not random, but principled. In the remainder of this chapter, I propose a resolution of this dilemma.

6.2 Principles of Ordering

In section 6.1, I showed that while there is variability in the ordering of lexical items both within a language and across the family, this variation is more limited than might be expected given the quotations at the beginning of that section. The variation between languages is mimicked by that within some of the individual languages. I now turn to my major goal, to examine ordering in more detail. I argue that in general, the uniformity and variability observed in section 6.1 follows from the scopal principle introduced in chapter 3.

6.2.1 The Principle of Scopal Ordering

Recall that I assume that scopal relations are structurally represented, and specifically, that an element that has scope over another element must c-command that element (see, for instance, Langacker 1969, Reinhart 1976). I also assume right-to-left directionality. Assuming hierarchical ordering, the following two basic orders of major categories can be defined for the Athapaskan family.[2]

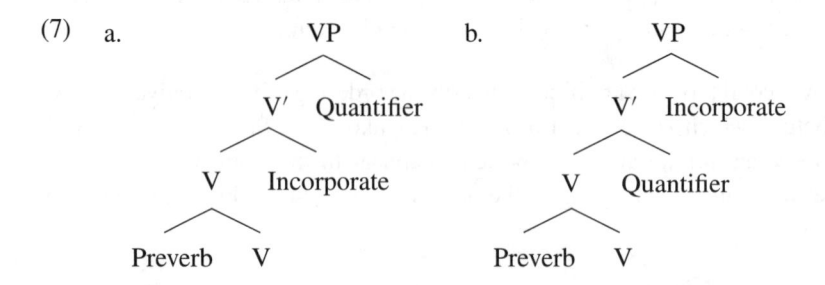

(7) a.
```
            VP
           /  \
         V'    Quantifier
        /  \
       V    Incorporate
      / \
  Preverb V
```

b.
```
            VP
           /  \
         V'    Incorporate
        /  \
       V    Quantifier
      / \
  Preverb V
```

In the trees in (7), the quantifiers and incorporates c-command the preverbs as the former are structurally superior to the latter.

Imposing hierarchical structure is not in and of itself sufficient to establish why the lexical items show limited orderings: structure alone does not represent an advance over a template if there is no particular reason for the ordering. The question that arises then is why only certain c-command relationships are found among the lexical items in the Athapaskan family. For instance, why are the preverbs always the most deeply embedded? It is here, I will argue, that scope becomes important.

6.2 Principles of Ordering

Recall from chapter 3 the scope principle, repeated in (8).

(8) When one morpheme is in the scope of another, the morpheme with greater scope must c-command morphemes within its scope.

I now turn to a more detailed consideration of scope and what it means; see also the discussion in chapter 3. One way of looking at scope is in terms of subset relations, with a more general item commanding a more specific one. This type of proposal is common in the literature. Brunson 1989, 1992, for instance, proposes that the preposing of English prepositional phrases is governed by a principle similar to that in (8). She argues that in English sentences with two or more thematically dependent prepositional phrases, the preposing properties of these prepositional phrases differ. The semantically more general one can easily be preposed, as in (9b) and (10b), while the semantically more specific one cannot be, as in (9c, 10c). (Note that with contrastive focus, either of the prepositional phrases can be preposed; Brunson's discussion is based on cases with noncontrastive preposing.)

(9) a. John talked to Mary at 3 o'clock on Tuesday.
    b. On Tuesday, John talked to Mary at 3 o'clock.
    c. *At 3 o'clock, John talked to Mary on Tuesday.
(10) a. John waited for Mary on the bench in the park.
    b. In the park, John waited for Mary on the bench.
    c. *On the bench, John waited for Mary in the park.

Brunson points out that the meaning relationship between the prepositional phrases in sentences such as those in (9) and (10) is asymmetrical, with one being in a subset relationship to the other. For instance, in (9), 'on Tuesday' is more general than 'at 3 o'clock' since the former contains the latter. Similarly, in (10), 'in the park' is more general than 'on the bench.' The more general phrase has greater privileges of occurrence than the more specific one – it can be preposed as well as occur postverbally. The more specific phrase, on the other hand, is not easily preposable. Brunson proposes that a relationship of government holds between the general and specific parts of preposed constructions, with the general part governing the more specific part. She provides evidence for this claim based on a variety of constructions and languages.

The notions of general and specific proposed by Brunson and the notion of scope in (8) are very similar. If a principle such as (8) is part of universal grammar, then ordering consistent with it need not be stipulated as part of the grammar of a particular language. It is when ordering does not follow from (8), for whatever reason, that it becomes necessary to make language-particular statements about ordering beyond directionality.

The principle in (8) not only makes a prediction about what happens when two items are in a scopal relationship with each other; it also makes a prediction about ordering when two items do not enter into a scopal relationship. In particular, there is no reason to expect any fixed ordering in this case – two elements that are not scopally related could appear in either order.

6.2.2 Directionality

The scopal principle tells us that given two elements A and B, if A is in the scope of B, then B must c-command A. But scope alone is inadequate to determine morpheme ordering; the position of the c-commanding element to the right or left of the element in its scope is also important. I assume (chapter 5) that the verb stem is in the 'wrong' position in Athapaskan languages, but that otherwise underlying morpheme order is as it appears on the surface (but see chapter 7). As the structure in (2) of chapter 3 shows, I assume that Athapaskan languages are head-final, with an element of greater scope to the right of one within its scope.

The remainder of this chapter is organized as follows. I begin by examining the ordering within classes – preverbs, quantificational elements, and incorporates. I then look at ordering among the preverbs, quantificational elements, and incorporates overall.

6.3 Ordering within the Preverbs

As discussed in chapter 4, preverbs indicate information about manner and relation; they also include aspectual information (chapter 11). It is possible for a verb to contain more than one preverb; see Kari 1989, 1990, Morice 1932, Reichard 1951, Rice 1989, 1991, Sapir and Hoijer 1969, Young and Morgan 1987, and Young, Morgan, and Midgette 1992. The meaning associated with combinations of preverbs may be idiosyncratic, as in (11).

(11) a. Ahtna (Kari 1990)
s preverb, *ta* preverb
s-ta-de-l-nen
preverb-preverb-qualifier-voice/valence-stem
'It (compact object) got lost.' (447)
s-ta-ni-yaa
preverb-preverb-aspect-stem
'He went away.' (325)

6.3 Ordering within the Preverbs

    b. Navajo
    na 'upward, rising', *tsí* 'mental process, thought' (Young, Morgan, and Midgette 1992:849)
    n-tsi-ni-sh-tláád
    preverb-preverb-qualifier-1sg Subject-stem
    'I get nervous, become apprehensive, upset, get jumpy.' (Young and Morgan 1987:680)

While Kari 1990 identifies the form *sta* in (11a) as morphologically complex, he does not provide a meaning for either of the individual pieces. In the Navajo example, Young and Morgan assign meanings to each of the pieces in question, but the meaning of the whole does not appear to derive from the meaning of the parts.

However, combinations of preverbs within a single verb word where the meaning is compositional are also found, and it is these combinations that are the focus of discussion in this section. It is possible that preverbs combine far more freely than suggested here. Reichard 1951, for instance, notes that in presenting paradigms she does not include combinations of lexical items where the semantics is completely transparent.

6.3.1 Fixed Ordering: Specific before General

One can imagine that verb words with two (or more) preverbs could exhibit a variety of different relationships between the preverbs and the verb stem. One possibility is that two preverbs create a compound that then combines with the stem, as in (12).

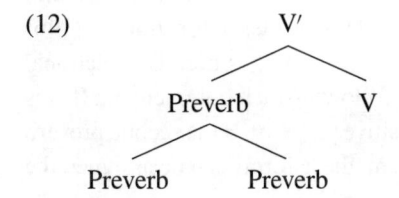

(12)

```
              V'
             /  \
         Preverb  V
         /    \
     Preverb  Preverb
```

An alternative possibility is that one preverb modifies the stem directly and that the second modifies the entire preverb-verb structure, as in (13).[3]

(13)

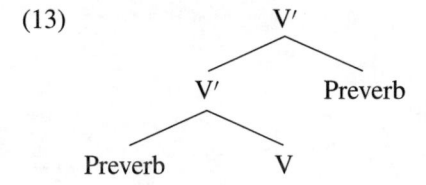

```
              V'
             /  \
           V'   Preverb
          /  \
      Preverb  V
```

The evidence for these structures would be, of course, indirect since the verb stem surfaces at the right edge of the verb word, and the ordering does not actually differ. Thus, patterning must be used to support these different structures.

Consider first the compounding structure in (12). The first preverb may be comparable to the complement of a postposition and the second relational in nature. Alternatively, the first may specify a manner in which the second is carried out. Finally, the first preverb may be logically entailed by the second. It is possible that these constructions have different structural relations that result in the same surface order; I assume for the sake of simplicity that the complement and the modifying structures are the same. Note also that I have not assumed a hierarchical relationship between the preverbs in (12); it is directionality that is important here.

First consider the complement-preverb cases. Combinations of such preverbs in Slave are shown in (14).

(14) Slave: location–relation
   a. **te-ká-y**į**-ya**
      water-out of-aspect-sg. go
      'S/he got out of water.' (Rice 1989)
   b. **teh-k'e**-ts'e-ne-tah
      water-around-human Subject-qualifier-stem
      'look around in water, feel around in water with stick' (Howard 1990:393)

The forms in (14) show that preverbs specifying location precede those specifying relational concepts of direction, source, and position. For example, in (14a) *teh* 'water' is a location and *ká* 'out (of)' specifies a direction; in (14b) *teh* specifies the location while *k'e* represents a relative position. The relational items share properties with postpositions, following their complement. If A is the first preverb (the complement of a transitive preverb), B the second preverb (the transitive preverb), and C the verb stem, these forms can be assigned the structure [[A B] C].

Other languages illustrate similar patterns. Some examples involving more than one preverb are given in (15) for Ahtna, in (16) for Carrier, and in (17) for Navajo.

(15) Ahtna (Kari 1990)
   a. **ti-k'e**-ni-yaa
      trail-on-aspect-sg. go perfective
      'He came to a trail.' (*ti* 'trail' + *k'e* 'on') (335)

6.3 Ordering within the Preverbs

    b. **ti-c'a**-ni-yaa
    trail-away from-aspect-sg. go perfective
    'He went into the woods.' (*ti* 'trail' + *c'a* 'away from') (335)

    c. **ta-tes**-ni-yaa
    water-across-aspect-sg. go perfective
    'He went over a portage.' (*ta* 'water' + *tes* 'over') (334)

(16) Carrier (Morice 1932)

    a. **tša-ha**-d-ez-yê
    mouth-from-qualifier-aspect-stem
    'take food away from one's own mouth' (*tša* 'mouth' + *ha* 'from')
    (I:629)

    b. **khwen-the**-thi
    house-amidst-stem
    'There is a road.' (*khwen* 'house' + *the* 'amidst') (I:635)

(17) Navajo (Young and Morgan 1987)

    a. **ta-na**-'a-sh-gizh
    water-around-unspecified Object-1sg Subject-stem
    'I thicken it (mush, cream of wheat) by stirring.' (701)

    b. bi-**zá-k'í**-dee-sh-nííh
    3 possessor-**throat, neck-on**-qualifier-1sg Subject-act with hands
    'I choke him (with the hands).' (*bi* 3, *zá* 'throat, neck'+ *k'í* 'on') (57)

In the Carrier verbs, the complement of the second preverb is a noun rather than a preverb; this is also the case in the Navajo form in (17b). The same semantic relationship holds in these languages as in Slave: preverbs specifying location (e.g., woods, shore) precede those specifying direction, source, and position (e.g., towards, from, arrival at, on, in, among).

In addition to a relational preverb following its complement, the first preverb can be interpreted as more specific than the second one. This is illustrated in (18) and (19).

(18) Ahtna (Kari 1990)

    a. O-yi-ts'i
    'out from inside O' (*yi* 'inside' (specific) + *ts'i* 'from' (general))
    (414)
    i-**yi-ts'i**-'i-l-tset
    disjoint anaphor-**inside-from**-epenthetic-voice/valence-stem
    'He ran out from inside it.'

b. O-ta-ts'i
     'from among O' (*ta* 'among' + *ts'i* 'from')
     u-**ta-ts'i**-ł-ts'i-hw-di-ni-laa
     3 Object-**among-from**-preverb-preverb-areal-qualifier-aspect-stem
     'He winnowed them (leaves) from it (berries).' (414)
  c. O-ta-t'a
     'between flat surfaces of O'
     ts'ede **ta-t'ah**-n-ez-c'et'-i
     blanket **among-into small enclosure**-qualifier-aspect-stem-suffix
     'sheet' (that which extends between blankets) (340)
(19) Carrier (Morice 1932)
  a. O-the-ha
     'from among O'
     u-**the-ha**-s-ʼaih
     3 Object-**among-from**-1sg Subject-stem
     'I choose from amongst them.' (*the* 'among' + *ha* 'from') (II:78)
  b. O-ye-ha
     'from inside O'
     u-**ye-ha**-(ye)-s-ʼaih
     3 Object-**inside-from**-(aspect)-1sg Subject-stem
     'I extract, take out (marrow, etc.).' (*ye* 'inside' + *ha* 'from') (II:83)

In these examples the first of the preverbs is more specific than the second in the sense that it delimits the domain defined by the second.[4]

Another type of relationship found between preverbs is a modifying one. All of the constructions in (20) are cases where the second preverb is *ní* 'terminative, arrival at an endpoint'. The first preverb specifies the manner in which that endpoint is achieved.

(20) Slave (Howard 1990)
  a. **łé-ní**-ts'-i̜-'a
     in half-terminative-human Subject-aspect-stem
     'fold' (9)
  b. **séé-ní**-eni-ts'-i̜-h-thi
     good-terminative-mind-human Subject-aspect-valence-stem
     'think over, get straightened in mind' (148)
  c. **xǫ-ní**-a-go-ts'-i̜-h-thi
     spouse-terminative-iterative-areal-human Subject-aspect-valence-stem
     'get married, establish home' (182)

6.3 Ordering within the Preverbs

    d. **łaá-ní**-ts'-į-tséh
       dead-terminative-human Subject-aspect-stem
       'kill with spear' (567)

    e. O **k'e-ní**-da-go-dé-nį-'ǫ
       on-terminative-word-areal-qualifier-aspect-stem
       'S/he accused, blamed (placed words on).' (Rice 1989)

    f. O **k'e-ní**-nį-dhah
       on-terminative-aspect-stem
       'S/he put pl. O back together.' (Rice 1989)

Similar examples from Carrier and Navajo are given in (21) and (22), respectively.

(21) Carrier (Morice 1932)
    a. **sû-nê**-nî-s-yai
       well-terminative-aspect-1sg Subject-stem
       'I am marriageable.' (grow to proper point for marriage) (I:622)

    b. **sû-nê**-ne-s-tlê
       well-terminative-aspect-1sg Subject-stem
       'I arrange, adjust, fix up, set in order, organize.' (I:622)

(22) Navajo (Young and Morgan 1987)
    a. **tsi'-ha**-ha-sh-łááh
       aimlessly, chaotically-up out, start to-areal-1sg Subject-stem
       'I disturb the peace, cause a commotion, 'raise hell'.' (734)

    b. damǫ́ǫ biiłkáhí 'ólta'   biniiyé sii'nilígíí bi-ł
       Monday   school   board   3.with
       'ah-**a-ni**-ná-há-sh-kah
       reciprocal-**toward-terminative**-iterative-qualifier-1sg Subject-stem
       'I meet with the rest of the members of the school board on Monday.' (39)

These forms suggest that a more specific preverb precedes a more general one. For instance, in 'kill with spear' in (20d) the second preverb indicates termination of an activity and the first indicates the manner of termination, namely termination in death. A similar pattern is found in 'think over' in (20b); here the second preverb indicates termination while the first specifies the type of ending, namely in something being straightened or good. The example 'accuse, blame' in (20e) is similar. The verb without *k'e* indicates coming to an end of a verbal action; the preverb *k'e* then indicates the goal of this activity. In these cases, then, the first preverb delimits the domain defined by the second.

Another set of examples illustrates another way in which preverbs can be related. The first preverb expresses motion into or closing something, while the second expresses motion out of something. They thus express opposing relationships, similar to prefix combinations found in the English words *disentangle* and *disembark*.

(23) Slave (Howard 1990)
   a. -**t'áh-ká**-ts'e-d-í-le
      into-out of-unspecified human Subject-qualifier-qualifier-stem
      'unharness, take out of harness (e.g., dog team)' (315)
   b. -**dáh-ká**-'e-ts'e-de-chu
      close-open-unspecified Object-unspecified human Subject-qualifier-stem
      'open (e.g., container)' (67)

(24) Carrier (Morice 1932)
   a. **ta-ha**-de-s-thih
      into-out of-qualifier-1sg Subject-stem
      'I open a door once.' (I:622)
   b. u-**nê-ha**-de-s-'aih
      3 Object-**around-from**-qualifier-1sg Subject-stem
      'I take off from around its (e.g., neck) for first time.' (II:65)
      cf. u-**nê**-de-s-'aih
         3 Object-**around**-qualifier-1sg Subject-stem
         'I put (hat) on his head (for first time, once, as to try it).' (II:39)
   c. u-**ta-ha**-na-'-de-ne-s-tlê
      3 Object-**orifice-from**-iterative-unspecified Object-qualifier-qualifier-1sg Subject-stem
      'I unload (gun).' (take back (*na*) something (') round (*n*) from (*ha*) its (*u*) orifice (*ta*)) (II:73)
      cf. u-**ta**-na-'-de-ne-s-tlê
         3 Object-**orifice**-iterative-unspecified Object-qualifier-qualifier-1sg Subject-stem
         'I load (a gun) with shot.' (*ta* 'orifice') (II:74)

The ordering of these preverbs too seems to follow from a scopal relationship: an opening necessarily entails that a closed state preceded and the removal of something entails a preceding state in which it was on. In terms of the notions of general and specific, the opening or removal entails the previous closed state or location, making the former more general. This type of relationship

6.3 Ordering within the Preverbs

falls under the general rubric of specific/general if this can be extended to include entailed/nonentailed.

Another interesting case of a scopal relationship comes from the positioning of the Ahtna preverb *cin'* 'pretend'.

(25) Ahtna (Kari 1990)
    a. da-z-tsaan
       preverb-aspect-stem
       'He died.' (367)
       da-cin'-de-l-tsaan
       preverb-pretend-qualifier-voice/valence-stem
       'He pretended to die.' (367)
    b. i-'eł   **s-ka-cin'**-hw-de-l-'aan
       disjoint anaphor-with   **preverb-preverb-pretend**-areal-
                                 qualifier-voice/valence-stem
       'He pretended to fight with him.' (72)
    c. **na-cin'**-de-c'ots'
       preverb-pretend-qualifier-stem
       'He pretended to wash something.' (128)

In these verbs, the preverbs *da*, *s-ka*, and *na* are listed as part of the lexical entry. The preverb *cin'* 'pretend' appears where predicted by the scopal ordering hypothesis – it has the first preverb and stem in its scope and appears to their right. Note that this item introduces a new event and in this sense is verbal rather than preverbal; see note 3.

Similar, more productive examples are found in languages that have a lexical item expressing inceptivity. This morpheme focuses on the point of inception, differing from the functional inceptive morpheme that marks the initial span of a situation (see chapter 11). The event that begins is defined by the verb stem and preverbs to the left of the inceptive.

(26) Sekani: inceptive *whè* (Hargus 1988)
    a. k'è-whè-n-ə-s-dah
       around-inceptive-qualifier-qualifier-1sg Subject-sg go
       'I start to walk around.' (163)
    b. O hǫ́-na-**whè**-nį-la
           out-iterative-**inceptive**-aspect-stem
       'S/he started to take plural/ropelike O back out.' (165)

(27) Babine-Witsuwit'en: inceptive *o* (Hargus 1996)
dus **ne**-ne-**o**-ï-l-ggït
cat **down**-iterative-**inceptive**-qualifier-voice/valence-stem
'The cat started to crawl back down.'

(28) Carrier: inceptive *hwe* (Morice 1932)
ł-qa-na-**hwê**-łe-rhe-l-tě
reciprocal-**preverb**-iterative-**inceptive**-negative-qualifier-voice/valence-stem
'They do not commence to beat one another again.' (II:161)

In (27), for instance, the event that started is crawling (stem) back (*ne*) down (*ne*); the inceptive is the rightmost preverb. In (28), what begins is that the subjects fail to commence beating one another again.

These examples can be assigned the structure in (29).

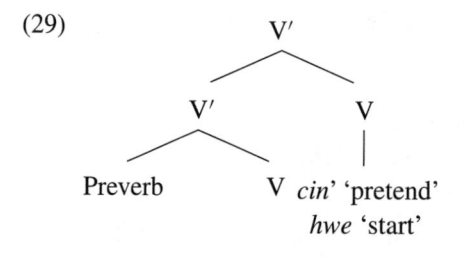

(29)
```
              V'
            /    \
          V'      V
         /  \     |
    Preverb   V  cin' 'pretend'
              hwe 'start'
```

The second preverb, labeled V here, is predicative, introducing a new event, and this morpheme can be considered to be a verb rather than a preverb. The higher verb takes the lower verb and preverbs associated with it in its scope, and the higher and lower verbs share arguments and aspect (see chapter 7). Notice that in the examples containing both the inceptive and the iterative, as in (26b), (27), and (28), the iterative has scope only over the lower verb, and appears to the left of the inceptive. Notice too that in the Carrier example in (28), the negative negates the inceptivity and appears at the right edge. I return to discussion of the inceptive and negative preverbs in section 6.8.

6.3.2 Unrelated Preverbs

I have discussed cases of two preverbs with predictable ordering, where the first is either an argument of the second, specifies the manner in which the second is met, is more specific than the second, entails the second, or is predicated of the second. One can imagine another kind of situation, one in which the preverbs are unrelated to each other in any way. In some cases it is difficult to identify whether one preverb is more general than the second, entails the second, and so on. Some Slave examples of this type are provided in (30).

6.3 Ordering within the Preverbs

(30) Slave (Rice 1989)
    a. **ká-tá**-h-tɬah
       out of-to shore-aspect-stem
       'S/he got out on shore.' (*ká* 'out of' + *tá* to shore')
    b. **ɬǫ-dah**-e-tle
       circle-up and down-epenthetic-stem
       'S/he is dancing in circle.' (*ɬǫ* 'circle' + *dah* 'up and down')

The scope hypothesis has nothing to say about ordering in such cases. The examples in (31) provide further strong evidence that two preverbs do not always enter into a scopal relationship.

(31) Slave (Rice 1989)
    a. O   **sǫ-ra**-d-é-'ǫ
       circle-around-qualifier-aspect-stem
       'S/he turned three-dimensional O over in hand, fiddled with three-dimensional object.' (*sǫ* 'circle' + *ra* 'around')
       O **ra-sǫ**-d-é-'ǫ   same glosses and translation as (31a)
    b. **na-ɬǫ**-ts'e-d-é-'éh
       continuative-circle-human Subject-qualifier-aspect-stem
       'turn in circles on water' (*na* continuative + *ɬǫ* 'circle')
       ɬǫ-na-ts'e-d-é-'éh   same glosses and translation as (31b)

In these examples, each verb contains two preverbs that are not fixed in order. The meanings of the two preverbs bear no scopal relationship to one another – one does not delimit the other, one is not more general than the other – and thus free ordering is possible.

The order of preverbs does not appear to be random, but a consequence of general semantic properties requiring, to speak generally, that a more specific preverb precede a more general one. The variability in ordering between preverbs that do not have a relationship to one another in at least some languages lends support to the scopal principle – it is only under certain semantic conditions that the absence of fixed ordering is possible.

Imagine constructing a template to order the preverbs. Kari 1989:40 divides preverbs into three positions, remarking that "compounding is possible, so the position can include one or two morpheme boundaries." Recall that in Kari's view, the template is not a reflection of word formation, but of surface ordering. While a template can be constructed to account for ordering relationships that are invariant due to a fixed semantic relationship between items, it cannot account for the variable ordering that we observe in the absence of fixed relationships. Furthermore, the template account has little to say about differences in orderings that reflect differing scopal relationships. I turn to these in the next section, in a discussion of Navajo.

6.3.3 Theme/Goal Arguments

The preverbs discussed so far designate relational concepts, manner, and predication. In this section I examine another preverb, identified as *í* in Navajo, *e* or a null element in Slave, and a null element in Ahtna. This is a transitive preverb that is translated 'against' in Navajo (Young and Morgan 1987). Despite this gloss, the preverb in question does not generally involve relation, but is empty in meaning, marking a theme or goal argument. The ordering of this preverb and its complement differs among the languages. In Navajo the thematic relation that the complement of this preverb bears to the verb determines the ordering of the preverbs. In Ahtna and Slave, on the other hand, it is the grammatical role of the complement that determines the preverb's placement: it occupies the position of oblique arguments.

I begin with Navajo. Young and Morgan put all preverbs in a single position, their position 1b, which includes "postpositions, adverbial-thematic material (both adverbs that are part of the basic lexical entry and those that function derivationally), and nominals" (Young and Morgan 1987). If these elements were strictly ordered by a template, one might expect fixed orderings of the elements within this position. However, when the postpositions and Young and Morgan's adverbial-thematic elements (i.e., preverbs) are examined, this is found not to be the case. Rather, postpositions and their complements can either precede or follow adverbial-thematic elements.

Consider first the following Navajo forms.

(32) Navajo (Young and Morgan 1987)
 a. na-ni-sh-tin
    around about-qualifier-1sg Subject-handle wooden O
    'I coach him, give him instructions, teach him.' (566)
 b. b-**í-na**-bi-ni-sh-tin
    3 Object-**against-around about**-3 Object-qualifier-1sg Subject-stem
    'I show it (b-í) to him (b), show him how, teach him by showing him how.' (223)
 c. b-**í-na**-sh-tin
    3 Object-**against-around about**-1sg Subject-stem
    'I teach it (*b-í*) to him, show or point it out to him.' (227)

The verbs in these examples are idiomatic in meaning; (32a) means, literally, 'I handle him/her.' It includes a single preverb, *na*, translated by Young and

6.3 Ordering within the Preverbs

Morgan as 'around about'. The examples in (32b,c) differ from (32a) in containing two nonagentive arguments; both mean 'I handle him/her against (*í*) it'. They differ in whether a direct object pronoun is present when the subject is non-third person and the object is third person; see chapter 10 for some discussion. Teaching or showing is conceived of as handling someone so as to give them something. When considered in terms of thematic roles, the direct object is the one handled, or the theme; the oblique object in (32b,c) is not a theme, but perhaps a location. Here the preverb *í* (and its complement) precedes the preverb *na* 'around about.'

While in (32) the preverb *í* and its complement precede another preverb, productive cases are also found in which this postpositional preverb and its complement follow another preverb. In each of the following examples, the first element of the verb is a preverb followed by a complement (*b* in these examples) of a second preverb, *í*. Here and in what follows, 'YM' and 'YMM' stand for Young and Morgan 1987 and Young, Morgan, and Midgette, respectively.

(33) Navajo
   na-b-**í**-sé-yil
   around about-3 Object-**against**-aspect/1sg Subject-shove, push
   'I pushed it around, pushed it about (e.g., wheelbarrow).' (YM 521)

(34) **'ahá**-b-**í**-z-ní-ł-táál
   apart-3 Object-**against**-qualifier-aspect/1sg Subject-valence-kick object, kick into space
   'I kicked it apart.' (YM 521)

(35) **'a**-b-**í**-dzíí-go'
   away out of sight-3 Object-**against**-qualifier/aspect/1sg Subject-move with forceful impetus, tumble, rush, spill, butt, collide
   'I rammed, butted, tackled, lunged against it, bumped it.' (YMM 214)

(36) **ch'í**-b-**í**-z-ní-ł-táál
   horizontally outward-3 Object-**against**-qualifier-aspect/1sg Subject-valence-kick object, kick into space
   'I kicked him out, threw him out, 'bounced' him.' (YM 281)

(37) **tá**-b-**í**-d-fi-yil
   here and there-3 Object-**against**-qualifier-aspect/1sg Subject-shove, push
   'I pushed it around here and there (e.g., car, wheelbarrow).' (YM 697)

In these examples, the verbs have a transitive translation. However, they lack structural direct objects. The complement of the preverb *í* resembles a direct object in terms of its thematic relationship to the verb. In particular, despite its oblique form, it is in a direct semantic relationship with the verb, functioning as the theme, and not, like most preverb complements, in an oblique thematic relationship with the verb. The postposition *í* is thus similar to English *of* in *be fond of*, providing case marking to an argument. In the verbs just discussed, then, the complement of *í* represents the theme of the verb. The lexical items in these verbs appear to have the structure in (13), where the second preverb has the verb stem and first preverb in its scope; see section 6.7.3 for discussion.

Similar, but slightly more complex, Navajo examples are given in (38) and (39).

(38) bi-**ghá**-b-**í**-ní-yil
   3 Object-**through**-3 Object-**against**-aspect/1sg Subject-shove, push
   'I pushed it (*b-í*) through (*ghá*) it (*bi*).' (YM 186)

(39) bi-**na**-b-**í**-sé-yel
   3 Object-**around about**-3 Object-**against**-aspect/1sg Subject-shove, push
   'I pushed, shoved it (*b-í*) around (*na*) it (*bi*) (e.g., building).' (YM 703)

These verbs again include two preverbs. The second, *í*, has the theme as complement; the first (*ghá* 'through' in (38); *na* 'around' in (39)) has a location as complement. This is, as we saw in chapter 4, a typical role for a complement of a transitive preverb – it can indicate locations with respect to relations. In Navajo, when the complement of *í* bears the relation of theme to the verb, it appears after other preverbs, but when a complement bears an oblique thematic relation to the verb, mediated by a preverb, it precedes that preverb.

The generalization that I have made is that the position of a transitive preverb can vary in Navajo depending upon the thematic relationship of the complement to the verb. Consider now cases with two transitive preverbs. The theme is to the right of oblique thematic roles; in scopal terms, the theme has oblique roles in its scope. This ordering parallels one that is frequent in other languages. Larson 1988, for instance, proposes that thematic marking is assigned by a hierarchy of thematic relations as in (40), which he adapts from Carrier-Duncan 1985. See Fillmore 1968, Givón 1984, and Jackendoff 1972 among others for similar hierarchies.

(40) AGENT > THEME > GOAL > OBLIQUES (manner, location, time, ...)

6.3 Ordering within the Preverbs

Following others, Larson argues that the lowest role on the thematic hierarchy is assigned to the lowest argument in constituent structure, and so on. In the case of head-final Navajo, lowest should correlate with leftmost, and themes should be the rightmost of the nonagentive arguments. This is exactly what we see in Navajo. Themes follow other preverbs; relations lower than theme precede other preverbs. Another scopal principle is thus at play here – thematic relations that are higher on the thematic hierarchy appear to the right of those that are lower on the hierarchy.

Consider next the position of the thematic arguments with respect to other preverbs. As seen, they follow. I postpone full discussion of this fact until section 6.7.3, where I argue that this is the expected position for incorporated arguments. Recall that the preverb that marks these themes has no real semantic content, but serves to introduce an entity.

Another class of verbs that occurs with the preverb í is slightly more complex. In these verbs, an unspecified direct object, ', is present. Young and Morgan 1987 suggest that this pronominal is part of the lexical entry of the verb in these cases.

(41) **ha**-b-í-'-íí-ł-jizh
    out-3 Object-**against**-unspecified Object-aspect/1sg Subject-valence-compress, crush, squeeze, dent
    'I squeezed him out, forced him off (his land).' (YM 372)

(42) **ha**-b-í-'-íí-shiizh
    out-3 Object-**against**-unspecified Object-aspect/1sg Subject-poke, jab
    'I gouged it out (as with chisel).' (poke unspecified object on it)

(43) **na**-b-í-z-'-d-ii-ł-don
    down-3 Object-**against**-qualifier-unspecified Object-qualifier-aspect/1sg Subject-valence-cause an explosion, shoot (a gun)
    'I knocked it down (by shooting it).' (YM 168, YMM 146)

In these verbs, the unspecified object ' is a type of cognate object with the role of theme. For instance, in (43) the unspecified argument represents the explosion. The complement of í is a theme also, however, in that it is the entity affected by the event; in (43) again, this complement of í refers to the thing that was knocked off. If the complement of í is indeed a second theme, then these cases parallel those in (33)–(40).[5] The direct object (unspecified ') indicates the theme; the complement of í further specifies the theme, reflecting the ordering specific before general.[6]

Carrier exhibits a similar phenomenon to Navajo. In the gloss to (44) 'instrumentality' is Morice's term.

(44) Carrier (Morice 1932)
na-p-ê-es-khat
down-3 Object-**instrumentality**-1sg Subject-stem (I:559)
'I knock it (composite fabric) down.' (I:637)

Here the preverb *na 'down'* precedes a pronoun that is semantically a theme of the verb.

In Navajo and Carrier a semantically empty transitive preverb marking a theme appears to the right of other preverbs; when the complement marks an entity that is filling another thematic role (e.g., location), it appears to the left of other preverbs. The existence of this construction raises many questions – for example, why are these not simple transitive verbs – but the ordering of elements follows from the thematic hierarchy.

The facts of Slave are slightly different. In Slave, verbs similar to those in Navajo and Carrier occur either with the cognate preverb, *e*, or a null preverb (arguments of the latter are considered to be structural oblique objects because of their form and position; see Rice 1989). This preverb can appear in verbs in the absence of an independent direct object.

(45) a. tłį **he**-k'é-dí
    dog **preverb**-preverb-handle
    'S/he keeps the dog.' (Rice 1989:752)
  b. m-**e**-ká-de-h-tse
    3 oblique Object-**preverb**-preverb-inceptive/aspect/1sg Subject-valence-handle
    'I pushed it out.' (Rice 1989:747)

Here 'dog' in (45a) and 'it' in (45b) are complements of a preverb, *he* in (45a) and *e* in (45b), and the verbs have no overt direct object.

This preverb can also occur in the presence of an internal argument, either the areal (*go*) or the unspecified (*'*); see chapter 10.

(46) a. s-**e**-ní-**gó**-nį-h-the
    1sg Object-**preverb**-preverb-**area**-aspect-valence-stem
    'It happened to arrive for me.' (Rice 1989:749)
  b. y-**e**-ní-'e-nį-h-k'é
    disjoint anaphor-**preverb**-preverb-**unspecified Object**-aspect-valence-stem
    'S/he shot it dead.' (Rice 1989:751)

In (46a), *go* 'area' functions as subject, while in (46b) ' 'unspecified object' is a grammatical direct object. Both contain the preverb *ní* 'terminative.' The

6.3 Ordering within the Preverbs

theme argument in these examples is structurally an oblique object rather than the expected direct object.

Rice 1989 summarizes the use of the preverb under discussion here, *e* or empty in form, as follows:

(47) a. Some verbs are subcategorized to take this preverb.
  b. If a ditransitive verb occurs with a direct object, ' 'unspecified' or *go* 'areal', as theme, its goal is often expressed by an oblique object, the object of a preverb *e* or a null preverb.
  c. In verbs with the subject ' 'unspecified' or *go* 'areal', a second thematic role is expressed as an oblique of a preverb *e* or a null preverb.

Rice 1989 treats the verbs with internal arguments (e.g., (46)) as having a theme, the internal argument, and a goal, the complement of the preverb. An alternative analysis is possible in the case where the internal argument is a direct object, as in (46b) – these could parallel the Koyukon example discussed in note 5, where the direct and oblique objects both refer to the theme.

Consider now the position of this preverb and its complement with respect to other preverbs. With one exception, it occurs to the left of other preverbs. For instance, in (45), it precedes the preverb *k'é*, and in (46) it precedes the preverb *ní* 'arrival at a point, termination.' The one exception is shown in (48), from Rice 1989.

(48) **du**-b-e-go-d-é-lį̇
   negative-3 Object-**preverb**-areal-qualifier-aspect-stem
   'S/he disappeared.' (it (*go*) does not (*du*) exist of him (*b*)) (755)
   du-b-e-go-d-i-h-shǫ
   negative-3 Object-**preverb**-areal-qualifier-aspect/1sg Subject-valence-stem
   'I forgot it.' (I do not (*du*) know it (*go*) of it (*b*)) (776)

In these verbs, a preverb *du* 'negative' precedes the object. In both these cases, the verb includes an inner argument, *go* 'areal'. This negative morpheme is used productively in some Slave dialects as a general sentential negator and is not part of the verb word. In a very few verbs, as in (48), it is part of the verb word. It is not productively used, and it must be lexically specified which verbs it combines with morphologically.

Ahtna has parallel examples. Kari 1989 uses the abbreviation 'P' for an oblique object; in (49) a null preverb occurs with a second preverb, *na*, which Kari identifies as reversative.

(49)   P-na#n-D-taa   'help P' (Kari 1989:64)

The arguments discussed in this section have two characteristics: structurally, they are complements of transitive preverbs, semantically they are themes. One fact holds of all languages examined: when more than one nonagent argument is present, the theme follows thematic relations that are lower on the thematic hierarchy in (40), as predicted by the hierarchy given Athapaskan directionality.[7] Beyond this, we find a pocket of difference between the languages with respect to the placement of this transitive preverb. In Navajo and Carrier, it follows other preverbs when its complement serves as theme, taking the position of theme with respect to the other preverbs (section 6.7.4). In this case, semantic factors win out in determining its placement. In Slave and Ahtna, on the other hand, this preverb and its complement precede other preverbs. This is a typical syntactic position for transitive preverbs – they appear at the left edge of the verb word, as can be seen by the position of postpositions to the left of adverbs in the verbal templates. Even though the arguments of these verbs are themes, syntactic ordering wins out over semantic factors in these languages.

6.3.4   Conclusion

The conclusion to be drawn from this section is that the ordering of preverbs is neither totally fixed nor totally free. Rather, their ordering is, overall, a consequence of general semantic properties – if a preverb with greater scope and one within its scope co-occur, ordering is fixed, with, to put the scope hypothesis in the broadest of terms, a more general preverb to the right of a more specific one. The variable ordering of the preverb *í* in Navajo is particularly striking. It appears before or after other preverbs, depending on the semantic relationship of its complement to the verb. When it precedes, the complement is a thematic relation lower on the thematic hierarchy than the theme; when it follows, the complement fills the role of theme. In Navajo, the semantic relation of the complement of this preverb to the verb determines the placement of the preverb. In Slave and Ahtna, on the other hand, structural factors override semantic ones, and the transitive preverb appears at the left edge of the verb word independent of the semantic function of its complement.

Consider now the template hypothesis. To account for the ordering of *í* in Navajo with other preverbs, a template must be devised that allows this item to precede or to follow other preverbs. Its position is not random,

6.4 Ordering within the Quantificational Elements

but depends upon semantic relationships between its complement and the verb stem. The template hypothesis can perhaps be salvaged, but it misses generalizations captured by the scope hypothesis. Ordering among preverbs therefore provides strong evidence for the scope hypothesis over the template hypothesis.

6.4 Ordering within the Quantificational Elements

I now turn to an examination of ordering among the quantifiers (iterative and distributive). Recall from chapter 4 that the iterative contributes to event structure, and that the distributive modifies arguments. Given that these quantifiers function in different systems, variable ordering might be expected, and indeed, both possible orderings, iterative-distributive and distributive-iterative, occur.

6.4.1 Variable Ordering within a Language

Variation in the ordering of quantifiers within a language is reported in Ahtna and Sekani. In Ahtna the most frequent ordering is iterative-distributive, but the ordering distributive-iterative is possible (see Kari 1990:40).

(50) da-**na-n**-ku-ghii-ł-tl'u'
preverb-**iterative-distributive**-3pl Object-aspect-1sg Subject/valence-stem
'I tied them up again.' (Kari 1990:40)
ts'i-ta-**n-na**-xii-ghe-ł-tses
preverb-preverb-**distributive-iterative**-pronoun-aspect-valence-stem
'He ironed them again.' (Kari 1990:40)

Kari does not note a meaning difference between the orderings. I argued in chapter 4 that the scopal domains of the iterative and the distributive differ – the iterative has scope over the event, while the distributive has scope over arguments. Since these do not interact, variability without associated semantic differences is not surprising.

Variable ordering within a language is found in a particularly dramatic way in Sekani. In this language, evidence for the ordering of the distributive and the iterative is often difficult to interpret. Consider the following examples (Hargus 1988). Note that the iterative sometimes surfaces as nasalization on the preceding vowel.

(51) Sekani (Hargus 1988)
    a. che-**na-dò̜**-ghə-ghəs
       into water-**iterative-distributive/iterative**-human plural Subject-stem
       'They habitually run into the water separately.' (179)
    b. ni-**na-dǫ́**-ts'-ə-d-ì-'ah
       raise-**iterative-distributive/iterative**-human Subject-qualifier-qualifier-stem
       'We habitually lift compact O separately.' (179)
    c. **yà-na-dò̜**-ts'-ì-kwi
       distributive-iterative-distributive/iterative-human Subject-qualifier-stem
       'We vomit again separately.' (180)

Hargus argues for the order distributive-iterative on phonological grounds. However, on the surface the order is iterative-distributive-iterative, as in (51a,b), or even distributive-iterative-distributive-iterative, as in (51c); see section 6.7.4 for discussion of dual marking of the iterative. In Sekani, there is little evidence for a fixed ordering between these two quantifiers.

6.4.2 Variable Ordering across Languages

While some languages allow more than one ordering of quantifiers, in others the ordering appears to be fixed. It is possible that variation is underreported; forms containing both the iterative and distributive are not commonly found in the sources. Assuming the correctness of the sources, Dena'ina is reported as an iterative-distributive language and Carrier as a distributive-iterative language, as shown in (3).

6.4.3 Summary

Given variation both within and between languages in the ordering of quantifiers, nothing specific can be said about their ordering. The variability can be attributed to the fact that they are part of different systems – the iterative is an A-quantifier that is part of the event system, while the distributive is a D-quantifier that is part of the argument system – and thus are not in a potential scopal relationship with one another.

6.4.4 Navajo Quantifiers: Iteratives Revisited

Young and Morgan 1980, 1987 recognize several quantificational elements in Navajo: reversionary (*ná* 'back'), semeliterative (*náá* 'again, another'),

6.4 Ordering within the Quantificational Elements

iterative (*ná* 'customarily, repeatedly'), and distributive plural (*da*). They report fixed ordering among these. Navajo is particularly interesting as what I have called iterative elsewhere appears to consist of three distinct items in this language, and thus their ordering is worthy of study.

The forms that Young and Morgan label reversionary, semeliterative, and iterative are illustrated in (52)–(54).[8] The reversionary represents a return to a previous state, and is often translated as 'back' or 're-'. It can appear with either intransitive or transitive verbs that contain a state as part of their event structure. These examples are not fully glossed; the morpheme in question is in boldface. The morphophonemics are complex and can safely be ignored.

(52) Reversionary ('back'): *ná* (Young and Morgan 1987)
    a. kintahgóó **ná**-n-í-s-dzá
       'I went back to town, returned to town.' (58)
    b. naaltsoos **ná**-n-í-'ą́
       'I gave the book back to, returned the book to him.' (58)
    c. **ná**-nee-z-dá
       'He sat back down, resumed a sitting position.' (58)
    d. ch'é-**é**-di-'-n-í-ł-dláád
       'The sun came back out.' (58)
    e. ch'é-**é**-n-í-s-dzid
       'I woke back up, reawakened.' (60)
    f. ní-**ná**-hi-d-i-sh-tah
       'I sprang back up.' (60)
    g. taah **ná**-sh-í-ł-teeh
       'He's putting me back into the water.' (62)

The semeliterative *náá* translates as 'again' and represents a single repetition of an event. There is a regular process in Navajo by which a syllable of the form CV combines with *na* to give CVV. At least historically then the semeliterative *náá* derives from *ná* + *ná*. I assume that it is a single morpheme rather than a derived item synchronically.

(53) Semeliterative ('again'): *náá* (Young and Morgan 1987)
    a. ch'í-**náá**-di-'-n-í-ł-dláád
       'The sun came out again (a single repetition).'
    b. ni-**náá**-hóó-ł-tą́
       'It rained again, it rained some more.' (60)

c. ch'í-**náá**-n-í-s-dzá
      'I went out again.' (60)
   d. naaltsoos b-aa **náá**-n-í-ą́
      'I again brought the book to him.' (60)
   e. ní-**náá**-hi-d-ii-sh-tah
      'I again sprang up.' (60)

Finally, Young and Morgan's iterative is used with a customary stem form (chapter 11) and is translated as 'repeatedly'. Like the reversionary, this morpheme has the form *ná*.

(54) Iterative: *ná* (Young and Morgan 1987)
   a. taah   **ná**-sh-í-ł-tééh
      into water **iterative**-1sg Object-aspect-valence-stem
      'He repeatedly (and customarily) puts me into the water.' (62)
   b. 'e'e'áahgo dibé tah   **né**-i-ni-ł-ka'
      evening   sheep water **iterative**-disjoint anaphor-aspect-valence-stem
      'In the evening he repeatedly and customarily drives the sheep to water.' (62)

Some of the adverbs co-occur. In particular, Young and Morgan note the co-occurrence of the reversionary and the semeliterative and of the semeliterative and the iterative, as in the following examples.

(55) Reversionary plus semeliterative (Young and Morgan 1987)
   a. chí-**ní-náá**-di-'-n-í-ł-dláád
      'The sun came back out again (reverted another time).' (58)
   b. ch'í-**ní-náá**-ní-s-dzid
      'I again woke (back) up.' (60)
   c. ní-**ní-náá**-hi-d-ii-sh-tah
      'I again sprang back up.' (60)
(56) Reversionary plus iterative (Young and Morgan 1987)
   a. **ní-ná**-sh-í-ł-tééh
      'He repeatedly puts me back into the water.' (62)
   b. di-**ná-á**-d-í-sh-jah
      'I repeatedly rekindle the fire.' (62)
   c. **ní-ná**-sh-dááh
      'I repeatedly return.' (156)

6.4 Ordering within the Quantificational Elements

On the other hand, Young and Morgan 1980:153 note that the semeliterative and iterative do not co-occur for semantic reasons; the iterative requires more than a single repetition while the semeliterative involves a single repetition.

The need for a template giving the ordering reversionary-semeliterative-iterative must be questioned. The ordering of the first pair can be established from examples like (55). While the reversionary and the iterative co-occur, as in (56), they are identical in form so it is difficult to determine the ordering relationship on the basis of phonological form.[9] Semeliterative and iterative do not co-occur, nor, as expected, do all three.

The claim that the reversionary and iterative are distinct lexical entries must also be questioned. In Athapaskan languages generally, verb stems are marked for aspectual information; see chapter 11. Young and Morgan describe Navajo verb stems as having aspectual forms including imperfective, perfective, optative, and repetitive (customary). When the distribution of the reversionary and the iterative, which are identical in form, is examined with respect to stem form, differences appear. The reversionary (and semeliterative) occur with imperfective, perfective, and optative stems. The iterative, on the other hand, is restricted in distribution, occurring with what Young and Morgan term a repetitive stem (1987:156). Thus, with imperfective, perfective, or optative stems, the form *ná* has a reversative reading, but with repetitive stems it has an iterative reading. This complementary distribution suggests that we are dealing with a single morpheme, and that the construction determines the exact reading associated with the item. Thus, *ná*, which appears to have two meanings, is not associated with two distinct lexical entries, but with a single one. With a repetitive stem, *ná* reinforces the customary meaning. With a nonrepetitive stem, it indicates a return to a former state.

(57) repetitive stem + *ná* = repeatedly (iterative)
other stem + *ná* = back (reversionary)

I will refer to this single lexeme, as reversionary *ná*.

Now consider the ordering of reversionary *ná* and semeliterative *náá* ('again'). The first indicates a return to a former location, state, or condition, the second simple repetition. Suppose that ordering is related to scope. The ordering reversionary-semeliterative has the reading of a reversion recurring: repetition presupposes return. The ordering semeliterative-reversionary, on the other hand, is not interpretable because in order to do something again, or repeat it, it is necessary that it have been done once. The reversionary thus cannot have scope over the semeliterative. While ordering appears to be fixed, the semantics of the morphemes involved allows no other ordering. A template describes the order, but provides no reason for it; the scope hypothesis predicts the only possible order.

Finally consider examples with two occurrences of *ná*, reversionary and iterative, as in (56). Young and Morgan propose two positions since two occurrences of *ná* are possible. In examples such as (56), with the proposed order reversionary-iterative, the reading is that the return is repeated; the reverse order is not interpretable. The scope hypothesis gives a principled reason for the order that is proposed, while the template hypothesis provides no principled basis for deciding upon an order of these two elements.

6.5 Ordering within the Incorporates

While a verb generally allows only a single incorporate, a few cases are cited with more than one incorporate. An example from Koyukon is given in (58).

(58) Koyukon (Axelrod 1990:183)
    b-okko   ne-**tlaa-tl'oo ɬ**-k'e-ts'e-de-n-le-tsoɬ
    3.in search of   go and return-**head-rope**-unspecified Object-human Subject-qualifier-qualifier-aspect-flexible object moves
    'We go around with rope tied to our necks in search of it.'

Both incorporates are entities. One is a participant argument (*tl'ooɬ* 'rope') and the other (*tlaa* 'head') a nonparticipant. While conclusions cannot be drawn from one example, the order is consistent with the thematic hierarchy in (40), with a theme to the right of a location. Another instance of more than one incorporate, from Dogrib, is given in (59).

(59) **whà-da**-go-ts'e-tsǫ̀
    mouth-beak-areal-human Subject-be dirty
    'talk dirty, swear' (Saxon, personal communication, 1997)

Both of these incorporates appear to specify locations. With such limited data, it is difficult to determine what the constraints are on the ordering of incorporates, and I shall not address this question further.

It may be that recognizing that more than one incorporate is possible within a verb word could eliminate the position that Kari 1990 terms 'thematic' for Ahtna, a position that follows the incorporates. Kari places one morpheme in this position, *x#gh* 'held, attached, constrained on one end, tethered, pivoting'. If this morpheme is an incorporate that compounds with a second incorporate, this odd property of Ahtna could be eliminated.

6.6 Summary

I have examined ordering within the preverbs, the quantifiers, and the incorporates. The ordering of preverbs and the ordering of the Navajo A-quantifiers provide particularly compelling evidence for the scope hypothesis, which provides an account for why ordering is as it is. The template hypothesis, on the other hand, describes the ordering, but potentially allows for other possible orderings that are not found.

6.7 Ordering among Constituents

In this section I turn to the ordering relationships among preverbs, quantifiers, and other material within the lexical items.

6.7.1 Ordering of Preverbs and Quantificational Elements

I argued in chapter 5 that the verb stem originates within the verb phrase, as a sister to the preverbs. As discussed in that chapter, there is evidence that the preverb-stem unit falls within the scope of the quantifiers – these modify the preverb-stem complex and not the stem or prefixes alone. Given the scopal principle, one expects the quantifiers to c-command the preverbs, and thus to follow the preverbs. Since the quantifiers have scope over the preverbs, the fixed order of these items is not surprising: it is a result of the fixed scopal relationship between the preverbs and the quantificational elements.

For the template hypothesis, on the other hand, ordering of morphemes is not a reflection of word formation but simply represents a post–word formation template. Since the template hypothesis makes no particular prediction regarding the ordering of these elements, it fails to account for the fixed ordering across the family.

6.7.2 Ordering of Preverbs and Event Incorporates

Event incorporates follow preverbs, as in (60)–(62).

(60) Slave (Rice 1989)
 k'ína-shin-e-d-a-da
 preverb-song-adverbial suffix-qualifier-aspect-voice/sg. go
 'S/he walked around singing.'
 cf. k'ína-ye-da
  preverb-situation aspect-voice/sg. go
  'S/he walked around.'

(61) Carrier (Morice 1932)
    a. **ne-cen**-dez-ya
       preverb-song-qualifier/aspect/1sg Subject-sg. walk
       'I walk singing.' (II:131)
    b. **ne-ɬez**-dez-ya
       preverb-urine-qualifier/aspect/1sg Subject-sg. walk
       'I walked urinating.' (II:135)
    c. **tso-dîz-yin**
       weep-qualifier/aspect/1sg Subject-stand
       'I weep while standing, stand up weeping.' (II:130)

(62) Ahtna (Kari 1990)
    a. **ɬu-tsax**-d-a-l-yaaɬ
       preverb-cry-qualifier-aspect-voice/valence-sg. go
       'He is walking around crying.' (374)
    b. **ti-seɬ**-d-ghe-l-ggaac
       preverb-shout-qualifier-aspect-voice/valence-run out
       'S/he ran out shouting.' (455)

Consider the semantics of these verbs. They involve two distinct but simultaneous events (with a single marking for argument and event structure). For instance in (60a) the actor is walking around and singing at the same time. The incorporate provides information about one of these simultaneous events (e.g., singing, urinating, crying, shouting, etc.) and the preverb-verb stem (e.g., walking around, sitting) about the other. The simultaneity of the events is clearest in the translations of Morice 1932 for (61c) – either verb can be the main verb in the translation. There are some hints that the verb stem realized at the right edge of the verb word is in some ways subordinate to the incorporate. This is not unexpected if the structure is [[preverb-stem] incorporate] with the incorporate having scope over the stem (recall that the verb stem at the right edge has raised from its position as sister to the preverb). First, in iterative forms, it is the preverb-stem that is necessarily iterated rather than both verbs; see the examples in (77) of section 6.7.4. Second, at least in Carrier, the verb stem is often given a subordinate translation by Morice, as in the examples in (63).

(63) Carrier (Morice 1932)
    a. **ne-tlo**-dez-**ya**
       preverb-laugh-qualifier/aspect/1sg Subject-**sg. go**
       'I laugh walking.' (II:143)

6.7 Ordering among Constituents

b. u-**rwe-tlo**-ne-s-'ih
3 Object-**preverb-laugh**-qualifier-1sg Subject-**steal**
'I stealthily laugh at.' (II:143)

In these and other examples from Morice 1932, the incorporate is translated as the main verb. Although the converse option – translating the stem as the main verb – would make no major meaning difference in (63a), it would incorrectly yield 'I steal in a laughing way' as a translation for (63b), which has as its main event stealing, not laughing. Thus, simultaneity of events does not require them to be coordinate; one could still be subordinate, and it appears that it is the incorporate that indicates the primary event, at least in Carrier. Generalizing from Carrier, these facts suggest that the preverb-stem is a complement of the incorporated verb. If this is the case, then the placement of the incorporate to the right of the preverb is a general consequence of scope and directionality. Again, the template hypothesis has nothing particular to say about why ordering is similar across the family as it allows any ordering.

6.7.3 Ordering of Preverbs and Entity Incorporates

Now consider the relationship of entity incorporates to preverbs, beginning with participant arguments. These occur in a constant order across the languages with incorporates: entity incorporates, like event incorporates, follow preverbs. (I ignore argument incorporates that are complements of preverbs.) The argument incorporates fill the roles of theme or agent of the preverb-verb stem; they are structurally subjects or direct objects. Consider first agent incorporates, or subjects, as illustrated in the Ahtna forms in (64). The noun *łi* 'dog' representing the verb's agent, or subject, is incorporated.

(64) Ahtna (Kari 1990)
 a. **łi**-yi-z-'ał
    dog-disjoint anaphor-aspect-stem
    'A dog bit him.' (280)
 b. ka-na-**łi**-de-l-ghos
    preverb-iterative-**dog**-qualifier-voice/valence-stem
    'The dogs are howling now and then.' (207)

Agents usually are subjects and as such originate as a sister to the verb phrase, or as the highest element within a verb phrase if subjects are considered to originate within the verb phrase (on this issue in Athapaskan languages, see Rice and Saxon 1994, Saxon and Rice 1993, and chapter 10). Subjects relate to the preverb-verb as a whole rather than to a piece of this unit, and thus their positioning to the right of the preverbs is understandable.

Now consider incorporated themes that are structural objects. The Slave verb in (65) contains the preverb *ní* 'terminative, arrival at a point' and the incorporated stem *yati* 'word'. The incorporate *yati* is an object of the complex *ní-'a* 'place default object' rather than of just the verb stem, 'handle default object.'

(65) ní-**yati**-dé-ni̜-'o̜
 preverb-**word**-qualifier-aspect-stem
 'S/he blamed (placed words).'

The question arises of why the object follows preverbs rather than preceding them. Given the structure that I proposed in (2) in chapter 4, why does the object c-command the verb and preverb both? We have seen a parallel in Navajo, where themes follow preverbs while oblique arguments precede them (section 6.3.3). The idea that the object c-commands the verb may be surprising since, in many ways, a verb determines characteristics of its object. However, Larson 1988 and Marantz 1984, among others, have argued that a direct object c-commands a verb and an oblique relation. Some Athapaskan facts can be adduced in favor of this claim. First, a parallel can be drawn with the ordering of quantificational elements with the preverb-stem. I argued that the quantifiers have scope over the preverb-verb stem complex because their meaning applies to the meaning of that whole complex. The incorporates (and objects generally) are arguments of the complex, not just of the stem, as discussed in chapter 4. For instance, the object of a preverb-verb like 'cut (verb) in two (preverb)' is an object of the whole, not just of 'cut,' (nor is it an oblique object of 'in two'). An argument to the left of a preverb is an argument of that preverb alone.

Another reason to think that it is reasonable for incorporates to c-command the verb-preverb unit has to do with the noun classification system. In many Athapaskan languages, as pointed out by Kari 1990:33 for Ahtna, "to use [a – KR] noun in combination with a verb it is necessary to know how the noun is marked for gender and classification." I refer to 'gender' as a noun class system; see chapter 12. What is important is the system that Kari calls the classification system. In Athapaskan languages, the classification system refers to co-occurrence restrictions between nouns and a set of verbs known as classificatory verbs, or verbs of handling and location. These stems occur only with particular object types. Kari 1990:33 gives the following example.

6.7 Ordering among Constituents

(66) Ahtna
tiz'aani   ti-ni-**'aan**
fishtrap   water-aspect-**place default object**
'He placed the fishtrap under the water.'

The verb stem *'aan* is a default verb, appearing with objects that are not otherwise classified in the classificatory system. This stem can be used for a fishtrap; it could not be used if it were a fishnet that was placed under water; in that case, the stem *niic*, which refers to the handling of a clothlike object, would be employed (Kari 1990:107). If the verb stems are viewed as a type of classifier (see, for instance, Axelrod 1996), it is possible to see this selection process as one where the theme of the verb selects the stem. If this view is correct, then we have direct evidence that the incorporated object takes the verbal complex in its scope, justifying a structure in which the object c-commands the verbal complex. Since, by hypothesis, the preverb and stem form a constituent, the position of the object to the right of the preverb is not surprising. Note that the position of the theme-marking preverb *í* and its complement in Navajo is also after other preverbs. Similar arguments can be adduced for it taking the preverb-stem in its scope.

One final set of entity incorporates remains to be considered, the nonparticipant roles. Some examples are given in (67); see also chapter 4.

(67) a. Slave (Rice 1989)
ná-**da**-go-yee
preverb-**mouth**-areal-stem
'S/he joked (played by mouth).'
cf. ná-go-yee
preverb-areal-stem
'S/he played.'
b. Carrier (Morice 1932)
ne-**khĕ**-n-thez-'ih
preverb-**foot**-qualifier-aspect/1sg Subject-stem
'I set out, depart, leave noiselessly.' (II:133)

These incorporates provide information about how the event is carried out, and, since the event is defined by the stem and preverbs both, they take the preverb-stem in their scope.

The ordering preverb-incorporate, whether the incorporate represents an entity or an event, is thus consistent with the general principle of scope.

6.7.4 Ordering of Quantificational Elements and Incorporates: Iteratives

I now consider the quantifiers and their ordering with respect to incorporates. Reasons for their ordering with respect to preverbs were established in chapter 5. The question of their ordering with respect to incorporates is particularly interesting as here we find great variation both within and among the languages, as discussed in section 6.1.

Recall from chapter 4 and from section 6.1 that the iterative contributes to the event structure of a verb, specifying a return to a previous state or a repetition. The distributive, on the other hand, refers to argument structure, specifying that an entity is to be interpreted as plural and, often, as individuated. This difference between the iterative and distributive is important in considering their ordering with respect to other elements.

As discussed in section 6.1, there is variability across the family as to the placement of quantifiers. In the languages in which the quantifiers are always adjacent to each other, the ordering is preverb-quantifier-incorporate. In other languages, the quantifiers need not be adjacent. For instance, Beaver and Sekani allow the orderings of quantifiers and incorporates in (68).

(68) incorporate-iterative-distributive
    iterative-incorporate-distributive

The variable placement of adverbs in Athapaskan languages is not surprising as adverbs show considerable variation in placement crosslinguistically. For instance, Jackendoff 1972 notes that an English adverb like *frequently* may occur in the positions illustrated in (69a) with no discernible meaning differences, and Ernst 1997 notes the positions in (69b) for the adverbs *probably* and *frequently* as opposed to *soundly*.

(69) a. John frequently dropped his cup of coffee.
    Frequently(,) John dropped his cup of coffee.
    John dropped his cup of coffee frequently.
 b. (Probably) she (probably) has (probably) been (*probably) sleeping (*probably)
    (Frequently) she (frequently) has (frequently) been (frequently) sleeping (frequently)
    (*Soundly) she (*soundly) has (*soundly) been (soundly) sleeping (soundly)

Jackendoff 1972 argues that the variable placement of sentential adverbs like *frequently* can be accounted for if they are transportable, or can be placed

6.7 Ordering among Constituents

in various positions in the sentence.[10] Ernst 1997 relates adverb positions in English to their scopal possibilities.

I begin by examining the ordering of the iterative with the incorporates. A possible analysis of the iterative is that it is a transportable adverb and as such can occur in more than one position. Some Slave examples illustrating the variable placement of the iterative are given in (70).

(70) Slave (Howard 1990)
    a. Incorporate + iterative
       dah-**dze-na**-łé-ts'e-de-tthe
       preverb-**heart-iterative**-dual number-human Subject-qualifier-stem
       'start in fright, be startled repeatedly (heart went up repeatedly)' (462)
       Iterative + incorporate
       dah-**na-dze**-łé-ts'e-de-tthe
    b. Incorporate + iterative
       na-**ła-na**-'e-ts'e-de-tłe
       preverb-**rope-iterative**-unspecified Object-human Subject-qualifier-stem
       'drag, lead (rope, animal on leash) repeatedly' (523)
       Iterative + incorporate
       na-**na-ła**-'e-ts'e-de-tłe

The iterative in Slave may appear to the right or the left of an incorporate. More than one occurrence of the iterative is also possible, as in the Slave verbs in (71), where the iterative surfaces as nasalization on the vowels.

(71) Slave (Howard 1990)
    a. goh-dá-ká-'e-ts'e-de-tsi
       areal-preverb-preverb-unspecified Object-human Subject-qualifier-stem
       'break into, through (house)' (574)
    b. preverb/iterative-preverb-iterative
       góh-dǫ-kǫ-'e-ts'e-de-tse
       areal-preverb/**iterative**-preverb/**iterative**-unspecified Object-human Subject-qualifier-stem
       'break into, through (house) repeatedly' (574)
    c. goh-dá-ká-'e-ts'e-de-zhí
       areal-preverb-preverb-unspecified Object-human Subject-qualifier-stem
       'break into, through (house)' (638)

d. preverb/iterative-preverb/iterative
góh-dǫ-kǫ-'e-ts'e-de-zhí
areal-preverb/**iterative**-preverb/**iterative**-unspecified Object-human Subject-qualifier-stem
'break into (house) again' (639)

The variable placement of the iterative can be attributed to its transportable nature, a frequent property of adverbs. Significantly, it is not freely transportable; it never occurs, for instance, to the left of all the preverbs (except in the lexicalized use, the so-called reversative; see chapter 4). Its placement is not fixed, as predicted by the template hypothesis, but not completely free either. It is thus worthwhile to explore whether the scope hypothesis might account for the transportability of the iterative. I will examine two cases, the positioning of the iterative with respect to preverbs and its positioning with respect to incorporates, and then relate these to scope.

So far, I have assumed that the iterative appears to the right of preverbs. However, this is not always true. There are counterexamples containing verbs with two preverbs where the second one entails the first (see discussion concerning (23) and (24)). Consider the Slave forms in (72).

(72) a. preverb/iterative-preverb
góh-dǫ-**ká**-'e-d-a-chú
area-**preverb/iterative-preverb**-unspecified Object-qualifier-aspect-stem
'S/he opened the door again.'(Howard 1990:70)
b. preverb/iterative-preverb/iterative
góh-dǫ-kǫ-'e-ts'e-de-zhí
area-**preverb/iterative-preverb/iterative**-unspecified Object-human Subject-qualifier-stem
'break into (house) again' (Howard 1990:638)

In (72a), the iterative follows the preverb *dá* 'close, in' but precedes the preverb *ká* 'out'; this verb means something along the lines of 'S/he handled wood (door) from in a location to out again.' Another way of thinking of this is: s/he moved a wooden item (i.e., door) from being in a closed state (*da*) again (*na*) to being in an open state (*ka*). This would give a translation of 'open again.' The iterative can appear in both places as well, as in (72b).

Now consider examples with a customary reading.

6.7 Ordering among Constituents

(73) a. preverb-preverb-iterative
go-**dá-ká-na**-'e-de-de-we
area-**preverb-preverb-iterative**-unspecified Object-qualifier-qualifier-stem, customary
'The door is always opening.' (Rice 1989:672)
b. preverb/iterative-preverb/iterative
góh-**dǫ-kǫ**-'e-ts'e-de-tse
area-**preverb/iterative-preverb/iterative**-unspecified Object- human Subject-qualifier-stem, customary
'break into (house) repeatedly' (Howard 1990:574)

In this case, the iterative can also appear in two positions. First, it can occur after each preverb, as in (73b). In this way it is like (72b) with the 'again' reading. It can also appear after the second preverb alone, as in (73a). When the verb is customary (signaled by the stem; see chapter 11), the iterative does not precede the second preverb (cf. (72a)). This is predicted by the scope hypothesis as in order to open the door customarily. It must have been in both the closed state and the open state previously; this contrasts with the iterative, where it is the closed state that must have been repeated.[11] Thus, while the iterative is transportable, it is only transportable within the limits of maintaining scopal relations.

The second question that arises returns us to the major topic of this section, the ordering of incorporates and the iterative. The Slave examples in (70) suggest that the iterative and incorporates are relatively free in their order. This is true also in Beaver and Sekani, where the iterative and incorporates appear in either order. The examples in (74) and (75) involve incorporation of objects, or semantic themes.

(74) Sekani (Hargus 1988)
a. Incorporate-iterative
nà-**xeł-na**-d-i̧-t-'ah
down-**pack-iterative**-qualifier-2sg Subject-voice-stem
'You sg. put pack down again.' (177)
Iterative-incorporate
nǫ̀-**na-xeł**-d-i̧-t-'ah
down/iterative-**iterative-pack**-qualifier-2sg Subject-voice-stem
b. Incorporate-iterative
łughe **chǫ-na**-'ə-də-ghə-s-łeł
fish **guts-iterative**-unspecified Object-inceptive-aspect-1sg Subject-stem
'I will take guts out of another fish.' (177)

Iterative-incorporate
ɫughe **na-ch**ǫ-'ə-də-ghə-s-ɫeɫ
fish **iterative-guts**-unspecified Object-inceptive-aspect-1sg Subject-stem

(75) Beaver (Randoja 1990)
 a. Incorporate-iterative
 je-**gwòt-na**-dànà-ghə-s-t-'ǫ
 preverb-**knee-iterative**-distributive-plural Subject-aspect-voice-stem
 'They bumped their knees again.'(134)
 Iterative-incorporate
 je-**na-gwòt**-nà-ghə-s-t-'ǫ
 preverb-**iterative-knee**-distributive-plural Subject-aspect-voice-stem
 b. Incorporate/iterative
 nà-sǫ-də-də-t-'a
 preverb-**sun/iterative**-qualifier-qualifier-voice-stem
 'The sun (*sa*) goes down customarily.'[12] (135)
 Iterative-incorporate
 nǫ̀-sa-də-də-t-'a
 preverb/**iterative-sun**-qualifier-qualifier-voice-stem

The surface order of elements in these languages is thus as in (76), where the iterative can either precede or follow the incorporated argument.

(76) (iterative) incorporate (iterative)

These forms, like the Slave forms, show us that within a language, the ordering of the incorporate and the iterative is not fixed. Why might this be?

 As discussed in chapter 4, the iterative is part of the event system; it modifies, or has scope over, events rather than arguments. This suggests that the relationship between incorporated nouns, which are arguments, and the iterative, which relates to events, need not be fixed – these elements are part of different subsystems. Since the iterative relates to events, it must c-command the event over which it has scope. But since it does not relate to arguments, its position with respect to arguments is not predictable, but idiosyncratic. Thus in some languages it precedes incorporated arguments, in some it follows them, and in some the ordering of these two elements is variable. The scope hypothesis makes no particular prediction as to the ordering of the iterative and the incorporated nouns since they are part of different systems. Here it is simply necessary to learn for each language what the order (or orders) is.

6.7 Ordering among Constituents

Nonparticipant arguments are similar to participant arguments in terms of ordering relationships with the iterative: the iterative may precede or follow the incorporate.

(77) a. Carrier (Morice 1932)
Iterative + incorporate
na-kwe-d-îs-terh
iterative-foot-qualifier-1sg Subject-stem
'to be returning on one's knees' (II:135)
b. Beaver (Randoja 1990)
Incorporate + iterative
k'è-'**ize-na**-də-da
preverb-**slush snow-iterative**-qualifier-stem
'S/he walked around in slush again.' (135)
Iterative + incorporate
k'è-**na-'ize**-də-da
preverb-**iterative-slush snow**-qualifier-stem

The nonparticipant locations and instruments occupy the same positions as do other entities with respect to the iterative; again, variability is not surprising.

In contrast to incorporated arguments, incorporates that function to add a new event are expected to enter into a semantic relationship with the iterative. Thus, before leaving incorporates, I look at event incorporates and the iterative. Some Ahtna and Carrier examples are given in (78).

(78) a. Ahtna (Kari 1990)
na-c'udyiis-de-l-yaa
iterative-whistle-qualifier-voice/valence-stem
'He returned whistling.' (439)
b. de'eni ku-**na-cehw**-d-ghi-ł-nen
den pronoun-**iterative-moving as group**-qualifier-aspect-
valence-stem
'They rushed in a group back into the den.' (113)
c. **na-xaeł**-c'-a-ł-deł
iterative-pack-unspecified Object-aspect-valence-stem
'He is packing back some things.' (146)
d. Carrier (Morice 1932)
na-cen-dî-z-yał
iterative-singing-qualifier-aspect-stem
'to be returning while singing' (II:131)

e. **na-cen**-de-thez-yaih
iterative-singing-qualifier-aspect-stem
'leave, depart again, set back, while singing' (II:131)

In these examples, the iterative precedes the event incorporate. Notice that it is a single event, the going, that is repeated in these cases. In (78a) the actor may or may not have whistled on the way out, in (78b) we have no indication of whether the group in question left as a group or as individuals, and in (78c) packing may or may not have occurred on the way out. In these cases, then, the positioning of the iterative to the left of the incorporates is easily interpretable: it has scope over the preverb-stem (recall that the stem originates as sister to the preverb), but not over the event specified by the incorporate.

Could the examples in (78) receive an alternative translation in which the iterative has scope over both events? That is, could they mean 'he came whistling again', 'they rushed into the den in a group again', and 'he is packing some things again'? I have not found a single example that is unambiguously of this type – all but one case in which the incorporate is clearly not an entity involve a repetition of the single event specified by the preverb-stem. The one exception, where the event incorporate might be included in the repeated activity, is from Beaver.

(79) Beaver (Randoja 1990)
   a. Incorporate + iterative
      k'è-**səle-na**-də-tl'e
      preverb-**yell, shout-iterative**-qualifier-run
      'S/he is yelling and running again.' (135)
   b. Iterative + incorporate
      k'è-**na-səle**-də-tl'e
      preverb-**iterative-yell, shout**-qualifier-run
      same as (79a)

The translation is not clear – it could be just the running that is repeated, or both the yelling and running could be repeated. Note the position of the iterative in (79a). The semantics requires additional investigation.

In general, then, the iterative precedes event incorporates, and, consistent with this ordering, has no scope over the event defined by the incorporate, but only over that expressed by the preverb-verb stem.

One final example of an entity incorporate requires consideration. There is some indication that the position of the incorporate and iterative may be frozen in Ahtna. This can be seen in (80).

6.7 Ordering among Constituents

(80) Ahtna (Kari 1990)
na-da-xu-x-ngi-'aak
iterative-mouth-pronoun-pronoun-qualifier-stem
'They tricked them again.' (78)
da#O+d+n+Ø+'aak   'deceive, trick, fool O'

The basic lexical entry includes the incorporate *da* 'mouth'. This entity plays a nonparticipant role here and is not grammatically a direct object. Notice that it follows the iterative *na*. This is unexpected, assuming that *da* is part of the basic lexical entry.

6.7.5 Ordering of Quantificational Elements and Incorporates: Distributives

I now turn to the ordering of the distributive and the incorporates. I know of only one case in which variable ordering is reported within a language.[13] Thompson 1977 gives the example in (81), commenting that "for some reason which I cannot identify, the *ne* [distributive – KR] seems to be quite mobile."

(81) Koyukon (Thompson 1977)
  a. **qanaa-na**-asi-tliyh
     word-distributive
     'I stammer.' (59)
  b. **na-qana**-asi-tliyh
     distributive-word

While variation in the ordering of these items is not reported in other languages (but see note 13), when we look across the family we find that two orderings exist – in some languages the distributive precedes incorporates (e.g., Ahtna) while in others it follows them (e.g., Dena'ina, Tsuut'ina, Beaver). Why might this be? With the iterative, I suggested that the iterative and entity incorporates are free in their ordering because the iterative has to do with events while the incorporates have to do with entities. This explanation extends to the variable ordering of the distributive with event incorporates. However, the free ordering of entity incorporates and the distributive cannot follow from such an explanation, as both are part of the argument system – the distributive has to do with entities. Why then can the distributive appear on either side of the entity incorporates, depending on language?

The answer to this question seems to lie in the semantics of the incorporates. There is not extensive work on the semantics of noun incorporation in Athapaskan languages. Axelrod 1990 is a notable exception, and Morice 1932 on Carrier and Rice 1989 on Slave contain some comments on the semantics of this group. Each of these authors notes semantic differences between examples where a noun is incorporated and ones where it is not. Some have noted a minimal difference between the reading of a verb with an incorporate and one with the same noun as an external object (Tuttle 1996 on Salcha). Axelrod 1990, in a detailed study of incorporated nouns in Koyukon, argues that meaning differences exist between verbs with incorporated nouns and those with external nouns. She examines both agentive and theme (patientive) incorporates; I will look only at themes. According to her, incorporation of a theme in Koyukon "allow[s] the verb to express a characteristic activity with clearly defined procedure and goal ... the action seems to be more focused on an expectable or implied result" (Axelrod 1990:190). Examples are given in (82).

(82) Koyukon (Axelrod 1990)
    a. do-**haał**-tle-'onh
       up-**trap**-aspect-stem
       'A trap is set up there.' (191)
    b. nee-**kkun'**-daa-nee-tonh
       to a point-**wood**-qualifier-aspect-stem
       'S/he built a woodpile, stocked up on wood.' (191)

Incorporated themes, Axelrod argues, are used to express characteristic activities where the incorporate is acted on in a typical way, and incorporation functions to "provide the lexicalized expression of a typical activity" (1990:193). Axelrod further points out that the analytic expressions, where the noun is external to the verb word, "individuate the activity, bringing the pieces into sharper focus" while the forms with incorporated patients express "conceptually unitary activities (Mithun 1986:35)" (1990:191).

Consider the relationship between a typical, unitary activity and distributivity. The distributive indicates something special about an entity. It marks a plural, which might be seen to reduce individuation, but at the same time it marks an individuated plural – each – rather than a group or collective plural. Thus, the functions of incorporation and distributivity are in conflict: the incorporated theme is non-individuated, whereas the distributive would force individuation. In the presence of an incorporated theme and the distributive, distributivity over the theme is not possible. Thus, their ordering is not fixed, as they cannot bear a scopal relationship to one another.

Overall, then, while the distributive modifies arguments, the semantics of incorporated arguments is such that the distributive cannot quantify them. Thus, their ordering is not fixed, and the variable order that we find is not unexpected.

6.8 The Other Lexical Items (Negative, Inceptive)

As discussed in chapter 4, two other types of lexical items exist in some languages, a negative and an inceptive. Here I look briefly at the ordering of these elements.

(83) incorporate-iterative-distributive-**inceptive**   Sekani
      iterative-incorporate-distributive-**inceptive**   Sekani
      iterative-multiple-*negative*-incorporate-**inceptive**   Babine-
      -distributive   Witsuwit'en
      distributive-iterative-**inceptive**-incorporate-*negative*   Carrier

First consider the negative. It appears simply to negate the proposition – it does not narrow the scope from the proposition to a particular element of the proposition. Accompanying the negative in Babine-Witsuwit'en and Carrier are two further elements: a functional item that marks negation and a negative enclitic; see chapter 11. This is shown for Babine-Witsuwit'en in (84). The negative suffix is in boldface, the lexical negative is italicized, and the functional negative is underlined.

(84) Babine-Witsuwit'en (Hargus 1997:401)
      Root: *'a* 'compact object is located'

Imperfective	Perfective	
sə-'ay	in-'a'	positive
w-e̱-'a-**h**	*w*-e̱-'a-**l**	negative

Many Athapaskan languages of Alaska and British Columbia have a negative functional item and enclitic without a lexical item that marks negation (see Leer 1996 for discussion).

As just mentioned, the negative form of a verb word simply involves negation of the proposition. In order to narrow the scope of negation, it is necessary to use a phrasal negative. Assuming that the lexical negative affects the entire proposition and not just a constituent, the position of the negative in Carrier, at the right edge of the lexical items, is not surprising. However, the position of the negative in Babine-Witsuwit'en is surprising. Given the placement of the lexical negative with respect to the iterative, one might expect the inceptive to be outside its scope. But this is not the case, as (85) illustrates.

(85) a. ne-**we**-o-nə-s-qat
        down-**negative**-inceptive-inceptive-negative-snow, negative
        'It hasn't started to snow.' (Hargus 1997:390)

The verb stem *qat*, the preverb *ne*, and the inceptive *o* are all in the scope of a negative element, but the ordering does not reflect this. This example thus appears to violate the scope principle. But recall that negation is not marked in just one place in the Babine-Witsuwit'en verb. As (84) shows, not only is there a lexical negative, but negation is also marked by a functional item (*s* in (85)) and an enclitic. If the scope of negation is determined by the placement of these items with respect to the lexical items, then exactly the occurring propositional reading is predicted. Apparently, then, if the scope of negation is determined by an enclitic the negative lexical item is not part of the scope system and its position is not important, at least in Babine-Witsuwit'en. Its position must be determined in an alternative way.

Finally, consider the inceptive. In Sekani, this element is at the right edge of the lexical items, in Carrier it is followed by incorporates and the negative, and in Babine-Witsuwit'en it precedes only the distributive. The inceptive lexical item co-occurs with a functional item *n* in both Sekani and Babine-Witsuwit'en. In other languages such as Slave, this functional item marks inceptivity in some aspects without the additional lexical item.

It is difficult to determine whether or not the inceptive enters into the scope system or not. Its position suggests that it may. Its position with respect to the distributive is not relevant since the distributive is part of the argument system, while the inceptive is part of the event system. It is, in essence, at the right edge with respect to other morphemes with which it interacts. On the other hand, independent marking of inceptivity by a functional item is found. In addition, the inceptive in Babine-Witsuwit'en has an odd ordering with respect to one preverb. This inceptive appears with activity and accomplishment verbs (see chapter 11). Hargus 1997 shows that the inceptive, which normally follows all lexical items except the distributive, can sometimes be the first item of the verb. This happens when the preverb 'ə, usually translated as 'so, thus', is present in the verb.

(86) Babine-Witsuwit'en (Hargus 1997)
   a. **'ə-t'əχ**
      'S/he is working.' (392)
   b. **'ə-geɣ**
      'It happens/happened.' (392)

This preverb precedes the iterative and the negative, as in (87).

(87) a. **'ə-ne-s-dleɣ**
      preverb-iterative-1sg Subject-stem
      'I fixed it.' (made it so again [*ne*]) (Hargus 1997:392)

6.8 The Other Lexical Items (Negative, Inceptive)

b. **'ə-we**-s-dlil
preverb-negative-1sg Subject-stem
'I didn't make it.' (*we* negative) (Hargus 1997:392)

However, the inceptive must precede the preverb 'ə in the absence of other lexical items.

(88) a. **ho-'ə**-z-n-i-ɬ-'ɛ'n
inceptive-preverb-human Subject-qualifier-aspect-valence-stem
'We started to work on it.' (Hargus 1997:393)
b. **ho-'**-n-i-ge y
inceptive-preverb-qualifier-aspect-voice/stem
'It started to happen.' (Hargus 1997:393)

In the presence of other lexical items (iterative, multiple, negative), the position of the inceptive is not rigidly fixed.

(89) a. Preverb + iterative + inceptive
'ə-ne-ho-z-n-in-le y
preverb-iterative-inceptive-human Subject-qualifier-aspect-stem
'We started to fix it, make another.' (Hargus 1997:393)
b. Inceptive + preverb + iterative
ho-'-ne-n-i-s-dle y
inceptive-preverb-iterative-qualifier-aspect-1sg Subject-voice/stem
'I started to fix it, make another.' (Hargus 1997:393)

The variation in (88) and (89) is not consistent with the template hypothesis, which requires a fixed order. On the face of it, it also is not compatible with the scope hypothesis as the inceptive should have scope over the preverb and thus follow it. However, as mentioned, functional material (*n*) always co-occurs with *ho*, making it difficult to identify just which part of the verb carries the meaning of inceptivity. (Based on comparative facts, functional *n* is used in other languages to indicate inceptivity/inchoativity; a cognate of *ho* is not always found.) Suppose that the meaning inception is part of the entry of the *ho-n* combination. If so, *n* takes scope over the lexical complex of the verb, and correctly predicts the reading assigned in the inceptive. If the lexical inceptive is not part of the scope system, the free ordering in (89) is not so surprising. It is reminiscent of English intensifiers (cf. *You used to really cry a lot* vs. *You used to cry really a lot*) and of the transportable adverbs in (69). The fact that inception is elsewhere marked in the verb makes this a reasonable hypothesis. If, however, this inceptive is part of the scope system, Babine-Witsuwit'en provides evidence against the scope hypothesis.

To summarize, the negative in Babine-Witsuwit'en initially presents a serious problem to the scope-based analysis of morpheme order developed in this chapter. However, since negation is marked elsewhere by a syntactic suffix (see chapter 11) and since the lexical negative does not narrow the scope of negation, it is not clear that it is part of the scope system, in which case its position is arbitrary. Moreover, the inceptive can occur in more than one location depending upon what it combines with. This too seems to present an insoluble problem for the scope-based account. Like negation, however, inceptivity is marked elsewhere in the verb. It is thus not clear that the lexical inceptive is part of the scope system.

6.9 Summary

Consider now the lexical items as a whole. This complex consists of two or three major categories: preverbs, quantifiers, and, in some languages, incorporates. These are not homogeneous categories; the latter two contain morphemes expressing both entities and events. An inceptive and negative also occur in some languages. Preverbs, quantifiers, and incorporates show some iterability. The structure in (90) is appropriate for this complex, although it does not capture the variation in order that occurs.

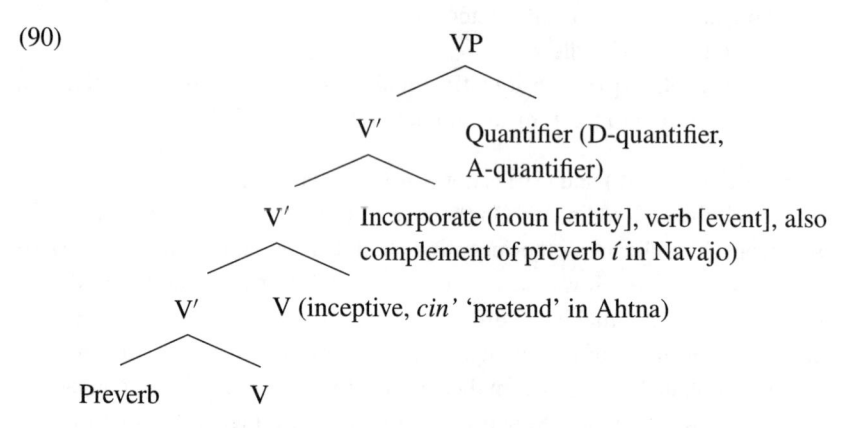

(90)

```
                        VP
                       /  \
                     V'    Quantifier (D-quantifier,
                    /  \              A-quantifier)
                  V'    Incorporate (noun [entity], verb [event], also
                 /  \                complement of preverb í in Navajo)
               V'    V (inceptive, cin' 'pretend' in Ahtna)
              /  \
        Preverb   V
```

The structure in (90) differs from that in (7) by specifying syntactic functions of some of the elements. Some items that are analyzed as preverbs are, in fact, verbs (Ahtna *cin'* 'pretend') or case markers (Navajo *í*), and incorporates are of two types: entities, which are syntactically either arguments or adjuncts, and events, which are syntactically noninflectable verbs.

We have further seen that the ordering possibilities among these elements are quite limited. I have argued that it is not an accident of history that the

6.9 Summary

patterning is so similar across the family, but that the fixed ordering is a consequence of scopal relations. When morpheme A has morpheme B within its scope, A must c-command B, appearing to its right. If either A can have B in its scope or vice versa, variable ordering, with different interpretations, is found. Finally, when A and B do not have a scopal relationship to each other, their ordering is often free, with no relationship between meaning and order, even within a language. If ordering properties are viewed strictly as a result of a language-particular template, then an important cross-family generalization is missed. In the absence of a scopal relationship, ordering becomes a language-particular idiosyncratic property, that must be accounted for in a language-particular way, be it by a template, phrase structure rules, alignment constraints, or some other device. Since an individual language may exhibit variation, whatever device is invoked must allow some flexibility; this suggests that a template is too restricted as it requires fixed rather than variable ordering.

Based on the observations in this chapter, we can conclude that a child encountering an Athapaskan language must know the following to cope with the lexical items:

(91) a. An element of greater scope appears to the right of elements within its scope.
b. Items not related by scope may appear in a free order or in an order that must be fixed for, or stipulated for, the language.

From (91) follow the properties in (92).

(92) a. Ordering of the categories
b. Ordering within the categories
c. Possible variation in absence of scope

In the absence of a scope relationship, other factors (e.g., phonological) may contribute to determining the ordering of lexical items, as in the case of the inceptive in Babine-Witsuwit'en, or the ordering may simply be idiosyncratic. The scope hypothesis allows one to separate out what ordering is principled and what is not. Strikingly, the principled orderings are repeated in language after language across the family; the interactions that are not related by scope vary across it.

7

Voice/Valence

In this chapter I consider the markers of voice/valence in Athapaskan languages. Including discussion of these morphemes in a section entitled lexical items might seem surprising to someone familiar with languages of the family as these morphemes share properties with functional items: they have the phonological shapes of functional items rather than of lexical items, and they occur at the right edge of the functional complex, while the lexical items occur to the left. I argue in this chapter that the voice/valence markers are functor predicates (see Ritter and Rosen 1993 for this term) – that is, they are predicates that take arguments or play a role in interpreting arguments. One of these morphemes, *ł*, marks valence – it is a causativizer. The second, *d*, is an indicator of voice – it specifies middle voice. A third, *l*, is a portmanteau combining properties of the others: it both causativizes and marks middle voice. The voice/valence elements are syntactically verbs that require a verb phrase complement. As such, they are properly discussed under the rubric of lexical rather than functional items. Once the properties of the voice/valence markers are established, I turn to their ordering properties. I argue first that they originate within the verb phrase, just as other lexical material does. I argue further that more than one voice/valence element can appear within a verb. When this is the case, the ordering is not phonologically determined (as argued, for example, by Hargus 1995a), but rather is a consequence of the semantic relationship between voice and valence.

Following a brief discussion of assumptions, I turn to the productive function of the voice/valence elements. While examining the function of these morphemes might seem unnecessary in a discussion of morpheme order, without an understanding of their functions, an understanding of their scopal properties is not possible.

7.1 Background Assumptions

Before beginning discussion of the voice/valence elements, I present several assumptions about lexical entries that underlie my analysis. Following a traditional assumption in the Athapaskan literature and in recent theoretical work by Cowper 1995, Cummins 1996, and others, I assume that a lexical entry of a verb includes material that must be present in all forms of the verb and that is not subject to change. Material that is not constant is not part of the lexical entry. This is a standard assumption in the Athapaskan literature; see, for instance, Rice 1989 on the definition of verb theme (basic lexical entry). Second, I assume that a verbal lexical entry has three major components: information about the number of required arguments (argument structure, including thematic and aspectual roles), event structure, and semantic content (qualia structure); see chapter 4. Third, I assume that nonlexical arguments can be added syntactically. Fourth, I make another assumption that is common in the Athapaskan literature, that the voice/valence morphemes have, in large part, broad but single identifiable functions (see Kibrik 1993, 1996, McDonough 1989, Rice forthcoming b, and Thompson 1996a, for instance, for discussion). Thus, while d, for example, appears to serve many roles, it has only a single lexical entry with different readings arising depending upon the construction that it appears in. This principle is taken up in recent work on the lexicon. Bouchard 1995, Carter 1988, and Cowper 1995, for example, argue that a typical lexical entry is underspecified, containing only essential semantic information. Cowper 1995 further argues that if a unified entry, without disjunctions or optional elements, is not available for a single phonological form, then two lexical entries are required.

The distinction between thematic roles and aspectual roles requires further comment. Thematic roles include those of agent, experiencer, theme, goal, source, location, and the like, and express a particular role played by an argument with respect to a verb. A second type of relationship between an argument and a verb can be recognized, an aspectual role (e.g., Grimshaw 1990, Ritter and Rosen 1993, Tenny 1994), or the aspectual role that an entity plays in the event. For instance, causatives typically add an initiator to an event (see Cummins 1996, Ritter and Rosen 1993, section 7.2.1 of this chapter), and nouns may serve to delimit an event. In this chapter I argue that the voice/valence elements contribute to the aspectual side of argument structure rather than to the thematic side.

7.2 Productive Uses

Markers of voice/valence, traditionally called classifiers, have long been a topic of inquiry in the Athapaskan literature (e.g., Axelrod 1996, Goddard 1905, Hoijer 1946a, Kibrik 1993, 1996, Rice, forthcoming b, Thompson 1996a). These elements have been identified as having two roles: they can be productive, performing causativizing and middle voice functions, or they can be idiosyncratic, listed with a particular lexical item.

The three overt voice/valence markers *ł*, *d*, and *l*, all function productively. In this section I examine these productive functions, showing that *ł* affects valence by adding an argument that is an initiator without specified thematic content, *d* marks middle voice, and *l* combines the functions of the other two, indicating both middle voice and causativity. See Kibrik 1993, 1996 for a similar claim; he uses the term transitivity indicators to replace the term classifier, while I use the term voice/valence.

The reader should keep the complex morphophonemics of the Athapaskan verb in mind in this chapter. I have boldfaced the voice/valence marker whenever possible, but its presence is often obscured.

7.2.1 Causativizer

I begin with the causativizer *ł*. The examples from Ahtna in (1) show that this marker can be added to a verb with different lexical voice/valence markers; see section 7.4. Voice/valence elements are in boldface.

(1) Ahtna (Kari 1990)
    a. lexical entry: G-Ø-t'aes
                         'roast, fry, bake' (347)
                         c'etsen' t'aes
                         'Meat is roasting.'
       causative: O-G-**ł**-t'aes
                         'roast, fry, bake' causative
                         c'e-**ł**-t'aes
                         unspecified Object-causative-roast
                         'S/he is roasting something.'
    b. lexical entry: G-**d**-caats
                         'be rendered, liquefied' (111)
                         s-**t**-caats
                         situation aspect-voice-be rendered
                         'It was rendered, liquified.'

7.2 Productive Uses

    causative: O-G-ł-caats
                        'render O (fat, fish heads), melt O (snow), liquefy
                        (fat, berries, snow)' causative
                        yi-ł-caats
                        disjoint anaphor-causative-render
                        'S/he rendered it.'

The examples in (1) illustrate the productivity of the *ł* valence marker. In the discussion to come, I detail the major uses of this element, drawing examples from several languages.

7.2.1.1 Intransitive Verbs with Theme Subjects

The causativizer can be added to an intransitive verb with a theme subject. The theme represents the endpoint of an event; the causativizer provides the event with an initiator. In the data throughout this chapter, the voice/valence markers are highlighted when they are transparent on the surface. I do not give morpheme-by-morpheme breakdowns or glosses here; the goal is to focus on the voice/valence markers. The morphophonemics is complex; see the various grammars for detailed discussion.

(2)   Koyukon (Jones and Jetté, forthcoming)
        intransitive Ø: too daadle-tsʉhtl
                              water
                              'Water made a splashing sound.'
        causative ł: too de-ł-tsʉhtl
                              'S/he caused the water to make a splashing sound,
                              he made the water make a splashing sound.'
(3)   Ahtna (Kari 1990)
        intransitive Ø: tsaey tnez-k'e'
                              tea
                              'The tea cooled off, became tepid, cooled.' (257)
        causative ł: itne-ł-k'e'
                              'S/he cooled it off.' (257)
        intransitive Ø: uyinaltaeniz-c'eł
                              'His biceps got pulled.' (124)
        causative ł: yi-ł-c'eł
                              'S/he tore it once.' (124)
        intransitive *d*:   c'ezes gha-dloz
                              'The skin got crumpled.' (164)

        causative ł: ighi-ł-dloz
'S/he softened it by crumpling.' (164)
        intransitive Ø: nen' ghighi-na'
'The earth was shaking.' (288)
        causative ł: łts'ii ts'abaeli dghe-ł-naa
wind tree
'Wind is moving the trees.' (288)

(4)   Slave (Rice 1989)
        intransitive Ø: we-gǫ
'It is dry.'
        causative ł: yé-**h**-gǫ
y disjoint anaphor + ´ situation aspect + h
causativizer = gǫ 'dry'
'S/he dried it.'
        intransitive Ø: ré-zhǫ
'It grew.'
        causative ł: re-**h**-shǫ
'I raised it, grew it.'
        intransitive *d*: satsónébehchiné k'ína-tłah
metal   sled
'The car goes around.'
        causative ł: satsónébehchiné k'ína-**h**-tłah
'S/he drives the car around.'

(5)   Navajo (Young and Morgan 1987G)
        intransitive Ø: yi-béézh
'It is boiling.' (119)
        causative ł: yi-ł-béézh
'S/he is boiling it.'
        intransitive *l*: yi-l-zhoł
'It's sailing along (as a cloud).' (119)
        causative ł: yoo-shoł
'S/he is dragging it along (as a trunk).'
        intransitive Ø: na'ni-yęęsh
'Something flows about in a meandering fashion.'
(119)
        causative ł: na'ni-ł-hęęsh
'S/he is making something flow about in a
meandering fashion.'

(6) Hupa (Golla 1970)
  intransitive Ø: daw
           'melt'
  causative ɬ: ɬ-daw
           'melt' (transitive)
  intransitive Ø: gyas
           'break, snap'
  causative ɬ: ɬ-gyas
           'cause to break, snap'
  intransitive Ø: xɪs
           'drop, fall'
  causative ɬ: ɬ-xɪs
           'send dropping, falling'

The examples in (2)–(6) involve event verbs (see chapter 11). Stative verbs and transitions are also subject to causativization when the subject is a theme. Two verb types occur in (7)–(12). One class, verbs of location or position, is a type of resultative. When such a verb is causativized, the reading is usually 'keep, maintain in a position', specifying an initiator and possessor. The second type is descriptive verbs; when these are causativized, an initiator is introduced and a transition is specified, as marked in the stem. These verbs become events through causativization.

(7) Koyukon (Jones and Jetté, forthcoming)
  intransitive Ø: hedaadle-tl'ee
           'They are staying, sitting.'
  causative ɬ: yeh hʉdaa-**tl**-tl'ee
           'S/he keeps them in the house.'
  intransitive Ø: nelaan le-kkonh
           'The meat (in dish) is there.'
  causative ɬ: yeh yee-**tl**-kkonh
           'S/he has it (dish of food) in the house.'
  intransitive Ø: hedenaadle-tl'ee
           'They sat down.'
  causative ɬ: hʉdenaa-tl'ee
           'S/he sat them down, made them sit down.'
  intransitive Ø: ne-dlogge
           'It is light in weight; he is nimble, agile, light.'
  causative ɬ: yee-ɬ-dlogge
           'S/he keeps it light.'

(8) Hupa (Golla 1970)
    intransitive Ø: si-'an
        'It (sg. object) is lying.' (76)
    causative ł: si-ł-'an
        'have sg. O lying motionless, possess'
    intransitive Ø: ni-Ø-Won'
        'be good' (76)
    causative ł: O ni-ł-Won'
        'cause O to be good'
    intransitive Ø: ti-Ø-ch'e'
        'Wind starts to blow.' (201)
    causative ł: O ti-ł-ch'e'
        'cause (wind) to blow, cause O to blow like the wind' (202)

(9) Slave (Rice 1989)
    intransitive Ø: bet'ádé-'a
        'post extends, sticks up'
    causative ł: yet'ádé-**h**-'a
        'S/he has a post stuck up.'
    intransitive Ø: the-da
        'S/he sits.'
    causative ł: yé-**h**-da
        'S/he has him/her sit.'

(10) Navajo (Young, Morgan, and Midgette 1992)
    intransitive Ø: si-dá
        'S/he is sitting.'
    causative ł: bisíní-ł-dá
        'You keep him/her seated.'
    intransitive Ø: 'íí-'á
        'pole/tree extends away out of sight, sticks up into air' (1)
    causative ł: 'íí-ł-'á
        'I held slender rigid object so it extends away into space.' (2)
    intransitive Ø: di-bááh
        'It is turning gray.' (41)
    causative ł: yiish-bááh
        'I am turning gray.'

7.2 Productive Uses

(11) Ahtna (Kari 1990)
   intransitive *d*: di-t-baets
   'It turned tan, brown, blond.' (103)
   causative *ł*: detse' tatni-ł-baets
   'She dyed her hair blond.'

(12) Carrier (Morice 1932)
   intransitive Ø: ezte-tsen
   'We are dirty.' (II:282)
   causative *ł*: ezte-ł-tsen
   We dirty someone.'
   intransitive *l*: hanî-l-ṭuz
   'He is bald.' (II:282)
   causative *ł*: hanuheznî-ł-ṭuz
   'We make you pl. bald.'

Kibrik 1993:56 suggests that the primary meaning of causatives of statives is "causing an existential/locative state to be maintained, controlling a Goal in a postion" – these are resultatives. Secondary to the major point here, when a stative is causativized, it remains a state; when a descriptive is causativized, it becomes a transitional, or an event, aspectually.

The examples in this section include both events ((2)–(6)) and states ((7)–(12)). Based on these verbs, the following generalizations can be drawn.

(13) When the causativizer is added to an event, it adds an initiator of the event.
   When the causativizer is added to a state it:
   a. creates a resultative of a locative verb, adding an initiator
   b. adds an initiator of a transition to a descriptive verb (makes the state into an event)

The causativizer adds an initiator, independent of the number of the verb's arguments (whether the event is intransitive or transitive), of the thematic role of the argument added (e.g., agent, possessor), and of the aspectual class of the verb (see chapter 11).

7.2.1.2 Intransitive Verbs with Agentive Subjects

When intransitive verbs with agentive subjects are examined, we see a split in the family. Some languages allow the simple causative construction seen so far (Ahtna, Carrier, Koyukon), some allow causativization of such intransitives, but require what Hale and Platero 1996 term a 'complex causative' construction (Navajo), and some do not generally allow the verbal causative construction with agentive transitives (Slave).

Consider first Ahtna, Koyukon, and Carrier. The examples in (14)–(16) show that the complement of the causativizer can be an intransitive verb with an agentive subject.

(14) Koyukon (Jones and Jetté, forthcoming)
    intransitive Ø: e-tsah
        'S/he cries.'
    causative ł: deketl'e e-ł-tsah
        'He makes his younger brother cry.'
    intransitive Ø: tleenee-baatl
        'S/he walked out energetically, in a huff.'
    causative ł: tleeyeenee-ł-baatl
        'S/he jerked him out.'
    intransitive Ø: hedo'eel-zoot
        'S/he slid into/inside the house.'
    causative ł: hedoyeenee-ł-zoot
        'S/he slid it into the house.'
    intransitive Ø: le-dlets
        'S/he urinated.'
    causative ł: ghee-ł-lets
        'S/he caused (her child) to urinate.'

(15) Ahtna (Kari 1990)
    intransitive *d*:   gha-t-na'
        'S/he was working.' (288)
    causative ł: ighe-ł-na
        'S/he is making him work.' (288)
    intransitive Ø: ni-yaa
        'S/he arrived.' (422)
    causative ł: gaa sni-ł-yaa
        'S/he made me walk here.' (423)
    intransitive Ø: nc'e-dlo'
        'S/he is laughing.' (163)
    causative ł: nsc'e-ł-dlo'
        'S/he makes me laugh.'
    intransitive Ø: tez-kaen
        'S/he started off in a boat.' (239)
    causative ł: c'etsen' nini-ł-kaen
        'S/he transported the meat (by boat).'

7.2 Productive Uses

(16) Carrier (Morice 1932)
    intransitive Ø: ne-pĕ·
                        'S/he swims.' (II:282)
    causative ł: neye-ł-pĕ·
                        'S/he makes him swim.'
    intransitive Ø: e-yał
                        'S/he is going on.' (II:282)
    causative ł: yî-ł-yał
                        'S/he causes him to go on.'
    intransitive Ø: es-sâr
                        'I weep.' (II:285)
    causative ł: O î-ł-tsâr
                        'I caused O to weep.'

These intransitives have an agent/initiator; the causative adds a second initiator to the event.

Navajo too allows causatives of intransitive verbs with agentive subjects.

(17) Navajo
    intransitive Ø: 'awéé' naa-ghá
                        baby
                        'The baby is walking around.' (Hale and Platero 1996:4)
    causative ł: 'awéé' nabiish-ł-á
                        'I am walking the baby around.'
    intransitive Ø: 'awéé' yi-dloh
                        'The baby is laughing.' (Hale and Platero 1996:5)
    causative ł: 'awéé' biyeesh-dloh
                        'I am making the baby laugh.'
    intransitive Ø: heesh-áá́ł
                        'I step along, shuffle along.' (YMM 674)
    causative ł: biyee-ł-sháá́ł
                        'I walk (baby) along (by holding its hand), move O along by 'walking' it (e.g., heavy refrigerator).' (675)
    intransitive Ø: yí-yóół
                        'The wind blows.' (YMM 724)
    causative ł: binii-sóół
                        'I make O bloat up, fill up O with gas (e.g., beans).'

intransitive Ø:	'íí-zhil
	'I drew in breath sharply, inhaled, gasped.'
	(YMM 773)
causative ł:	'ashíí-shil
	'It made me gasp for breath.'

The causative construction in these forms is distinct from that when the subject is a theme. The constructions differ in that when the subject is a theme no overt direct object pronoun is required in the causative (examples in (10)), while when the subject is an agent/initiator a direct object pronoun is required (examples in (17)). See Hale 1997, Hale and Platero 1997, and Rice, forthcoming b for a discussion of the differences between the constructions.

Finally, causatives of intransitives with agentive subjects are not common to all languages. This type of construction is not found in Slave, for instance.

(18) Slave (Rice 1989)
    intransitive Ø: yi̜-tse
                            'S/he cries.'
    causative ł: *seyi̜-h-tse
                            'S/he made me cry.'

A periphrastic construction is used instead.

(19) Slave periphrastic causatives (Rice 1989)
    a. bebí déh-w'a 'a-h-lá
       baby 3.burp   1sg.cause
       'I burped the baby.'
    b. he-h-tse 'a-se-ne-lá
       1sg.cry   2sg.make.1sg.
       'You made me cry.'
    c. na-d-éh-tła 'a-y-i̜-lá
       3.go back   3.make.3
       'He made him go away.'

In Slave, double initiators of events are not common within a single verb word. If a verb has an agent or initiator, causativization, or the addition of an initiator is not possible.

7.2.1.3 Transitive Verbs

Koyukon allows transitive verbs to be the complement in the causative construction.

7.2 Productive Uses

(20) Koyukon (Jones and Jetté, forthcoming)
    transitive *l*:   ts'eh nedaal-'onh
                      'S/he is wearing a hat.'
    causative *ł*:   ts'eh yendaa-ł-'onh
                      'S/he let him wear a hat.'
    transitive *l*:   eet needaal-tset
                      'S/he (quickly) put his hand there.'
    causative *ł*:   yaayedaanee-ł-tset
                      'S/he made him touch it, put his hand on it.'
    transitive Ø: k'eghee-zes
                      'S/he was drinking something (alcohol), sipping something (hot).'
    causative *ł*:   yek'e-ł-zes
                      'S/he is giving him something to drink.'

In these verbs, the added argument can be an agent/causer or an experiencer; the causee may or may not control or initiate the event in question. The shared property is that an initiator is added. The initiator of the original event is realized as an oblique object, while the theme remains a direct object.

In Ahtna, I have found only a few transitive verbs in Kari 1990 that enter into the causative construction. In these verbs, the original initiator does not exercise control over the event; control is held by the initiator introduced by the causativizer.

(21) Ahtna (Kari 1990)
    transitive Ø: O G-Ø-(y)aan
                      'eat O' (429)
    causative *ł*:   ic'e-ł-yaan
                      'S/he is feeding something to him.'
    transitive *d*:   O d-naan
                      'drink O' (290)
    causative *ł*:   iy'ghi-ł-naan'
                      'S/he gave him something to drink.'
    causative *ł*:   tuu ughe-ł-naan'
                      'I made him drink water.'

Morice 1932 lists a few transitive verbs that can be causativized as well, and readings are similar to those in Ahtna.

(22) Carrier (Morice 1932)
    transitive Ø: în-ˑaɬ
        'You sg. eat.' (II:283)
    causative ɬ: pê-î-ɬ-ˑaɬ
        'You sg. make him eat it, feed him.'
    transitive *d*:   eh-tnai
        'You pl. drink.' (II:283)
    causative ɬ: pê-e-ɬ-tnai
        'You pl. make him drink it.'

In Navajo these same two transitive verbs enter into the causative construction, and again the new initiator shows control.

(23) Navajo (Young, Morgan, and Midgette 1992)
    transitive Ø: yish-dlą́
        'I drink O, eat O (soup).' (153)
    causative ɬ: O biish-dlą́
        'I make P drink O.'
    causative ɬ: bi'yíí-ɬ-dlą́ą́'
        'I gave P a drink, fed P (baby, lamb), watered P.'
    transitive Ø: yí-yą́ą́'
        'I ate.' (692)
    causative ɬ: biyíí-są́ą́'
        'I fed O (food) to P (baby).'

Koyukon appears to be the only language that has a productive morphological means of forming causatives of transitives. In other languages, morphological causatives of transitives are limited to a few verbs.

7.2.1.4 Further Differences among the Languages

I have summarized the major productive functions of the causativizer; see Kibrik 1993 for discussion of additional uses. I have argued that the causativizer can take the following types of verb bases:

(24) Bases for causativization
    1. Intransitive verb with patient argument: all languages
    2. Intransitive verb with single agent argument: Ahtna, Koyukon, Navajo
    3. Both intransitive verb and transitive verb (productive): Koyukon

There is a hierarchy according to which intransitive verbs with theme arguments are the most likely to be causativized and transitive verbs the least likely to be causativized. This hierarchy is not a surprising one. Intransitive

7.2 Productive Uses

verbs with theme arguments are the most likely to undergo causativization because they contain no lexically specified initiator of the event that they depict. Eventive dyadic verbs include an initiator in their lexical representation, and thus are the least likely to allow the addition of an argument that specifies an initiation.

The causativizer has a clear aspectual role: it adds an initiator. In terms of thematic roles, that initiator can be an agent/causer, an experiencer, or a possessor. The initiator's thematic content is not fixed, but rather is determined through the context.

The languages also differ in what kind of causer is possible. To begin with the most limited case, in all languages the causer can be human. I will not repeat examples here; this is shown in many of the earlier examples. In some languages, a nonhuman that is capable of control can be a causer. This is true of Ahtna and Koyukon.

(25) Ahtna (Kari 1990)
 intransitive *l*: naagha-l-'uuts
  'I am relaxed.' (93)
 causative ɬ: tuu nilaeni nasghi-ɬ-'uuts'
  'The beer limbered me, relaxed me.'
 intransitive *l*: na-l-ghaex
  'It is melting.' (214)
 causative ɬ: naghaay kaghi-ɬ-ghaen
  'It (nature) thawed out the frogs.'
(26) Koyukon (Jones and Jetté, forthcoming)
 intransitive Ø: k'edeghee-lee'
  'He sang.'
 causative ɬ: sotseeyh ek'ede-ɬ-lee
  'Happiness is making him sing.'
 causative ɬ: gheeno' yedenaa-**tl**-dlut
  'It became full of maggots (maggots brought it to a boil).'

In other languages (e.g., Slave), it appears that the causer is limited to humans. Thus, in all languages the causee, or initiator of the event, can be human, while in some languages, the initiator can be nonhuman, but something with volitional force.

Although conditions on the use of the causativizer differ from language to language, a major function across the family is to add an argument. While this added role is an initiator of the event, circumstances of the language and the verb determine further thematic properties that are involved. The lexical restrictions on the causativizer's use must be stated for each language, but its general function is similar across the family.

7.2.1.5 Position of the Causativizer

I now examine where the causativizer fits in the syntactic structure of the verb. It introduces an argument without specific lexical semantic content as to the thematic role that it assigns. Specifically, it can introduce an agent/causer, experiencer, or possessor, among others; these share in being initiators of events. The causativizer also requires a proposition. It is multifaceted: it is functional in that it has no independent lexical semantic content in terms of thematic roles that it allows (rather, the content is determined by what it combines with), but it is verblike in that it affects argument structure. Ritter and Rosen 1993 examine similar morphemes in English (the verb *have*) and Japanese (the morphological causativizer-*sase*), and I essentially adopt their analysis for the Athapaskan causativizer. Basically, it is a verb that takes a verb phrase complement, and that requires a single nominal argument without specific thematic content, but with aspectual content (being an initiator). This accounts for the range of meanings that can be assigned to it depending upon construction. Ritter and Rosen term such elements functor predicates since they combine properties of functional elements and properties of predicates. I follow them in using this terminology.[1]

Why should a causativizer be analyzed as a verb? Baker 1988 argues that morphological causativizers are verbs in many languages. Verbs take arguments; the causativizer is associated with arguments in that it adds an argument.[2] The properties of the causativizer in Athapaskan languages are similar to those of verbs in other languages, and an analysis of the causativizer as a verb has specific precedent in the Athapaskan literature also (see Embick 1997, Hale and Platero 1996).[3]

The syntactic configuration that the causativizer enters into is important given the scope hypothesis. I suggest that this predicate enters into the syntactic structure in (27), where the causativizer introduces a VP complement that has an initiator as its subject.

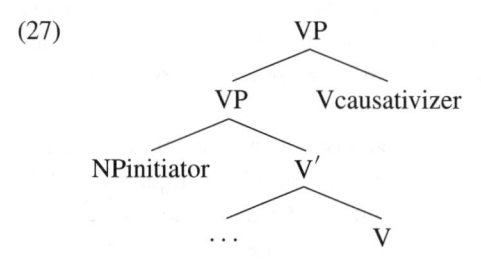

(27)
```
                VP
               /  \
             VP    Vcausativizer
            /  \
     NPinitiator  V'
                 /  \
                ...   V
```

7.2 Productive Uses

There are several reasons to propose that the causativizer takes a VP rather than a full sentence as its complement. First, there is only one set of functional features associated with the entire verb. Since functional projections are outside of VP (see chapter 5), if the complement of the causativizer is a VP rather than a full sentence, it should not contain more than a single set of inflectional material. This contrasts with an independent causativizing verb, which has its own set of functional features. The periphrastic causative construction is illustrated in (28). Note that the glosses are not morpheme-by-morpheme glosses, but rather convey the overall sense of the verb.

(28) Slave
   a. ná-'e-ge-de-dló   'a-go-thí-dhę
      human plural Subject laugh   1pl Subject cause 3pl Object
      'We keep them laughing.' (Rice 1989:1303)
   b. tł'otsę   hehtse   'aseh'į
      onion   1sg Subject cry   cause 1sg Object
      'Onions make me cry.' (Rice 1989:1305)

In this construction each verb contains its own functional material. The higher verb clearly introduces a complete sentence; the difference in patterning between it and the functor predicate is predicted if the functor predicate has the structure in (27).

Support for the structure in (27) also comes from case properties of the nouns involved. While each verb has its own arguments in the periphrastic construction, this is not true of the functor predicate construction, which is a single clause with respect to the case marking of arguments. Basically, with intransitive verbs, the subject of the functor predicate has subject marking, and the subject of the lower verb is a direct object or takes accusative case. With transitive verbs, on the other hand, the subject of the functor predicate is nominative, the subject of the lower verb is oblique, and the object of the lower verb remains an object (see (20) and (21)). In the last example in (21), for instance, the morphology is as follows: *tuu* 'water' is a direct object, *u* is an oblique object marking the subject of the lower clause, and the first person singular subject of the causative verb combines with the causativizer. If two sentences were involved, there would be no reason not to expect two independent subject markings.

As discussed in chapters 4 and 6, some Athapaskan languages include a negative in their functional complex. The negative has scope over both the causativizer and the causativized verb, but cannot negate either part independently, based on examples in the Ahtna (Kari 1990) and Koyukon (Jones and Jetté, forthcoming) dictionaries. In order to negate either piece of the construction alone, the periphrastic construction would be required.

In conclusion, while the Athapaskan causativizer patterns as an independent verb, it does not take a sentential complement but rather a VP complement.

Returning to the structure in (27), we can account for the surface adjacency of the verbs if they combine through verb incorporation (Baker 1988), with the lexical verb suffixing to the functor predicate. Baker argues that incorporation obeys structural conditions: incorporation results from X^0 movement, which, in the case of causatives, adjoins one verb head to another. Thus the verb stem raises from its position low in the tree to adjoin to the causativizer. The resulting verb complex raises further, creating the marked surface order with this verb complex separated from material within the verb phrase and following the functional material.

Now consider the position of the functor predicate with respect to the other verbal material. I have suggested that this predicate is embedded beneath the functional categories as the highest element in the verb phrase. This is expected. The causativizer has the lexical verb and its arguments and adjuncts within its scope. It introduces its own argument in most cases, but in other cases acts to impose a different interpretation on the argument.

To summarize, I have analyzed the causativizer as a functor predicate, without intrinsic thematic content but being an initiator aspectually, along the lines argued by Ritter and Rosen 1993 for English and Japanese. The thematic interpretation is parasitic upon the interpretation assigned to the arguments of the combined functor and verb.

7.2.2 Middle Voice

Two further voice/valence elements can be identified in all Athapaskan languages, d and l. The element d has a similar function in all languages: it is used in reflexive, reciprocal, passive, and iterative forms of verbs, among others. Kibrik 1996 identifies d and l as detransitivizers, Thompson 1989, 1996a suggests that they mark middle voice, and Arce-Aranales, Axelrod, and Fox 1994 argue that they indicate middle diathesis, with active voice. In this section I follow the basic proposal of these linguists, arguing that the productive d marks middle voice, and that l marks middle voice and causativity. In other words, l combines the functions of d and $ł$, as has long been recognized in the Athapaskan literature (e.g., Hargus 1988, Kari 1976, Rice 1989, Stanley 1969). I propose that d is a functor predicate that contributes to

7.2 Productive Uses

the interpretation of the sentence, but does not contribute an argument. Unlike the causativizer, it has no valence, but is a voice marker, providing a particular interpretation to its propositional complement. Specifically, it requires 'low elaboration' of an entity involved in the event that serves as its complement or of the event itself. Just as the causative contributes to the understanding of the event, providing an initiator, middle voice too helps understand the event, marking low elaboration.

I begin by defining middle voice. I follow Cummins 1996, Kemmer 1993, and others in relating voice to aspectual roles. Middle voice, according to Kemmer 1993, has to do with relative elaboration of an event or state. Kemmer defines the property of relative elaboration as "the degree to which the facets in a particular situation, i.e., participants and conceivable component subevents in the situation, are distinguished" (1993:208). Prototypical events or states with low elaboration are reflexives and reciprocals, where the initator and the affected entity are the same. Middles fall somewhere in between prototypical two-participant events, or events in which "a human entity (an Agent) acts volitionally, exerting physical force on an inanimate definite entity (a Patient) which is directly and completely affected by that event" (Kemmer 1993:50), and prototypical one-participant events where "the conceptual differentiation of Initiating and Endpoint facets is utterly non-existent: there is no Endpoint, but simply one participant of which a state or action is predicated" (Kemmer 1993:73). Middles typically involve two participants that are not differentiated or an aspect that is not clearly divided into an initiation and a conclusion. The event participants can be thought of in terms of their aspectual role – the initiator, be it an agent or a source, and endpoint, be it theme or goal, are not differentiated. The aspectual roles rather than the thematic roles that can be assigned to entities thus are useful here, as they were for the causatives, as they allow a general statement of the function of middle voice.

Based on her crosslinguistic study, Kemmer identifies a large number of semantic domains as potentially requiring middle morphology. These include reflexives, reciprocals, middle passives, translational and nontranslational motion, change in body posture, facilitative structures, grooming, other body actions, positionals, cognition middles, perception middles, and spontaneous middles. Not all languages choose to mark all of these domains as middles morphologically, but middles encompass this full range of meanings.

In the following discussion I examine constructions in which the d element occurs, showing how they meet the general criteria discussed by Kemmer for middle voice (see Kibrik 1996, Rice, forthcoming b, and Thompson 1996a for detailed discussion).

7.2.2.1 Reflexives: Initiator and Endpoint Not Differentiated

A reflexive shares with a prototypical two-participant event the fact that one entity affects or acts on another entity, but it is distinguished from a prototypical two-participant event in that the two entities are referentially identical, yielding an instance of low elaboration because the participants are not differentiated. Some examples are given in (29)–(34). In the lefthand column, the structure in question and the lexical voice/valence marker are given; the phonology is complex, so this information is necessary to understand the verb. The reflexive marker and the middle voice marker are both in boldface (when possible).

(29) Ahtna (Kari 1990)
    transitive Ø: tl'ogh t'aas
                      tl'ogh 'grass' + t'aas 'cut, imperfective'
                      'S/he is cutting grass.' (341)
    reflexive *d*:   **d**-es-t'as
                      de reflexive + s aspect = d middle + t' as 'cut, perfective'
                      'S/he cut her/himself.'

(30) Koyukon (Jones and Jetté, forthcoming)
    transitive Ø: yeghee-ghonh
                      ye- 3 Object + ghee aspect = ghonh 'make, kill pl.'
                      'S/he made them, killed them, beat them up.'
    reflexive *d*:   **ho**-he-**do**-**de**-ghonh
                      ho reflexive + he 3 plural Subject + d reflexive + o aspect = de middle + ghonh 'make, kill pl. O'
                      'They killed, overexerted themselves.'

(31) Slave (Rice 1989)
    transitive Ø: dahyedį́-lu
                      dah preverb 'up' + ye 3 Object + d noun class + į́ aspect = lu 'handle rope'
                      'S/he hung it.'
    reflexive *d*:   dah-'**ede**-dí-**d**-lu
                      dah preverb 'up' + 'ede reflexive + d noun class + í aspect = d middle + lu 'handle rope'
                      'S/he hung him/herself.'

7.2 Productive Uses

(32) Navajo (Young and Morgan 1987)
    transitive Ø: yi-ch'id
                        'S/he's scratching it.' (YM 69)
    reflexive *d*:   'ádí-ch'id
                        'S/he's scratching herself/himself.'
(33) Hupa: no change to *d* (Golla 1970:108)
(34) Carrier (Morice 1932)
    transitive Ø: ûs-ṭah
                        'I beat it (with stick, rod, etc.).' (II:353)
    reflexive *d*:   udedez-ṭah
                        'I beat myself.'

7.2.2.2 Reciprocals: Initiator and Endpoint Not Differentiated

Reciprocals, like reflexives, require middle voice. These too involve low elaboration of the participants in that the subject is both the origin and the target of the action.

(35) Ahtna (Kari 1990)
    transitive Ø: ggax kubii-ghaan
                        'Rabbits are killing them.' (204)
    reciprocal *d*:   dzuuggi na-**niɬ**-gha-**d**-ghaan
                        'The princesses killed each other.'
(36) Koyukon (Thompson 1996a)
    transitive Ø: yeto-ts'eyh
                        'S/he will pinch him/her once.' (355)
    reciprocal *d*:   **neeɬ**-heeto-**de**-ts'eyh
                        'They will pinch each other once.'
(37) Hupa (Golla 1970)
    transitive Ø: O ni-Ø-yod
                        'chase O' (81)
    reciprocal *d*:   ya-**n**-**ɬ**i-ni-**di**-yod-i
                        'chase one another'
(38) Navajo (Young and Morgan 1987:9)
    transitive Ø: yi-ghą́
                        'S/he's killing them.' (69)
    reciprocal *d*:   '**ah**i-gą́
                        'They're killing each other.'

(39) Slave (Rice 1989)
    transitive Ø: náyenii̧-ta
                          'S/he kicked him/her.' (634)
    reciprocal *d*:   ná-'**eɬe**-na-ta
                          'They kicked each other.'

7.2.2.3 Indirect Reflexives: Initiator and Location Not Differentiated

Indirect reflexives are related to two- or three-participant events; they differ from direct reflexives in that the actor and an oblique argument are identical, thus lowering the elaboration of the event.

(40) Koyukon (Jones and Jetté, forthcoming)
    indirect reflexive *d*:   **ed**e-nodo-**de**-tson'
                                 ede reflexive # no 'splash on' # d-gh thematic + de middle + tson' 'defecate'
                                 'He defecated on himself.'

(41) Navajo (Young and Morgan 1987)
    transitive Ø: béé-ghaz
                              'I scraped it off it.' (69)
    indirect reflexive *d*:   '**ád**-éés-gaz
                              'I scraped it off myself.'

(42) Slave (Rice 1989)
    transitive ɬ: yek'ená'eneyi̧-h-tse
                             'S/he washed it.' (handled O (water) on it)
    indirect reflexive *l*:   '**ede**-k'ená'ena-tse
                             'S/he bathed herself/himself.' (handled O (water) on self)

In Slave, indirect reflexives and reciprocals are found with a few postpositions; indirect reflexives and indirect reciprocals do not occur in the middle voice in some languages.

7.2.2.4 Indirect Reciprocals: Initiator and Location Not Differentiated

Indirect reciprocals, like indirect reflexives, indicate that the origin of the event and an oblique target are identical to each other.

(43) Slave (Rice 1989)
    transitive ɬ: bek'ená'enii-h-tse
                             'I washed him/her.'
    indirect reciprocal *l*:   '**eɬe**-k'ená'ekena-tse
                             'They washed each other.'

7.2 Productive Uses

Indirect reciprocals, like indirect reflexives, are less likely to require middle voice.

7.2.2.5 Self-benefactives: Initiator and Recipient Not Differentiated

Self-benefactives are a type of indirect reflexive in which the agent performs an action for his or her own benefit (Thompson 1996a:356), creating low elaboration of arguments.

(44) Ahtna (Kari 1990)
    transitive ɬ: ize-ɬ-ghaen
                                'He killed it.' (213)
    self-benefactive *l*:   i-**d**-ze-**l**-ghaen
                                  'He killed it for his own benefit.' (131)

(45) Koyukon (Thompson 1996a)
    transitive ɬ: le-tl-baats
                                  'I boiled it.' (356)
    self-benefactive *l*:   **d**-aalge-baats
                                  'I boiled it for myself.'

(46) Slave (Rice 1989)
    transitive Ø: nį-lu
                                  'You sg. sew.'
    self-benefactive *d*:   **de**-nį-**d**-lu
                                  'You sg. sew for yourself.'

(47) Carrier (Morice's appropriative) (Morice 1932)
    transitive Ø: thĕnes-ʼaih
                                  'I take something out of the house.' (II:334)
    self-benefactive *d*:   thĕ-**d**i-s-ṭ-aih
                                  'I take something out of the house for myself.'
    transitive Ø: nênes-khaih
                                  'I put the contents in an open pan.' (II:334)
    self-benefactive *d*:   nê-**d**î-s-khaih
                                  'I put the contents in an open pan for myself, for my own use.'

7.2.2.6 Incorporated Body Parts: Endpoint Part of Initiator

Many northern Athapaskan languages allow incorporation of body parts. Middle voice may accompany body part incorporation when, as Axelrod 1988 argues, the verb marks the movement of the body part in a typical manner. This, as Thompson 1996a:357 points out, is not surprising since something that affects one part of the body affects the entire self.

(48) Ahtna (Kari 1990)
    other incorporate Ø: **c'edzi**-gha-'aał
        'It (four-legged animal) is running along.' (74)
    body part incorporate *d*:   its'e **laa-t**-'aas
        hand
        'He is waving his hand at him.'

(49) Koyukon (Thompson 1996a)
    non-incorporated Ø: de-**lo'** neenee-'onh
        refl-hand
        'S/he put her/his own hand there.'
    body part incorporate *d*:   nee-**lo'**-ee-**t**-'onh
        hand
        'S/he put her/his own hand there, at rest.'

(50) Tsuut'ina (Cook 1984)
    non-incorporated Ø: sí-**tsì** dìnìsís-'ó
        head
        'I turned my head.' (136)
    body part incorporate *d*:   dígá **tsì**-dìnìsí-**t**-'ó
        'I turned my head.'

7.2.2.7 Mediopassives: Initiator and Endpoint Not Differentiated

The term 'mediopassive' is used in two senses in the Athapaskan literature. First, Young and Morgan 1987 use it to refer to situations where an object, either direct or oblique, is part of the subject, but the reflexive construction is not used. These verbs include noun class markers – either *d*, referring to sticklike objects (arms and legs), or *n*, referring to small round objects (head).

(51) Ahtna (Kari 1990)
    transitive Ø: nayghi-'aan
        'S/he brought it down.' (71)
    mediopassive *d*:   na-**n**-da-**t**-'aan
        'S/he put it (his hat) on herself/himself.' (72)

(52) Navajo (Young and Morgan 1981)
    transitive Ø: yiih yiyíí-'ą́
        'S/he put three-dimensional object into it.' (227)
    mediopassive *d*:   yiih **n**-oo-**t**-'ą́
        'S/he put his head into it.'

7.2 Productive Uses

(53) Slave (Rice 1989)
    transitive Ø: O teni̧-'o̧
        'S/he put three-dimensional O in water.'
    mediopassive *d*:   te-**d**-ę́-se
        'S/he put her/his own hand in water.'

'Mediopassive' is also used to refer to cases where a reflexive is understood, but not overt.

(54) Koyukon (Jones and Jetté, forthcoming)
    transitive Ø: noyele-tl'oonh
        'S/he dressed him/her (e.g., child).'
    mediopassive *d*:   nolse-tl'oonh
        'I dressed.'

(55) Ahtna (Kari 1990)
    transitive Ø: nayiz-tl'uun
        'S/he gave him/her clothes.' (365)
    mediopassive *d*:   nas-tl'uun
        'S/he got dressed.'

(56) Slave (Rice 1989)
    transitive ł: ráyere-h-tł'o̧
        'S/he dresses him/her.'
    mediopassive *d*:   ráre-tł'o̧
        'S/he dresses herself/himself.'

7.2.2.8 Spontaneous Middles (Anticausative): Initiator Suppressed

Thompson 1996a shows that many constructions in Athapaskan languages can have either a passive or a spontaneous middle translation. He calls the latter anticausatives, with inanimate endpoints and no implied initiator or agent. Passives, on the other hand, have an implied initiator. He speculates that the Athapaskan passives (see section 7.2.2.9) developed out of spontaneous middles (Thompson 1996a:359).

(57) Koyukon
    transitive Ø: dekenh denaal-yes
        'S/he broke the stick.'
    middle *l*:   dekenh denaałe-yes
        'The stick broke, the stick was broken.'

7.2.2.9 Passives: Initiator Suppressed But Implied

Athapaskan languages form passives through the use of middle voice marking and, generally, suppression of the agent. It is often pointed out (e.g., Kibrik 1996, Thompson 1996a) that passives have an implied, but suppressed, agent. Suppression of the agent creates low elaboration of the event.

(58) Ahtna (Kari 1990)
    transitive Ø: ighi-ghaan
                        'S/he made them.' (130)
    passive *d*:   a-**d**-ghaan
                        'They were made.'
    transitive Ø: ighi-yaan'
                        'S/he ate it.' (429)
    passive *d*:   **d**-aan
                        'It is being eaten.' (130)

(59) Hupa (Golla 1970)
    transitive Ø: O adverb-Ø-liW/la
                        'move O (several, rope) somewhere' (79)
    passive *d*:   adverb-wi-**di**-la
                        'several, rope have been moved somewhere'
    transitive Ø: O adv-Ø-mił/metł'
                        'throw O (several in bunch)' (79)
    passive *d*:   adverb-**di**-mił
                        '(several in bunch) move precipitously, fly, throw themselves'

(60) Navajo (Young and Morgan 1987)
    transitive Ø: yiz-tał
                        'S/he gave him a kick.' (121)
    passive *d*:   yis-tał
                        'S/he was given a kick.'
    transitive Ø: yizh-t'éézh
                        'S/he blackened it/him.' (121)
    passive *d*:   yish-t'éézh
                        'It was blackened.'

(61) Koyukon (Thompson 1996a)
    transitive ł: neeto-ł-dzes
                      'S/he will hit you once.' (360)
    passive *l*:   eeteghee-**l**-dzes
                      'You will be hit once.'

7.2 Productive Uses

      transitive Ø: k'oonghee-haanh
                            'S/he picked berries.' (360)
      passive *d*:   kehoodenee-**de**-haanh
                            'All (the berries) were picked.'

(62) Slave (Rice 1989)
      transitive Ø: léyi-ghe
                            'I cut it.'
      passive *d*:   léye-ge
                            'It was cut.'
      transitive Ø: sek'é' į́-la
                            'S/he confirmed me (handled unspecified objects on me).'
      passive *d*:   sek'é'í-ya
                            'I was confirmed (unspecified objects were handled on me).'

(63) Carrier (Morice 1932)
      transitive ł: des-rĕl
                            'I plane it.' (II:286)
      passive *d*:   de-krĕl
                            'It is planed, it can be planed.'
      transitive Ø: nes-˙a
                            'I deceive O.' (II:286)
      passive *d*:   nes-ṭ-ah
                            'I get deceived.'

7.2.2.10 First Person Plural Subjects

Some Athapaskan languages have a morpheme that marks a first person plural subject. First person plurals can be thought of as involving low elaboration in that they involve a number of initiators working as a collectivity. This element occurs with the *d* middle voice marker.[4]

(64) Navajo (Young and Morgan 1987)
      third plural subject Ø: t'óó 'aha-yóí
                                      'They are many.' (114)
      first person plural *d* ('):   t'óó 'ahonii-'-yóí
                                      'We are many.'
      first person singular Ø: yah 'íí-'ą́
                                      'I carried it inside.' (114)
      first person plural *d*:   yah 'ii-t-'ą́
                                      'We carried it inside.'

(65) Slave (Rice 1989)
    first person singular Ø: heh-'á
                                           'I eat.'
    first person plural *d*:   hí-t-'á
                                           'We eat.'
    first person singular Ø: leh-xe
                                           'I cut it.'
    first person plural *d*:   lehí-ge
                                           'We cut it.'
(66) Hupa (Golla 1970)
    third person Ø: ch'e'i-ya'n
                                           'He eats it.' (303)
    first person plural *d*:   k'i-**di**-yan
                                           'We eat.' (71)

In Galice (Hoijer 1966), both the first and second person plural forms require middle voice when the verbs has lexical ɬ.

(67) Galice (Hoijer 1966)
    first person singular ɬ: dash-ɬ-bad
                                         'I boil it.' (325)
    second person singular ɬ: niN-ɬ-bad
                                           'You sg. boil it.'
    first person plural *l*:   di-l-bad
                                          'We boil it.'
    second person plural *l*:   do'o-l-bad
                                           'You pl. boil it.'

7.2.2.11 Iteratives: Initiator and Endpoint Not Differentiated

Most Athapaskan languages have a construction known as the iterative (see chapter 4). The iterative has the form *na* (or cognate) and has more than one reading: return to a previous state (often translated 'back') and repetition of an event (generally translated 'again' or 'another'). It may co-occur with a customary aspect stem in most languages. When combined with an intransitive verb, middle voice is found; it is unusual to find middle voice iteratives with transitive verbs. The iterative construction with intransitive verbs is the nonparticipant argument parallel to the reflexive and reciprocal in the participant argument system; it indicates that the endpoint is identical to the point of initiation.

7.2 Productive Uses

(68) Ahtna (Kari 1990)
    noniterative Ø: ni-yaa
                            'He arrived.' (422)
    iterative d: **na**-'i-**d**-yaa
                            'He returned.' (291)

(69) Koyukon (Jones and Jetté, forthcoming)
    noniterative Ø: ne-yo
                              'S/he arrived.'
    iterative d: **no**-'ee-**de**-yo
                            'S/he came back.'

(70) Navajo (Young and Morgan 1987)
    noniterative Ø: sé-łį́į́'
                            'I became.' (122)
    iterative d: **ní**-sís-**d**-łį́į́'
                          'I reverted, turned back (into).'
    iterative d: **náá**-sís-**d**-łį́į́'
                          'I again became.'
    noniterative Ø: baa ní-yá
                            'I went to him.' (122)
    iterative d: baa **ná**-nís-**d**-zá
                          'I returned to him.'
    iterative d: baa **náá**-nís-**d**-zá
                          'I again went to him.'

(71) Hupa (Golla 1970)
    noniterative Ø: adverb-xo-Ø-'aW/'an
                            'pl. Subject run somewhere' (80)
    iterative d: adverb-**na**-xo-**di**-'aW/'an
                          'pl. Subject run back somewhere'

(72) Slave (Rice 1989)
    noniterative Ø: dé-'éé
                            'S/he starts off by boat.'
    iterative d: **ra**-de-**t**-'éé
                          'S/he starts off again, starts back by boat.'
    iterative d: **ra**-**t**-'ó
                          'S/he goes customarily by boat.'
    noniterative Ø: 'ane-lee
                            'You sg. do it.'
    iterative d: 'a-**ra**-ne-**d**-lee
                          'You sg. do it again.'

Note that with transitive verbs, the points of initiation and ending are not rendered identical by the iterative, and thus middle voice is not found.

7.2.2.12 Errative: Initiator Control Suppressed

A construction used to indicate unintentional action, the errative, is found in many Athapaskan languages.[5] Axelrod 1993:108 provides the following definition: "doing the activity referred to by the verb excessively or incorrectly and being unable to stop or escape from the consequences." Morice 1932 II:327, who appears to be the first to use the word 'errative', points out that the errative in Carrier "quite often connotes a reflex idea not only of impropriety, but of unwished for consequences for the subject of the verb." The errative occurs with a qualifier *n* as well as with the *d* middle element. Thompson 1996a:362 suggests that low elaboration is involved in the errative given the unintentional character of the action; normally the agent causes the event, but in the errative this agency is suppressed. In particular, the agent may control the beginning of the event, but does not control the endpoint.

(73) Ahtna (Kari 1990)
    nonerrative Ø: kahghi-yaa
                           'S/he spoke out.' (285)
    errative *d*:   kah-**n**-es-**d**aa
                           'S/he accidentally spoke it.'
    nonerrative *ł*:   ite-ł-na'
                           'S/he swallowed it.' (286)
    errative *l*:   it-**n**-e-**l**-na'
                           'S/he choked on it.' (285–286)

(74) Koyukon (Axelrod 1993)
    nonerrative Ø: k'eghee-hon'
                           'S/he ate.' (108–109)
    errative *d*:   k'e-**n**-aał-**d**-on'
                           'S/he overate.'
    nonerrative Ø: ghee-do'
                           'S/he was sitting, staying.' (109)
    errative *d*:   **n**-aałee-**d**o'
                           'S/he started staying and couldn't make her/himself leave.'

7.2 Productive Uses

(75) Carrier (Morice 1932)
    nonerrative ∅:   es-ṭên
        'I work.' (II:327)
    errative *d*:   e-**n**-es-ṭên
        'I work uselessly, wrongly, make a mistake, err.'
    nonerrative ∅:   thas-ˑaih
        'I put something in the water.' (II:328)
    errative *d* :   tha-**n**-es-**ṭ**-aih
        'I put the wrong piece in the water.'

The Navajo aspectual form that Young and Morgan call the prolongative has the same semantics as the Alaskan errative and requires middle voice marking and the qualifier *n*.

(76) Navajo 'prolongatives' (Young, Morgan, and Midgette 1992)
    nonerrative ∅:   'i'nish-'aał
        'I start to chew.' (28)
    errative *d*:   ná-**n**-ésh-**t**-'aal
        'I ate too much, got stuffed.' (29)
    nonerrative ∅:   haash-chééh
        'I start to cry.' (70)
    errative *d*   nadí-**n**-ísh-chééh
        'I cry and cry, prolongedly.'
    nonerrative ∅:   nínít-chozh
        'I finished eating.' (90)
    errative *d*:   ná-**n**-ésh-chozh
        'I ate too much of O, overate on O.'

7.2.2.13 Repetitive/Perambulative: Endpoint of Event Suppressed

Intransitive verbs in what is called the perambulative aspect in Koyukon and the repetitive aspect in Slave take middle voice.

(77) Koyukon (Jones and Jetté, forthcoming)
    motion ∅:   ts'enee-datl
        'We arrived.'
    perambulative *d*:   **kk'o**-ts'ee-**de**-daał
        'We are traveling around.'

(78) Slave (Rice 1989)
continuative ∅:   náwhe-ya
                   'S/he made a return trip.'
repetitive *d*:   **k'ína**-ye-**d**a
                   'S/he walked around.'

In this aspect, the event is not a distinct, discrete one – the endpoint is suppressed – and thus middle voice is not inappropriate. Thompson 1996a:364 coins the term 'antitelic' for this function to indicate a suppressed goal. It is interesting that in the distributive aspect, where a series of discrete arguments are involved rather than a collective, middle voice is not found (see chapter 11).

7.2.2.14   Interim Summary

Middle voice is marked by an affix *d*. I use the term middle voice, as the affix appears in a variety of constructions that are unified in that they indicate low elaboration of events or arguments: there is no distinction between initiator and endpoint, or one is not elaborated. While *d* has a single function, middle voice, it is used in several constructions that are differentiated by extra material in all but the passive and spontaneous middle, as in (79).[6]

(79) Construction of middles

passive	no other morphological material
reflexive	reflexive direct object prefix
reciprocal	reciprocal direct object prefix
indirect reflexive	reflexive oblique object prefix
indirect reciprocal	reciprocal oblique object prefix
incorporated body part	incorporate
self-benefactive	*d* prefix
plural subject	subject marking
iterative	*na* iterative
customary	customary stem (*na* iterative prefix optional)
errative	*n* prefix
repetitive/perambulative	preverb (e.g., *kk'o* Koyukon, *k'ína* Slave)

Meaning is constructionally determined; the middle voice marker simply designates low elaboration, but not the specific reading to be assigned; this must be derived from the context. Rampant homonymy is avoided because interpretation is constructional. Not too surprisingly, however, some ambiguities are found, as in (80).

7.2 Productive Uses

(80) Koyukon ambiguities (Jones and Jetté, forthcoming)
    a. neeɬ'ek'ehe-l-onh
       'They are feeding each other, one is feeding the other.'
    b. ede-k'e-l-zes
       'He is drinking by himself, giving himself something to drink.'
    c. de-'aak   dle-tseenh
       reflexive.dress
       'S/he made herself a dress, her dress was made.'

7.2.2.15 The Syntactic Structure Associated with Middle Voice

The syntactic structure associated with middle voice also requires attention. I suggest that, like the causative, middle voice is a verb that takes a VP complement. Middle voice differs from the causative, however, in taking a proposition, but not introducing an argument. This analysis raises several questions. First, why should middle voice be considered to be a verb? It, unlike the causative, does not add an argument, but interprets something in the lower clause, in tandem with other material in the verb. Verbs that do not introduce arguments, but provide a point of view of the main event or add a flavor to an argument, occur in other languages as well, as the English examples in (81) illustrate (thanks to Leslie Saxon for this suggestion).

(81) a. The rain appeared / seemed / tended to fall.
    b. John tended to sleep late.

English verbs 'appear, seem, tend' take a proposition as complement, but introduce no further arguments. Middle voice, like the verbs in (81), introduces a particular interpretation of the complement. In this way, then, it is like a verb. It is also verblike in selecting for certain verbs (see section 7.5).

Second, why is middle voice considered to take a VP complement rather than a sentential complement? Just as the causativizer takes a VP, so does middle voice – only one set of functional material is present, rather than the two expected when two sentences are found. Again as with the causative, in languages with a negative as part of their functional complex, the negative does not negate either part of the structure independently.

Finally, how is the specific middle voice function assigned? The functor predicate itself simply informs that something in the complement is lowly elaborated. This predicate, in construction with further material in the clause, determines the particular reading.

7.2.2.16 Summary

I have argued that *d*, a marker of middle voice, is a functor predicate. It appears on its own in passives, and in combination with another item in other middle constructions, where *d* indicates low elaboration and the additional morpheme indicates how low elaboration is interpreted. Syntactically, I have suggested that it is a verb which takes a proposition, or VP. Unlike the causativizer, it does not introduce a new argument, but adds an interpretation to the lower verb.

7.3 Middles and Causatives

So far, we have seen evidence for morphological marking of middles and causatives in Athapaskan languages. In this section I return to questions of ordering and examine situations which involve a middle and a causative both. I begin with an uncommon case, situations where two overt voice/valence markers are present on the surface, and then address the common case, where a single voice/valence marker is present on the surface, but both a middle and a causative meaning are contained within the verb.

7.3.1 Overt Double Voice/Valence in Navajo

Young and Morgan list a few cases with two voice/valence markers in Navajo.

(82) Navajo double voice/valence (Young, Morgan, and Midgette 1992)
l middle:	yi-l-woł
	'He is going along flexing, he is running along.' (885)
ł causative:	'ahání-ł-hod
	'I broke it in two by flexing it.'
ł + *l* causative of middle:	yiyoo-ł-wol
	'S/he is causing it to run along, s/he is running it along.'

In the middle form, only *l* is present; in the causative only *ł* is. In the causative of the middle, there is an overt causativizer (*ł*), but *l* is also present. This can be seen from the presence of voicing on the stem-initial consonant ([w] rather than [h]); it would be voiceless, as in the causative form, if *l* were not present.

Another Navajo example is given in (83).

(83) Navajo (Young, Morgan, and Midgette 1992)
d:	ndish-'-na'
	'I got up.' (885)
ł + *d*:	nábidii-ł-'-na'
	'I stood it back up (e.g., fallen corn plant).'

7.3 Middles and Causatives

In the first example, *d* occurs, as can be seen by the presence of a glottal stop preceding the stem-initial *n*. In the second example, this *d* is still present, and the causativizer is as well. Thus, in these two examples of causatives of middles, both a lexical middle marker (*d*, *l*) and a causative marker surface.

This is not the norm in Navajo (see, for example, Young, Morgan, and Midgette 1992:885 for discussion). In general, when a verb is a causative of a middle, just the causativizer is present on the surface. This can be seen in the examples in (84).

(84) Navajo: single voice/valence phonologically
    lexical *l*:   hani-l-gháásh
                  'It bubbles, boils, comes to a boil.' (YMM 234)
    causative *ł*: 'anii-ł-haazh
                  'I brought it to a boil.'
    lexical *l*:   'iil-zhood
                  'It slides away out of sight.' (YMM 786)
    causative *ł*: 'iish-shood
                  'I drag it away out of sight (heavy long, trunk, sled).' (787)
    lexical *d*:   hodii-'-nááh
                  'Area starts to move or shake.' (YMM 420)
    causative *ł*: hodiish-nááh
                  'I cause area to shake.'
    lexical *d*:   yish-jį́įh
                  'I turn black, become tarnished, get sunburned.' (YMM 782)
    causative *ł*: yish-shį́įh
                  'I dye O black (wool), color O black, oxidize O, turn O black.'

In the causatives, the lexical *l* or *d* is missing. This can be seen in the verbs with lexical *l* by the voicelessness of the stem-initial fricative. It can be seen in the verbs with lexical *d* by the absence of the so-called D-effect (glottal before *n*; stop counterpart of fricative). Thus, in Navajo, the surface double voice/valence forms may represent the historical state, but synchronically the forms with double voice/valence must be regarded as marked.

7.3.2 Overt Double Voice/Valence in Hupa

Hupa is different from Navajo in providing two overt markings of voice/valence in a way that is somewhat productive.

Consider first iteratives. These take *d* middle voice, as in (85).

(85) Hupa double voice/valence (Golla 1970)
intransitive Ø: adverb-xo-Ø-'aW/'an
                 'pl. subject run somewhere' (80)
middle *d*:   adverb-na-xo-**di**-'aW/'an
                 'pl. subject ran back somewhere'

If the verb has a lexical voice/valence marker with phonetic content, two voice/valence markers surface.

(86) Hupa double voice valence (Golla 1970)
intransitive ł: O wi-ł-teł
                 'move sg. person along' (87, 119)
middle ł-*d*:   O na-wi-**ł-di**-tel
                 'move sg. person back along'
intransitive *l*: wi-l-dał
                 'sg. runs along' (87)
middle *l-d*:   na-wi-**l-di**-dał
                 'sg. runs along back'

Double marking of voice/valence is found in other cases as well. The examples in (87) show causatives of stative verbs; these yield possessives, where the resultant state implies a prior event. What is interesting about these causatives is that they contain not just the causativizer, but optionally include a middle voice marker as well.

(87) Hupa double voice/valence (Golla 1970)
intransitive *l*: si-l-q'as
                 '(stones) lie thrown' (158, 191)
causative ł-*d*: O si-**ł-di**-q'as
                 'have O (stones) lying thrown'
(88) Hupa double voice/valence – analogy (Golla 1970)
intransitive Ø: si-da
                 'sg. animate sit, dwell'
causative ł (*d*): O si-ł-da / O si-**ł-di**-da
                 'have O sitting, own a pet' (192)

Golla suggests that in the first type of these forms, (87), the stative verb is historically a middle derived from a transitive; hence the presence of a middle voice element and the causativizer. The second class (*si-ł-di-da* in (88)) he proposes was derived analogically from the first; here the middle voice marker is variable.

7.3 Middles and Causatives

A particularly complex form is shown in (89).

(89) Hupa causative of passive (Golla 1970)
 transitive ɬ: Oɬ-tiW
  'move (one person) somewhere' (181)
 passive l: l-ten
  '(one person) has been moved somewhere' (181)
 causative ɬ-d: **ɬ-di**-ten
  'have (one person) moved somewhere' (182)

Here a passive is formed through the addition of d, yielding l, and a further causative is formed on the passive, yielding the compound voice/valence marker.

7.3.3 Covert Double Voice/Valence

One might expect that middles of causatives and causatives of middles should generally be possible, even if markings for both do not surface because of, for instance, constraints on possible consonant clusters in a language. This is indeed the case. In this section I examine forms marked for both voice and valence. The trees in (90) show the general situation. Basically, a middle formed on a causative has the l voice/valence marker while a causative formed on a middle has the ɬ voice/valence marker.

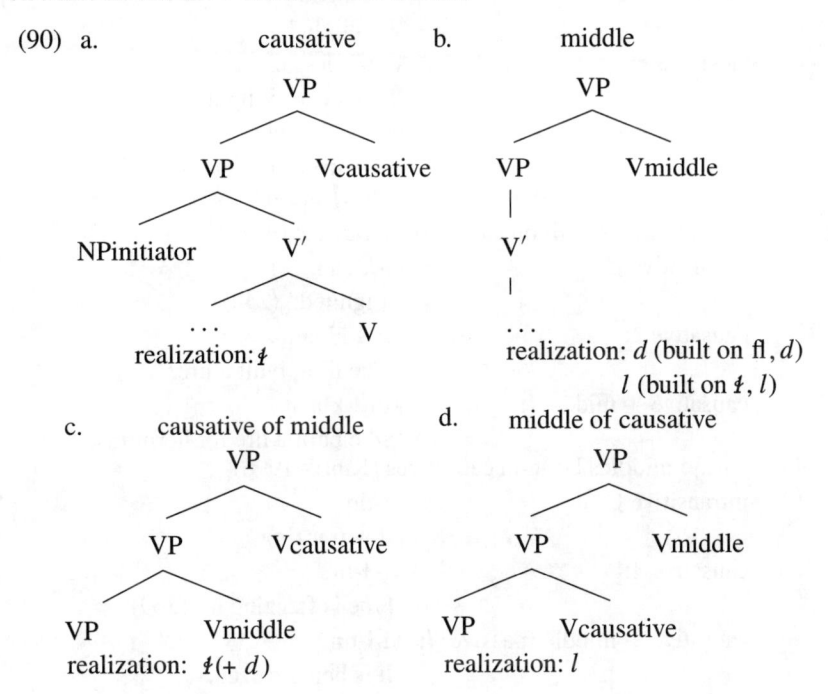

(90) a. causative
 [VP [VP NPinitiator V' [... V]] Vcausative]
 realization: ɬ

b. middle
 [VP VP Vmiddle]
 realization: d (built on fl, d)
 l (built on ɬ, l)

c. causative of middle
 [VP [VP VP Vmiddle] Vcausative]
 realization: ɬ(+ d)

d. middle of causative
 [VP [VP VP Vcausative] Vmiddle]
 realization: l

7.3.3.1 Middles Built on Causatives

Having sketched the general situation, I turn to specific examples, beginning with middles built on causatives. In the expression 'causative + middle', I mean that the middle is built on a causative as in (90d).

(91) Koyukon middles built on causatives (Jones and Jetté, forthcoming)
      intransitive Ø: tsaanee-let
                                'S/he woke up.'
      causative ɬ: ts'aayeenee-ɬ-let
                                'S/he woke her up.'
      causative + middle *l*: ts'aahodee-let
                                'S/he woke her/himself up.'
      intransitive Ø: e-tsah
                                'S/he cries.'
      causative ɬ: deketl'e e-ɬ-tsah
                                'S/he makes his younger brother cry.'
      causative + middle *l*: yede-l-tseh
                                'S/he makes him cry for his own satisfaction, by his own selfishness.'
      intransitive Ø: ne-dlogge
                                'It is light.'
      causative ɬ: yee-ɬ-dogge
                                'S/he keeps it light.'
      causative + middle *l*: beɬ de-l-dlogge
                                'S/he keeps her/his sleep light (is a light sleeper).'

(92) Ahtna middles built on causatives (Kari 1990)
      intransitive Ø: di-k'aan
                                'It ignited.' (248)
      causative ɬ: idi-ɬ-k'aan
                                'S/he lit it, built a fire.'
      causative + middle *l*: i'di-l-k'aan
                                'S/he built a fire for her/himself.'

(93) Navajo middles built on causatives (Kibrik 1996)
      intransitive Ø: yi-tin
                                'It is freezing.'
      causative ɬ: yi-ɬ-tin
                                'S/he is freezing it.' (269)
      causative + middle (passive) *l*: yi-l-tin
                                'It is being frozen.'

7.3 Middles and Causatives

(94) Carrier middles built on causatives (Morice 1932)
    intransitive Ø: es-ŝar
                           'I weep.' (II:285)
    causative ł: î-ł-tsâr
                           'I cause O to weep.'
    causative + middle (passive) *l*:   î-l-tsâr
                           'I am made to weep.'
    intransitive Ø: nes-yĕh
                           'I grow.' (II:285)
    causative ł: nes-yĕh
                           'I raise O.'
    causative + middle (passive) *l*:   nez-yĕh
                           'I get raised.'

(95) Hupa middles built on causatives (Golla 1970)
    intransitive ł   ł-cay'
                           'get dry' (177)
    causative ł   O ł-cay'
                           'dry O'
    causative + middle (passive) *l*:   O l-cay'
                           'O has been dried.'

Here we see basic intransitives, with causatives built on them, and then a middle. The combination of a middle built on a causative is uniformly marked by *l*. Hupa allows a recausativization, where we see the dual voice/valence marking, with *d* marking the middle voice and *ł* the further causativization.

7.3.3.2 Causatives Built on Middles

There are also causatives built on middles (90c). These are most obvious in Hupa.

(96) Hupa causatives built on middles (Golla 1970)
    transitive ł: O ł-taq'
                           'count O' (170)
    middle (passive) *l*:   O l-taq'
                           'O is counted'
    middle + causative ł-*d*:   O **ł-di**-taq'
                           'cause O to be counted'

In (96), a causative is built on a passive, which derives from a transitive. In the following example, two causative derivations occur, with a middle (passive) sandwiched between.

(97) Hupa: a complex derivation (Golla 1970)
    intransitive ɬ: ɬ-cay'
                                                 'get dry' (177)
    causative ɬ: O ɬ-cay'
                                                 'dry O'
    causative + middle (passive) l: O l-cay'
                                                 'O has been dried.'
    causative + middle + causative ɬ-d: O ɬ-di-cay'
                                                 'have O dried'

I have not found many clear examples of causatives of derived middles in other languages, although causatives of lexical middles are rampant and always occur with the causativizer (ɬ) on the surface. There could be a phonological reason for this. Notice that in Hupa, the plain causative and the causative of the middle form differ in that the plain causative has just the ɬ valence marker while the causative of the middle has marking for both middle voice and causativity. In the other languages, overt double marking is not common. Thus, the causative and the causative of the middle would look the same. It would be worthwhile to examine causatives to see if they can be ambiguous in meaning between a reading where the complement is a transitive or a middle.

Let us now return to the ordering hypotheses. We have seen the following structures:

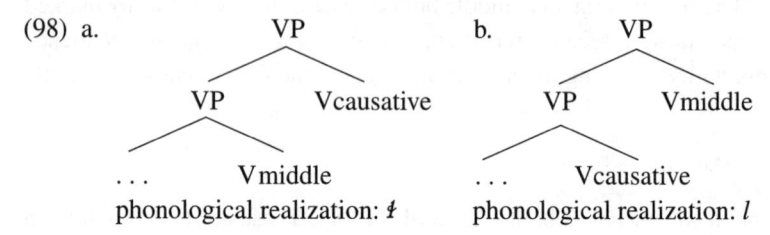

(98) a.   VP   b.   VP
             ┌─────────┴─────────┐   ┌────────┴────────┐
            VP   V causative   VP   V middle
       ┌────┴────┐   ┌────┴────┐
      ...   V middle   ...   V causative
       phonological realization: ɬ   phonological realization: l

Verb words that include both causative and middle marking do not conflate with each other, as might be predicted by the template hypothesis; Hargus 1995a, for instance, suggests that the voice/valence elements appear in a fixed order. The scope hypothesis, on the other hand, correctly predicts that the realization of a causative built on a middle will be distinct from that of a middle built on a causative. This is exactly what we find, providing support for the scope hypothesis.

7.4 Idiosyncratic Nature

In previous sections, I assumed that a lexical entry includes a voice/valence marker; each voice/valence element (Ø, ɬ, d, and compound l) can be part

7.4 Idiosyncratic Nature

of the lexical entry. It is generally assumed in the Athapaskan literature that voice/valence elements are found idiosyncratically as well as productively (see Axelrod 1998, Kibrik 1995, Thompson 1996a for recent discussions). In this section I discuss briefly why voice/valence markers must be considered to be part of the lexical entry synchronically. The reasons are twofold: first, verbs in a semantic class are compatible with the range of voice/valence elements, and second, some stems occur with more than one voice/valence marker with no clear meaning difference. All data here are from Ahtna, but similar facts are reported across the family.

First, basic transitives can appear with any of the four voice/valence elements.

(99) Transitives (Kari 1990)
O G-Ø-ghaan
'make pl. O, kill pl. O' (204)
O G-ł-tsii
'make sg. O' (204)
O d-naan
'drink O' (290)
O G-l-daetl'
'eat pl. O' (261)

The middle voice hypothesis might account for the presence of *l* in 'eat pl. O' – there is low elaboration of the object – but the verb 'make pl. O, kill pl. O' does not have this marking. The verb 'make sg. O' has the causativizer. This is not surprising for a basic transitive verb, but all of these verbs are transitives.

Similar patterning is found with intransitives. The full range of voice/valence markers is possible. The examples in (100) show intransitive verbs with agentive subjects.

(100) Ø-bae   'sg. swim on surface' (101)
    ł-yaał   'jump, move, run quickly, vigorously; bird lands' (423)
    d-tsaak'   'pl. run, leap, jump' (368)
    l-tlet   'sg. run, leap, jump' (355)

The singular and plural of 'run, leap, jump' differ by the presence of the causativizer only. It is possible to explain some of these forms by the middle voice hypothesis, but just which are middle voice and which are not, and which of those that are have *d* and which have *l* seems idiosyncratic synchronically. A historical explanation is perhaps possible (see Axelrod 1998, Kibrik 1993, 1996, Thompson 1996a).

Intransitives with theme subjects likewise appear with the full range of elements.

(101) G-Ø-t'aes
    'roast, fry, bake' (347)
    G-ł-kaets'
    'Enclosed object moves independently, falls.' (241)
    G-d-caats
    'be rendered, liquefied' (111)
    G-l-ts'et
    'Animate or compact object moves independently, falls.' (408)

Similar properties are found in other classes of verbs. The choice of voice/valence does not appear to correlate with semantic properties in descriptive or locative verbs.

(102) descriptive
    G-Ø-k'ats'
    'weather, inanimate is cold' (253)
    G-ł-caax
    'be big, large, tall, high, great in quantity or volume' (109)
    G-d-gak'
    'be dirty' (179)
    G-l-ggaak
    'be stout, fat, thick, big in girth' (189)
(103) locative
    Ø-tae
    'sg. animate lie, recline' (328)
    ł-taets
    'pl. animate lie, recline' (331)
    d-l-ts'ii
    'pl. sit, stay' (412)

In verbs relating to eating, all four voice/valence markers are possible.

(104) O G-Ø-(y)aan
    'eat O' (429)
    O G-Ø-tsaet
    'eat, gulp whole O' (377)
    O ł-k'on
    'gnaw, eat O (bone) with crunching noise' (259)

7.4 Idiosyncratic Nature

O **d**-naek
'devour O, eat O greedily' (297)
O G-l-ghel
'eat pl. O' (218)

The presence of *d / l* in the verbs 'devour O' and 'eat pl. O' might be considered to be middle voice, but one might expect 'eat, gulp whole O' to be middle voice as well. Some of these verbs have overt marking for causativity, but not all of them do, and although some of the marking for voice/valence is predictable, overall it is idiosyncratic.

Some verbs allow more than one voice/valence marker. The verbs in (105) are found with two different voice/valence markers. Kari 1990 finds no clear grounds for determining when one or the other is selected.

(105) a. G-n-Ø/ł-yaa
'grow, grow up, mature' (420)
b. G-**l/d**-baats'
'be found, circular (with *n* noun class marker), be cylindrical (with *d* noun class marker)' (99)
c. G-l/ł-bets
'be wide, broad' (106)
ł: uk'e'sdeyaani de-ł-bets
    'The table is wide.'
l: tsaani uk'e hwne-l-bets
    'The bear's track is wide.'

Kari remarks in several cases that the variation in voice/valence marking is baffling.

The range of facts just discussed argues against the claim that voice/valence is synchronically transparent semantically for a given verb – the particular voice/valence marking is idiosyncratic. Subpockets of transparency for voice/valence can be found within the verbal lexicon (e.g., Axelrod 1998, Kibrik 1993, 1996), but there are numerous cases where the voice/valence marker must simply be memorized as part of the lexical entry of the verb.

Based on the assumption that the voice/valence elements mark valence and voice, they must, in some cases, be regarded as unpredictable and idiosyncratic – there is no direct synchronic correlation between the morphological form of the voice/valence marker and the basic voice/valence type of the verb since all verb classes can appear with each voice/valence marker. Given that these elements have been identified as indicating voice/valence (or something closely related) by all linguists who have investigated them, I do not pursue alternative hypotheses that assign them different functional status here. In at least some cases, the use of voice/valence markers is lexicalized.

7.5 The Lexical Entry

The voice/valence markers then are both highly productive and lexically listed. This raises an important issue: what does the lexicon look like with respect to voice/valence?

It is usually assumed in the Athapaskan literature that a verbal entry includes an indication of argument structure (transitivity) and voice/valence (see, for instance, the lexicons compiled by Kari 1990 for Ahtna and by Young, Morgan, and Midgette 1992 for Navajo). The inclusion of a marking of voice/valence is unusual if voice/valence elements are higher verbs, as argued in sections 7.2.1.4 and 7.2.2.15, since lower verbs do not subcategorize for what higher verb they take. Instead, it is properties of the higher verb that determine properties of the embedded clause. This is clearly the case with the productive causativizer where conditions on the type of lower verb that it can take differ from language to language within the family, as discussed in section 7.2.1. It is also the case with middle voice where there are restrictions, for example, on the types of verb that can be passivized (see Rice forthcoming b), and properties of the lower verb determine exactly how middle voice is to be interpreted. A unified treatment of voice/valence elements is available if the restrictions are stated on the voice/valence elements rather than on the verbs: a particular voice/valence element takes a particular verb stem as a complement.

I assume the following model. In the lexicon, the idiosyncratic voice/valence–verb stem combinations form phrasal idioms, with voice/valence functor predicates selecting for certain verb stems (or verb complexes; I will use the term 'stem' for both). The interpretation of the voice/valence marker and stem as a unit is lexically listed, as befits an idiom. They are in this way parallel to phrasal idioms in English: a listing like 'kick the bucket' receives its lexically listed idiomatic reading rather than the constructional reading that is assigned to the same phrase when the concatenation is syntactic. For instance, the Ahtna entry [[*tsaak'*] [*d*]] 'plural run, leap, jump' is listed in the lexicon with a meaning assigned to the entire form and not to the individual pieces. Such a verb can enter into a syntactic construction with a functor predicate, with the lexical meaning of the idiom combining with that contributed by the functor predicate to yield a predictable meaning. For instance, the Ahtna [[*caats*][*d*]] 'be rendered, liquefied' combines with the causativizer to yield the semantically transparent 'render O, liquefy O.' Voice/valence elements thus can be part of a lexical entry, and are commonly so, creating a phrasal idiom containing two verbs. They can also be introduced syntactically and provide a productive meaning.

Some evidence supports the claim that the major difference between idiosyncratic and productive voice/valence has simply to do with the level, lexical or syntactic, at which it is introduced, and that both occupy the same position syntactically. Whether voice/valence is part of the lexical entry or syntactically introduced, it patterns identically with respect to other restrictions. One of these restrictions concerns the marking of perfective viewpoint in structures where the highest verb is middle voice, either lexical or productive. In many Athapaskan languages, perfective viewpoint is not overtly marked by a prefix when the highest verb is the middle voice element (see chapter 9 for brief discussion). Hopper and Thompson 1980, in a discussion of transitivity and its correlates, suggest that one facet of transitivity has to do with aspect: high transitivity correlates with presence of perfective aspect and low transitivity with its absence. The intuition behind this is the following. Highly transitive verbs have objects, which provide an endpoint to the event. Perfectivity, which focuses on an endpoint, is thus appropriate for highly transitive verbs. But in middle voice verbs, the event is lowly elaborated, and the endpoint is not distinct from the initiation of the event. There is thus no distinct boundary, or endpoint, to the event in middle voice verbs, and perfectivity is less relevant. Whether the middle voice element is lexically present or syntactically introduced, this same restriction holds of the absence of perfective viewpoint marking in middle voice forms. This restriction can be stated simply if middle voice always occupies the same position syntactically – this position does not license the perfective prefix. Interpretation of this element as productive or not depends upon whether the middle voice element is part of the lexical entry or not.

7.6 Summary

I have argued that the voice/valence markers are verbs, functor predicates, that take VP complements. Both are involved in defining aspectual roles. The causativizer takes both a proposition and an initiator argument, whereas the middle voice marker takes a proposition and indicates that some element within that proposition is lowly elaborated. Which element this is is determined by material in the proposition. Morphological causative and middle forms in Athapaskan languages thus each contain two verbs, differing from periphrastic forms in that there is only a single set of inflection for the entire complex. The verb stem must raise, suffixing to the functor predicate. Such a process is argued to exist in many languages (Baker 1988). The verb formed through verb incorporation then raises further. This is a property of Athapaskan languages that sets them apart from other languages; it is here that their major idiosyncrasy lies. However, given this idiosyncrasy, the placement of the voice/valence elements to the left of the verb stem is not surprising. Raising creates a discrepancy between underlying scopal relationships and surface word order.

The odd position of voice/valence and the verb stem then is one way in which ordering questions arise. The possibility of marking for both voice and valence raises a second question concerning ordering. Middles can be formed on causatives and causatives on middles in Athapaskan languages. The scope hypothesis correctly predicts that the different orderings are reflected in different phonological realizations. The template hypothesis, on the other hand, stipulates a single ordering in the case of multiple voice/valence elements, a situation that is not in fact found.

8

Summary: Lexical Items

In this second part of the book, I have argued for the following points concerning overall ordering of morphemes:

- The verb stem originates within the verb phrase rather than at the right edge of the verb. Under this assumption, the ordering of verbal elements fits the pattern identified in typological studies of languages of the world.
- The voice/valence morphemes are functor predicates that originate within the verb phrase. Under this assumption, the argument-affecting properties of voice/valence are accounted for, as is the fact that they do not occur with independent argument structure.
- The stem raises to the voice/valence markers, and this unit in turn raises to the right edge of the verb phrase. This assumption is required to place the verb and voice/valence markers, a phonological constituent, in the correct position on the surface.

It is in these ways, and these ways only, that the surface ordering of the elements of the verb differs from their more abstract ordering.

I have further argued for the following points about ordering within the lexical items. Within the lexical complex of the verb, the scope hypothesis provides an account of fixed as well as variable orderings. Variable orderings are of three types. First, the orders A-B and B-A can both be interpreted, but have different readings. In this case, the semantic relationship between A and B is not fixed. Examples of this are the middle voice and causativizer, and the ordering of the reversionary with respect to the semeliterative in Navajo. Second, the orders A-B and B-A can both be interpreted and have the same reading. In this case, A and B do not enter into a semantic relationship. This was illustrated with respect to some of the preverbs; I also attributed the variable ordering of the iterative and the distributive to the fact that they quantify over different systems. They thus do not enter into a scope relationship, and free ordering is expected. Finally, variable ordering can occur across languages when either a semantic or a structural account of ordering is possible – depending upon language, either semantic or structural factors prevail. This, I argued, accounts for the different placement of the complement of the case marking preverb in Navajo and Slave.

The semantic relationships that regulate morpheme order within the lexical span of the verb include the following:

- More general items follow more specific items.
- Modified items follow modifying items.
- Entailing items follow entailed items.
- Themes follow oblique thematic relations.

A template account can, with some careful attention to detail, perhaps be designed in such a way that it describes the ordering found among the lexical items. However, such an account ignores the facts discussed in this part of the book. Specifically, ordering is identical across the languages when semantic relationships between lexical items are involved, but differs across the languages in the absence of such relationships. The template account allows for a wider range of possible orderings across languages than is actually found, but at the same time has difficulty accounting for variation, whether determined by scope considerations (e.g., orderings of voice/valence) or due to the absence of a scope relation (e.g., iterative and distributive). The scope principles that I invoke are not in any way strange or unusual, but are properties that are important cross-linguistically. The template provides a convenient description and is useful in many ways, but it has, at least for the lexical span of the verb, little explanatory value.

PART III

THE FUNCTIONAL ITEMS

9

An Introduction to the Functional Elements

In this part of the book, I examine the functional items and their ordering. Whether the ordering of functional items follows from scope has been a point of controversy; see, for example, Anderson 1992, Baker 1992, Halle and Marantz 1994, Lapointe 1996, and Speas 1991a,b for discussion. Baker 1992 discusses this issue, asking: "The question is whether this kind of syntactic motivation can be extended to inflectional morphology ... the plausibility of this approach depends on the degree to which the order of inflectional morphemes seems syntactically well-motivated" (102–103). Baker suggests that there are two reasons to pursue a hypothesis according to which the ordering of inflectional elements is principled. First are empirical considerations based on Bybee's research (1985a, 1985b). Bybee, in a crosslinguistic study of inflectional affix ordering, finds universal tendencies that she explains in terms of iconicity, or relevance to the verb. Speas 1991, in a small survey, finds similar results, as do Foley and van Valin 1984. This is one reason to believe that there are principles underlying the ordering of functional items. The second consideration that Baker brings to bear is methodological. A theory in which the ordering of inflectional elements reflects syntactic embedding allows for a restricted interface between syntax and inflection, whereas a theory in which the order of inflectional elements is idiosyncratic and language-particular makes no predictions.

In this part of the book, I investigate this issue with respect to the functional part of the verb of Athapaskan languages and argue that to a large degree the ordering of functional items in Athapaskan languages has a principled basis. While features of functional items are generally considered to be grammatical and are called morphosyntactic features, I speak in terms of the semantics of these items, taking person/number/gender features, aspectual features, classificatory features, and so on to mark properties of meaning.

In the remainder of this chapter I provide a very brief overview of this portion of the verb. Chapter 10 examines the pronominal system, chapter 11 the aspectual system, and chapter 12 the qualifier system. Such a study is required to understand ordering relationships as it is necessary to know what it is that is being ordered. Chapter 13 then returns to the major point of the book: what ordering relationships are found, and are they principled?

Recall from chapter 2 that the general template for the functional items is as in (1).

(1) direct objects – number subjects – qualifiers – situation aspect – viewpoint aspect – agreement (1/2 person) subjects

This group of morphemes is called conjunct prefixes in the Athapaskan literature. As noted in chapter 4, they share phonological properties. First, they have similar canonical forms: they are generally a single segment, usually a consonant (with epenthesis of vowels); in tone languages they seldom have a lexical tone. Second, they combine with each other, and some show portmanteau realizations. This set is usually divided into two phonological domains, with the direct objects and number subjects forming one domain, and the rest forming a second.

A note of caution is in order before proceeding with this span of the verb. First, the morphophonemics of the functional complex is intricate, particularly of the qualifier-aspect-subject span. These elements frequently combine with each other, and the phonological processes involved often seem highly idiosyncratic. See the grammars, Hargus and Tuttle 1997, McDonough 1990, Rice 1993, and others on the complexities of this portion of the verb. In addition, many vowels in this part of the verb are argued to be epenthetic (see Hargus and Tuttle 1997 and references therein for recent discussion), making it difficult to divide words into morphemes. I do not discuss the elaborate morphophonemics and must beg the reader's indulgence in accepting the morphological breakdowns that I give. Second, qualifiers are often part of the lexical entry of the verb, and no meaning can be assigned to them on their own. When meaning is relevant, I draw my examples from clear cases.

I now conduct a quick survey of the content of each of the positions. Direct objects are part of the argument system (see chapters 4, 10), and indicate object person, number, and gender. In general, direct objects realize affected arguments, whereas nonaffected ones are realized as oblique objects. We will see in chapter 10 that object forms can also function as subjects; the term 'object' is a misnomer, and 'accusative case' or 'internal argument' better describes the status of these items.

An Introduction to the Functional Elements 177

Number subjects are also part of the argument system and include human plural number and unspecified/first person plural human subject prefixes. The terms 'third person subjects' and 'deictic subjects' are often used in the Athapaskan literature for elements in this position; the former is a misnomer because many of the languages allow a first person plural reading for the unspecified human subject; see chapter 10.

The group of morphemes labeled 'qualifiers' represent the least understood and most heterogeneous part of the verb. The term 'qualifier' was introduced by Kari 1989, based on Jetté 1906.[1] It includes noun class markers, verb class markers, subsituation aspect markers, an element indicating voice, and lexically frozen items. See chapters 11 and 12.

The morphemes that I term noun class markers are generally called gender in the Athapaskan literature (e.g., Kari 1989, 1990, 1992, Thompson 1993); however, they are similar in nature to classifiers in other languages. I call them noun class markers rather than classifiers because of the use of the word classifier in the Athapaskan literature for another category, namely the elements that mark voice and valence (chapter 7). Qualifiers also include markers of subsituation aspect; these are part of the aspect system and indicate categories such as inceptive, conative, and inchoative. I use the term 'subsituation' as these aspects do not define an event on their own, but rather focus on a piece of an event.

Noun class markers and subsituation elements have largely the same phonological shapes and exhibit identical phonological patterning. For instance, in Ahtna *n* classifies objects (roundish objects, liquids, rope or stringlike objects) and indicates termination ('assume a position'), whereas *d* classifies objects (stick, tree, leaf, plant, bark, pitch; cup, dish, basket; feather, hair, fur; enclosed liquids, lake, puddle, pus, afterbirth, breast, egg; word, song, story, news, name; day, day's journey, units of time; fire, smoke, star) and indicates self-benefactivity (along with the so-called D-effect; see chapter 7). In Slave *d* classifies woodlike objects and oral objects (e.g., song, story) and indicates benefactivity as well as having the subaspectual function of marking inceptivity.

Finally, as remarked earlier, qualifiers are often without meaning and are listed as part of the lexical entry of the verb.

The next two positions are part of the aspect system, indicating situation aspect and viewpoint aspect. These are not traditional terms in the Athapaskan literature, where these elements are instead called mode or aspect (subsituation aspect), conjugation (situation aspect), and mode or aspect (viewpoint aspect). I justify the use of the terms in (1) in chapter 11. What I call situation aspect indicates four major aspectual categories: accomplishments, achievements, activities, and semelfactives; see chapter 11.

Finally there are morphemes that mark perfective aspect and optative mode; the absence of an overt morpheme or the reflex of the Proto-Athapaskan reduced vowel schwa (see Hargus and Tuttle 1997) signals imperfective. I call this viewpoint aspect, but it is a heterogeneous class of mutually exclusive forms indicating viewpoint aspect or modality.

Subject markers indicate first person singular, second person singular, second person plural, and, in some languages, first person plural. Slave forms are shown in (2).

(2) first person singular   tu h-e-**h**-dǫ   'I drink water.'
     second person singular   tu **ne**-dǫ   'You sg. drink water.'
     cf. third person   tu h-e-dǫ   'S/he drinks water.' (null)
     first person duo/plural   tu h-**í**-dǫ   'We drink water.'
     second person duo/plural   tu h-**ah**-dǫ   'You pl. drink water.'

The forms in (2) can be identified as subject markers in imperfective, optative, and middle voice perfective viewpoint paradigms. Perfective viewpoint verbs with ∅ and ɬ voice/valence (see chapters 7 and 11) are more complex in some languages. For instance, in the perfective viewpoint of a ∅ or ɬ verb, first person singular subject and perfective viewpoint surface as a portmanteau *i* in Slave, with no trace of *h*; the second person plural has the form *a* rather than the *ah* in (2). With d/l voice/valence verbs, on the other hand, perfective viewpoint is not overtly marked (chapter 7). The two perfective viewpoint forms are compared for Slave in (3). The lefthand column includes a prefix marking perfective (often combined with person); the righthand column does not include a prefix marking perfective. Boldface indicates the viewpoint aspect and subject markers in the lefthand column and the subject markers in the righthand column (perfective viewpoint is not present here).

(3) ∅, ɬ valence   *d* middle voice, *l* voice/valence
     y-**i**-'á   'I ate.'   ye-**h**-dǫ́   'I drank.'
     y-**i-ne**-'á   'You sg. ate.'   y-**į**-dǫ́   'You sg. drank.'
     y-**į**-'á   'S/he ate.'   ye-dǫ́   'S/he drank.'

Facts such as these suggest that perfective viewpoint and subject form a portmanteau in non-middle voice verbs. They also have implications for the distribution of the perfective; see McDonough 1990 and Rice 1993 for discussion.

One more function is indicated in this portion of the verb in some languages, namely negation. See chapter 11 for discussion.

An Introduction to the Functional Elements 179

I now turn briefly to the morphology of the stem in Athapaskan languages. Roots in Athapaskan languages may often be used either nominally and verbally; some Slave examples are given in (4). See chapter 11.

(4) Slave (Rice 1989)
    dzéh   'gum, be gummy'
    fí   'head, action with head'
    xáh   'club, beat with club'
    tł'o   'grass, be grassy'
    shį   'song, sing'

The root is a formal unit; it is used in a stem form in verbs. Stem formation can involve two components, an overt suffix and a particular consonant-vowel form or syllable shape. I will speak of stem suffixation patterns, but it should be kept in mind that more than just straightforward suffixation can be involved. For instance, the shape of the stem can be affected (e.g., some aspects require long vowel forms; others obligatorily have short vowels); see Leer 1979 for detailed discussion. A few examples of Ahtna aspect suffixes are given in (5).

(5) Ahtna (Kari 1990:70)
    'aa   'classify compact object, root form'
    'aa**n** 'classify compact object, neuter imperfective,
           achievement perfective'
    'aa**s** 'classify compact object, achievement imperfective'
    'a'   'classify compact object, distributive'
    'aał   'classify compact object, progressive'

The suffix-*n* indicates the perfective in certain aspects, -*s* the achievement imperfective, a final glottal stop the distributive, and - ł the progressive. See chapter 11 for further discussion of the aspect system and these suffixes.

This provides a very brief introduction to the functional elements. These elements interact with both the argument system and the aspect system of the languages. I begin the journey into the functional items by looking at the pronominals.

10

Pronominals

Both subject and object pronominals are found within the verb in all Athapaskan languages. Their ordering is particularly puzzling, especially when subjects are considered. As discussed in chapter 9, subjects occur in two positions in the verb, with first and second person subjects in one slot and third person subjects in another (see below for refinement of this statement). A major distinction is thus made between first and second persons, or speech act participants, and others. Why should this be the case? Objects do not appear to parallel subjects; all objects occur in the same slot. Why should subjects and objects differ in this way? Finally, while objects generally precede third person subjects, this is not always true. Why is this the case? In this chapter I address these questions concerning pronominals. I postpone discussion of the ordering of pronominals with respect to other functional items until chapter 13, focusing here on the ordering of pronominals with respect to each other.

Before beginning, a brief note on the status of these elements is in order. There is lively debate in the Athapaskan literature as to whether pronominals within the verb are pronominal arguments or functional in nature (e.g., Cook 1996, Jelinek and Willie 1996, Potter 1997, Rice and Saxon 1994, Sandoval and Jelinek 1989, Saxon 1986, 1989a, b, Speas 1990, 1995, Thompson 1996b, Tuttle 1996, Willie 1991, Willie and Jelinek 1996). I make the assumption, one that I do not believe to be critical to the main point, that pronominals are functional items that indicate agreement and number.

10.1 Subject Form Pronominals

Recall from chapter 9 that subject pronouns appear in two positions in the verb: first/second person subject forms are at the right edge of the functional complex, whereas third person subject markers and, in some languages, the

10.1 Subject Form Pronominals

first person plural/unspecified subject marker, immediately follow direct objects. This raises an immediate question with respect to the pronominals: why, in all Athapaskan languages, does subject marking appear in two verbal positions? Given the scope principle, and assuming that all subject inflection is of the same type, this asymmetry in positioning is unexpected; see Lapointe 1997 for discussion relating to Navajo. In this section I argue, after Rice and Saxon 1994 on Slave, that the assumption that first/second person subject inflection on the one hand and third person subject inflection on the other are the same kinds of entities is incorrect. Rather first/second person subject inflection represents agreement, including features of person, number, and gender, while third person subject inflection represents number and gender, but not person. Rice and Saxon 1994 call the former Agreement and the latter Number. It is the absence of person in 'third person' forms that is of interest, and in the following discussion I concentrate on arguments for this claim. I begin by summarizing in (1) the features that Rice and Saxon 1994 propose for these third person pronouns in Slave. The phonological forms are given in the first row, and the relevant features are listed in the first column.

(1) Pronominal features of third person subject inflections (Slave)[1]

	k/g/gh	ts'	Ø
Number	plural	±plural	±plural
Gender	human[2]	human	±human
Specificity	specific	±specific	specific
Definiteness	±definite	±definite	±definite

First and second person subject inflections in Slave have the features in (2). Again, the first row gives the Slave phonological forms.

(2) Pronominal features of first and second person subject inflections (Slave)

	h	n	i-d	ah
Person	1	2	1	2
Number	singular	singular	plural	plural
Gender	human	human	human	human
Specificity	specific	specific	specific	specific
Definiteness	definite	definite	definite	definite

Rice and Saxon 1994, based on this evidence, present arguments that first/second and third person inflection represent different functional categories, and I summarize some of these in what follows.

10.1.1 Subject Inflection in Slave

First/second person subject inflection and third person subject inflection, commonly called deictic subjects in the Athapaskan literature, are fundamentally different in many ways in Slave. These include discourse functions, positions in which they occur, obligatoriness, morphological affinities, and syntactic patterning. I examine discourse functions, positions, obligatoriness, and syntactic patterning in the sections that follow; see Rice and Saxon 1994 for additional arguments.

10.1.1.1 Discourse Functions

A major difference between first/second person on the one hand and third person on the other has to do with discourse function – first/second persons are speech act participants, while third persons are unspecified actors. Many linguists have noted that first/second person and third person have a differential status. For instance, Benveniste 1971:216 states, "Person belongs only to *I/you* and is lacking in *he*," and Moravscik 1978:353 remarks that "There is some indication that, of the three persons, the first and second constitute a natural class as opposed to the third." Benveniste 1971, Moravcsik 1978, and Ritter 1995, among others, enumerate ways in which first/second and third person pronominals differ across languages. For instance, in Hungarian first and second person plural pronouns are synthetic while third person plural pronouns are analytic (Moravcsik 1978:354). In English, third person singular is the only pronominal that manifests gender and that has a special verbal form. A split between discourse participants and others thus is commonly reported in languages of the world. Benveniste's claim is particularly relevant – third person pronouns are distinct from the others in not including person. This is the point taken up by Rice and Saxon 1994 and argued for here.

10.1.1.2 Position

The superficially most obvious difference between the first/second and third person inflection is the one that I am trying to account for: third person inflections are found in a different position from first/second person inflection. This can be clearly seen in the paradigm in (3). The subject inflections are in boldface.

(3) 'hide' (optative) (Rice 1989:555)
   ní-né-o-**h**-'į̂   1singular *h*
   ní-né-**ǫ**-'į̂   2singular nasalization

10.1 Subject Form Pronominals

ní-n-**úú**-'į̃	1dual/plural *úú*
ní-ná-**ah**-'į̃	2dual/plural *ah*
ní-né-o-'į̃	3 (unmarked)
ní-**ke**-n-éo-'į̃	3dual/plural *k*
ní-**ts'**e-né-o-'į̃	unspecified *ts'*

First/second person subject inflection directly precedes the verb stem and voice/valence, and appears at the right edge of the functional items, whereas third person subject inflection appears further to the left, preceding *n*, a qualifier that is part of the lexical entry of this verb. These paradigmatic forms do not provide evidence for the claim that first/second person inflection is a different kind of entity from third person inflection. They serve, instead, to illustrate the problem: why do the two sets of pronouns appear in different positions?

10.1.1.3 Obligatoriness

A major difference between first/second person subject inflection on the one hand and third person subject inflection on the other concerns their paradigmatic status. In Slave, first/second person subject inflection is obligatory, as can be seen in the forms in (4). The subject inflections are in boldface; as the ungrammatical forms show, the same reading cannot be achieved if the subject inflection is not present in the verb. The parenthesized independent pronouns are optional; the sentences are unacceptable with an external pronoun but without the verb-internal inflectional marking.

(4) a. (sį̃) jǫ ná-**h**-dé
   1sg here preverb-**1sg Subject**-stem
   'I live here.'
   *(sį̃) jǫ ná-dé
  b. (nį̃) jǫ ná-**ne**-dé
   2sg here preverb-**2sg Subject**-stem
   'You sg. live here.'
  c. (naxį̃) jǫ ná-**í**-dé
   1pl here preverb-**1pl Subject**-stem
   'We live here.'
  d. (naxį̃) jǫ ná-**ah**-dé
   2pl here preverb-**2pl Subject**-stem
   'You pl. live here.'

Third person subjects, on the other hand, display a different set of properties. A similar reading can be obtained whether an inflectional element is present or not. I generally gloss *ts'* as 'HSubject' for human subject and *g* as '3pl Subject.'

(5) a. Ø: dene jǫ ná-dé
person here preverb-stem
'People live here.'
b. *ts'* dene jǫ ná-**ts'**e-dé
person here preverb-**HSubject**-stem
'People live here.'
c. *g* dene jǫ ná-**ge**-dé
person here preverb-**3pl Subject**-stem
'People live here.'

The verb in (5a) contains neither of the overt number morphemes (I use the term 'number' after Rice and Saxon 1994, anticipating the conclusion to this section), but nevertheless can receive a third person plural interpretation, the verb in (5b) is marked with the unspecified human subject prefix *ts'*, and that in (5c) is marked with the third person plural human subject prefix *g*. Cook 1996 and Saxon 1993 discuss the semantic and discourse contexts of these affixes in closely related languages. Rice and Saxon 1994 suggest that these morphemes, like subject agreement morphemes, are functional and obligatory; however, their semantics and discourse properties are not yet well enough understood to determine the exact conditions of their appearance. The element *ts'* appears to include the speaker, while *k/g* indicates that a group rather than individuals is important. What is important is that number subjects, unlike first and second person subjects, do not require obligatory overt inflection. This is the first piece of evidence that first/second person inflection includes marking for person – they must appear in order to mark that person, while number inflection does not include an indication of person – no single overt morphological realization of third person must be present.

The nonobligatory status of the human plural *k/g* for a third person plural interpretation can be seen in two more ways. First, the presence of this morpheme requires a third person human plural reading, but its absence does not rule out such a reading. This can be seen in (6b), where in the absence of *k/g* the subject is ambiguous with respect to number and gender of the subject, except as determined by context.

10.1 Subject Form Pronominals

(6) a. **gi**-i̧-tse
3pl Subject-aspect-cry
'They (human or dogs) cried.'
b. i̧-tse
aspect-cry
'He, she, it, they (human, nonhuman) cried.'

This finding is reinforced when verb stems requiring inherently plural themes are considered; the stem *de* 'plural go' in (7) is an example. In the presence of *k/g*, the subject is necessarily third person plural and human; in its absence, a nonhuman interpretation is also allowed.

(7) a. rí-**ke**-ré-ni̧-de
preverb-**3pl Subject**-qualifier-aspect-pl. go
'They (human) landed.'
b. rí-ré-ni̧-de
preverb-qualifier-aspect-pl. go
'They (human, nonhuman) landed.'

The different paradigmatic status of number subject inflection from first/second person subject inflection can also be seen in textual examples exhibiting alternations between number forms. For example, in (8), the first occurrence of the verb 'kill' has the human subject *ts'* and the second has the human plural *k*, although both have the same referent, the Chipewyans. The pronouns are in boldface; I do not give morpheme-by-morpheme glosses for all words here, but rather gloss the words as a whole.

(8) 'eyi go-ts'ę 'ekúhnįe **łe-ts'**e-gǫ dzá 'agǫt'e gots'ę
that area-from then **HSubject**-kill bad it is and
k'áts'eleht'ineke sı̨́i dene **ke**-ghǫ
Chipewyan focus person **3pl Subject**-pl.kill
'In those days, they (*ts'*) killed each other and it was bad. The Chipewyan (*k*) killed people.' (Rice 1989)

Similar examples are given in (9). (9a) has *gh* (an alternative form of *k/g*, the plural human marker) in the first clause and *ts'* in the second. (9b) has an unmarked number in the first clause and *gh* in the second clause. (9c) has *ts'* followed by *gh*, and (9d) has *ts'* followed by an absence of marking. In all of these cases, the referent of each pair of subject markers is shared.

(9) a. tsá   k'á-**ghe**-ndetah   éhsán nóghe   keeh
       beaver **3pl Subject**-looked for then wolverine tracks
       wo-**ts'**-a'in
       HSubject-saw
       'They (*gh*) were looking for beaver when they (*ts'*) saw wolverine tracks.' (Moore and Wheelock 1990:146)
   b. ... dets'ín mbeti   at'in,   mo   úh, mbetá   úh a-**ghe**-t'in
       where 3-parents be   mother and 3.father and **3pl Subject**-be
       edaghodíh-í   sóon
       know-relative clause marker   then
       'He knew where his parents (Ø) had been, his mother and his father (*gh*) had been, then.' (Moore and Wheelock 1990:207)
   c. ndeda   etthén   ní'e-**ts'**e-dintse, i   tl'a, ts'ído, tl'a, edu dene
       2sg for meat   **HSubject**-left and well child well not person
       e-**ghi**-nht'e   úh
       3pl Subject-be and
       'They (*ts'*) left meat for you, but well, children (*gh*) are not really people.' (Moore and Wheelock 1990:164)
   d. dinh-**ts'**e-dinla.   thidi   mbek'eh   anda-**ts'**e-dla,
       HSubject-threw in fire   embers 3-on   **HSubject**-did again
       nda-**ts'**e-ndéhtin.   eyi   dene   ayínlá   íin   tl'a
       HSubject-went back to bed that person did   before well
       ke   onki   ayeh'in
       shoe two   has
       'He (*ts'*) threw them on the fire and stirred (did) the embers, and (*ts'*) went back to bed. That man (Ø) who had done it, well, he (Ø) had two pairs of moccasins.' (Moore and Wheelock 1990:177)

While the presence of first/second person inflection is determined by strictly syntactic conditions, this is not true of number inflection, where overt marking may be present, but exactly which one is determined by semantic and contextual factors.

The evidence presented so far shows that first/second person inflection differs from number inflection in terms of its obligatoriness: number inflection does not mark person in the way that first/second person inflection does.

10.1.1.4 Semantics of Number

Having established an asymmetry between first/second and number inflection, I now turn to the semantics of number. It is often remarked in the Athapaskan

10.1 Subject Form Pronominals

literature that the prefix *ts'* and its cognates are reminiscent of French *on* 'one'. The range of functions of this pronominal is illustrated in (10). See Saxon 1993 for detailed discussion of the use of *ts'* in the very closely related languages of Chipewyan and Dogrib.

(10) *ts'* 'unspecified human'

    a. Unknown but referential actor
        'e-**ts'**e-de-h-shú
        unspecified Object-**HSubject**-qualifier-valence-whistle
        'Someone is whistling.' (Rice 1989:624)

    b. Nonspecific actor
        yahtı̨kǫ́   go-**ts'**e-h-tsı̨
        church   area-**HSubject**-valence-build
        'A church is being built.'

    c. Generic actor
        'eyi   go-ts'ę   'ekúhnie   łe-**ts'**e-gǫ   dzá   'agǫt'e
        that   areal-from   then   reciprocal-**HSubject**-fight   bad   preverb-
                                                                                              areal-be
        'At that time there were wars.' (Rice:1342)
        'ı̨t' ǫ́ k'e k'ína-**ts'**e-da   nı̨dé   ná-we-h-kw'ę
        leaf on preverb-**HSubject**-walk   if   preverb-qualifier-valence-
                                                                         make sound
        'When you walk on leaves, they make a noise.' (Rice 1989:1053)

    d. Indefinite actor
        ts'ído   ehdah   a-**ts'**e-di-d-leh
        child   too   preverb-**HSubject**-reflexive-voice-make
        'Children too can find their own way.' (Moore and Wheelock 1990:109)

    e. Singular definite actor
        kíi   aidihdah   **ts'**e-tin-á   a-e-**ts'**e-d-í-d-la
        just   on purpose   **HSubject**-sg.sleep   preverb-unspecified
                                                                                           Object-**HSubject**-
                                                                                           reflexive-aspect-make
        'He pretended to sleep.' (Moore and Wheelock 1990:176)

    f. nonsingular definite actor
        xehtl'unh t'áh,   k'é-'e-**ts'**e-h-geh
        packstrap with   preverb-unspecified Object-**HSubject**-valence-
                                                            pack
        'They (2) packed stuff back with packstraps.' (Moore and Wheelock 1990:173)

se-yéh-ká-**ts'**e-de-deh
1sg Object-preverb-preverb-**HSubject**-qualifier-outdistance
ehsóon wondejid on, a-h-t'e
in case frightening even though preverb-1sg Subject-be
'I am afraid that they are outdistancing me.' (Moore and Wheelock 1990:162)

g. First person plural actor
'eyáhdi hé ná-go-**ts'**e-ye
ball with preverb-area-**HSubject**-play
'Let's play ball.' (Rice 1989:624)

I continue to use the term '(unspecified) human' for this morpheme. By this I mean that whether it has specific or nonspecific reference is not lexically specified, but rather determined by the context. In this respect, it differs from first/second person subject inflection, which always refers to a specific individual(s), as in (2).

The morpheme *k/g/gh* marks a plural human subject, which can be either indefinite or definite, as the examples in (11) illustrate.

(11) *k/g* human plural

a. Nonsingular indefinite actors
go-weri wha deneke beká t'á zǫ 'ekwę́
areal-before long people spear with only caribou
ła-**ke**-h-de
preverb-**3pl Subject**-aspect-kill pl Object
'Long ago people used to kill caribou only with spears.' (Rice 1989:1337)

b. gáa, łínt'onh dene tín-**ghe**-ni-h-the
yes all person preverb-**3pl Subject**-aspect-valence-suffer
'Yes, all the people had started to suffer.' (Moore and Wheelock 1990:115)

c. Nonsingular definite actors
Elise gots'ęh Jean Marie t'oo t'á
and paddle with
nahe-ts'á-**ge**-'e ekúh ...
1pl ObliqueO-preverb-**3pl Subject**-visit [boating] when
'When Elise and Jean Marie paddled in to visit us, ...' (Thom and Blondin-Townsend 1987:102)

10.1 Subject Form Pronominals

d. i   dedhóo   nda-**ghe**-de-dzed
that young man preverb-**3pl Subject**-qualifier-hunt
'The two [Star] men were always hunting.' (Moore and Wheelock 1990:104)

10.1.1.5 Summary

I have argued that first/second person subject inflection and number inflection differ in morphological, syntactic, and semantic ways, suggesting a category difference. Following Rice and Saxon 1994, I adopt the view that the asymmetry between them concerns the presence of person; the formal difference between them is whether they instantiate the functional category of Agreement (first/second persons) or Number (third person). I have, again following Rice and Saxon 1994, further proposed that Agreement markers are inherently marked for person, number, and gender, whereas Number markers are unmarked for person, including only number and gender. While Number does not include person, I continue to use the term 'third person' for convenience.

10.1.2 Syntactic Asymmetries in Slave

Assuming that first/second person subject inflection involves Agreement and third person subject inflection Number, differing by whether person is included, one might expect differences in syntactic patterning between the persons. Such differences are found. With first/second person subject inflection, the relationship between the pronominal inflection and its specifier NP is one of agreement; with third person inflection, the relationship is not of agreement, but rather of mutual elaboration of semantic properties.

Slave is a pro-drop language, as the examples in (4) show. The use of an external pronominal subject is optional, and these subjects, when present, are interpreted as emphatic or contrastive (Rice 1989). The pronouns enter into coordinate constructions in an interesting way. In (12), the first sentence of each set has a noun phrase consisting of a noun and a pronoun as subject. The second example illustrates that the pronoun can be dropped in this context, just as it is when it is the sole subject. That the subject involves a conjoined phrase is made clear from the obligatory presence of the conjunction. The final example of each set illustrates that the absence of the conjunction results in ill-formedness. If first/second person subject inflection represents agreement, this is not surprising, since the verb has plural subject agreement, but the NP with which it agrees is overtly singular, and without the conjunction, the NP is not second person.

(12) a. Simon hé   ni̜   hé juice ná-**ah**-dí
         and 2sg. and   preverb-**2pl Subject**-buy
         'You and Simon buy juice.'
     Simon hé juice ná**ah**-dí
     *Simon juice ná**ah**-dí
  b. Jimmy gots'ęh si̜i̜   tehk'áa 1200 a-thí-dlá
         and   1sg.   muskrat   preverb-**1dual Subject**-do
     'Jimmy and I got 1200 muskrat.' (Thom and Blondin-Townsend 1987:109)
     Jimmy gots'ęh tehk'áa 1200 athídlá
     *Jimmy tehk'áa 1200 athídlá
  c. sedené   shu nahezhaa   dech̜tah   go-níh-thí-zhǫ
     1sg.husband and 1pl-child   bush   3pl Object-qualifier-
                                             1dual Subject-grow
     'My husband and I raised our children in the bush.' (Thom and Blondin-Townsend 1987:117)
     *sedené nahezhaa dech̜tah goníhthízhǫ

Number subject inflection patterns differently: there is no agreement between a subject NP and the verb. This can be seen in a variety of ways. First, a nominal subject marked with the plural nominal enclitic *ke* need not occur with a plural subject pronoun; rather the two forms are independent. This can be seen in the following examples. Both the nominal clitic and the subject inflection may be present, as in (13a), one or the other may be present, as in (13b,c), or neither may be present, as in (13d). All sentences are grammatical on the same reading.

(13) a. John beya-**ke**   'eyá   **ke-yi̜**-lé
         3-son-**plural**   sick   **pl Subject**-aspect-be
         'John's sons were sick.'
     b. John beya-**ke**   'eyá   yi̜-lé
         3-son-**plural**   sick   aspect-be
     c. John beya   'eyá   **ke-yi̜**-lé
         3-son   sick   **pl Subject**-aspect-be
     d. John beya   'eyá   yi̜-lé
         3-son   sick   aspect-be

While overt noun phrases can be coindexed with third person subjects, as the example in (14) shows, this is not so with first and second persons.

10.1 Subject Form Pronominals

(14) *t'ere yi-tse
    girl aspect/1sg Subject-cry
    'I, as a girl, I cried.' (cf. Willie 1991:109–110 on Navajo)

A second reason for believing that the relationship between number inflection and its subject NP is not agreement concerns the patterning of Number under coordination. In each of the examples in (15), the subject noun phrase necessarily has a real world singular referent. Yet the verb contains the human plural subject inflection k/g, and the meaning that obtains is one in which the subject is a group defined by the named individual.

(15) a. setá   názé-ɬe-**ke**-dé-h-tɬa
       1sg-father   hunt-dual-**3pl Subject**-inceptive-aspect-1, 2 go
       'My father and he went hunting.'
   b. mbetá   sóon   dá-**ghe**-já   élính
       3-father then   what-**pl Subject**-aspect-do dubitative
       wo-k'e-nde-a-de-dah
       area-on-mind-unspecified Object-qualifier-sg. go
       'He was always thinking about what his father's people might have been doing.' (Moore and Wheelock 1990:207)
   c. duhdei ehtsée   e-**ge**-ni-h-sud-i
       here   grandfather unspecified Object-**3pl Subject**-aspect-valence-
                                        drag-suffix
       'My grandparents have passed this way dragging (toboggan).'
       (Moore and Wheelock 1990:135)

These sentences do not show a grammatical relation of agreement between two entities; rather, a group is defined by the named individual. The specifier-head relationship is clearly quite different for agreement and number inflection.

10.1.3 Ordering Properties: Beginnings of an Account

I have argued following Rice and Saxon 1994 that the two verbal positions traditionally identified as housing subjects are both functional, but that two functions are involved, Agreement with first/second person subject markers and Number otherwise. First/second person inflectional markers are specified for person; third person is unmarked for person. These categories also differ in terms of gender: first/second person inflection is inherently marked for human gender; third persons differ in gender. Finally, first/second person includes a marking for number; the third person human plural is necessarily plural, while the other Number markers take on a reading for number based on their context. I thus follow Rice and Saxon 1994 in their conclusion that these are not the same sorts of items, but represent two distinct functional categories, Agreement and Number. Thus, one part of the ordering problem is solved: subject inflection is in two places in the verb because subject inflection is not homogeneous, but rather involves two types of functional elements.

A second question concerns the ordering of these two types of inflectional elements. Ritter 1995, in a study of Hebrew, proposes that two subject categories are required in that language, Agreement for first/second person subjects and Number for third person subjects, as in Slave. She argues that these categories are layered with Subject Agreement above Aspect and Number below it. In their work, Rice and Saxon 1994 note that the hierarchical position of Agreement and Number is identical in Hebrew and Slave, as shown in (16).

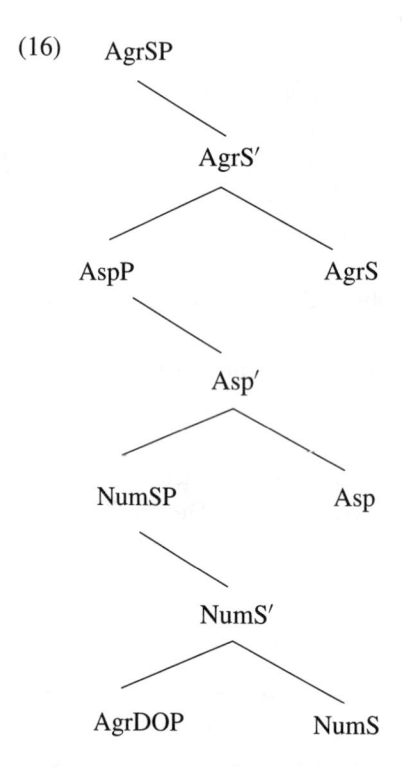

(16)   AgrSP
          /   \
              AgrS'
              /   \
           AspP   AgrS
           / \
              Asp'
              / \
          NumSP   Asp
           / \
              NumS'
              /   \
          AgrDOP NumS

There is thus precedent in other languages for ordering Subject Number lower than Subject Agreement. Why might this be?

In order to answer this question, it is necessary to examine an additional asymmetry between first/second person and third person. Partee 1987 argues that first/second person pronouns are presuppositional. Ritter 1996 reaches a

10.1 Subject Form Pronominals

similar conclusion, arguing that first/second persons are inherently referential. Jelinek 1993, following Hockett 1966, calls them local, referring to the speech act participants. Third persons, on the other hand, are not presuppositional (Partee 1987), not inherently referential (Ritter 1996), and nonlocal, or outsiders (Jelinek 1993, following Hockett 1966). The two classes differ in that third persons must be assigned a referent to be interpreted, while first/second persons are not assigned an external referent as they are inherently referential. Diesing and Jelinek 1995 and Jelinek 1993 assume that presupposition distinguishes first/second persons from third persons and propose a structural difference between presuppositional and non-presuppositional arguments. They argue that presuppositional arguments must be higher than non-presuppositional arguments at Logical Form. In some languages, this split is reflected in the actual ordering of elements in the syntax; in other languages, it is an abstract property of Logical Form.

Assume that the structural distinction proposed by Diesing and Jelinek 1995 is correct. If in Athapaskan languages the split in positioning subjects is syntactically visible, then the difference in position of first/second person subject inflection as opposed to third person subject inflection receives an account – the ordering reflects the higher position of presuppositional (first/second person) than of non-presuppositional (third person) pronominals. The positioning of Agreement as distinct from Number then is a reflection of universal semantic constraints on position with respect to the property of inherent referentiality. The generalization in (17) can be drawn, using Ritter's term referentiality:

(17) inherently referential subjects > inherently nonreferential subjects

This is to be read that inherently referential subjects c-command inherently nonreferential subjects; in Athapaskan languages this translates to inherently referential subjects following inherently nonreferential subjects. Specifically, first/second persons are inherently referential and follow aspect; third persons are inherently nonreferential and precede first/second person subjects. An important question remains unanswered, however: what determines the exact positions – why is placement on either side of aspectual material important? There are several positions for the functional elements that would all be consistent with the generalization in (17). I address this topic in chapter 13.

10.1.4 Summary

I now summarize the syntactic consequences of the arguments made so far. In first/second person contexts, subject agreement, AgrS, is found, while in number contexts, number, Num, occurs instead. Given this, part of the mystery of two subject positions is solved. The split of subject inflection in the Slave verb between two positions is not so unusual as the two positions house different morphological categories: agreement and number. Further, the ordering of these categories may reflect a universal semantic requirement that inherently referential material c-command inherently nonreferential material. If this is correct, then the ordering of the categories in the Slave verb is not an idiosyncrasy that requires stipulation but instead reflects a general crosslinguistic pattern.[3]

10.1.5 Beyond Slave

Other languages are similar to Slave in yielding evidence that subjects are of two functional categories. While evidence concerning the syntactic facts illustrated for Slave (section 1.3) is not available in the literature on other languages,[4] the other kinds of information are easily obtainable, and I summarize these here. First, consider position. As discussed in chapter 2 and appendix 1, two positions for subject inflection are found across the language family, with first/second person subject inflection (ignoring first person plural subject for now) in one position and third person subject inflection in another.

10.1.5.1 Paradigmatic Status

One argument from Slave for separating agreement and number was based on paradigmatic status – marking is obligatory for first and second person, but not for third person. Paradigmatic status in other languages is similar: first/second person singular and second person plural subject inflection is required, while third person subject inflection is optional (I return to first person plural subjects). Cook 1996 demonstrates the optionality of number subject inflection for a number of languages; some examples are given in what follows.

(18) Chipewyan *he* human plural subject (Cook 1996)
    a. hubenéné   ts'ǝn   na-**he**-dh-del
        3pl-homeland   to   preverb-**3pl Subject**-aspect- pl. Subject go
        'They went to their homeland.' (95)
    b. dəne   łą   ye-k'eniye   dzeré-dit
        person   many   disjoint anaphor-after   preverb-plural
                                                            subject go
        'Many people followed him.' (94)

10.1 Subject Form Pronominals

   c. náane   deníye   na-t'ath   náane   tθ'i   kún   **he-ł-tsi**
     some   moose   preverb-cut   some   also   fire   **3pl Subject-**
                                                                                                                                                              valence-make
     'Some of them cut the moose and others made fire.' (94)

Third person plural inflection is overtly marked in (18a) both through the human plural marker and the verb stem. In (18b) it is marked in the stem. In (18c) it is not marked on the first verb but is marked by *h* on the second one.

(19) Tsuut'ina *gi* human plural subject (Cook 1996)
     a. úwat'iyi **giyi**-zì-s-yí-là
        and   **plural** disjoint anaphor-qualifier-aspect-kill-suffix
        na-**gi**-dì-s-t'ǫz-la
        preverb-**3pl Subject**-qualifier-aspect-dual subject go-suffix
        'They (2) killed him and walked back home.' (96)
     b. ts'ídó-**kúwá**   ísina   náá-'ół-la
        girl-plural   as for   preverb-swim-suffix
        'The girls were swimming.' (96)

The third person human plural subject is overtly marked in (19a), and the second verb stem ('dual subject go') indicates that the subject is dual. In (19b) plurality is marked on the subject by the clitic *kúwá*, but is not marked on the verb.

(20) Chilcotin *ji* human plural subject (Cook 1996)
     a. 'an 'eguh 'esquax qwenjah na-ni-ŝ-day
        now then children floor   preverb-qualifier-aspect-dance
        'Then the children danced on the floor.' (96)
     b. deni   'esquax   **ji**-n-zun   a'eyen   ya-**ji**-n-lin
        person children **3pl Subject**-aspect- they   preverb-**3pl**
                                 good   **Subject**-as-
                                                                                                             pect-be
        je-ne-dash   ha-gwe-t'in
        3pl Subject-qualifier-dance   preverb-areal-happen
        'The people turned into handsome children and were dancing around.' (97)

In (20a) number is not marked on the verb but is marked on the subject, while in (20b) the three verbs contain the human plural subject marker *j*.

The conclusion from these examples is identical to that drawn for Slave – third persons are not obligatory in the way that first and second persons are.

10.1.5.2 Semantics

Turning to the semantics of these elements, the range of meanings exhibited by third person subject inflection in Slave is also found elsewhere. Thompson 1989a summarizes the general functions of the unspecified human subject prefix in Athapaskan languages as in (21).

(21) general functions of unspecified human subject
   a. unspecified or indefinite human or personified animal (unknown, nonspecific, or nonreferential)
   b. first person plural
   c. proximate third person human (specific, definite, usually in contrastive context)

These uses have been illustrated for Slave; I argued that the core specified feature is human, and that other features follow from context. The same can be seen in other languages. See in particular Saxon 1993 for detailed discussion of Dogrib and Chipewyan.

Tenenbaum 1978 provides the following meanings for these elements in Dena'ina.

(22) Dena'ina (Tenenbaum 1978)
   ch' first person plural, 'someone' subject
   a. First person dual/plural
      ch'e-chegh
      HSubject-stem
      'We two are crying.' (62)
      ch'-u-yuł
      HSubject-aspect-stem
      'We are walking along.'
   b. Unspecified singular subject (used when identity is not known, person cannot be seen)
      ch'e-chegh
      HSubject-stem
      'Someone is crying.' (62)
      ch'-u-yuł
      HSubject-aspect-stem
      'Someone is walking along.'
   c. Impersonal subject
      ch'u-yuł-a
      HSubject-stem-negative suffix
      'Don't walk around.' (115)

10.1 Subject Form Pronominals

    d. **ch'**e-qe-nax-a
       HSubject-area-stem-negative suffix
       'Don't talk.' (115)

As in Slave, if the unspecified human subject in Dena'ina is unmarked for person and specificity, the range of readings can be derived from the context.

Willie 1991 and Young and Morgan 1987:76–77 show that the Navajo fourth person or impersonal, *j*, which is cognate with the unspecified human subject, has a similarly wide range of uses. The examples in (23) show that it can refer to a single definite actor, a generic actor, a nonspecific actor or actors, a first person, and a second person among others. See the references for discussion and further examples.[5]

(23) Navajo *j*
    a. Impersonal subject
       chidí bi-ne'jígo doo   n-**ji**-née   da
       car b-behind neg   preverb-**HSubject**-play neg
       'Don't play behind cars.' (YM 77)
    b. First person
       'ashiiké   ń-**j**-ó-dle'   laanaa da-n-ii-dzin
       boy-pl   iterative-**HSubject**-aspect- wish   distributive-
                become   qualifier-1dual
                                                               Subject-wish
       'We wish that we could become boys again.' (literally: we wish that one or people could turn back into boys) (YM 77)
    c. Polite, deferential
       ha'át'íísh   **dz**i-n-í-zin
       what   **HSubject**-qualifier-aspect-want
       'What do you want?' (literally: what does he/she want?) (YM 77)
    d. Quotative
       yóó-'a-**jí**-í-yá   **ji**-ní
       preverb-unspecified Object-**HSubject**-aspect-sg. go **HSubject**-said
       'They said that person is lost.'

The human plural in Dena'ina is similar to Slave in its function as well in marking third person plural human subjects. It can also be used indefinitely, without regard for number, as in (24b).

(24) Dena'ina *q* plural human (Tenenbaum 1978)
    a. Unmarked plural subject
       qe-chegh
       human plural Subject-stem
       'They two are crying.' (66)

sh-**qi**-z-teł
1sg Object-**human plural Subject**-aspect-stem
'They kicked me once.'

b. Indefinite human subject, especially if person can be seen but identity is unknown
qe-chegh
human plural Subject-stem
'Someone is crying.' (67)
hyu-dna-**q**-i-luq
preverb-1pl Object-**human plural Subject**-aspect-stem
'Somebody paid us.'

Number inflections thus share similar properties across the family: they have core features associated with them (HSubject = human, unmarked for person, number, specificity, definiteness; 3pl Subject = human, plural (generally), specific; unmarked for person), with finely grained detailed meanings determined through as yet poorly understood factors (Saxon 1993) and in all languages, they are not obligatory in the same way that non-third person inflection is. In addition, other languages show the alternations between number subjects illustrated for Slave in (8) and (9); see Cook 1996 for discussion. Their properties therefore differ from those of the first/second person inflections, which obligatorily include marking for person, number, gender, specificity, and definiteness.[6]

10.1.5.3 First Person Plurals

The hypothesis that speech act participants are morphologically marked by Agreement and unspecified actors by Number faces a major hurdle when first person plural subjects are taken into account. I have concentrated on Slave, a language in which first/second person inflection is clearly marked in a different position from number inflection regardless of number. But this is not true of all Athapaskan languages; in fact it is not even completely true of Slave. In all Athapaskan languages, first person singular, second person singular, and second person plural subject inflection is marked at the right edge of the functional complex, as in Slave. Also, the human plural (cognate with Slave *k/g/gh*), if it exists in the language, follows the objects, as does the morpheme that I have called unspecified human number, cognate with Slave *ts'*. The problem in many languages has to do with the marking of first person nonsingular subjects. While languages like Slave clearly have first person

10.1 Subject Form Pronominals

nonsingular agreement, marked by an affix cognate with Slave *í-d*, in some languages the cognate marks only first person dual, and first person plural is marked by the cognate of Slave *ts'*. In still other languages all first person nonsingular subjects are marked by the morpheme cognate with the Slave *ts'*, and *í-d* has no cognate.[7]

In this section I address first person nonsingulars, considering *ts'* cognates in particular. I begin by continuing with Slave. I have treated *ts'* as unmarked for person. It is also used in many Slave dialects as a first person plural, as in (25).

(25) a. shé-**ts'**-u-ye
food-**HSubject**-optative-plural eat
'Let's (plural) eat.' (Rice 1989:624)
b. ná-**ts'**-u-dé
preverb-**HSubject**-optative-plural go
'Let's (plural) make a trip.'
c. **ts'**e-ji̱
HSubject-sing
'We pl. sing.' (Bearlake dialect)
cf. h-**í**-ji̱
epenthetic-**1dual Subject**-sing
'We two sing.'

In all Slave dialects, *ts'* can indicate a first person plural subject. In the Bearlake dialect *í-d* is restricted to first person dual subject; *ts'* is a human subject (of any number) and a first person plural subject. Rice and Saxon 1994:186 note that in this dialect "*ts'*, in addition to its 'third person' functions, is the exclusive marker of first person plural, a role which is permitted by the fact that the morpheme is not inherently specified for person." Rice and Saxon 1994 thus find support for the claim that number inflections are unspecified for person in this use of the unspecified human subject as a first person plural. This pattern is found in other languages including Babine-Witsuwit'en, some Carrier dialects (Poser, personal communication, 1998), and Sekani (Hargus 1988; see discussion below).

In other languages (e.g., Ahtna, Dena'ina, Koyukon), the human subject is the only morpheme used to express first person dual/plural reference (see Story 1989 and Willie and Saxon 1995). As Willie and Saxon point out, in these languages, verbs marked with the unspecified subject are "systematically ambiguous, having the interpretation 'we,' as well as indefinite reference to 'someone' or 'people,' and possibly definite reference." That this is the case in Dena'ina can be seen from the examples in (22): while *ch'* clearly marks first person plural, it has other functions as well. This is also true in Ahtna, where Kari 1990:398 assigns to the morpheme that he labels first person plural the meanings 'we, someone, first person plural subject, unspecified human subject.' The phonological form varies by context.

(26) Ahtna (Kari 1990:8)
   a. ugheli **ts'**i-laen
      fine **HSubject**-be
      'We are fine.' (398)
   b. yet **'s**-ne-z-yaał
      there **HSubject**-qualifier-aspect-stem
      'We camped there, someone camped there.' (398)

Kari also notes that unspecified subject inflection is common in nominalized verbs in Ahtna, and provides examples such as (27).

(27) a. **ts'**e-t-naan-i
        HSubject-voice-drink-suffix
        'beverage (that which we drink)' (Kari 1990:398)
     b. u-k'e-**'s**-de-l-ts'iiy-i
        3 Object-on-**HSubject**-qualifier-voice/valence-pl. sit-suffix
        'bench (that on which we sit)' (398)

Thompson 1989b shows that the Koyukon cognate is similarly multifunctional.

(28) Koyukon (Thompson 1989b)
   a. **ts'**i-nee-ł-'aanh
      HSubject-qualifier-valence-see
      'We/someone/she/he is looking at him/her/it.' (11)
   b. **ts'**i-l-do
      HSubject-voice/valence-sit
      'We/someone/she/he is sitting.' (11)

Willie and Saxon 1995 cite Thompson 1990, who identifies the unspecified human subject as a proximate third person. As they say, "from an indefinite someone or group of people, and the notion of a proximate third person, it is just a short move semantically to first person plural, since the group

10.1 Subject Form Pronominals

of people most proximate to any speaker is bound to be the group of people to which the speaker belongs – that is, first person plural" (Willie and Saxon 1995). Thus, the 'unspecified' human subject does seem to be unspecified for person. The fact that it can be a first person nonsingular is consistent with this. The fact that it is in some languages used exclusively for first person plural also follows; given that there is no way to express this grammatical category through Agreement, it can be expressed only through Number.

I began this discussion in order to show that the distinction between Number and Agreement is found across the family. The marking of first person plural subjects poses a problem since first person plural is expected to be expressed as Agreement rather than as Number. However, the systematic ambiguity of the *ts'* cognate supports the claim that Agreement and Number should be separated, with the *ts'* cognate representing Number across the family.[8]

10.1.5.4 One Further Pattern: Sekani First Person Plurals

I have identified two major patterns for marking first person nonsingular forms. One has distinctive first person singular and first person plural inflection at the right edge of the functional complex. In languages with this pattern, the unspecified human inflection can also be used as a first person plural. The second pattern has no distinctive marker that is restricted to first person plural; instead a single form, human number, is used for both unspecified human subject and first person nonsingular subject inflection.

A further pattern occurs in Sekani. In Sekani, first person plural and unspecified subject are marked exclusively by *ts'*, although Hargus notes that this morpheme is rarely used as an unspecified subject. It is also found as the subject of nominalizations.

(29) a. ła-**ts'**-i̧-tsùz
preverb-**HSubject**-aspect-stem
'We plural gave each other clothlike object.' (Hargus 1988:85)
b. k'e-**ts'**-ə-ni̧-t'ats
preverb-**HSubject**-aspect-stem
'We plural cut O in half.' (101)
c. 'ə-**ts'**-ə-gò̧'
unspecified Object-**HSubject**-stem
'dried meat' (unspecified subject dries unspecified object) (208)

d. dah-'ə-**ts'**a-h-ya-i
preverb-unspecified Object-**HSubject**-aspect/voice/valence-stem-suffix
'glasses' (unspecified subject has unspecified object located above on self) (210)

The Sekani first person dual inclusive subject form, Hargus 1988:126 argues, is marked discontinuously.[9] (30) gives some examples.

(30) a. u-**sə**-n-**ɨ**-be
qualifier-**dual number**-qualifier-**1dual Subject**-stem
'We dual pick berries.' (Hargus 1988:95)
b. ghu-ya-'ə-**sə**-n-**ɨ**-t-'ǫ
3pl Object-preverb-unspecified Object-**dual number**-aspect-**1dual Subject**-voice-stem
'We dual hired them.' (98)
cf. ya-'ə-nį-'ǫ
preverb-unspecified Object-aspect-stem
'S/he hired him, her.'
c. **sə**-gh-**ɨ**-gǫ
dual number-aspect-**1dual Subject**-voice/kill pl.
'We dual killed pl. object.' (99)
cf. ə-ghǫ
aspect-kill pl.
'He/she kills pl. object.'

Hargus identifies the first part of this form, *s*, as a number element and the second part, *i*, as a first person nonsingular subject. I interpret this to mean that Sekani allows number and agreement to co-occur so long as a reading can be assigned, as predicted by the structure in (17). The dual number marker *s* is neither redundant nor incompatible with first person nonsingular agreement, but rather further delineates the type of nonsingularity specified by the agreement element *i*.[10] But items that are obligatorily singular are incompatible with dual marking, and thus the dual number marker does not co-occur with singular forms.

10.1.6 Summary

Subject inflection in Athapaskan languages is unusual in that it occupies two positions. As many have pointed out, first/second person subject inflection

10.2 The Status of Object Inflection

always "comes after all other prefixes, and thus immediately in front of the stem (or class marker)," while third person subject inflection "can be followed by other prefixes" (Golla 1985:38). Following Rice and Saxon 1994, I have argued that the fundamental difference between the two types of subject inflection is that the first/second person inflection elements are true agreement markers, while number subject inflection is unmarked for person, having features of number and gender only, and instantiates the category Number. This hypothesis provides a partial answer to the question of why subject inflection occurs in two sites – subject inflection is not a homogeneous class, but involves different kinds of functional material. The existence of this pattern in other languages, with agreement and number in different syntactic locations, suggests that we are dealing with a general property of language and not an idiosyncratic property of Athapaskan languages.

10.2 The Status of Object Inflection

The functional category of object inflection has yet to be considered. Having differentiated Agreement from Number in subject inflection, the question arises as to whether this distinction holds for object inflection as well. I have postponed discussion of object inflection because insight into subject inflection helps to understand object inflection. I propose in this section that subject and object inflection are parallel in nature: both show a split between first/second person, or speech act participants, and third person. The proposal that inherently referential arguments differ from inherently nonreferential ones has been made for pronouns in general, and thus it is not surprising to find that objects as well as subjects pattern differently depending on person.

One clue to the different status of first/second and third person subject inflection was position: the two types of subject occur in distinct locations in the verb. It is this very fact that makes subjects in Athapaskan languages worthy of study. The facts are different with objects: there is no ordering evidence for dividing object inflection into two categories. However, an examination of its paradigmatic and syntactic properties suggests that object inflection, like subject inflection, falls into two distinct classes.

10.2.1 Obligatoriness

I start with a discussion of obligatoriness of inflection, again concentrating on Slave. Consider first/second person object inflection, which is identical in patterning to first/second person subject inflection. In particular, it is obligatory, and in its absence a reading of the object as first or second person is not possible. This is shown in (31). (31a) has a first person singular object, *s*. (31b) illustrates that its absence rules out a reading of the object as first person singular. (31c,d) differ from (31a,b) in the presence of an overt object, *seni̱* 'first person singular'. The pronominal inflection is required, even in the presence of this overt pronoun.

(31) a. rá-**se**-re-yi̱-h-t'u
preverb-**1sg Object**-qualifier-aspect-valence-punch
'S/he punched me.'
b. *rá-re-yi̱-h-t'u
(on reading 'S/he punched me.')
c. seni̱ rá-**se**-re-yi̱-h-t'u
1sg. preverb-**1sg Object**-qualifier-aspect-valence-punch
'It's me that s/he punched.'
d. *seni̱ rá-re-yi̱-h-t'u

Parallel facts obtain for other objects, as shown in (32).

(32) a. rá-**ne**-re-yi-h-t'u
preverb-2sg Object-qualifier-aspect/1sg Subject-valence-punch
'I punched you sg.'
b. *rá-re-yi-h-t'u
(on reading 'I punched you sg.')
c. neni̱ rá-**ne**-re-yi-h-t'u
you sg. preverb-**2sg Object**-qualifier-aspect/1sg Subject-valence-punch
'It's you sg. that I punched.'
d. *neni̱ rá-re-yi-h-t'u
e. (raxeni̱) rá-**raxe**-re-yi̱-h-t'u
1 pl/2pl preverb-**1/2pl Object**-qualifier-aspect-valence-punch
'S/he punched you pl/us.'
f. *(raxeni̱) rá-re-yi̱-h-t'u

Number objects differ in their paradigmatic patterning from first/second person objects. These divide into two different types, anaphors and nonanaphors. The anaphors include a reflexive, a reciprocal, and a disjoint anaphor (see Rice and Saxon 1991, Saxon 1984, 1986; but see Saxon 1995 on the pronominal status of anaphors). The anaphors are specific in reference. The

10.2 The Status of Object Inflection

reflexive *'ede* is used when the subject and object are coreferential. As shown in (33), it is invariant and receives its person interpretation from its antecedent.

(33) a. dah-**'edé**-de-h-d-lú
preverb-**reflexive**-qualifier-aspect/1sg Subject-voice-stem
'I hung myself.' (Rice 1989:634)
 b. -ghá-**'edé**-nį-tį
preverb-**reflexive**-aspect/2sg Subject-stem
'You sg. gave yourself (to O).' (523)
 c. ná-**'ede**-n-a-t'u
preverb-**reflexive**-qualifier-aspect/voice/stem
'S/he hit him/herself.' (634)
 d. -ghá-**'edé**-n-í-tį
preverb-**reflexive**-aspect-1pl Subject-stem
'We gave ourselves.' (523)
 e. -ghá-**'edé**-n-ah-tį
preverb-**reflexive**-aspect-2pl Subject-stem
'You pl. gave yourselves.' (523)
 f. -ghá-**'ede**-g-į-tį
preverb-**reflexive**-3pl Subject-aspect-stem
'They gave themselves.' (523)
 g. -ghá-**'ede**-ts'-į-tį
preverb-**reflexive**-HSubject-aspect-stem
'One gave oneself.' (523)

The reciprocal is similar: it can occur with any subject that can be construed as plural (Rice 1989:634).

(34) a. ká-**łe**-ts'-a-kw'i
preverb-**reciprocal**-HSubject-aspect-stem
'We pinched each other.'
 b. ná-**'ełe**-n-a-ta
preverb-**reciprocal**-qualifier-aspect-stem
'They kicked each other.'
 c. ná-**'ełe**-ne-y-í-ta
preverb-**reciprocal**-qualifier-aspect-1pl Subject-stem
'We kicked each other.'

The disjoint anaphor *y* (the name is due to Saxon 1984) is used when the subject is third person and the object is a non-coreferential third person.

It occurs in Slave and most northern languages only in the absence of an object noun, as in (35). The first form of each data set contains an object pronoun; the second form contains an object noun but no object pronoun. The anaphor is in boldface.

(35) a. i. Mary ná-**ye**-ni-į-tá
preverb-**disjoint anaphor**-qualifier-aspect-stem
'Mary kicked him/her/it (sg/pl).'
ii. Mary John ná-ni-į-tá
preverb-qualifier-aspect-stem
'Mary kicked John.'
iii. Mary tthe ná-ni-į-tá
stone
'Mary kicked the stone/s.'
b. Mary gá-**y**-u-re-h-tę
area/preverb-**disjoint anaphor**-qualifier-qualifier-valence-stem
'Mary taught him/her.'
Mary ts'ǫ́dani gá-h-u-re-h-tę
child area/preverb-epenthetic-qualifier-qualifier-valence-stem
'Mary taught the child.'

This morpheme marks third person as distinct from all other persons. It is used as a direct object in Slave only if the subject is also third person (and specific; *ts'* does not occur with this object), indicating a second third person. (In this sense it is similar to an obviative.) These anaphors are distinguished from first/second person objects: first/second person object inflection is used to refer to speech act participants regardless of the person of the subject; the person of the anaphors, on the other hand, is dependent on, and determined by, the person of the subject.[11]

While the disjoint anaphor does not in general co-occur with nominal objects, there is one condition under which it does: namely when the nominal object is third person plural human. The plural disjoint anaphor is *go*. Like the subject *k/g*, it may but need not be present, as shown in (36a,b), respectively.

(36) a. ts'ǫ́dani-ke ká-**go**-de-n-é-zhú
child-pl. preverb-**pl Object**-qualifier-qualifier-aspect-chase
'S/he chased the children out.'

10.2 The Status of Object Inflection

b. ts'ǫ́dani-ke ká-de-n-é-zhú
child-pl.　preverb-qualifier-qualifier-aspect-chase
'S/he chased the children out.'

Its presence implies a human object; if it is absent, the object may be human or nonhuman. In (37b), the disjoint anaphor *y* occurs.

(37) a. ła-**go**-nį-h-dé
preverb-**pl Object**-aspect-valence-kill pl.
'They killed them (human).'
b. ła-**yé**-nį-h-dé
preverb-**disjoint anaphor**-aspect-valence-kill pl.
'They killed them (human/nonhuman).'

The anaphoric form *go* marks a human, plural, specific object, noncoreferential with the subject. The semantics of this morpheme parallel that of the human plural subject *k/g* except for anaphoricity, a property that does not occur in subjects. While *y* is simply disjoint anaphoric and specific, *go* in addition includes plural number and human gender in its meaning. The disjoint anaphors do not mark agreement since they are not obligatorily present in third person contexts; they instead indicate number, gender, and specificity.

Sentences with third person direct objects and first and second person subjects remain to be considered. In this context, a third person nonhuman object never has an overt marker; a third person human object may be marked by *b*, but need not be. The semantic and discourse conditions for *b* remain to be explored. See Rice 1999 for some discussion.

(38) a. ná-ni-i-ta
preverb-qualifier-aspect/1sg Subject-stem
'I kicked him/her/it.'
ná-**be**-ni-i-ta
preverb-**3 Object**-qualifier-aspect/1sg Subject-stem
'I kicked him/her.'
b. gá-h-u-re-h-tę
area/preverb-epenthetic-qualifier-qualifier-1sg Subject/valence-stem
'I teach him/her/it.'
gá-**b**-u-re-h-tę
area/preverb-**3 Object**-qualifier-qualifier-1sg Subject/valence-stem
'I teach him/her.'

Third person plural human specific objects may be marked by *ku/ki/gi/go* (depending on dialect) when the subject is first/second person. The verb stem in (39) requires that the theme argument be plural.

(39) a. ts'e-**ku**-nį-wa
preverb-**human pl Object**-aspect/2sg Subject-stem
'You sg. wake them up.'
b. t'ere ts'e-**ku**-nį-wa
girl
'You sg. wake the girls up.'
c. t'ere ts'e-nį-wa
'You sg. wake the girls up.'

The form *b* marks humanness alone when it is an object, while *ku* and its dialect variants in addition to indicating gender also mark plural number. Both indicate specificity.

The semantics of the third person direct objects is summarized in (40). The unspecified *'e* is included for completeness.[12]

(40)
	y	go	b	ku	'e
Anaphoricity	anaphoric	anaphoric	nonanaphoric	nonanaphoric	nonanaphoric
Number	±plural	plural	non-plural	plural	±plural
Gender	±human	human	human	human	nonhuman
Specificity	specific	specific	specific	specific	nonspecific

Number object inflection is similar to number subject inflection. In both, number has a different paradigmatic status from first/second persons: the sense of first/second person is conveyed only by the overt presence of a morpheme, but the sense of number does not require the appearance of a morpheme. Objects thus fall into two categories with respect to whether they mark person or not, as subjects do. To maintain the parallel with subjects, I call the categories Object Agreement and Object Number.

10.2.2 Syntactic Asymmetries in Slave

Just as coordination facts for subjects depend upon whether a first/second person is involved as a conjunct, they also do for objects. This can be seen by comparing the examples in (41) and (42). (41a) contains an explicit first person singular pronoun, which can be dropped, as in (41b). The conjunction, however, is required, as shown in (41c). In (42) with a third person plural reading, the stated NP is overtly singular, and the conjunction is not needed. The object form *raxe* in (41) marks a first or second person plural object.[13]

10.2 The Status of Object Inflection

(41) a. Mary seni̧ hé ra-**raxe**-re-yi̧-h-t'u
      1sg   with preverb-**1/2pl Object**-qualifier-aspect-valence-
                          stem
    'S/he punched Mary and me.'
  b. Mary hé ra-**raxe**-re-yi̧-h-t'u
    'S/he punched Mary and me/you.'
  c. *Mary ra-**raxe**-re-yi̧-h-t'u
    (okay as 'Mary punched you-pl/us.')

(42) se-tá   rá-**go**-re-yi-h-t'u
     1sg-father   preverb-**human pl Object**-qualifier-aspect/1sg Subject-
                          valence-stem
    'I punched my father and him/her/them.'

Object inflection, like subject inflection, divides into two types. First/second person inflection includes person, number, and gender features, which are inherently specific, and exhibits syntactic properties of agreement. The number inflections may be anaphoric or not; in addition they include features of number, gender, and specificity. The syntactic patterning of first/second person objects in coordinate structures shows properties of agreement, just as in the case of the subjects; the patterning of number forms is not one of agreement, but of elaboration.

First/second person subject inflection and number subject inflection clearly appear in two positions in the verb, separated by other functional material. The evidence discussed in this section suggests that the objects are associated with a structure parallel to that of the subjects, as in (43). Note that I have ordered Object Agreement above Object Number; although there is no evidence for this, it follows from the principles discussed in section 10.1.3.

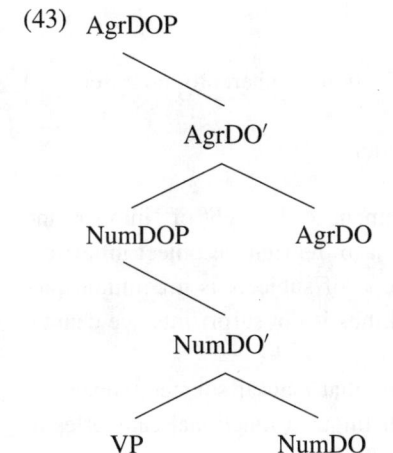

(43)
```
        AgrDOP
           \
            AgrDO'
           /     \
       NumDOP   AgrDO
       /    \
           NumDO'
           /    \
         VP    NumDO
```

Evidence from morpheme ordering for two subject inflection positions is not available for object inflection since first/second person object inflection is not separated from number object inflection by other functional material. Unlike subject inflection, object inflection is therefore traditionally treated as occupying a single position in the verb template.

10.2.3 Beyond Slave

Other Athapaskan languages parallel Slave in a number of ways with respect to object inflection. Most noticeably, as in Slave, first/second person object inflection is obligatory, while third person inflection is not obligatory in the same way.

In general, then, for both subject and object inflection there is evidence for two categories, Number and Agreement. A difference in category type is suggested by the different paradigmatic status. Syntactic evidence from coordination in Slave shows that first/second persons have agreement properties while third persons show different properties. Agreement, or first and second person, includes inherent marking for person as well as number, gender, and specificity; Number, or third person, is unmarked for person.

10.3 On Noncanonical Subjects

The next question concerns the ordering of subject and object inflection with respect to each other. We are in a position to provide a partial answer to this question: subjects, be they Agreement or Number, are hierarchically superior to, or have scope over, objects. Thus, two generalizations are possible at this point regarding ordering of pronominals.

(44) a. inherently referential subject inflection > inherently nonreferential subject inflection
    b. subject inflection > object inflection

(44a) accounts for the ordering of Agreement to the right of Number, and (44b) for the ordering of subject inflection to the right of object inflection. The placement of objects within the scope of subjects is a common pattern found in languages of the world and thus is not surprising; see chapter 13.

In this section I examine the positions that clausal subjects appear in. I argue that not only is it necessary to distinguish functional categories of

10.3 On Noncanonical Subjects

Agreement and Number, but also to identify VP-internal and VP-external positions for subjects. These two structural positions for subjects have been argued to exist in general (see, for instance, Fukui and Speas 1986, Koopman and Sportiche 1991, Kuroda 1988, Sportiche 1988) as well as for Athapaskan (see Rice 1993, 1999, Rice and Saxon 1994, Saxon and Rice 1993). The clausal subjects considered so far are structurally external to the verb phrase and functionally salient (Leer 1990) or topics rather than foci (e.g., Willie and Jelinek 1996). A second class of subjects is structurally internal to the verb phrase and functionally nonsalient (Leer 1990), or focus (Willie and Jelinek 1996). Some arguments for VP-internal subjects are presented in this section (see also Rice, forthcoming a, Rice and Saxon 1994, Saxon and Rice 1993). The inflectional expression of agreement and number with VP-internal clausal subjects differs from that with VP-external clausal subjects. This examination of clausal subjects therefore allows consideration of another ordering problem, the ordering of inflection linked to internal subjects on the one hand and objects on the other.

In this section I follow Rice 1993, 1999, Rice and Saxon 1994, and Saxon and Rice 1993 in proposing that Athapaskan languages have two classes of clausal subjects. One is a prototypical clausal subject – these are typically agentive, human subjects; I call them canonical or external subjects. The second type of clausal subject has distinct properties – these tend to be nonagentive and nonhuman, and they are nonsalient in the discourse or represent focused items; I call these noncanonical or internal subjects. In this section I argue, following Saxon and Rice 1993, that the first subject type occupies a position structurally external to the verb phrase and the second type one internal to the verb phrase. The inflection associated with external subjects is the subject inflection discussed earlier in this chapter (be it Agreement or Number), but the inflection associated with internal subjects shows morphological properties of object rather than subject inflection. The existence of internal clausal subjects is thus important: it is relevant to just what the content of the verbal positions generally called 'subject' and 'object' is, and it bears critically on the ordering issue as verbs can be inflected for both an internal subject and an object.

The clausal subject positions are illustrated in (45). SA is the external position for first and second person subjects, SB the external position for number subjects, and SD is the VP-internal subject position, OC and OE are object positions. See Rice 1999 for details.

(45)

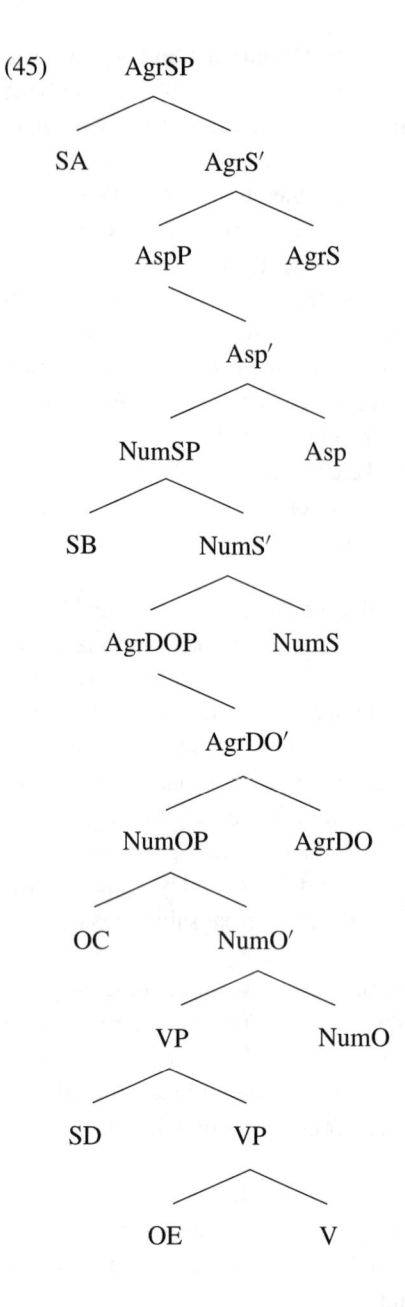

```
                AgrSP
               /     \
             SA      AgrS'
                    /     \
                 AspP     AgrS
                    \
                    Asp'
                   /    \
                NumSP   Asp
                /   \
              SB   NumS'
                   /    \
              AgrDOP   NumS
                   \
                   AgrDO'
                  /      \
               NumOP    AgrDO
               /   \
             OC   NumO'
                  /    \
                VP    NumO
               /  \
             SD   VP
                  /  \
                OE   V
```

A variety of types of syntactic evidence argues for two subject positions. These include idioms, incorporated nouns, and anaphora, and I turn to these

10.3 On Noncanonical Subjects

now. See Rice and Saxon 1994 and Saxon and Rice 1993 for further development of these arguments.

10.3.1 Idioms

Idioms provide evidence for a VP-internal subject position. Marantz 1984 remarks on the crosslinguistic rarity of idioms in which the subject of a transitive verb contributes to the idiom's meaning. The converse type of idiom, where the object contributes, is common, as in the English idiom 'kick the bucket.' Marantz assumes that the domain of idioms is the VP; if the verb phrase does not include the subject, then the rarity of the first type of idiom follows. In Athapaskan languages, however, subject idioms are found. Some examples are given in (46)–(48).

(46) Slave (Rice 1989)
    a. mbeh   se-dhé-h-xį
       sleep   1sg Object-qualifier/aspect-valence-kill sg.
       'I am sleepy.' (literally 'Sleep killed me.') (932)
    b. raxǫ   'a-y-į́-lá
       snowblindness preverb-disjoint anaphor-aspect-affect
       'S/he is snowblind.' (literally 'Snowblindness affected him/her.') (929)

(47) Ahtna (Kari 1990)
    a. naaɬ   s-de-ɬ-ghaen
       sleep   1sg Object-inceptive-valence-kill
       'I am getting sleepy.' (literally 'Sleep is starting to kill me.') (213)
    b. c'eyuuni   si-z-kat
       ghost   1sg Object-aspect-slap
       'I have a birthmark.' (literally 'A ghost slapped me.') (232)
    c. naaɬ   s-t-ni-ɬ-ts'aax
       sleep   1sg Object-qualifier-aspect-valence-open
       'I yawned.' (literally 'Sleep opened me.') (401)

(48) Navajo (Young and Morgan 1987)
    haastiin tó   bi-is-xį́
    man   water   3 Object-aspect-valence/kill
    'The man drowned.' (literally 'The man, water killed him.') (266)

Adopting Marantz's assumption concerning the phrase structure of idioms, these idioms pattern as if both the subject and verb were contained within VP at some level, and they can therefore be taken as evidence for a VP-internal subject position.

10.3.2 Incorporated Subjects

Incorporated nouns are found in many Athapaskan languages; see chapter 4. All languages with incorporates permit incorporated patients and some also allow incorporated agentive subjects of transitive clauses, as discussed in chapter 4.

Incorporated agentive subjects of transitive clauses are illustrated in (49) and (50) from Ahtna and Koyukon, respectively.

(49) Ahtna (Kari 1990)
    a. te-**ta**-yi-ni-ł-taen
       preverb-**water**-disjoint anaphor-aspect-valence-stem
       'S/he drowned.' ('**Water** carried her/him underwater.') (329)
    b. **łi**-yi-z-'ał
       dog-disjoint anaphor-aspect-stem
       'A **dog** bit him/her once.' (79)
    c. ni-c'a-**łts'i**-i-d-i-ł-t'ak
       preverb-preverb-**wind**-disjoint anaphor-qualifier-qualifier-valence-stem
       'The **wind** lifted it up.' (411)
    d. ka-**naał**-s-te-ł-taen
       preverb-**sleep**-1sg Object-inceptive-valence-stem
       'I am starting to fall asleep.' ('**Sleep** started to handle me up.') (289)

(50) Koyukon (Axelrod 1990)
    a. haa-**tseh**-ye-dee-ł-taanh
       preverb-**tears**-disjoint anaphor-qualifier/aspect-valence-stem
       'S/he went away crying.' ('**Tears** carried him/her off.') (185)
    b. kk'o-**ełts'eeyh**-yee-dzoyh
       preverb-**wind**-disjoint anaphor/aspect-stem
       'The **wind** is moving them around.' (185)
    c. no-**tenh**-ye-taa-tł-gghet
       iterative-**ice**-disjoint anaphor-qualifier-aspect/valence-stem
       '(The cracking of) **ice** scared him/her back off.' (186)

Agentive nonhuman incorporated subjects can also occur with intransitive verbs.

10.3 On Noncanonical Subjects

(51) Slave (Rice 1989)
    a. k'e-**tsi**-i-tɬa
       preverb-**snow**-aspect-stem
       '**Snow** drifted.' ('**Snow** went around.') (653)
       cf. k'e-e-tɬa
       'S/he walked around.'
    b. tá-rah-**xeníh**-e-'ó
       preverb-iterative-**raft**-epenthetic-stem
       '**raft** comes ashore (customarily)' (place name) (664)
       cf. tá-ts'e-'é
       'One comes ashore.'

Incorporated subjects are rare crosslinguistically. Baker 1988:83 predicts that such incorporates are impossible under the assumptions that a noun phrase whose head is incorporated into the verb is lexically governed by the verb and that subjects are not so governed. If the subject NP is within the VP, then it can be incorporated. This is a second bit of evidence that clausal subjects can be VP-internal.

10.3.3 Word Order

Certain word order facts also suggest that clausal subjects can be internal to the VP. SOV is considered to be the basic word order in Athapaskan languages. However, OSV word order is also possible. Some examples of OSV order in Ahtna are given in (52).

(52) Ahtna (Kari 1990)
    a. u-daghos   tuu   k'e-n-de-z-c'et'
       3-gunwales water preverb-preverb-qualifier-aspect-reach
       'Water reaches its gunwales.' (125)
    b. n-yuu'   ggas   ni-ghi-laa
       2sg-clothes dirt preverb-aspect-stem
       'Dirt got on your clothes.' (260)

Agreement facts suggest that the object noun in these sentences is not dislocated outside the clause. If it were, one would expect an overt expression of object Number in the verb, but this is not present. Assuming that the direct objects are within AgrSP, the existence of sentences with OSV word order suggests that the subjects in these examples must be within the VP.

10.3.4 Interim Summary 1

Facts from idioms, incorporated nouns, and word order suggest that subjects can be external or internal to the verb phrase. In the next sections, I discuss marking of VP-internal subjects. The subjects discussed in section 10.1 are in an external position and show subject marking. Internal subjects are different – they show object marking. The forms are summarized in a somewhat simplified way in (53), using Slave and Ahtna as exemplars. With third persons, I indicate forms when two third persons are involved.

(53) Subject and object inflectional forms

	External subject		Internal subject		Object	
	Slave	Ahtna	Slave	Ahtna	Slave	Ahtna
1sg.	h	s			s	s
2sg.	n	i			n	n
1pl.	í-d	–			nax	ne
2pl.	ah	oh			nax	nhw
3 on 3 transitive	Ø	Ø	Ø	Ø/y	y/b	y/b
	ts'	ts'	go	hw	go	hw
	k	k	go	hw	go	hw

The morphological form of subjects ultimately relates to the major issue at hand: if there are two VP-internal pronominals, an object and an internal subject, what is the ordering of the inflection associated with them, and why?

10.3.5 Anaphora

An interesting source of evidence for two clausal positions for subjects comes from anaphora. So far the discussion of ordering of inflectional items has focused on subject inflection relating to external subjects. Evidence from anaphora allows for a discussion of inflectional marking in connection with two VP-internal arguments, subject and object.

The evidence to be discussed in this section comes from the patterning of the disjoint anaphor (see Saxon 1984, 1986), a number form with the limited distribution of an anaphor that must be interpreted as disjoint in reference to the subject. This anaphor has the morphological form *y* or cognate, as discussed in section 10.2. Surprisingly, the anaphoric pronoun can appear as subject inflection in some northern Athapaskan languages when the subject is nonsalient or focused; see Leer 1990, Saxon and Rice 1993, and Thompson 1989a, 1996b for discussion. Assuming that anaphors occur only under conditions of c-command, these subjects must then be c-commanded by some other

10.3 On Noncanonical Subjects

noun phrase within the clause: a noun phrase in canonical subject position is not c-commanded by any of its clausemate noun phrases, but a VP-internal subject may be.

Consider the following facts from Koyukon. The disjoint anaphor is in boldface. In the gloss, the topic is italicized and the noun represented by the disjoint anaphor, the focus, is in boldface.

(54) a. **y**-egh nee-nee-yo
    disjoint anaphor-to preverb-aspect-walk
    '*He* walked up to **him** (disjoint anaphor).' (Thompson 1989a:40)
  b. *b*-egh nee-yee-nee-yo
    3 ObliqueO-to preverb-**disjoint anaphor**-aspect-walk
    '**He** (disjoint anaphor) walked up to *him*.' (Thompson 1989a:41)

These sentences illustrate intransitive verbs with oblique objects. (54a) is a common clause type: the subject is morphologically null, and the oblique object is marked by the disjoint anaphor *y*. In this example, the subject is topical (see Leer 1990, Saxon and Rice 1993, Thompson 1989a). In (54b), on the other hand, it is the verb that contains the disjoint anaphor *y*, which now unambiguously marks the subject. This is clear because the verb in (54) is intransitive, with an oblique rather than a direct object. Notice that the oblique object is *b*. Thompson 1989a, 1996b argues that when the disjoint anaphor occurs as a subject, it signals a nonsalient or focus subject, or one that is less salient or topical than the other argument in the sentence. Saxon and Rice 1993, in an examination of structural positions of clausal subjects, argue that assuming a VP-internal position for a clausal subject that triggers the presence of the disjoint anaphor accounts for its presence – it is c-commanded by a non-coreferential third person within its clause – as well as for its semantics – VP-internal subjects are focused or nonsalient whereas VP-external subjects are topics or salient.

Similar facts are found in others of the languages. In each case, the verbs are intransitive, the first example has an unmarked subject, and the second example has the disjoint anaphor as a subject. 'DA' stands for 'disjoint anaphor.'

(55) Ahtna (Kari 1990)
  a. **i**-'eł na-'i-d-yaa
    oblique **disjoint anaphor**-with iterative-epenthetic-voice-stem
    '*He* returned with **him** (DA).' (419)
  b. u-'eł y-a-yaał
    3 ObliqueO-with **disjoint anaphor Subject**-aspect-stem
    '**He** (DA) is walking with *him*.' (419)

(56) Dena'ina (Tenenbaum 1978)
    a. **y-eł**   nu-ta-s-d-yu
       oblique **disjoint anaphor**-with iterative-inceptive-aspect-voice-
                                   stem
       '*She* started coming back with **him** (DA).' (83)
    b. nunigi   v-eł   yu-cheł
       fox   3 ObliqueO-with **disjoint anaphor Subject**-stem
       'The **fog** (DA) was lifting with *her*.' (83)

(57) Tsuut'ina (Cook 1984)
    a.   ɣ-à-'íh
       oblique **disjoint anaphor**-preverb-stem
       '*He* does like **him**.' (201)
    b. m-a-yi-t'íh
       3 ObliqueO-preverb-**disjoint anaphor Subject**-stem
       '**It** (DA) does like *him*.' (201)

The major point of these examples with oblique objects is to show that the disjoint anaphor can, in some languages, function as either subject or object inflection, depending on syntactic and semantic factors. Subject inflectional forms are found when the argument with which the inflection is linked is clause external; object forms occur with any internal argument regardless of its syntactic function, subject or object.

     I next consider transitive verbs.

(58) Koyukon
       a. ye-tl'o   ye-ghee-ł-taanh
          oblique **disjoint anaphor**-to   **disjoint anaphor Object**-aspect-
                                           valence-stem
          '*He* gave **it** (DA) to **him/her/it** (DA).' (Leer 1990:28)
       b. ye-tl'o   be-ye-ghee-ł-taanh'
          oblique **disjoint anaphor**-to   3 Object-**disjoint anaphor Subject**-
                                           aspect-valence-stem
          '**He** (DA) gave *him* to **her/it** (DA).' (Leer 1990:28)
       c. be-tl'o   ye-ye-ghee-ł-taanh
          3 Object-to   **disjoint anaphor Object-disjoint anaphor**
                                    Subject-aspect-valence-stem
          '**it** (DA) gave **him** (DA) to *her*; **it** (DA) to *him*.' (Leer 1990:28)
       d. ye-nee-ł-'aanh
          disjoint anaphor Object-qualifier-valence-see
          '*He* is looking at **him** (DA).' (Thompson 1989a:40)

10.3 On Noncanonical Subjects

    e. *b*e-ye-nee-ł'aanh
    3 Object-**disjoint anaphor Subject**-qualifier-valence-see
    'It (DA) is looking at *him*.' (Thompson 1989a:40)

In (58b, e) two object forms, *b* and *y*, appear within the verb. Similar facts are found in other languages, as in (59) and (60).

(59) Ahtna (Kari 1990)
    a. i-na-ł-'aen
       disjoint anaphor Object-qualifier-valence-see
       '*He* is looking at **it/him** (DA).' (86)
    b. *b*i-i-na-ł-'aen
       3 Object-**disjoint anaphor Subject**-valence-see
       'It (DA) is looking at *him*.' (96)

(60) Dena'ina (Tenenbaum 1978)
    a. chi-y-da-ł-yuq
       preverb-disjoint anaphor Object-qualifier-valence-stem
       '*He* (man) killed **him** (man, DA).' (69)
    b. tiqin chi-*ve*-y-da-ł-yuq
       wolf preverb-3 Object-**disjoint anaphor Subject**-qualifier-valence-stem
       '*The wolf* (DA) killed **him**.' (69)

The examples in (58b), (58e), (59b), and (60b) are verbs with internal subjects and topical direct objects. Notice that in these examples, both *b*, representing the direct object, and *y*, representing the internal subject, are present, and occur in the order object-subject.[14] Structurally, these examples can be understood as follows. If the subject is VP-internal (SD in (45)) and the object above it (in OC in (45)), the c-command relationship between the subject and object is one of asymmetrical c-command, with the object c-commanding the subject. A single verb can contain two inflections that are morphologically object forms, namely *b* and *y*, in the order *b-y*, where the first is linked to the object and the second to the subject. Thus, what is generally identified as object marking, or accusative case (Kibrik 1996), more accurately can be said to indicate inflection linked to a VP-internal argument, regardless of its grammatical relation to the verb.

A brief comment on the semantics of the forms (58)–(60) is in order. The sentences in each set express the same propositional content, but differ in informational structure: when the subject is marked by *y*, it is of lower topicality/saliency than the object (Kari 1990, Leer 1990, Thompson 1989a).

The proposed structural account mirrors the semantic facts by placing topical subjects external to the verb phrase and nontopical, focus subjects internal to the verb phrase.

In examples with an internal subject and a direct object, ordering is an interesting issue. First, consider which subjects can be internal. The data is consistent with the claim that only number subjects serve as internal subjects with transitive verbs, and that first/second person subjects never do.[15] The inherent topicality of first and second persons accounts for this: they always meet the conditions for external, or canonical, subjects. Now consider the ordering of the inflectional elements linked to internal subjects and objects. The ordering of inflectional elements is, with an exception to be discussed in section 10.5.2, object-subject. This ordering, then, is identical to the ordering of an external subject with an object: syntactic pressures regulate this ordering.[16]

10.3.6 Interim Summary 2

I have presented four arguments for two subject positions, based on idioms, incorporation, word order, and anaphora; see Saxon and Rice 1993 for further discussion. Not all these types of evidence are found in all languages. Idiomatic evidence exists in all languages of the family, while evidence from incorporated nouns is, naturally, limited to those languages with incorporates (chapter 4). The evidence from anaphora varies across the family. In a discussion of the distribution of *y* across the languages, Rice and Saxon 1991 note that several variables are involved in its distribution in a language, including the position of the licensing noun phrase and semantic conditions on canonical subjects. In addition, many other types of evidence point to the existence of two subject positions. These include evidence from the distribution of *y/b* as oblique object inflection, the patterning of the unspecified inflectional morpheme (from Proto-Athapaskan *k'*), and the patterning of the areal morpheme. See Rice, forthcoming a, for discussion of some of these. In the following section, I examine another instance of two inflections licensed by VP-internal arguments, the case of the Navajo semipassives.

10.3.7 Navajo Semipassives

Navajo has a type of passive construction that Young and Morgan 1987 call an agentive passive; this construction has also been called semipassive, passive II, passive B, and impersonal – see Kibrik 1996 for full discussion. I follow Kibrik 1996 in using the term semipassive. This semipassive is illustrated in (61).

10.3 On Noncanonical Subjects

(61) a. Active: 'asdzą́ą́   'ashkii   tá-né-í-z-giz
               woman   boy   preverb-preverb-disjoint
                                       anaphor-aspect-stem
            'The woman washed the boy.' (Kibrik 1996:270)
    Semipassive: 'ashkii   táá-*bí*-'-dí-s-giz
                         boy   preverb-*b Object*-**unspecified**-middle-
                                  aspect-stem
            'The boy was washed.' (Kibrik 1996:270)

  b. Active: ni-sh-hash
                        2sg Object-aspect-bite
                        'It bit you sg.' (Kibrik 1996:280)
    Semipassive: *n*i-'-di-sh-ghash
                        2sg *Object*-**unspecified**-middle-aspect-bite
                        'You have been bitten.' (Kibrik 1996:280)

  c. Semipassive: *sh*i -'-di-l-zhééh
                        1sg Object-**unspecified**-middle-voice/valence-shave
                        'I am being shaved.' (YM 143)
                        *n*i-'-di-l-zhééh
                        2sg Object-**unspecified**-middle-voice/valence-shave
                        'You sg. are being shaved.' (YM 143)
                        *b*i-'-di-l-zhééh
                        b Object-**unspecified**-middle-voice/valence-shave
                        'He is being shaved.' (YM 143)
                        *nih*i-'-di-l-zhééh
                        1/2pl Object-**unspecified**-middle-voice/valence-
shave
                        'We/you dpl are being shaved.' (YM 143)

The semipassives are middle voice forms (see chapter 7) with an unspecified subject ' (in boldface in (61)). The theme (italicized in (61)) is animate. Young and Morgan 1987:143 point out that the construction generally requires a human theme, but that logical objects that represent personified animals and inanimate objects in human form (e.g., dolls) may enter into the construction. The construction uses *b* as third person object, and there is an additional morpheme *d* that may relate to middle voice or be a part of the subject in this transitive construction (see also Young and Morgan 1987:143). While much in these passives remains mysterious, one aspect is clear – the unspecified subject is not external, as is also noted by Young and Morgan 1987 and by Kibrik 1996. Two major sources of evidence suggest this. First, the third person object has the form *b* in these examples rather than *y*. The expected object form when the subject is internal to the verb phrase is *b*; see

Rice, forthcoming a, for arguments. Second, the semantics of the unspecified subject suggests that it is VP-internal. As discussed by Thompson 1991, this morpheme is nontopical semantically. If it is true that nontopical arguments are structurally internal to the verb phrase (see section 10.3.5), then its semantics supports this position. The semipassive examples thus indicate the possibility of two internal arguments in Navajo, object and unspecified subject, in that order.

10.3.8 Summary

I have argued that subjects are not a unitary phenomenon in the Athapaskan family: functionally subject marking within the verb may represent Agreement or Number, and structurally subjects may be canonical (VP-external) or noncanonical (VP-internal). While the conditions concerning which subjects can and must be external vary across the family, there are shared patterns – salient/topical subjects are generally external, and agentive human subjects are normally external. Internal subjects tend to be nonsalient, or less salient than some other argument or to represent focus; they are often inanimate. External and internal subjects differ in morphological markings, with external subjects showing subject inflection and internal subjects showing object inflection.

10.4 A Return to the Ordering Questions

This excursus on the positions of clausal subjects was necessary in order to continue discussion of the ordering of pronominal inflection. In this section I examine verbs with two such elements, beginning with verbs with an object and an external subject. The only external subjects that I consider are those marked by NumS. I assume these to be external subjects for two major reasons. The first is morphological – if they were internal, they should have the same form as the objects do, but the marking of subject and object Number is distinct, as can be seen for a number of languages in (62).

(62)

Language	Human plural External	Human plural Internal	Unspecified human External	Unspecified human Internal
Slave	k/g	gi/go/ku	ts'	go
Dogrib	g	gi	ts'	go
Navajo	–	–	j	ho
Koyukon	he	heye/hebe	ts'i	dinaa[17]/hʉ
Tsuut'ina	gi	giyi/gimi	ts'i	gu

10.4 A Return to the Ordering Questions

The second reason for considering NumS inflection to be licensed by an external argument is that the subjects marked by NumS share semantic characteristics with typical external subjects – they are obligatorily human and salient, or topical.[18]

With an exception to be discussed in section 10.5.2, whenever NumS is present in a verb with an object, either NumDO or AgrDO, the ordering is invariably object-subject inflection. This can be seen in the following forms, chosen from a variety of languages, where AgrDO represents first/second person objects and NumDO third person objects.

(63) AgrDO NumS
rá-**se**-**ke**-re-yį-h-t'u
preverb-**1sg Object-human plural Subject**-qualifier-aspect-valence-stem
'They punched me.' (Slave)

(64) NumDO NumS
k'a-**h**a-l-dlaanh
unspecified Object-human plural Subject-aspect-stem
'They had caught (the bear).' (Koyukon; Thompson 1991:65)

With internal subject arguments also, the ordering is object-subject. NumDO references the internal subject; it is labeled NumDO because of its morphological form.

(65) AgrDO NumDO (i.e., object-subject)
ni-'-di-sh-ghash
2sg Object-unspecified Subject-middle-aspect-stem
'You sg. have been bitten.' (Navajo; Kibrik 1996:280)

(66) NumDO NumDO (i.e., object-subject)
ni-**bi**-'-dee-l-tlah
preverb-3 **Object-unspecified Subject**-middle-voice/valence-stem
'He was stopped.' (Navajo; YM 123)
be-ye-nee-ł-'aanh
3 Object-disjoint anaphor Subject-qualifier-valence-stem
'It (DA) is looking at him.' (Koyukon; Thompson 1989a:40)

In the examples discussed so far, the statement that the ordering is object-subject inflection can be maintained. It does not matter if the subject is external (morphologically NumS) or internal (morphologically NumDO), nor does it matter whether the object is first/second person (AgrDO) or third person (NumDO). Whenever two pronouns co-occur, they appear in the order object-subject.

(67) subject > object inflection

This hierarchy is stated syntactically, in terms of grammatical relations, rather than in semantic terms, whether thematic or aspectual. This is because all subjects behave alike in terms of ordering, independent of their information status – topic or focus – or their thematic role – agentive subjects of verbs like 'hit' and 'dance' and theme subjects of verbs like 'grow' and 'be good' have identical subject marking despite their different relationships to the verb.

10.5 Problems for Object-Subject Inflection Ordering

While object-subject inflection is the common ordering, a number of exceptions exist. These are of four types. First is the construction 'third person plural acting on third person singular.' Second is the construction 'unspecified subject acting on third person singular' in some languages. Third are phonologically conditioned metatheses, and fourth is the problem of ordering in Hupa and Kato.

10.5.1 Third Person Plural Acting on Third Person Singular

The existence of an inflectional form meaning 'third person human plural acting on third person singular' provides the first problem for the claim that pronominal ordering is always object-subject. I begin by considering examples of this construction from a variety of languages. One might expect to find the ordering *y-k* and its cognates, with the disjoint anaphor followed by the third person human plural Number. But this is not what occurs. Instead, the subject precedes the object, as in (68). In some of these languages, a form is found that transparently combines the third person human plural subject and the disjoint anaphor (Chilcotin, Ahtna, Dena'ina, Tsuut'ina, Koyukon); in other cases, a portmanteau exists (Slave, Dogrib, Tututni). I do not attempt to gloss this form yet, and simply repeat its phonological form, in boldface, in the gloss.

(68) a. Chilcotin
        na-**jeye**-ni-lh-tin
        iterative-**jeye**-aspect-valence-stem
        'They brought him back.' (Cook 1996:104)

10.5 Problems for Object-Subject Inflection Ordering

b. Ahtna
 kii-na-ł-'aen
 kii-qualifier-valence-stem
 'They are looking at it.' (Kari 1990:229)

c. Dena'ina
 qey-tu-ł-jeq'
 qey-inceptive/aspect-valence-stem
 'They will punch him several times.' (Tenenbaum 1978:76)

d. Tsuut'ina
 gìyì-'ás
 gìyì-stem
 'They'll kick him.' (Cook 1984:200)

e. Koyukon
 go dinaa yił   sołt'aanh yił   **hay**i-nee-ł-'aanh
 this man conjunction woman conjunction **hay**i-qualifier-
                                          valence-stem
 'This man and woman are looking at him.' (Thompson 1991:70)

f. Slave
 rá-**ki**-re-yį-h-t'u
 preverb-**ki**-qualifier-aspect-valence-stem
 'They hit him/her.' (Rice 1989)

g. Dogrib
 ts'èko   nà-**gi**-rį-į-kà
 woman   preverb-**gi**-qualifier-aspect-stem
 'The women slapped him.' (Saxon 1995)

h. Tututni
 xi-ɣə-'ał
 xi-aspect-stem
 'They two are carrying it.' (Golla 1976:223)

The marking of 'third person plural on third person singular' is complex, involving a *y* component and a *g* (*j, q, k, h, x*) component. The problem is that they come in an unexpected order, *g-y*, or subject-object inflection. This is clearest in the forms from Chilcotin, Tsuut'ina, Koyukon, Ahtna, and Dena'ina; it is slightly less clear in Slave, Dogrib, and Tututni, where a phonological reduction has occurred.

While this form appears to be a counterexample to the claim that morpheme ordering is object-subject inflection, there are further considerations that are important in determining its status. In the following discussion, I follow Saxon 1995 on Dogrib and argue that this item, which I will refer to as *kii*, is complex, but not as a consequence of a metathesis of subject and object inflection (see, e.g., Cook 1996 for this point of view). It is rather a plural disjoint anaphor, and requires that a nonplural object be distinct in reference from any member of the plural subject. It does not consist of object inflection followed by subject inflection (or vice versa), but is rather an anaphoric object with plural marking. If *k* and its cognates simply mark human plural and are not marked as subjects, the positions can be seen as a consequence of scope: the disjoint anaphor and the human plural are in a relationship such that the latter modifies the former. The ordering human plural-disjoint anaphor is therefore expected since the plural modifies the disjoint anaphor. In view of this conclusion, I will refer to this item as a plural disjoint anaphor.

So far I have given examples of verbs with third person plural subjects and third person singular direct objects containing the *kii* form. The form has an interesting distribution: it appears not only as a subject-direct object combination, but also as the possessor of a nonsubject and as the object of a postposition when the subject is third person plural and the other argument is third person singular. This can be seen in (69) and (70).

(69) Third person human plural subject acting on third singular possessor
    a. Slave
       ki-tá   rá-ke-re-yi̧-h-t'u
       pl disjoint anaphor-father   preverb-human plSubject-qualifier-aspect-valence-stem
       'They hit his/her father.' (Rice 1989:210)
       gi-mǫ   ts'ę́   ná-dí
       pl disjoint anaphor-mother   to   preverb-stem
       'They are helping his/her mother.'
    b. Dogrib
       Joe hi̧ Moise hi̧ **gi**-tà   gha   elà
       and   and   **pl disjoint anaphor**-father   for   boat
       whe-h-tsi̧
       aspect-valence-stem
       'Joe and Moise built a canoe for her father.' (Saxon 1995)
    c. Chilcotin
       gwanes   guyen   **jeye**-lhghedex   gatŝ'in
       that is why   that person   **pl disjoint anaphor**-siblings   everyone
       yax
       that way
       na-**jeye**-ni-lh-tin
       iterative-**pl disjoint anaphor**-aspect-valence-stem
       'That is why his brothers and sisters, everyone, brought him back.'
       (Cook 1996:104)

10.5 Problems for Object-Subject Inflection Ordering

(70) Third person plural subject acting on third singular oblique
    a. Slave
        ki-ts ę̃   rá-ke-dí
        pl disjoint anaphor-to   preverb-human plSubject-stem
        'They are helping him/her.' (Rice 1989:273)
    b. Dogrib
        gi-t'à   elà   dè-h-ɬi
        pl disjoint anaphor-with   boat   qualifier/aspect-valence-stem
        'They stitched canoes with it.' (Saxon 1995)
    c. Tsuut'ina
        giyi-nák'à   γi-yáɬ
        pl disjoint anaphor-behind   aspect-stem
        'They are walking behind him.' (Cook 1996:101)
    d. Ahtna
        kii-gha   l-soɬ
        pl disjoint anaphor-about   voice/valence-stem
        'They are lying about it.' (Kari 1990:229)
    e. Dena'ina
        qey-ch'   ta-z-datl'
        pl disjoint anaphor-to   inceptive-aspect-stem
        'They started walking towards him.' (Tenenbaum 1978:83)

These examples provide a clue that this pronominal is unusual. Notice that although these verbs have semantic third person plural human subjects, plural human subject inflection need not occur in the verb, as shown in (69b–c) and (70b–e): the inflection appears as object of a postposition and possessor, where subject marking is completely unexpected.

These data show another interesting characteristic of *kii*. Not only does it occur in unexpected positions, but, in these positions, it can appear together with the human plural number subject *k* and cognates, as in (69a) and (70a). If it were a concatenation of *y* and *k*, the co-occurrence of *kii* and *k* would be surprising. I return to this point.

The facts are still more complex, at least for some languages. The following patterns are found, as illustrated by Tsuut'ina and Dogrib; see Cook 1996 for discussion.

(71) Tsuut'ina (underlying rather than surface forms) (Cook 1996)
    a. γi-nák'à   gi-γi-yáɬ
       disjoint anaphor-behind   **human plural Subject**-aspect-stem
       'They are walking behind him.' (101)

    b. **giɣi**-nàk'à   gi- ɣi-yáɬ
       pl disjoint anaphor-behind   **human plural Subject**-aspect-stem
       'They are walking behind him.' (101)
    c. **giɣi**-nák'à   ɣi-yáɬ
       pl disjoint anaphor-behind   aspect-walk
       'They are walking behind him.' (101)

(72) Dogrib (Cook 1996)
    a. ye-ghà-ge-e-nda
       disjoint anaphor-preverb-**human pl Subject**-qualifier-stem
       'They look at him/her.' (103)
    b. **gi**-ghà-ge-e-nda
       pl disjoint anaphor-preverb-**human pl Subject**-qualifier-stem
       'They look at him/her.' (103)
    c. **gi**-ghà-e-nda
       pl disjoint anaphor-preverb-qualifier-stem
       'They look at him/her.' (103)

These examples show that with oblique objects, one of three constructions is possible. The perhaps expected construction contains a third person plural human subject and the disjoint anaphor as object, as in (71a) and (72a). In addition, the plural disjoint anaphor can occur as oblique object, either with the human plural subject, as in (71b) and (72b) or without, as in (71c) and (72c).

These properties of *kii* suggest that it is not simply a concatenation of the disjoint anaphor and human plural subject inflection. If it were, it should not be able to occur in positions that it does (e.g., possessor, oblique), and it should not be able to co-occur with human plural subject inflection as this is already included within the form.

Saxon, in a detailed analysis of *kii*, argues that its Dogrib realization, *gi*, is a plural disjoint anaphor, parallel to the disjoint anaphor *y*. She further assumes that it is structurally complex, containing both the disjoint anaphor as head and the human plural element as this head's specifier. Consider the nature of an anaphor – it is dependent on another argument. The reflexive indicates that the subject and the second argument are coreferential, the disjoint anaphor signals that the subject (or c-commanding argument) and the second argument are non-coreferential, and the plural disjoint anaphor indicates that a plural subject and a second argument are non-coreferential. If the item under question is an anaphor, the distribution can be accounted for.

10.5 Problems for Object-Subject Inflection Ordering

It, like the reflexive and reciprocal, cannot be a subject.[19] The occurrence of human plural subject inflection with the disjoint anaphor when the anaphoric relationship holds between the subject and an oblique object or possessor is also accounted for, as the morpheme in question is an anaphor and thus can co-occur with a subject.

The idea that the human plural component simply marks human plural number and not subject is reinforced by patterns found in several languages. For instance, the human plural component can combine with other number objects, as in (73).

(73) a. Dena'ina (Tenenbaum 1978)
qev third person plural object (= *qe* human plural + *v* object)
qev-ch'-ghi-'an
qev-HSubject-aspect-stem
'We saw them.' (75)
b. Tsuut'ina (Cook 1984)
gimi third person plural object (= *gi* human plural + *mi* object)
gìmì-ts'à-'ás
gimi-HSubject-stem
'Somebody will kick them.' (200)
c. Slave (Rice 1989)
kede third person plural reflexive possessor (= *ke* human plural + *de* reflexive)
kede-sǫ ts'ę́ 'e-ke-de-tl'é
kede-grandmother to unspecified O-human plural-qualifier-stem
'They write to their grandmother.' (210)
d. Koyukon (Thompson 1990)
hebe third person plural object (= *he* human plural + *be* object)
hebe-tl-'aah
hebe-valence-stem
'I am looking at them.'
e. Babine-Witsuwit'en (Hargus 1995a)
hebə third person plural object (= *he* human plural + *bə* object)
hebə-z-ni-z-gwət
hebə-human Subject-qualifier-aspect-stem
'We poke them in the face.'

In all of these compound prefixes, it is striking that the human plural number portion precedes the other pronominal, which clearly marks number nonsubjects. If the human plural number is not a subject lexically but is unmarked for category, these constructions can be understood – the human plural number precedes the other pronominal because it modifies the pronominal.

There is one distributional gap that I have not yet discussed. In a transitive construction, *gi* and cognates never occur with either the human plural subject or the disjoint anaphor.

(74) Dogrib (Saxon 1995)
    a. **gi-è-h-tsį**   'They made it.'
    b. *ye-ge-h-tsį   (*disjoint anaphor + plural human subject)
    c. *ge-yè-h-tsį   (*plural human subject + disjoint anaphor)
    d. ***gi-ge-h-tsį**   (*plural disjoint anaphor + plural human subject)
    e. ***gi-yè-h-tsį**   (*plural disjoint anaphor + disjoint anaphor)

When a disjoint anaphoric relationship holds between a plural subject and an oblique object, as in (71) and (72) or a possessor, as in (69), variation is possible; when this relationship holds between a plural subject and a direct object, as in (74), variation is not found. Saxon 1995, in her analysis of Dogrib, argues that the disjoint anaphoric element must be nondistinct from NumS and so cannot occur with it, and it cannot co-occur with the disjoint anaphor *y* because they occupy the same position. As Saxon points out, in other contexts the disjoint anaphor is not part of the verb, so there is no conflict between the overt expression of the disjoint anaphor (as oblique or possessor) and that of the human plural subject.

I have argued that the 'human plural acting on third person' forms are not a concatenation of a subject and an object, but rather the human plural number element modifies the object. The form is a plural disjoint anaphor, consisting of plural marking and an anaphor, and is paralleled by other combinataions of the human plural with number object items. If the number element specifies the nature of the anaphor, the order plural-anaphor is not so surprising as it reflects the scopal relationship between the items.

10.5.2 Unspecified Subjects

A second counterexample to the generalization that subject inflection follows object inflection is found in some Alaskan languages, where when a verb has unspecified/indefinite internal subject inflection and a disjoint anaphor as direct object, they appear in the order subject-object. Examples are given in (75). The subject in these examples is a reflex of Proto-Athapaskan *c'*, which is labelled indefinite, unspecified, or of low topicality in the Athapaskan literature (see Thompson 1991 in particular).

10.5 Problems for Object-Subject Inflection Ordering

(75) Ahtna (Kari 1990)
    a. **c'i-i**-n-a-ł-'aen
       unspecified Subject-disjoint anaphor-qualifier-aspect-valence-stem
       'Something (animal c') saw him (i).' (121)
    b. ka-**c'i-i**-d-ghi-ggaats'
       preverb-**unspecified Subject-disjoint anaphor**-qualifier-aspect-stem
       'It (animal c') tore him (i) up.' (180)
    Koyukon
    c. **k'e-ye**-nee-ł-'aanh
       unspecified Subject-disjoint anaphor-qualifier-valence-stem
       'Something (k') is looking at him/her (y).' (Thompson 1989a:74)

Thompson 1991 argues that the unspecified subject indicates low topicality, is indefinite and nonreferential, and is used for unimportant inferrable information. In featural terms, I assume that it is a Number element that is nonspecific and nondefinite. It is unmarked for gender (it can be human or nonhuman depending on context, but is generally nonhuman; see Thompson 1991). The noun that licenses this element is, I assume, internal to the verb phrase. Its semantics is consistent with this analysis, as is its morphosyntactic patterning across the family. A VP-internal position for indefinites is common; see, for instance, Diesing 1992 for detailed discussion.

It is only the disjoint anaphor y object inflection that enters into this unusual ordering with k' unspecified; with b object inflection, the order is the expected object-subject, as the following Koyukon example illustrates.

(76) b Object $+ k$' unspecified Subject
    dinaa yił   sołt'aanh yił   **bi-k'**i-nee-ł-'aanh
    man conjunction woman   conjunction **3 Object-k' Subject**-qualifier-valence-stem
    'The man and the woman are looking at him.' (Thompson 1991:70)

The ordering unspecified subject-object is reminiscent of the third person plural subject acting on third person singular object discussed in section 10.5.1. However, it does not show the full range of patterning of the plural disjoint anaphor. For example, if the unspecified subject occurs with a disjoint anaphor oblique object, the expected forms are found rather than a special form parallel to *kii*.

(77) Ahtna (Kari 1990:423)
   i-tse   c'e-te-z-yaa
   disjoint anaphor-ahead   **unspecified Subject**-inceptive-aspect-stem
   'It (animal c') escaped, going ahead of him (i).'

Treating the odd ordering of the internal unspecified subject and the disjoint anaphor as a consequence of a complex lexical entry is therefore not an appropriate move.

I would like to suggest a different account for the ordering of the unspecified internal subject inflection and the disjoint anaphor. I propose that this ordering is attributable to properties of nonspecific/indefinite subjects. In the following discussion, I use the terms specific and definite interchangeably, and the terms nonspecific and indefinite as well. While there are important differences between definiteness and specificity, they are not relevant to the discussion here.

We have seen that referentiality, or presuppositionality, plays an important role in Athapaskan languages, with inherently referential or presupposed subjects (first and second persons) taking subjects that are not inherently referential or presupposed (number) in their scope; see section 10.1. Consider now the semantics of the inflectional elements under discussion in this section. As discussed in section 10.1, number is inherently nonreferential, or non-presuppositional, becoming referential through binding to an antecedent. The nonspecific/indefinite marker is never referential, however – it never has a specific, definite antecedent. Thus, when a number object and an unspecified subject co-occur, the situation parallels that with number subjects versus first/second person subjects. The nonspecific/indefinite marker is never referential, while referentiality is established by context for the third person. The ordering of these elements in languages such as Ahtna and Koyukon is thus reminiscent of the hierarchy referential > nonreferential, realized here as specific contextual reference > nonspecific/indefinite contextual reference.

So far, the ordering of subject and object inflection has suggested the hierarchy subject > object; the hierarchy referential > nonreferential was important in establishing the ordering of the two subject types. In languages where the unspecified subject licenses the disjoint anaphor, the hierarchy specific contextual reference > nonspecific/indefinite contextual reference interacts with the subject > object hierarchy, and the former is seen to be more important than the latter: an object can have scope over a subject just in case the subject is nonspecific/indefinite/nonreferential and the object is specific/contextually referential.

10.5 Problems for Object-Subject Inflection Ordering

One might ask why a nonspecific/indefinite subject precedes with *y* as object, but follows *b*; see the example in (76). The reason for the difference is that when the object is *b*, the subject is conjoined. I venture that this nominal subject cannot be internal to the verb phrase. Its Number marker is therefore forced to occupy the external subject position, and normal order obtains.

The existence of subject-object inflection ordering initially appears to be problematic and to lend support to the template hypothesis. However, the semantics of the subject-object ordering is constrained – it is found only when both a nonspecific/indefinite subject and a focused direct object are internal to the verb phrase and only in some languages. In other languages with internal unspecified subjects and specific direct objects, the ordering object-subject inflection is maintained, as in the Navajo semipassive form in (78) (see section 3.7). Recall that the object is *b* and the subject unspecified/indefinite'.

(78) **bi-'-d-oo-l-zį́į'**
Object-unspecified Subject-middle-aspect-voice/valence-stem
'S/he was blessed.' (YM 212)

I have hypothesized that two interacting factors are involved in determining subject position. One is syntactic: subjects have objects in their scope. However, specificity/definiteness is also a factor, and specific/definite/contextually referential forms have scope over nonspecific/indefinite/nonreferential ones. These principles yield contradictory results for nonspecific subjects and specific objects: subject > object requires the subject to have scope over the object, while specific/definite reference > nonspecific/indefinite reference requires the specific object to have scope over the nonspecific subject. The languages differ as to which hierarchy takes precedence. Ahtna and Koyukon prefer the semantic constraint, and Navajo prefers the syntactic one. Notice that when the order object-subject is disrupted, this occurs in only a very limited way and is controlled by just two factors. This fact argues against the template hypothesis, where random, arbitrary orderings of object and subject marking are allowed; it supports the scopal hypothesis, where universal principles determine ordering.[20]

10.5.3 Metathesis

Number material may be subject to metathesis. In Navajo, an unspecified human subject *j*, with a phonologically conditioned allomorph *zh*, called 'fourth person' in the Navajo literature, and an unspecified object ' are subject to metathesis under phonological conditions, namely when they precede a consonant beginning a functional prefix. This can be seen in the following examples.

(79) a. order: 'unspecified object + *j* subject
   n-'-**ji**-ł-go'
   'unspecified pokes around (something)' (YM 550–552)
   b. order: *j* (*zh*) subject + ' unspecified object
   dá-da-**zh**-'-di-nil
   'unspecified plugs up (holes)' (YM 297)
   c. order: *j* (*zh*) subject + ' unspecified object
   da-**zh**-'-d-oo-dis
   'They will be spinning (something).'

Both object-subject inflection and subject-object inflection orders are found, with the conditioning being morphophonological. The human subject is unmarked for specificity and definiteness, while the object is nonspecific and indefinite lexically. Thus, there is no reason to expect ordering other than object-subject. Moreover, assuming that the human subject *j* is always external to the verb phrase and the nonspecific/indefinite object is internal to the verb phrase, the ordering subject-object is not expected on any semantic grounds. In this case then, scope has nothing to say about the ordering, as it predicts the invariant ordering object-subject; instead phonological conditions take precedence over semantic ones to create the variable ordering.

Kari 1990:27 reports a similar phenomenon in Ahtna. He suggests that the unmarked ordering of the human subject and unspecified object is subject-object. However, in certain phonological environments, the reverse is found. The forms in (80)–(83) compare the ordering of *c'* unspecified object with different Number prefixes – ordering is variable depending on phonological conditions. The unspecified object and unspecified subject both have several phonologically predictable forms; see Kari 1990:27.

(80) Human plural subject *k*:
   Object-subject

   a. **i'**-**ke**-yaan
      i' object + *k* subject
      'They are eating something.'
   b. **i'**-**h**-t-a-yiił
      i' object + *h* subject
      'They will eat something.'

10.5 Problems for Object-Subject Inflection Ordering

    c. n-'-**ke**-l-ye'
       ' object + *k* subject
       'They are playing.'

(81) Human plural subject *k*:
Subject-object
h-c'e-yaan
h subject + *c'e* object
'They are eating something.'

(82) Unspecified human subject *ts*'
Object-subject

    a. **i**-'s-t-a-yiił
       i object + *'s* subject
       'We will eat something.'
    b. na-**y**-'s-ghi-ghaen
       y object + *'s* subject
       'We packed something down.'

(83) Unspecified human subject **ts'**
Subject-object
's-c'e-yaan
's subject + *c'* object
'We are eating something.'

Kari proposes that the unspecified subject and object metathesize under the following morphophonological conditions:[21]

(84) ts' + c'   → c' + ts'/ _ CV [([boundary before voice/valence)
    subject + object → object + subject

These two prefixes are reordered to yield object-subject order under the morphophonological condition that they precede an open syllable followed by voice/valence and stem. Kari also notes some dialect variation in the ordering of these morphemes.

    In both Navajo and Ahtna, morphophonological metathesis disrupts the normal order of morphemes. The surface order is controlled not by semantic factors, but by morphophonological factors. These facts do not favor a template, where ordering is predicted to be fixed arbitrarily. But they also fail to support the scope hypothesis, where ordering is predicted to be fixed by semantic or syntactic factors. Instead, morphophonological requirements take precedence over semantic or syntactic ones, obscuring the basic order.

10.5.4 Hupa and Kato: Subject-Object Ordering

Two Pacific Coast languages, Hupa and Kato, present problems for the claims made so far about ordering of object and subject inflection. In Kato, third person subject pronominals precede object pronominals, while in Hupa, the order of object pronominals and third person subjects is mixed, with subject-object order with some objects and object-subject with others.[22] I argue that the status of the third person pronouns in Hupa and Kato differs from that in the languages surveyed so far – they pattern as lexical items rather than as functional items.

Before examining questions of ordering, I survey the facts of Hupa. (I focus on Hupa because it is better documented.) First, as in other languages, first and second person subjects are at the right edge of the functional items, as in (85) (Golla 1970).

(85) a. 1sg Subject   wi-**W**-dahł   'I run along.' (69)
    b. 2sg Subject   si-**n**-da   'You sg. are sitting.' (71)
    c. 1pl Subject   k'yi-**di**-yan   'We eat.' (71)
    d. 2pl Subject   '-**oh**-te'č'   'You pl. come to lie down.' (72)

Third person subjects precede qualifiers and aspect. In addition to the general and human deictic illustrated in (86), Golla 1970 identifies a specific deictic and a place deictic, which I ignore in the following discussion.

(86) a. General deictic *yi*
       yi-xi-nehW 'It speaks.' (98)
    b. Human deictic *ch'i*
       yeh-**ch'i**-wiN-yay 'He went inside.' (100)

According to Golla 1970, *yi* marks a nonhuman subject capable of initiating an action and *ch'i* marks a human subject. The differences between null marking, *yi*, and *ch'i* are sometimes subtle and have to do with semantic factors; see Golla 1970, 1997, Rice and Saxon 1993, Thompson 1989a, and the following for discussion.

Golla divides objects into first/second and third person objects, illustrated in (87) and (88), respectively.

(87) a. *Wi*   first person singular
      ya:-**W**-oh-ł-tiW
      'You pl. pick me up.' (103)

10.5 Problems for Object-Subject Inflection Ordering

    b. *ni*   second person singular
       ni-W-yo'
       'I like you sg.' (104)
    c. *noh*   first/second person plural
       noh-W-yo'
       'I like you pl.' (104)
       noh-ch'i-ɫ-ca:n
       'He sees us/you pl.' (104)

(88) a. Ø   general deictic object
       de:-di-ŋ-'aW
             de: 'into fire' + d 'aspect' + ŋ 2sg S
       'You sg. put (single object) into the fire.' (105)
    b. *xwi*   human deictic object
       na:-**xwe**:-wa:s
       'I have shaved him.' (106)
       no-y-**xo**-ne:-yoh
       'It (dog) barks at him.' (107)
    c. *k'yi*   specific deictic object
       k'yi-W-wahs
       'I am whittling (something).' (107)

Golla 1970:56 proposes the order deictic subject-object for Hupa. Some examples are given in (89).

(89) a. **yi**-W**i**-ɫ-cin
       yi general deictic Subject + *Wi* 1sg Object
       'It sees me.' (99)
    b. ya-'-**k'yi**-ta-'aw
       'deictic human Subject + *k'y* unspecified Object
       'They sing.' (99)
    c. 'i-na-'-**Wi**-s-te:n
       'deictic human Subject + *Wi* 1sg Object
       'She raised me to standing position.' (103)
    d. **yi**-**Wi**-wi-ɫ-tehɫ
       yi general deictic Subject + *Wi* 1sg Object
       'It carries me along.' (103)
    e. na-'-**xo**-wi-Da:s
       'deictic human Subject + *xwi* human Object
       'He has shaved him.' (106)

f. no-**y-xo**-ne:-yoh
   y general deictic Subject + *xwi* human Object
   'It (dog) barks at him.' (107)
g. **ch'i-Wi-ł**-kis
   ch'i deictic human Subject + *Wi* 1sg Object
   'He hits me.' (1985:44)
h. **ch'i-xo-ł**-kis
   ch'i deictic human Subject + *xo* human Object
   'He hits him.' (Golla 1985:44)

With other objects (second person singular, first/second person plural), the order is object-subject.

(90) a. **ni-ch'**i-wi-ł-tehł
   ni 2sg Object + *ch'i* deictic human Subject
   'He carried you sg. along.' (104)
b. **noh-č'**i-ł-ca:n
   noh 1pl/2pl Object + *ch'i* deictic human Subject
   'He sees us/you pl.' (104)
c. 'a:-ya-**noh-č'**i-lah
   noh 1pl/2pl Object + *ch'i* deictic human Subject
   'They treated us/you pl. so.' (105)

The reciprocal partially precedes and partially follows.

(91) *n-łi* reciprocal
   (ya)-**n-ch'i-łi**-kis
   reciprocal-deictic human Subject-reciprocal
   'They hit each other.' (Golla, personal communication, 1997)

In sum, Hupa differs from the other languages in that the ordering of subject and object is not fixed – depending on the person of the object, it may precede or follow a third person subject.

Kato exhibits only subject-object order, suggesting two separate questions. The first concerns why the pronominals appear in Hupa and Kato in the order subject-object and the second concerns why there are cases where Hupa maintains the order object-subject (assuming that object-subject order is conservative).

I examine the second question first. The ordering object-subject in Hupa can perhaps be explained as the result of phonologically conditioned metathesis. The second person objects and the *n* part of the reciprocal, which all precede third person subjects, begin with a nasal; none of the other objects do.

10.5 Problems for Object-Subject Inflection Ordering

Nasals show other odd conditioning. For one thing, expected long vowels are not found before an object beginning with a nasal; for another, a nasal ending a lexical item sometimes appears after rather than before a following lexical item (Golla 1996:372). However, metathesis does not seem to be particularly motivated here; see Kibrik 1995 for discussion. An alternative hypothesis is that these forms show a grammaticized person hierarchy – providing a special position for second persons shows deference on the part of the speaker. But there is no particular evidence for this solution either. I will not attempt to answer the question of why only certain object pronouns precede the subjects in Hupa. Instead I focus on the first question – why is the order of the pronominals subject-object in Kato and, often, in Hupa?[23]

Given that Hupa and Kato differ from other Athapaskan languages in their ordering of objects and third person subjects, one must question whether the ordering object-subject is globally uniform. Perhaps it is idiosyncratic that the ordering is so consistently object-subject, and small clues in other languages for differences in ordering should lead us to expect the Hupa case, where the ordering must be stipulated, not just by category but by particular morpheme within a category. While yielding to stipulated ordering, and thus a template, is a possibility, some facts suggest that Hupa and Kato differ from the other languages in fundamental ways.

Hupa/Kato *ch'/tc'* differs from its cognates in many languages in two major ways. First, Thompson 1989a, b identifies the general form in Athapaskan languages as having the following range of functions: unspecified or indefinite human subject, proximate third person human subject (with specific and definite reference), first person plural subject, and second person deferential subject. In Hupa/Kato, on the other hand, this pronominal is referential, indexing only a discourse-prominent third person. Second, the Hupa/Kato cognate has a special form after a vowel-final disjunct prefix and before a consonant, reducing to a glottal stop, as illustrated for Hupa in (92).

(92) a. Word-initial
    ch'i-qa:l   'He walks along.' (Golla 1985:40)
  b. Following a consonant
    yeh-**ch'i**-win-yay   'He went in.' (Golla 1970:100)
  c. Preceding a vowel
    no:-**ch'**-o:-tiwh   'Let him put it (stick) down.' (Golla 1985:40)
  d. Following a vowel, preceding a consonant
    no-'-tiwh   'He puts it down.' (Golla 1985:40)
    no-'-ni-n-tan   'He put it (stick) down.' (Golla 1985:91)

Functional items do not show similar reductions to a consonantal form in similar environments. For instance, the vowels in boldface in (93) are always present despite being in the reduction environment just mentioned.

(93) a. ch'i-**di**-win-ta:n   'He took off, out.' (Golla 1970:41)
     b. ch'i-**ti**-na:wh   'He goes off.' (Golla 1970:49)
     c. ch'i-**ɬi**-xan   'She is sweet.' (Golla 1995)
     d. na-**ni**-W-cis te: 'I'll see you sg. again.' (Golla 1996:372)

In addition, the consonantal form of the pronoun appears only after a lexical item, as shown in (94).

(94) a. Following a lexical item
       'a-'-de'ine'
       '*a* 'thus' + *ch'i* human subject
       'He always said.' (Golla 1995)
    b. Following a functional item
       mi-ni-**ch'**i-s-loy'
       ni 2sg. object + *ch'i* human subject
       'He has tied you to it.' (Golla 1970:104)

While the cognate does exhibit allomorphy in some languages, the conditioning factors differ. For instance, in Babine-Witsuwit'en, the cognate item has two forms, *ts'ə* and *z*. The consonantal form occurs, as in Hupa and Kato, between a vowel and a consonant, but is found regardless of whether the preceding item is functional or lexical (Hargus 1995a).

(95) a. Preceding lexical item
       we-**z**-nə-l-gət
       'We're scared.'
    b. Preceding functional item
       həbə-**z**-ni-z-gwət
       'We poke them in face.'

In Navajo, too, the cognate morpheme has two major forms, one with a vowel and one without. Once again, the form without the vowel occurs between a vowel and a consonant, and the vowel may belong to a functional or lexical item.

The Hupa/Kato *ch'* subject thus patterns differently from a functional item in that it has a vowelless allomorph, while functional items in general do not. This vowelless allomorph is restricted in its distribution, which is determined by a combination of purely phonological factors (it must be preceded by a

10.5 Problems for Object-Subject Inflection Ordering

vowel and followed by a consonant) and structural factors (the vowelless form occurs only after a lexical item).

The subject *y* patterns similarly to *ch'*. Both have a special function and a special form after a lexical item. The *y* form has a special meaning, being used to refer to old people, outsiders, babies, boys, old people, dogs, prehuman beings, and some mythic beings (Goddard 1905); in general it is used to refer to a second third person subject (Golla 1997). The forms in (96) illustrate that *y*, like *ch'*, has a reduced counterpart *y*, which appears in the same environment as the reduced counterpart of *ch'*.

(96) Reduced form in V__C environment, where V is part of a lexical item
    a. ya-**y**-ky'a:n   'bunch of animals are eating' (Golla 1995)
       na-**y**-xi-ne:wh   'It speaks.' (Golla 1995)
    Full form in word-initial position
    c. **yi**-xi-ne:wh   'It speaks.' (Golla 1995)
       yi-xo-ne-ł-'ing   'It (dog) looks at her.' (Golla 1995)

Third person subjects differ in two ways from their counterparts in other languages. First, meanings are more restricted, and second, the environment for the reduced form is different. In particular, number subject pronouns differ phonologically from functional prefixes – they have reduced forms in certain phonological environments when following a lexical item; functional prefixes do not exhibit reduced forms. The Hupa reduced form fails to occur after a functional item; other languages allow reduced forms regardless of preceding morpheme type.

I have been arguing for a theory that incorporates semantically based structural representations. Such a theory cannot handle both object-subject order, as is general in Athapaskan languages, and subject-object order, as occurs in Hupa/Kato, if the pronominals are the same types of elements across the family. Suppose, however, that Hupa/Kato differ from the rest of the family in a fundamental way in that their third person pronominals are lexical rather than functional items. Some facts of these languages follow straight-forwardly from this analysis. If the pronouns are lexical items in Hupa/Kato, their positioning to the left of objects is expected: they are within the VP, being the highest material in this constituent. This is an appropriate position for subjects; it is the position in which incorporates, including subjects, appear in many Athapaskan languages; see chapter 4 (Hupa/Kato do not have incorporates). The objects, on the other hand, are functional, in the functional part of the verb, and are expected to follow lexical material given the structure that I have proposed. The order follows directly from structure rather than from the subject > object hierarchy.

Some other facts suggest that the Hupa/Kato elements might be pronouns. The question of whether pronominals function as inflection or as arguments has been much debated in the Athapaskan literature as well as in the syntax literature in general. It has been argued, with Athapaskan languages playing an important role in the debate, that languages divide into two types with respect to the status of pronouns: pronominal argument languages, where the pronouns function as arguments, and pronominal agreement languages, where the pronouns function as inflection; see Saxon 1989b for discussion. Pronominal argument languages (see, for instance, Baker 1996, Potter 1997, Sandoval and Jelinek 1989, Speas 1990, Speas and Yazzie 1996, Willie 1991) have been argued to exhibit syntactic properties including the following: optional overt nominals, free word order, discontinuous constituents, rich agreement morphology, internally headed relative clauses, and the absence of nonreferential quantified expressions (such as 'everyone', 'everything', 'no-one', 'nothing', 'every'); see the above references among others on this debate within the Athapaskan family. I have taken the position that in the Athapaskan languages pronouns are inflectional although the languages do exhibit some properties of pronominal argument languages (rich agreement, discontinuous constituents in some, internally headed relative clauses in some, absence of nonreferential quantified expressions). Navajo, the language most commonly argued to exhibit pronominal arguments (Willie 1991, Willie and Jelinek 1996) has been analyzed by others as showing pronominal inflection (see especially Speas 1995, Speas and Yazzie 1996; see also Potter 1997 on the closely related Western Apache).

While Hupa/Kato share most properties with the other languages of the family, they differ in two major ways. First, constituent order in Hupa/Kato is relatively free as compared to that of other Athapaskan languages. In most Athapaskan languages, constituent order within a clause is basically SOV, although postverbal nouns are found under certain circumstances; see Rice 1989 on Slave and Thompson 1996c on Koyukon. Golla 1970 notes that in Hupa constituent order is quite free except that a subject noun phrase precedes an object noun phrase. This is illustrated in (97).

(97) a. S O *ch'*- V
    da'ni-q'ad hay-yo:w   **camehstl'o:n**   **ce**
    just before that   **woman** (subject)   **stone** (object)
    dah-ya-'-a-'aW
    she picks up
    'Just before that woman picks up a stone.' (Golla 1970:296)

more accessible collection edited by Richard Posner, *The Essential Holmes* (Chicago: University of Chicago Press, 1992). Finally, see *Holmes and Frankfurter: Their Correspondence, 1912–1934,* ed. Robert M. Memel and Christine L. Compston (Hanover, N.H.: University Press of New England, 1996).

15 Holmes, "Profession of the Law," 472–73.
16 Holmes's address "Man and the Universe" is reprinted in Novick's edition of the *Collected Works* (vol. 3, 517–18), from which all of the quotations from this essay are taken.
17 This Nietzschean element has been especially well developed in David Luban, "Justice Holmes and the Metaphysics of Individual Restraint," *Duke Law Journal* 44 (1994):449.
18 Posner, "Introduction," in *Essential Holmes,* xxviii.
19 See Sanford Levinson and J. M. Balkin, "The 'Bad Man,' the Good, and the Self-Reliant," *Boston University Law Review* (1998).
20 Ralph Waldo Emerson, "Self-Reliance," in *Essays and Essays: Second Series,* ed. Morse Peckham (Columbus, Ohio: Merrill, 1969), 36–73. (Cited hereafter parenthetically in the text by page number.)
21 David Seipp, "Holmes' Path," *Boston University Law Review* 77 (1997):515, 542.
22 Ralph Waldo Emerson, "History," in Peckham, *Essays,* 9.
23 Thus, it has been suggested, Thoreau was an "embodiment of Emerson – not just his Emersonianism, but the process of its representation or 'acting out' . . . While the modern image of Thoreau stresses his autonomy, he was for his contemporaries (both the disconcerted and the appreciative ones) often a sort of 'applied' version of his mentor [Emerson]," nowhere more so than in his decision not only to write "Resistance to Civil Government," better known as "Civil Disobedience," but also to go to jail to register his refusal to collaborate with slavery. See Albert J. Von Frank, *The Trials of Anthony Burns* (Cambridge, Mass.: Harvard University Press, 1998), 104. Emerson himself, however, did not engage in such disobedience. Still, so fervent was his opposition to the Fugitive Slave Act, passed by Congress in 1850, that he seemed in his public statements to embrace civil disobedience. In an 1854 speech, he pronounced the act an "immoral law" and said that "an immoral law cannot be valid." See Ralph Waldo Emerson, "The Fugitive Slave Act," in *Selected Writings of Ralph Waldo Emerson,* ed. Brooks Atkinson (1950), 866. Nevertheless, Emerson had no illusions that the act was not valid law, and he denounced "[t]his filthy enactment" as "the most detestable law that was ever enacted by a civilized state," stating: "I will not obey it[,] by God." See Robert D. Richardson, *Emerson: The Mind on Fire* (Berkeley and Los Angeles: University of California Press, 1995), 498. Emerson scathingly attacked Massachusetts judges for their willingness to support slavery by enforcing the act. "What avails their learning of veneration? At a pinch, they are no more use than idiots" ("Fugitive Slave Act," 881). And he delivered a strong speech on 18 November 1859 on behalf of John Brown, even as Brown stood condemned to death for his raid on Harpers Ferry. See Emerson, "John Brown," in *Selected Writings,* 879–82.
24 Ralph Waldo Emerson, "Lecture on the Times," in *Complete Works* (Boston: Houghton Mifflin, 1984), vol. 1 at 282.
25 F. O. Matthiessen, *American Renaissance: Art and Expression in the Age of Emerson and Whitman* (New York: Oxford University Press, 1941), 65.
26 Ralph Waldo Emerson, *Journals,* ed. Edward Waldo Emerson and Waldo Emerson Forbes (Boston: Houghton Mifflin, 1909), vol. 7, 112.
27 I cannot resist the temptation to point out that Holmes's single most famous comment, at least within the legal community, is almost certainly his injunction that the life of the law

is rooted in experience rather than logic. Oliver Wendell Holmes, Jr., *The Common Law,* ed. M. Howe (Boston: Little, Brown [1881], 1963), 5. The key question then becomes to define what one means by "experience" and to decide how confident one can be in the existence of determinate lessons to be grasped from experience. If one cannot distinguish with any reliability between "illusion" and "reality," then a law ostensibly predicated on the latter may be just as likely to be reflective of the former.

28 Emerson, "Experience," 257, 259.
29 Emerson to Carlyle, in *The Correspondence of Emerson and Carlyle,* ed. Joseph Slater (New York: Columbia University Press, 1964), 394.
30 Emerson, "Montaigne: or, the Skeptic," in Whicher, *Selections from Ralph Waldo Emerson,* 284–301.
31 Emerson, "Fate," in ibid., 330–52. Cited hereafter parenthetically in the text by page number.
32 Emerson, "Montaigne," 300, 301.
33 Stephen E. Whicher, *Freedom and Fate: An Inner Life of Ralph Waldo Emerson* (Philadelphia: University of Pennsylvania Press, 1953), 124.
34 Felix Frankfurter to Morris Ralph Cohen, 14 May 1929, quoted in Lenora Cohen Rosenfield, *Portrait of a Philosopher: Morris R. Cohen in Life and Letters* (New York: Harcourt, Brace & World, 1962), 255.
35 Holmes to Lewis Einstein, 17 September 1917, in Oliver Wendell Holmes, *The Holmes–Einstein Letters: The Correspondence of Mr. Justice Holmes and Lewis Einstein, 1903–1935,* ed. James Bishop Peabody (New York: St. Martin's, 1962), 148.
36 Grant Gilmore, *The Ages of American Law* (New Haven: Yale University Press, 1977), 49.
37 See Robert Ferguson, "Holmes and the Judicial Figure," *University of Chicago Law Review,* 55 (1988):506.
38 Holmes, "Law and the Court" (1913), in Novick, *Collected Works,* vol. 3, 505–8. Cited hereafter parenthetically by page number in the text.

11

The Path Dependence of the Law

CLAYTON P. GILLETTE*

Any legal system that relies on precedent necessarily confronts conflicting objectives. Precedent constrains decision makers (judges and juries) who might otherwise have idiosyncratic preferences and permits the law's subjects to predict the consequences of their conduct.[1] But precedent simultaneously limits the capacity of decision makers to adjust to new conditions and, arguably, discourages detection of those changes by reducing the need for judges to justify their decisions, as long as they discern no novelty in the case they are deciding.[2] This tension between the conflicting characteristics of a precedential system both explains and disputes a major theme of *The Path of the Law*.[3] Much of that essay portrays tradition in the law as worthy of ridicule. While the villain is often legislators rather than judges, the phrases that Holmes employs to critique the use of tradition as a basis for decision ("the pitfall of antiquarianism" by which "tradition . . . overrides rational policy" [474, 472]) suggest that, in the adjudicative context, reliance on precedent does not simply frustrate legal evolution but subjects legal doctrine to misapplication and inappropriate extension (472–73).[4]

This view, however, appears distorted once one considers a broader range of Holmes's writings as commentator and judge. Notwithstanding the strong language in his celebrated essay, his earlier lectures on the common law and his judicial opinions reveal a more measured and more complex role for precedent in the development of legal doctrine. At times, judicial invocation of tradition, embodied in the practice of following precedent without further investigation into the propriety of the preexisting rule, played the role of scoundrel, but at times Holmes himself invoked tradition as a substitute for ad hoc analysis – the very sin against which *The Path of the Law* admonishes others.

---

* Thanks to Gillian Hadfield, Jody Kraus, Daryl Levinson, Liz Magill, and Steven Walt for comments on previous drafts. I am also grateful for comments I received from participants in conferences on *The Path of the Law* at the University of Iowa College of Law and Boston University School of Law.

My objective here is not to chide Holmes for inconsistency, certainly not for drafting opinions at odds with an essay written in the early stage of his judicial career. Taking *The Path of the Law* in isolation seems a dangerous strategy in evaluating Holmes's beliefs over his lifetime. Moreover, if precedential systems generate the conflicting values that I have mentioned, then there may be times when each of the values trumps the other, so that apparent inconsistencies may simply reflect the reality that a factor that dominated in one context was subordinated in another. Indeed, that is precisely the result implicit in Holmes's conception of economic reasoning in the law, which requires balancing the costs of tradition in any case against its benefits. On that understanding, whether precedent is ultimately overutilized or underutilized depends on the ease with which judges distinguish "bad" precedent from "good" and weigh precedents as applied in a given case.

Thus, rather than simply contrasting Holmes's hostile reaction to and hospitable use of precedent, my objective here is to explore the claim implicit in *The Path of the Law* about the hold that tradition has on law's content. A strong reading of Holmes's antipathy toward tradition would be that substantive doctrine, once established, becomes locked in or frozen. Legal doctrines that would have been adopted were decisionmakers writing on a clean slate are instead rejected or simply not considered. Law, on this theory, does not depend on a rational process directed at implementing a particular social, political, or economic view. Instead, it reflects contingencies that arose for reasons unrelated to current needs but that, once established, determine subsequent developments. Critically, Holmes implies, tradition does not simply displace reason but does so "after first having been misunderstood and having been given a new and broader scope than it had when it had a meaning" ("Path" 473).

The claim that law is path dependent, in the sense that prior doctrine determines the content of current doctrine, may be noncontroversial. Holmes's critique goes farther than a positive claim, however, and asserts that legal doctrines rooted solely in tradition are undesirable. At first glance, the Holmesian objection strikes one as odd. First, it seems incongruous in light of Holmes's insistence that the study of law consists of prediction ("Path" 457). One might imagine that binding litigants to previously adopted positions would enhance rather than diminish the predictive character of legal study.[5] What makes prediction possible is the ability to rely on future adherence to rules previously laid down, and that practice implicitly recommends following tradition. (This is not to deny Judge Richard A. Posner's claim that precedents are not the law, under the prediction theory; the law is only the prediction about what courts will say when a case comes before them.[6] Posner's interpretation suggests that a Holmesian legal system could evolve to meet the necessities of the particular time, as long as one trying to discern "the law" could determine when the need for certainty was overridden by the absence of fit between the preexisting rule and current social preferences. But even this understanding of the prediction theory of law admits that precedents, and hence traditions, "are essential inputs into the predictive process,"[7] in part because we expect judges to begin the analysis of current cases with attention to relevant precedents.)

Second, tradition might be thought to have some connection to desirable legal doctrine. Notwithstanding the overused analogy, much favored by Holmes,[8] to evolutionary biology, adaptations within the legal system are generated by human design, not by any external mechanism. Legal actors have the capacity to change law, either by judicial innovation or by overriding legislation. *The Path of the Law* demonstrates Holmes's recognition of exogenous influences on legal developments: most of our laws are "open to reconsideration upon a slight change in the habit of the public mind" ("Path" 466). Appeals to tradition impede change by privileging the status quo. In the face of the human capacity to create legal change when socially desirable but to retain traditions when they are preferable, one might imagine that the preservation of a tradition constituted some evidence that the tradition serves values important within the society (e.g., efficiency, fairness, commitment to community), and that such values override any adverse effects that the tradition might generate.[9]

Notwithstanding these difficulties with Holmes's apparent animosity toward precedent, I believe that *The Path of the Law* hints at a critique of tradition that we are only today reaching sufficient sophistication to use in striking the proper balance among the competing effects of tradition. In this essay, Holmes adopts a crude form of economic analysis that asks us to compare the social "costs" of legal change with the social benefits.[10] His naive economics assumes that those involved in the weighing of gains and losses make their calculations from the perspective of social welfare. His attack on tradition, therefore, initially poses a puzzle, for a proper judge would apply that same calculus to the decision to follow precedent. If decision making subsumes a process of weighing "the ends of legislation, the means of attaining them, and the cost" ("Path" 474), then the survival of tradition after the completion of that process is unproblematic. Thus, for the Holmesian attack to make sense, tradition must be seen either as an impediment to initiating the weighing process or a factor that receives weight disproportionate to actual social preferences. His suspicion of tradition reveals a conviction that judges are committed to prior decisions even when circumstances have changed sufficiently to warrant a modification of the existing legal rule.

In short, Holmes is reacting to what the literature of technology and innovation currently describes as the phenomena of "path dependence" and "lock-in effects."[11] The basic insight of these principles is that once a technology develops along a particular path and produces positive returns, alternatives are ignored. The consequences of following the existing path rather than an alternative, however, may be suboptimal, even if the initial path was optimal at the time that it was selected.[12] Nevertheless, once a choice has been made (and notwithstanding the economist's admonition to ignore sunk costs), exit may be difficult, in large part because others have made similar choices and to act in coordination with others seems superior to casting off on one's own. The result may be to save costs from an individual perspective but to impose significant costs in the form of forgone opportunities on society at large. So it is, Holmes implies, with law. Investment in precedent rewards judges, but only at the social expense of retaining legal rules that have long since failed to reflect the conditions for social progress. Indeed, much of what I want to say may explain Holmes's advocacy for judicial restraint.[13] If judges have incentives to extend traditions beyond their usefulness, so that law is determined largely by the preferences of an earlier time, then we may want to limit the scope of judicial intervention. If, on the other hand, judges have incentives to overcome precedent in situations where its preservation would be socially undesirable, then the stabilizing effects of tradition may be less problematic than the Holmes of *The Path of the Law* indicates.

I begin with a fuller examination of Holmes's views of tradition, in order to demonstrate his awareness of the richness of the subject. Implicitly, this section cautions against inferring too much from Holmes's essay in isolation. I then turn to the claim that allegiance to precedent generates overinvestment in tradition at the expense of social vicissitudes that warrant legal changes. This discussion illustrates that judges have more discretion over the use of precedent than naive conceptions of *stare decisis* suggest. That judges may select among precedents, however, does not mean that they will exercise that discretion. Judges may lack sufficient creativity to escape precedent or may accept precedent of dubious applicability. Either condition would lock us into rules laid down in prior decisions. But path dependence and lock-in are not necessarily cause for dissatisfaction. Where legal precedents simply solve coordination problems or where legal change would create improvements only by generating transition costs not worth incurring, constraints on judicial inventiveness serve a valuable function for the very reason that they lock in an existing legal rule. Thus, judges have significant latitude to use or to ignore precedent. In part IV, I discuss motivational theories to determine whether judges have systemic incentives to overutilize or underutilize precedent. I conclude in part V with the suggestion that Holmes's skeptical view of tradition is warranted, given the mix of judicial incentives.

A final prefatory note is in order. My use of the term "precedent following" does not presume that precedents are given a particular weight. There are substantial discussions of precedent that argue for attaching a range of weights to rules of *stare decisis,* either throughout a legal system or case by case.[14] I assume only that the presence of precedent is not completely determinative, that judges under some circumstances will be able to overturn or avoid precedent, and I ask only whether they have the incentives to interpret that authority broadly or narrowly.

I. Holmes the Traditionalist

The Path of the Law expresses Holmes's antipathy to tradition, which, translated into the judicial forum, constitutes an attack on precedent. Holmes implies that commitment to tradition would cause a judge to apply the rule dictated by a previous decision without exploring any justification for its application to the current case. He speaks of each generation's tendency to "simply obey a law of spontaneous growth," as if legal rules were handed to them with no roots in a reasoning process that might limit their applicability. He criticizes those who act or think unquestioningly because that is what "our fathers have done" ("Path" 470).[15] The concern that tradition will override rational policy (472) or interfere with tradeoffs inherent in legal rules ("the ends of legislation, the means of attaining them, and the cost" [474]) underlies Holmes's strident conclusion that a historical explanation for a rule of law, without more, "is revolting" (469). Indeed, one might infer that giving an historical explanation, even when combined with other explanations, would be cause for Holmes's revulsion. He contends that it would be even "more revolting" if the grounds on which the original rule was laid down had vanished, so that "the rule simply persists from blind imitation of the past" (469). But if that is the case in which following tradition is "more revolting," then presumably it is at least merely "revolting" when the reasons that generated the rule continue to apply. Even in that case, Holmes implies, judges must reconsider the merits of the rule, explore the extent to which its initial justification remains valid, and "recognize their duty of weighing considerations of social advantage" that attach to the rule (467).

It is this language that has led Anthony Kronman to portray Holmes as "contemptuous" of precedent.[16] But fuller consideration of Holmes's views reveals a more complex picture than accusations of "blind imitation" suggest.[17] Judges did not, in Holmes's view, perpetuate precedent without imposing some explanation on the rule they were applying. Rather, in a fashion more complicated than allegations of wooden application imply, judges created a contemporary justification for a rule that had developed previously for reasons that no longer obtained. To illustrate this judicial phenomenon, Holmes explicates the development of the legal principle that a material alteration of a written contract voids the contract against the party making the alteration (472–73).[18] Such *ex post* rationalizations, however, are more fully explored in the first lecture in *The Common Law*.[19] There Holmes demonstrates his understanding, perhaps as advanced for our own age as for his, that evolution is not equivalent to progress, but only to adaptation:

But just as the clavicle in the cat only tells of the existence of some earlier creature to which a collarbone was useful, precedents survive in the law long after the use they once served is at an end and the reason for them has been forgotten. The result of following them must often be failure and confusion from the merely logical point of view.[20]

The Holmes of *The Common Law,* however, seems more tolerant of the phenomenon than the Holmes of "The Path of the Law." In the former work, such logical gaps and *ex post* rationalizations seem inevitable, an intrinsic part of legal development.[21] Indeed, the Holmes of *The Common Law* finds the inconsistencies that result almost charming, so that calls for their abolition are futile insofar as they fail to consider that the law "will become entirely consistent only when it ceases to grow."[22]

The picture becomes more complex as we consider Holmes as judge. Holmes the judge systematically and sympathetically invoked tradition as a preferable constraint on the judicial role. Throughout his judicial career, Holmes suggested that tradition serves social functions, preservation of which warranted deference to previous judicial pronouncements in ways that rival his celebrated deference to legislative judgments.[23] Take, for instance, Holmes's brief opinion in *Stack v. New York, N.H. & H.R. Co.,*[24] a tort suit in which a lower court had refused to order the plaintiff to submit to a physical examination by a doctor to whom the plaintiff objected. In upholding the trial court, Holmes noted that no known precedent authorized judicial intervention. He admitted that recent increases in tort actions arguably represented a change in circumstances that warranted increased judicial involvement. Nevertheless, only a judge "careless or ignorant of precedent" would assume such authority:

We do not forget the continuous process of developing the law that goes on through the courts, in the form of deduction, or deny that in a clear case it might be possible even to break away from a line of decisions in favor of some rule generally admitted to be based upon a deeper insight into the present wants of society. But the improvements made by the courts are made, almost invariably, by very slow degrees and by very short steps. Their general duty is not to change, but to work out, the principles already sanctioned by the practice of the past.[25]

This seems a remarkable endorsement of tradition just three years after his criticism of reliance on tradition. It may be true that tradition alone does not warrant judicial devotion. But when judges determine what the law should be, Holmes implies, they play an institutional role as well as a substantive one, and the interaction between the two roles cannot be underestimated. Given the absence of any collective forum for judicial decision making and the subsequent capacity for judges to conflict with each other, tradition may play a more important role in adjudication than in legislation.

Or take *Gardiner v. Butler & Co.,*[26] in which Holmes deals tersely with two claims for damages after a lessee had gone into receivership. The first claim was predicated on an explicit damages clause in the lease, while the second, involving the same parties, was predicated on a general contractual claim, the lease being silent as to damages. Holmes recognized the logical similarity of the two cases but held that the first claim was provable in receivership whereas the second was not, on the grounds that "the law as to leases is not a matter of logic in vacuo; it is a matter of history that has not forgotten Lord Coke."[27] Thus, until state law on leases changed, there was no reason for courts, or at least the U.S. Supreme Court, to interfere with "the English tradition" on which that law was based.[28]

Judicial respect for tradition transcended deference to legal precedent. It also meant deference to social traditions, even if legal rules dictated by such traditions were ill suited to contemporary conditions. Take, for instance, *Laurel Hill Cemetery v. City and County of San Francisco*.[29] There Holmes rejected a claim that an ordinance prohibiting burial within the city limits was based on outmoded superstition. Recognizing that contemporary opinion was divided on the safety of cemeteries near residences, Holmes concluded that resolution of the issue could not depend on the reasoning of the justices but was dependent on matters other than "abstract theory."[30] "Tradition and the habits of the community count for more than logic. Since, as before the making of constitutions, regulation of burial and prohibition of it in certain spots"[31] had been a subject of social concern, one contesting such regulations would have to point to a more unified "consensus of civilized opinion"[32] in order for a court to overthrow a law predicated on the traditional position.[33]

Even where some have found Holmes less deferential, as in Constitutional challenges to legislation,[34] he sometimes rejected claims with a simple reference to the shibboleth of tradition. For instance, in *New York Trust Co. v. Eisner*,[35] executors of an estate claimed that a federal estate tax was direct and therefore subject to apportionment. In his brief dismissal of the claim, Holmes revealed an attraction both to precedent and to tradition generally:

> But that matter also is disposed of by Knowlton v. Moore, not by an attempt to make some scientific distinction, which would be at least difficult, but on an interpretation of language by its traditional use—on the practical and historical ground that this kind of tax always has been regarded as the antithesis of a direct tax; "has ever been treated as a duty or excise, because of the particular occasion which gives rise to its levy." Upon this point, a page of history is worth a volume of logic.[36]

Again, I use these examples of Holmes's deference to precedent and tradition not to show inconsistency, but to indicate complexity in his thought. Indeed, as I have suggested, the predictive theory of law implies more respect for tradition than a brief reading of *The Path of the Law* suggests. Reflection on Holmes's dual roles reveals him to be not so much an opponent of tradition as he is a proponent of reason. The two may occasionally be juxtaposed to one another. Reason suggests ad hoc analysis, while appeals to tradition suggest unthinking application. But nothing in the appeal to reason requires that every decision be subjected to review from first principles. As Holmes the judge recognized, judicial reexamination is a costly enterprise; and, as Holmes the essayist preached, comprehensive scrutiny of legal rules requires us

> to consider and weigh the ends of legislation, the means of attaining them, and the cost. We learn that for everything we have to give up something else, and we are taught to set

the advantage we gain against the other advantage we lose, and to know what we are doing when we elect. ("Path" 474)

If Holmes is to follow his own admonition to compare costs and benefits, reconsideration of a traditional rule itself is justified only if the expected value of doing so exceeds the costs of judicial inquiry.[37] If there is a high *ex ante* probability that reconsideration will systematically lead to application of the same rule, then reconsideration seems wasteful in the absence of special circumstances suggesting that the traditional rule is ripe for alteration. Holmes believed that judges who saw similar cases on a routine basis would be better able than juries, which saw only one such case, to discern the content of reasonable conduct in such cases.[38] So might judges who saw similar cases on a regular basis reasonably invoke their prior decisions without rehearsing all of their original justifications. Although this possibility raises the difficult issue of how to calculate the optimal search for changed circumstances, my concern here lies only in noting the possibility that even Holmes's crude cost–benefit analysis suggests that optimal investment may approach zero. If nothing else, such allegiance to precedent serves an economizing function insofar as it reduces judicial investigation. Thus reason and tradition need not be polar opposites, and even blind adherence to precedent may not constitute an "indefensible practice."[39] Indeed, given the admitted benefits that may flow from a precedential system, judges may defer to precedent too little rather than too much.

This conclusion, of course, assumes a probabilistic argument about the initial decision that is perhaps reflected in Holmes's complex mixture of admonitions to reexamine precedent and avoid wooden invocations of precedent. Deference to prior decisions makes sense only if one believes that reconsideration is unlikely to correct an erroneous decision; that is, that the original decision was likely to have been correct in ways that would also properly determine the subsequent decision. If the requirement to follow precedent is not absolute, the survival of a precedent might also suggest that sometimes one *can* infer ought from is, at least where there are forces that would cause shifts where they were appropriate. This explanation is consistent with the presumption that because judicial decisions have been correctly made, there is little reason to relitigate.[40]

But in the absence of a belief that some degree of reexamination is permissible, the probabilistic argument is troublesome. There is no reason to believe that a decision is more likely to be correct simply because it was made first.[41] Indeed, the subsequent decision may be more likely to be correct, because the judge making that decision will have seen the rule applied in a broader range of circumstances. The probabilistic argument is, therefore, troublesome as a defense of precedent and may even be circular. Accordingly, we cannot assume that the initial decision, standing alone, was more likely to be correct than a later, fully considered decision on the same issue. In a system that permits at least some reconsideration of the prior decision (e.g., when the rule of precedent requires only presumptive deference to the prior decision), however, repeat results may indicate correctness and justify reliance on the prior case, as long as there is no affirmative demonstration of changed circumstances. But the very requirement of some degree of precedent following deters thorough reconsideration. Since the possibility of reconsideration suggests that precedents retained for a long period of time are likely to be correct, the deterrent effect undermines the very probabilistic argument on which precedent might be thought to depend. Perversely, the stronger the presumption attached to precedent following (and thus, the less thorough the reconsideration of the rule in subsequent cases), the less we can rely on its survival to support a conclusion that the original decision was "probably" correct.

II. The Scope of Precedent

The claim that I wish to defend in the balance of this essay is that Holmes's critique of precedent reflected a concern about what we would today describe as "lock-in effects." Such effects preclude balancing the economizing and inhibiting effects of precedent. I use the term "reflected" advisedly, since I do not claim that Holmes had in mind the analysis that follows. I suggest only that my argument finds both inspiration and support in his rudimentary statement of an economic view of legal change and his more opaque suggestions about judicial incentives that determine the judicial use of precedent.

Before turning to judicial incentives, we need to recount the nature of precedent and what it means to be "locked in" by a preexisting "path." Examination of incentives reveals only what motivations judges are likely to have. My present concern is less with those abstract motivations than with their manifestation when judges apply legal doctrine. Thus, I examine the range of actions that judges might select when faced with potential precedents. I then turn to an examination of path dependence, in order to disaggregate the array of situations in which judicial discretion determines the application of precedent. My claim is that subsequent cases often depend on precedent either in trivial ways or not at all. Holmes's concerns about precedent, therefore, matter only if there exist nontrivial cases in which prior decisions determine the subsequent path that legal doctrine follows.

A. *Precedent and Judicial Discretion*

Facile explanations of precedent operate on the assumption that a judge, deciding a case today, looks to discover how judges confronted with similar fact situations have decided those cases in the past. The judge in the current case is at least presumptively bound to adhere to these decisions. Although, as I have indicated, a probabilistic argument supports precedent following, the requirement that judges apply prior decisions does not obtain its authority from probability alone. Were that the case, precedent would possess its binding authority by virtue of the continued justification that applied to the prior case. At the very least, a judge in a subsequent case would be warranted in examining whether the justification in the prior case continued to hold. Precedent, however, does not allow *de novo* examination once it is determined that the subsequent case falls within a factual description that is sufficiently similar to the prior case. Even decisions that ultimately reject the precedent must take that precedent into account as the starting point for analysis. To the extent that we believe that precedent has a binding nature, it must lie in the simple fact that it is a precedent rather than in the justification given for the prior case.[42]

Thus, precedent, when first laid down, not only provides reasons for subsequently following the same rule; it also compels rule following.[43] This compulsion both generates the greatest benefits for precedent and maximizes its costs. But this compulsion follows only when the subsequent case is, in fact, governed by the prior case. That is, each of the justifications commonly proffered for a system of precedent – fairness to actors bound by legal rules, efficient decision making, ties to tradition, ensuring certainty and predictability in legal doctrine, or conserving decisional resources[44] – flows from the requirement that the subsequent case be sufficiently "similar" to the prior case that it is appropriate to treat the two cases similarly. This requirement rests on two assumptions that may be either glossed over or ignored entirely in discussions of precedent. The first is that judges can readily discern what counts as precedent for what. The second, and related, assumption is that precedent is primarily a retrospective doctrine.[45]

Take first the notion that judges can determine what counts as precedent for what. The constraining function of precedent is obviously weaker to the extent that judges in the subsequent case have discretion to select what is and what is not properly considered precedent. A judge in such a case, therefore, must determine which facts in the subsequent case are relevant to its outcome. The judge must also discover prior cases in which some of the same facts were present and were relevant to those decisions. The fact that we are dealing with "similar" rather than identical cases means that the current case will not map perfectly with the prior cases but will bear at best the proverbial "family resemblance."[46]

The imperfect mapping of facts permits even a court that wants to portray itself as bound by precedent to foreclose claims of insufficient deference. This may occur in at least three ways. First, the process of determining which precedent governs the current case may be problematic because the current case bears sufficient similarity to multiple precedents that can be classified in conflicting ways. Imagine, for instance, a judge confronted with a case in which during a game of baseball one player intentionally throws a ball at the head of another. The judge is confronted with two lines of precedent that arguably govern the case. Let us assume that the first line involves cases in which ballplayers injured during a consensual game are governed by a rule of no liability. The second involves cases in which individuals who throw rocks and other missiles at each other without provocation face liability for battery. Whether the judge chooses to follow the first or second line of cases may depend on such matters as whether the judge believes that "beanballs" are part of the "game" of baseball, or whether foul play during a game is different from an attack. These decisional points, however, are not settled by a priori principles, but by the judge's decision to emphasize or deemphasize certain circumstances in the case. This is not to say that the decision to distinguish or not is unprincipled or indeterminate. Rather my claim is that principle may justify any of several outcomes. The result is that the reach of any particular rule of law is inherently fuzzy. At least in theory, a judge has significant latitude to break out of a particular line of precedent by following another. In doing so, even a judge who looks retrospectively "creates" precedent rather than "finds" it.

Second, a judge who desires to be perceived as attentive to precedent may seize on factual differences among cases to distinguish the legal rules that apply to them. This process permits not only the selection of a different rule, which might be seen as too radical a departure from precedent, but also the more subtle step of modifying the previous rule to create exceptions that leave the original rule intact in cases that are closer to the prior case. Assume, for instance, that in prior cases, banks that have issued letters of credit had been bound under bank custom to honor drafts drawn against the credit, notwithstanding certain nonconformities in documents accompanying the draft.[47] Such a custom might arise because banks understand that the relevant nonconformities did not threaten the likelihood that conforming goods have been shipped. A custom that arises in this way is likely to be efficient, because the banks that develop it will sometimes be advantaged and sometimes disadvantaged by the custom. Since the parties to the custom internalize both its costs and its benefits, there is reason to believe that it would not have developed unless it generated net benefits. Now assume that a judge, in a case where a bank has refused to pay against nonconforming documents, has observed that the custom arose during peacetime, while the nonconforming documents in the current case were presented during wartime. The judge might conclude that wartime increases the likelihood that the goods would not reach the purchaser. The judge in the case might find that the distinctions between shipment during wartime and peacetime warranted an exception to the prior cases. Conversely, the judge might conclude that nonconformity in documents did not itself indicate any defects in the shipment and that the bank was acting strategically in refusing to comply with custom. The point is not that one of these decisions is clearly correct. To the contrary, the point is that, because cases will not map onto each other perfectly, judges will have substantial leeway in determining whether distinctive facts constitute distinctions with a difference.

In Holmes's view, the frailty of judging often lies in just the opposite flaw – the tendency of judges to make insufficient distinctions. This is one way to understand the story that Holmes tells in *The Path of the Law* about the Vermont justice of the peace asked to adjudicate a suit brought by one farmer against another for breaking a churn. The justice considered the case but determined after perusing the statutes that he could find nothing about churns and gave judgment for the defendant (474–75). Perhaps the most puzzling thing about this story, however, is that it demonstrates the limitations of Holmes's preferred basis of decision making: appeals to reason. The success of those appeals cannot be greater than the judge's capacity to engage in the reasoning process. If his Vermont justice of the peace was incapable of reasoning farther than the story suggests, then economizing on the decision-making process may be perfectly appropriate.

Third, the judge in the subsequent case may seize on the linguistic imprecision of the precedent to conclude that a current case is not covered by the rule previously laid down.[48] Limitations of description and imperfect foresight may preclude a judge in a prior case from characterizing the grounds of decision with sufficient precision that it clearly includes or excludes the subsequent case. After all, the judge in the prior case was presumably attempting to decide that case, not to lay down a rule for hypothetical future cases with similar facts.[49] By "imprecision," I do not mean dicta that can be ignored in a subsequent case, but language that provides insufficient direction about its application to a subsequent case. Thus, the judge in the subsequent case, though attempting to be attentive to his or her obligation to follow precedent, may include facts not intended to be included by the judge in the prior case or may fail to include facts intended to be included. The classic example here is obscenity. But think, more mundanely, of ordinances that preclude "live entertainment" and that are directed at nude dancing. When Chief Justice Burger admonished that such ordinances should be allowed to stand because no one would construe them to "prevent a high school performance of 'The Sound of Music,'"[50] he was essentially saying that a judge in a subsequent case would be able to construe the imprecise scope of a prior case to exclude from the ban situations that the prior judge did not have in mind. There is, however, no reason to believe that the judge in the subsequent case will have the same interpretation of the imprecise phrase as the judge in the prior case. Indeed, if the description in the prior case was "imprecise," different individuals are likely to interpret its scope differently. Hence, there is significant reason to think that a subsequent judge could include such a performance within the ban, even if that is not the kind of performance the judge in the prior case had in mind when upholding the ban against nude dancing.

Each of these mechanisms for deviating from the rules of prior cases is enhanced by the fact that the decision to utilize precedent is made by the judge in the subsequent case.[51] Judges in the prior cases typically decide only the case before them and do not elaborate what variations in the facts would generate different results. Indeed, even if they did so, it is not clear that the judge in the subsequent case would be bound to follow what essentially was dicta in the prior case. By interpreting facts of a previous case as material or not, selecting which line of precedent governs the relevant one, or applying an imprecise locution to a particular set of facts, the judge in the subsequent case has a rather robust set of tools for determining the scope of precedent. That ability provides reasons for us to be less concerned about path dependence, since it permits distinctions that would limit the force of precedent when, in fact, it disserved the public interest. Indeed, where the judgment about when to apply precedent falls to the judge in the subsequent case, these interpretive tools indicate that the judge possesses the same discretion against which the doctrine of precedent was presumably invoked in the first place.

B. Precedent and Prospectivity

At this point, one may wonder why Holmes would be concerned about lock-in effects of tradition. If judges in subsequent cases have the tools to avoid wooden application of precedents, then why would they not use them? The second feature of precedent adds to this puzzle. The standard story of precedent asks why a judge in a subsequent case is bound by a decision in a prior, albeit similar, case.[52] To the extent that the doctrine of precedent imposes a constraint on future decisions, it raises the costs of generating contrary decisions in the future and therefore privileges the status quo. It is this attribute that gives precedent the beneficial characteristic of imposing relative certainty on a legal system. But the function of precedent is not simply to economize retrospectively.[53] Precedent possesses an additional prospective element. Litigants' incentives to overturn inefficient rules suggest that, from their perspective, the prospective element of precedent dominates.[54] A litigant, of course, searches for precedents that allow him to describe his conduct as similar to that of parties who received what was, from that litigant's perspective, a favorable outcome. But where the litigant expects to find himself engaged in the same conduct in the future, the more important value of precedent lies in its prospective effect. Those who can obtain a precedent that favors their view of the law not only obtain victory in the individual case, but also secure the benefits of a favorable decision that is itself privileged and costly to overturn. Thus, parties who enjoys these lock-in effects are willing to incur higher costs in order to obtain a favorable precedent. But this same possibility reduces the lock-in effect itself, since parties to the litigation will spend a greater amount to secure a new precedent, as long as they believe that the expenditure will be amortized over a sufficient period before opposing parties are willing or able to invest in a return to the original rule. Again, lock-in seems to be less of a problem than Holmes suggests, since, as evidenced by litigation campaigns ranging from civil rights issues to tobacco company liability, repeat players will invest in continued litigation until they receive favorable judgments.

III. Path Dependence and Precedent

A. When Path Dependence Matters

Path dependence in common law matters if decisions, once established as precedents, become so locked in that exit from them is too difficult, even though changed conditions would have led us to select a different rule if we were writing on a clean slate. But even if law is path dependent in the sense that former decisions dictate later ones, that result is trivial if the path does not affect the fit between the substantive law and the objective of the legal system. This may be because we are more concerned about having a rule by which to guide conduct than about having a particular rule, or because, although we wish to achieve a particular objective, we are uncertain what rule will accomplish that end. For instance, even if we value efficiency, we may be uncertain whether that objective would be obtained by assigning stolen goods to a good-faith purchaser or to the original owner of those goods, because it is not clear whether the original owner's ability to avoid theft is superior to the purchaser's ability to discern the provenance of the goods.[55] Thus, path dependence dictated by precedent would itself be a trivial problem unless the path determined by prior decisions locked us in to doctrine from which we could not feasibly escape on learning that it disserves the objective of the law. Especially in light of the tools available to resist lock-in effects, the mere existence of path dependence does not necessarily support Holmes's strong assertion that preexisting legal rules not only determine the result of subsequent cases, but do so detrimentally because they inhibit adaptation to changed circumstances.

In speaking of lock-in in this sense, I draw from the literature concerning path dependence in the development of technological standards.[56] Path dependence in this area describes the adoption of a standard based on technology available at the time of adoption that determines subsequent technological developments. Traditional examples are the size of light-bulb bases, the QWERTY typewriter, the narrow-gauge railroad, and VHS recording systems.[57] Such a standard becomes self-perpetuating, or locked in, when a critical mass of potential users must accept an improvement in order to amortize the substantial investment in its creation. The very function of the existing standard, however, impedes its acceptance. Standards solve coordination problems, allowing parties within an industry or users of a technology to interact with each other in ways that would not be possible if actors used variants of the standard. They are useful in industries that have the characteristics of network externalities, where cooperation and coordination among potential beneficiaries of the technology is facilitated if all accept the same standard for the technology. Once such a standard has been widely adopted and it generates positive returns, there is little incentive to use alternative technologies, even those that would have been selected in the absence of the existing standard. Any deviation from what others are doing frustrates participation in the network and will succeed only if a sufficient number of others also adopt the new standard. If others fail to accept the improved standard, the party who does switch outside the relevant network will be less able to coordinate with others in the industry. As long as all light bulb receptacles accept the same-sized light bulb, users of light bulbs can shift among light bulb manufacturers, who can increase their markets. A manufacturer who could make a bulb last twice as long by changing the size of the bulb's base would still face the difficulty of ensuring that enough other bulb and bulb-receptacle manufacturers would adopt the new standard to make the new product marketable and the costs of shifting to the new technology recoverable. Similarly, development of a superior alternative to VHS recording will be rejected unless potential users are confident that recordings will be available in the new format; alternatives to narrow-gauge railroads will be rejected if potential operators of those railroads fear that their trains will be unable to connect with others that fail to make the transition.

In the legal literature, Marcel Kahan and Michael Klausner have suggested that contract terms and transactional forms in corporate documents are path dependent in this way.[58] Once a term attains a meaning through customary use and potential ambiguities are resolved through litigation, attorneys have incentives to use those terms or transactional forms rather than to introduce new and potentially superior ones. The existing ones are well understood in the industry. Thus, those who might create or adopt improved standards will do so only if they can capture sufficient private benefits to offset the private costs of retraining, retooling, and purchasing the new standard. Add to this difficulty the incentives that managers have to eschew innovation, and the possibility of inertia in the face of potential social improvement is complete.[59] The result is that lock-in can generate what appears ex post to be inefficient results.

As I have implied, however, path dependence does not necessarily generate inefficiencies. As applied to legal rules, we should distinguish path dependence that impedes adoption of superior rules from path dependence in the trivial sense that a prior rule either (1) determines the selection of a particular rule among equally plausible candidates, or (2) causes selection of a legal rule that actually satisfies an accepted social objective. In either of these cases, the fact that one rule was selected over another rule in the past does not impose significant costs on the current legal regime; in addition, preservation of the existing rule avoids the costs that would accompany subsequent selection of an alternative legal rule (e.g., the costs of informing target actors and their legal advisers of the new rule).[60] Take, as an example of path dependence among equally plausible legal rules, any rule that is implemented to solve a coordination problem or that selects among a series of equally preferred possibilities, such as the proper period for filing an appeal from a final judgment. We may be indifferent as to whether that period is thirty days, forty-five days, or sixty days. We are not indifferent, however, as to the existence of a well-publicized and commonly accepted rule. Thus, once we select one rule from the set of plausible alternatives, that rule may stick, even if some of the reasons for its original choice (such as the need to ensure sufficient time for proofreading and getting documents from printers) are rendered obsolete by technological advances (such as the advent of overnight delivery and desktop publishing). The disappearance of the reasons that may have favored the initial selection does not necessarily warrant a shift to some alternative, because no justification for an alternative establishes that it would be superior to the existing rule. Thus, even if the extant legal rule is path dependent, that path dependency does not privilege a suboptimal rule.[61] In this situation, it may be perfectly appropriate to select among plausible rules solely on the basis that the selected rule "was laid down in the time of Henry IV."

Indeed, appeals to tradition may generate substantial benefits in this situation. Assuming that we are speaking of situations in which there is no clear social advantage to any particular alternative, any selection is likely to be based on grounds such as the preferences of the parties to the litigation in which the rule was initially established. This phenomenon suggests that cycling may occur because a rule that was not preferred in that litigation may be out of contention in subsequent litigation in which a third rule is adopted, even though the rule initially rejected would have been preferable to the third rule that was adopted.[62] Where multiple possible rules simply reflect equally plausible alternatives, the use of precedent may be a useful mechanism to avoid cycling among personally, as opposed to socially, favored alternatives.

Alternatively, tradition may favor extant legal rules even if they would not be selected today were we writing on a clean slate, because the change is not worth the cost of publication and implementation. Even if we regret our prior selection, the earlier choice may have been based on imperfect foresight rather than erroneous calculation of the net benefits of the rule at that time. Certainly tradition dictates the rule in such a case, but again, we should hesitate to criticize the rule on that basis. Think, for example, of the Uniform Commercial Code rule that treats separate branches of the same bank as separate banks for the purpose of deadlines for taking action with respect to the payment of checks.[63] The rule may have made substantial sense when it was first formulated. At that time, branches of the same bank may still have had difficulty making prompt exchange of documents relevant to the decision whether to pay a check. For instance, drawers whose signature cards are located at one branch of a bank could issue checks that are presented at other branches of the same bank. Because the decision whether or not to pay the check might have to await comparison of the signature on the check to the signature on the card, additional time might be required to send the check to the bank that possessed the relevant document. We can now foresee technological changes that would allow one branch to call up computerized facsimiles of signature cards that are physically held at another branch. That capability might justify a new legal rule treating all bank branches as part of the same institution for the purpose of the timing deadlines. Nevertheless, the costs related to passing the legislation in fifty states (or of having a period of time in which different rules exist in different states) might be sufficiently great to negate the marginal gains available from transition. In this case as well, it is difficult to imagine that Holmes would object to following tradition.[64]

The cases in which reliance on traditional legal rules is detrimental, then, must be cases in which the conditions that justified a preexisting rule have changed so much that (1) some alternative rule is now desirable, and (2) it would be worth incurring the transition costs, but (3) the existence of the current rule prevents the transition to the more desirable rule. For instance, the requirement to follow precedent would be considered both path dependent and locked in, in this strong and negative sense, if we believed that common law processes, devoid of precedent-following, would lead to the evolution of efficient legal rules (assuming, for the moment, that we valued efficiency in legal rules).[65]

There are independent reasons to believe that there are substantial constraints on efficient evolution in the common law.[66] And no one claims that the common law contains no inefficient rules. To the extent that precedent following does lock in those rules, tradition may saddle us with greater (or at least different) inefficiencies than would exist if courts were not required to follow precedent. Before concluding that lock-in is a significant problem in such cases, however, it is necessary to consider the mechanisms of path dependence. Even where following a previously established path would be problematic, lock-in should be avoidable if the path can be avoided when a superior alternative arises. Thus, our reactions to precedent should depend on whether application of legal rules is susceptible to the mechanisms that avert lock-in.

B. Inertia and the Conditions of Path Dependence

As I have indicated, the path-dependence literature suggests that standards may be locked in where a critical mass of potential users must accept an improvement in order to amortize the substantial investment in the creation of the improvement. Contrivances for solving the problem of inertia do exist, however. If the potential private gains from an improvement are sufficiently great, the creator or entrepreneur of the new standard can subsidize transition costs (e.g., by giving away free software, new light bulbs, or cellular phones) to increase the expected return from adopting the new standard. The entrepreneur may also subsidize or disseminate information that suggests that a large number of potential adopters will ultimately accept the standard, with the promise of high rewards for early adopters.[67] Risk-taking managers who are attracted to new standards may also counteract risk aversion in some cases.[68] Thus, even in an environment that might be thought most susceptible to lock-in effects, path dependence does not necessarily maintain inferior standards.

The evolution of legal rules may be even less susceptible to inertia than technological standards. Think of the conditions under which common law develops. One might initially believe that the public-good nature of law will frustrate legal change, since beneficiaries of the change will realize those same benefits without making any expenditure, if others incur the costs of creating the new law. But the public-good nature of law may simultaneously reduce the likelihood that inertia will dominate where a new legal doctrine would be an improvement. The possibility that an insufficient number of potential adopters would accept the improvement does not exist, because where law binds it binds all within its jurisdiction. Thus, those who might otherwise adopt a change in legal standards will not fail to do so out of fear that insufficient numbers of others will concur. Because no one shifts to the new legal rule unless all do, the prisoner's dilemma paradigm that is often applied to explain inertia in technological standards[69] is transformed into an Assurance Game. Potential litigants will have less concern that initiating litigation will cause the law they create to be inconsistent with laws created by others. When potential litigants do fear that legal change will detract from their ability to join networks, they may elect to litigate in multiple jurisdictions or to select a more centralized jurisdiction that can lay down a single law for a larger number of those in the relevant network. Additionally, some entrepreneurs in law, such as law professors and reform groups, may invest in urging legal change. Unlike manufacturers who might otherwise propose new standards, they do not have to bear any of the costs related to transition. At the same time, they obtain significant benefits (tenure, professional reputation) simply by advocating the reform.[70] As the discussion of the prospective role of precedent demonstrates, some repeat players will have substantial incentives to overcome precedent because they are personally disfavored by the existing rule of law and will benefit if they can convince lawmakers to adopt an alternative.

The incentives of litigants and others will not overcome tradition, however, if precedent is not institutionally susceptible to change, that is, if judges have neither the tools nor the inclination to overcome precedent. I have demonstrated earlier that judges possess the tools needed to break out of precedent by selecting among competing precedents, distinguishing cases on the basis of factual differences, and construing linguistic imprecision in a manner that makes precedent inapplicable to the current case. But the availability of these tools indicates only that judges are not locked in to a path created by prior decisions. It remains possible that they could be so constrained. Holmes's antipathy toward precedent is warranted if judges are motivated by incentives that systematically favor inappropriate following of precedent.

I am not suggesting that motivations for precedent following are always inappropriate. Judges may properly be driven to inertia by concerns for the network externalities of their decisions. In a limited jurisdiction, where members must interact with members of other jurisdictions, a judge may worry that deviation from widely accepted precedent will cause adverse network effects similar to those that exist when one party uses a variant of an industry standard. Assume, for instance, that a judge must decide under state law a case involving the liability of a company that manufactures a product that is sold throughout the country. Assume further that arguable precedents within the jurisdiction have laid down a rule of no liability and that similar rules govern in other jurisdictions. Even a judge who otherwise believed that there was a basis for distinguishing the precedent might be concerned that the effects of distinguishing could cause substantial dislocations for parties in the local jurisdiction when dealing with parties in other jurisdictions. This argument, of course, is an argument about the desirability of uniformity rather than one strictly of precedent. But a judge might believe that the desirability of maintaining uniformity warrants subordination of the arguments for breaking from precedent. Although cases in one jurisdiction do not serve as binding precedent elsewhere, they may be used as examples of persuasive decisions from other jurisdictions. Thus, we frequently see uniformity among jurisdictions in areas such as tort or contract law because a decision in any jurisdiction serves as a salient coordination point for the others. (Of course, this may manifest a trivial example of trivial path dependence. The costs of deviating from the standard simply may not be worth the benefits of carving out occasional exceptions.)

The fact remains, however, that the judge in such a case has discretion to follow precedent or not. The mechanisms for applying or rejecting arguable precedent, discussed earlier, indicate the breadth of that discretion. Hence, the scope of path dependence and the extent to which it will generate inferior legal rules depend on the incentives that judges possess either to favor or disfavor narrow application of precedent. I turn next to an investigation of those incentives.

IV. The Incentives of Judges

Our discussion to this point suggests that judges have tools to narrow the adverse effects of following precedent. In addition, given the possibility of nontrivial path dependence, they also have opportunities to avoid following an inefficient precedent. But discretion also means that judges may fail to select these tools and thus remain locked in to existing standards. That, of course, is Holmes's fear. But once we admit the possibility that judges will not perfectly apply Holmes's crude cost–benefit analysis, so that application of tradition varies from the ideal, it is equally plausible – contra Holmes – that the tools for distinguishing precedents will be overutilized, and that judges will be insufficiently deferential toward precedent.

Our final inquiry, therefore, is whether judges have incentives to take advantage of those tools when, but only when, deviation from precedent would be useful. As Gillian Hadfield has indicated,[71] motivational theories of the evolution of common law have not been well developed, at least in the literature concerning efficient evolution. The theories that have emerged assume either that judges pursue efficiency or that litigants, acting out of self-interest, tend toward efficiency. A more recent literature focuses on the incentives of judges and allows us to consider those incentives that have systemic effects on judges' use of precedent. I am concerned here only with systemic effects, not with incentives that judges may have in individual cases. Incentives that judges may have include bribes, personal interest in the outcome of a case, or, to use Holmes's example, irritability caused by gout. None of those incentives systematically favors a narrow or broad interpretation of precedent. A judge susceptible to bribery is as susceptible to a litigant who wants a particular line of precedent followed as to one who wants that line disregarded. Similarly, judges may be susceptible to other forms of personal gain, such as increasing their own future employment opportunities by making certain decisions. We may believe that judges are less susceptible than legislators to the entreaties of interest groups, perhaps because life tenure or high return rates for elected judges makes them less needful of those groups, perhaps because judges have fewer opportunities for logrolling (because they either vote singly or in panels that frequently change composition), perhaps because judges must give reasons for their decisions. But prospective employment opportunities do not systematically affect attitudes toward precedent, other than as a by-product of other objectives, such as reputation or fame. Finally, lower-court judges may be thought to have an incentive to avoid reversal, in part to avoid criticism from peers and in part to avoid investment of time in an enterprise (creating the judge's own precedent) that is easily undone.[72] But (and perhaps counterintuitively) this desire does not inexorably favor adherence to precedent. Although precedent following might be seen as the safer course, its effect depends on the incentives of the reviewing court. If that court favors precedent creation rather than precedent following, then a lower-court judge who departs from prior law is less likely to suffer reversal than one who adheres to existing doctrine. Thus, aversion to reversal does not systematically favor broad conceptions of precedent apart from an understanding of the incentives of judges generally. Nonetheless, given that appeals courts infrequently overrule prior opinions, concern for reversal will tend to generate adherence to precedent in lower courts.

Judges, of course, decide only cases that litigants bring before them. Even the judge who seeks to distinguish among cases or otherwise to break from tradition cannot do so until offered an opportunity by litigants. We have identified a variety of constraints that prevent even judges faced with real litigants from reaching too far to overturn precedent, since judges are limited as to what disputes they can hear (case or controversy requirements), the circumstances under which they can make decisions (mootness and jurisdictional requirements), and the breadth of the decisions they can lay down (pronouncements characterized as obiter dicta will not be binding). These doctrines may be mechanisms that insulate judges from interest groups and thus increase the probability that decisions reflect the public interest. But these doctrines similarly have implications for our conception of judicial incentives. If we believe that judges are insufficiently motivated to depart from precedent, then we might want to construe narrowly the limitations on judicial jurisdiction to make those departures. On the other hand, if we believe that judges have incentive to depart from precedent too frequently, then we might want to construe those doctrines more broadly.

Assume, then, that a legal rule established by precedent disserves society. Our earlier discussion suggests that judges (1) have the tools to distinguish the precedent and thus (2) are not locked in by the constraints that cause inertia in other settings. Certainly we would believe that publicly interested judges – those whose interests align perfectly with those of the society that the judges represent – would strive mightily to determine a precedent's appropriate application. Recall that this objective function would not necessarily mean full reexamination of the established rule in each case. Even Holmes's crude cost–benefit analysis suggests that the economizing functions of precedent following could override the desire for reexamination. It might be that judges suffer from intellectual limitations in discerning proper from improper application of precedent. But that characteristic would provide insufficient reason for railing against precedent, since those intellectual limitations would likely affect the same judges in their ability to decide cases from first principles without the guidance of precedent.

But then, some richer analysis is necessary to understand what might cause judges to ignore the conditions that require a change in path. Here again, it is useful to begin with Holmes. But this is not the Holmes of facile social cost–benefit analysis. Rather it is a Holmes more sympathetic to the possibility that individual actors who perform the necessary calculus may have incentives to deviate from the socially beneficial, and that those motivations may be manifest in attitudes toward precedent. In an 1872 "Book Notice," reviewing an article by Frederick Pollock on John Austin's definition of law, Holmes offered an early insight into the basis for predicting how judges would define the law. Judges were not simply purveyors of legal science but persons inspired by complex and flexible tools that could be used to reach a variety of results, given any set of facts. His response to the Austinian assertion of law as the command of the sovereign will manifested by judicial adoption was to demonstrate how custom and trade usage have the same compulsory power as formal law, and, more importantly, how judicial expression of that will constitutes little more than a "motive for decision" in future cases. For "[a] precedent may not be followed; a statute may be emptied of its contents by construction . . . It must be remembered . . . that in a civilized state it is not the will of the sovereign that makes the lawyers' law, even when that is its source, but what a body of subjects, namely, the judges, by whom it is enforced, *say* is his will."[73] The motives of judges serve as sources of law, but only insofar as they allow prediction of what the judge will say.[74]

This early view of Holmes is remarkable in two respects. First, it suggests a more activist capacity for judges than the locked-in judge of *The Path of the Law*. To predict the law is to predict what judges will say, but that prediction requires knowledge of far more than what other judges have said on previous occasions. When Holmes states that a precedent "may not be followed," he allows for the possibility not only of overrulings, but of refinements and exceptions. Second, Holmes, in discounting the role of arbitrary will as a predictor of law, still recognizes that the "singular" may affect what judges do, even if those singularities are not appropriate sources of law. Yet once we grant the capacity of judges to make fine distinctions, to ignore precedent, to be moved as much by "the political aspirations of the judge, or his gout"[75] as by statute or constitution, we have the rudiments of a more complete explanation of the significance of precedent.

Judges, like entrepreneurs, may have incentives to leave an accepted standard in place, notwithstanding its inferiority to an alternative. Or, judges may enjoy personal benefits that induce insufficient reliance on precedent. If judges overcome path dependence in trivial cases, then they impose the costs of disseminating information and implementing the new standard without generating sufficient offsetting benefits. If tradition privileges the status quo, it privileges the good along with the bad. But if judges distinguish precedent only in nontrivial cases of path dependence, then Holmes's objection to precedent following seems misplaced.

That leaves open, of course, the issue of what personal benefits and costs would influence judicial attitudes toward precedent. Judges, at least those at high levels of the state or federal judiciary, typically receive monetary rewards less than those they could receive in other uses of their talents, such as in the private practice of law. Thus, the economic assumption is that judges seek their offices in pursuit of nonmonetized benefits, the value of which exceeds the value of the monetized rewards that they have forgone. Our current, but crude, understanding of those benefits includes the possibility of leisure, of being involved in the process of making law, and of enhanced reputation.

These incentives cut in very different directions from the perspective of precedent following. Judges who seek leisure should want to invest as little time as possible in the decision-making process. The hypothesis that judges place value on leisure is reinforced by many of the characteristics of judging at both the federal and the state level: fixed pay, life tenure (or a high rate of return to office), inability to secure a residuum of their efforts,[76] and the limited ability to achieve fame (within either an expanding federal judiciary or a state judiciary that has less visibility and prestige than its federal counterpart). These characteristics all tend toward circumventing the rigorous analysis inherent in the effort of the Holmesian judge "to consider more definitely and explicitly the social advantage on which the rule they lay down must be justified" ("Path" 468). Tradition reinforces these tendencies, insofar as adherence to precedent reduces the need for creative effort and justifies the practice of simply citing cases deemed similar and following the rule laid down in them.

The result is that judges may underinvest in making fine distinctions by satisficing or settling on satisfactory, rather than optimal, legal rules.[77] Judges may select the first line of available precedent without determining whether a competing line of precedent has equal application. Although judges who follow precedent must still invest in the discovery of precedent,[78] the research necessary for that function may be less than the research necessary for full consideration of each case. Were that not so, the economizing justification for following precedent would have no weight. Here, Holmes's Vermont justice of the peace offers the caricature that contains a ring of truth. Although that justice purported to have examined the statutes, he found nothing about churns that would dictate his decision, thus revealing insufficient investment in decision making. Had he found a decision involving the theft of a churn in which the plaintiff had won, he might have given a decision for the plaintiff in his case involving the breaking of a churn on the rationale that the first churn case was binding precedent for the second, notwithstanding the dissimilarities between stealing and breaking. There is no reason that leisure-seeking judges will invest in distinguishing between cases in which the lock-in effects of precedent are trivial or nontrivial. Thus, Holmes seems rightly concerned that a doctrine of precedent following induces inappropriate lock-in if leisure maximization is judges' primary incentive.

The press of judicial reports, the lengthiness of opinions, and the increased number of dissents and concurrences in multijudge courts, however, indicate that a preference for sloth alone cannot explain judicial behavior. Rather, at least some judges write long and often (or have their clerks do so), because they wish to maximize some alternative objective, such as fame or reputation,[79] or participation in a law-making process. Reputation for excellence in judging may increase the availability of certain types of postjudicial employment (e.g., positions in high-paying law firms, teaching posts), opportunities for enhanced earning power (lecture invitations), emblems of professional respect (membership in professional associations, assignment of highly qualified law clerks), or opportunities for advancement within the ranks of judges.[80]

A concern for reputation generates a complicated set of actions. The same act that enhances reputation with one group may diminish it with another. Judges who wish to increase their reputation with their peers may simply want to clear their dockets quickly, so that they are not seen as imposing a heavy caseload on their colleagues. Judges with these incentives may spend little time rethinking established rules or questioning arguably applicable precedents. For others, however, enhancing reputation may require emergence from the pack of judges. These objectives might be thought to generate insufficient respect for precedent. Judges are less likely to develop reputations if their opinions fail to develop the law but only restate and apply the law laid down by others. If constrained by the past, therefore, judges will be less able to demonstrate subtlety in making distinctions, finding conflicts among competing lines of precedent, or adding refinements to previously imprecise locutions. To the extent that judicial reputation is generated by both practitioner and academic commentary, those commentaries are likely to focus on the novel and the extraordinary rather than on the wooden and mundane. One need not posit the extreme position that judges seek to create inefficient precedents in order to maximize citations by generating additional litigation;[81] a less heroic claim that judges seek professional acclaim is sufficient to contend that judges overinvest in distinguishing precedent.

These incentives are amplified by the prospective function of precedent. My account of prospectivity focused on its utility to litigants to bind future decision makers. The prospective function of a precedent also enhances the value of a decision to the judge who makes it. The force of tradition means that a judge able to write an opinion that survives the appellate process has created a rule that others will follow presumptively. If judges in subsequent cases take a retrospective view of precedent, they are likely to follow the rule laid down by the judge in the prior case, increasing his or her visibility and reputation.[82] Thus, a judge who uses precedent prospectively may see tradition as a tool for personal advancement rather than as a constraint. While there is, of course, a likelihood that judges in subsequent cases will be equally creative and thus distinguish the prior case, merely following the established rule deprives the judge in the prior case of reputational enhancement by subsequent citation. Even if subsequent judges choose to distinguish the precedent created by the prior case, they must at least discuss the case being distinguished, thus providing greater notoriety for the judge in that prior case.

These objectives suggest that there will be some judges, call them "rogue judges," who are likely to overinvest in creating new law; that is, they are likely to overutilize the tools of distinction that are available to them. I mean by this that they are likely to avoid path dependence in trivial cases as well as nontrivial ones. Recall that avoiding tradition in such cases imposes excessive costs by changing rules under circumstances that do not produce social advances. Rogue judges may make such overinvestments because they obtain personal benefits from the new decision but do not suffer the costs of rule changes. A requirement of adhering to precedent may be perceived as an effort to constrain rogue judges by causing them to internalize more of these costs, as by requiring them to justify deviations from precedent with more rigor than is necessary when a court simply follows an established rule.[83] But for at least some rogues, this requirement has a perverse effect. Judges who seek reputational advantage, or who benefit from participating in the lawmaking process, may treat opinion writing as a consumption good rather than a cost.[84] To the extent that this is true, complex opinions filled with fine distinctions will return greater benefits than opinions that simply cite preexisting law favorably. Thus, the very effort to constrain rogue opinions risks producing more of them.

Rogue judges may favor deviation from precedent for additional reasons. Judges may seek approval outside of their professional rank and within a broader political forum, perhaps motivated by the possibility of advancement in the political arena. Political recognition, however, is more likely to come from departure with precedent than from following it. Political support is likely to form because a group seeks to alter the status quo. Judges inclined to make such changes may be more attractive to those groups. While politically ambitious judges who preserve the status quo may be able to blame earlier decision makers for unpopular decisions and offer their own fidelity to law as a characteristic worthy of political support, they are unlikely to generate the same political enthusiasm as judges who demonstrate independence and commitment to a political agenda. Thus, political rogues may care more that their decisions are popular than that they are consistent with a preexisting body of law.

It is in this context that Holmes's appeal for flexibility in legal doctrine leads him into direct confrontation with tradition. When he insists that legal doctrine does not flow from "exact logical conclusions," so that determinations about preferable rules are not "good for all time" but are "open to reconsideration upon a slight change in the habit of the public mind" ("Path" 466), Holmes recognizes that resort to tradition suppresses the adaptation of legal rules to vicissitudes in public opinion. But this appears to be a virtue of precedent. Notwithstanding his epigrammatic description of his role as judge as helping his fellow citizens "go to Hell" if that is their desire,[85] little in Holmes's judicial writings indicates a willingness to follow popular movements uncritically. Perhaps one reason for favoring precedent is that tradition may itself be one of the institutional constraints that leads us to believe that courts can resist inconstancy in popular views.[86] In short, of the two functions of precedent with which I began this essay, constraining the scope of reconsideration may be more important.

Finally, tradition may serve as a constraint on the capacity of judges to receive entreaties of limited interests. To the extent that it limits opportunities for variation, the doctrine of precedent complements doctrines such as standing and ripeness, and restraints on advisory opinions (case or controversy requirements and limitations on declaratory judgments) that repress opportunities for judges to serve the idiosyncratic interests of particular groups. Situations in which parties are willing to bear the costs of litigation even though they are not directly interested in the specific facts that give rise to the litigation (standing and ripeness), or are unwilling to invest in the underlying activity that gives rise to litigation (advisory opinions) may suggest that those parties have idiosyncratic interests and are poor representatives of the social interests that we want the legal rule to reflect. Judges, of course, may use the same tools of interpretation that apply to precedent to circumvent these doctrines, such as by finding standing or ripeness in dubious circumstances. These doctrines, therefore, cannot fully restrain judges from hearing special pleas if they are otherwise inclined. But just as these doctrines limit such parties from coming before courts in the first place, so the doctrine of precedent inhibits judges who hear those appeals from making substantive decisions based on those interests. Combined with a requirement that judges explain their rationales, a requirement of precedent following serves as a signaling mechanism to indicate that deviations from established law have occurred. The requirement thus facilitates monitoring of potential rogue judges. Again, however, the existence of a monitoring device suggests that, in the absence of a precedent-following rule, judges will defer too little, rather than too much, to tradition.

V. Conclusion: Striking the Balance

Restraints and signaling mechanisms, of course, are not costless. Tradition is underinclusive insofar as it is drawn with fuzzy lines that make its content indistinct. It is overinclusive insofar as it locks in practices developed for an earlier time, perhaps for reasons long forgotten, and that would not have been adopted if considered afresh today. Precedent, as an embodiment of tradition, suffers from both these defects. Entrepreneurial judges who are capable of manipulating legal doctrine can easily escape; judges who substitute history for the rational study of law, or who recharacterize justifications for existing doctrine that evolved from different circumstances rather than ask whether the doctrine makes sense in the first place will find escape more difficult ("Path" 469).

Tradition, then, may be a mechanism for lock-in, as Holmes suggests. But lock-in effects in adjudication are not necessarily evil. The issue that remains is whether precedent is overutilized by judges who maximize interests unrelated to their assumed roles or underutilized by rogues. One might fear that rogue judges are the real villains. If exercise of judicial discretion can overcome the constraints of precedent as easily as I have suggested, then it may be that Holmes's concern was misplaced, because we should be more concerned with the effect of precedent as a constraint on rogues than as a tool for sloth. And if path dependence typically arises in cases where the rule dictated by the path is trivial, the fact that precedent binds judges may be untroublesome because the doctrine's economizing features outweigh any harm of overreliance on tradition.

But maybe Holmes was right after all. Given the capacity of the judge in the subsequent case to define and distinguish what he or she deems to be controlling precedent, there may be precious little we can do about rogue judges, once a case properly appears before them. Even if underinvestment in precedent by rogues threatens more damage than underinvestment by slothful judges, the ease with which precedent can be circumvented limits our capacity to use that doctrine to address the issue. Our controls on rogue judges must instead be directed at the variety of jurisdictional doctrines that prevent too many cases, especially those in which we think the parties' interests are idiosyncratic, from reaching courts in the first place. Accordingly, those cases in which precedent has a significant effect may, systematically, be those cases in which the greater threat is lazy judges rather than rogues. By signaling that mere citation to prior authority is an acceptable judicial practice, precedent may underwrite more judicial leisure than is acceptable. Absent more judges who (perhaps like Holmes) are able to strike the crude balance from a social perspective and to distinguish the trivial from the nontrivial cases of path dependence, maybe such rough judgments about the general tendency of judicial incentives is the most we can accomplish.

Notes

1 See Richard A. Wasserstrom, *The Judicial Decision* (Stanford: Stanford University Press, 1961). On the value of precedent for predictability, see Benjamin Klein, "Comment," *Journal of Law and Economics* 19 (1976):309.
2 On the willingness of at least some judges to underinvest in their decision making, see Richard A. Posner, "What Do Judges and Justices Maximize? (The Same Thing Everybody Else Does)," *Supreme Court Economics Review* 3 (1993):1.
3 Oliver W. Holmes, Jr., "The Path of the Law," *Harvard Law Review* 10 (1897):457 (cited hereafter parenthetically in the text as "Path"). "The Path" is reprinted in the Appendix to this volume with star paging.
4 In his judicial opinions, Holmes occasionally issued the same complaint about the arbitrary survival of legal doctrine. See E. Donald Elliott, "Holmes and Evolution: Legal Process as Artificial Intelligence," *Journal of Legal Studies* 13 (1984):113, 133–34.
5 See Klein, "Comment." A predictive view of the law does not necessarily require binding precedent. Prediction, for instance would include the capacity to foretell when courts would deviate from prior decisions. Nevertheless, one imagines that deviations would be infrequent, so that reliance on precedent would strengthen predictive capacities.
6 Richard A. Posner, *The Problems of Jurisprudence* (Cambridge, Mass.: Harvard University Press, 1990), 227.
7 Ibid.
8 Mark DeWolfe Howe, *Justice Oliver Wendell Holmes: The Proving Years, 1870–1882* (Cambridge, Mass.: Belknap Press of Harvard University Press, 1963), 43–50.
9 Holmes takes just this position at one point in *The Common Law*. See Oliver Wendell Holmes, *The Common Law* (Boston: Little, Brown, 1881), 26 (if a legal doctrine "were not supported by the appearance of good sense, it would not survive"). Note also Thomas Grey's conclusion that Holmes was "slow to depart from precedent," in large part because of his doubt that legal reforms would generate social progress. Thomas C. Grey, "Holmes and Legal Pragmatism," *Stanford Law Review* 41 (1989):787, 812.

I do not deny that there are powerful forces that allow legal rules to remain intact even when they disserve social values. Interest groups that obtain favorable legislation or judicial decisions may also maintain that legislation. Unless we believe that much of the lawmaking enterprise is dominated by special-interest groups whose conduct disserves the society, or that social conditions outstrip prevailing law, some presumption that existing law fits underlying social conditions seems appropriate.

10 "We learn that for everything we have to give up something else, and we are taught to set the advantage we gain against the other advantage we lose, and to know what we are doing when we elect" (474).
11 See, e.g., Lars Magnusson and Jan Ottosson, *Evolutionary Economics and Path Dependence* (Brookfield: Ed Elger, 1997); W. Brian Arthur, *Increasing Returns and Path Dependence in the Economy* (Ann Arbor: University of Michigan Press, 1994).
12 See Douglass C. North, *Institutional Change and Economic Performance* (Cambridge: Cambridge University Press, 1990), 76.
13 See, e.g., David Luban, "Justice Holmes and the Metaphysics of Judicial Restraint," *Duke Law Journal* 44 (1994):449, 489–501; Thomas C. Grey, "Molecular Motions: The Holmesian Judge in Theory and Practice," *William and Mary Law Review* 37 (1995):19.
14 See e.g., Steven J. Burton, *Judging in Good Faith* (Cambridge: Cambridge University Press, 1992), chapter 2, sections 3–4; Lewis A. Kornhauser, "An Economic Perspective on *Stare Decisis*," *Chicago–Kent Law Review* 65 (1989):63; Jonathan R. Macey, "The Internal and External Costs and Benefits of *Stare Decisis*," *Chicago–Kent Law Review* 65 (1989):93.
15 Two years later, Holmes continued this attack on tradition. Contending that the "true science of the law" depends on establishing postulates based on "accurately measured social desires instead of tradition," he demonstrated how a series of legal rules was based on historical artifacts that no longer justified their application. See Oliver Wendell Holmes, Jr., "Law in Science and Science in Law," *Harvard Law Review* 112 (1899):443, 452–55.
16 See Anthony Kronman, "Precedent and Tradition," *Yale Law Journal* 99 (1990):1029, 1035.
17 For the proposition that Holmes's epigrammatic style has led to oversimplified interpretations of his thought, see Grey, "Molecular Motions," 24.
18 See also Holmes, "Law in Science," 455 (discussing "the danger of inventing reasons offhand for whatever we find established in law").
19 Holmes, *Common Law*, 5–33.
20 Ibid., 31.
21 Here is Holmes's general account of the phenomenon:
    The customs, beliefs, or needs of a primitive time establish a rule or a formula. In the course of centuries, the custom, belief, or necessity disappears, but the rule remains. The reason which gave rise to the rule has been forgotten, and ingenious minds set themselves to inquire how it is to be accounted for. Some ground of policy is thought of, which seems to explain it and to reconcile it with the present state of things; and then the rule adapts itself to the new reasons which have been found for it, and enters on a new career. The old form receives a new content, and in time even the form modifies itself to fit the meaning which it has received. (Ibid., 8)
22 Ibid., 32.
23 On Holmes's deference to legislatures, see Luban, "Metaphysics of Judicial Restraint," 491.
24 *Stack v. New York, N. H. & H. R. Co.*, 58 N.E. 686 (Mass. 1900).
25 Ibid., 687.
26 245 U.S. 603 (1918).
27 Ibid.
28 Elliott also notes that Holmes, despite his appeal to reason, could sometimes be found on the side of "arbitrary historical rules." See Elliott, "Holmes and Evolution," 133. My claim is that there may be no necessary conflict between reason and appeal to arbitrary rules.

29 216 U.S. 358 (1910).
30 Ibid., 366.
31 Ibid.
32 Ibid.
33 See also *Lewin v. Folsom,* 171 Mass. 188 (1898), in which Holmes justified the grant of simple rather than compound interest on a judgment, "reasoning" that the law had demonstrated an "ancient unwillingness to allow compound interest."
34 See, e.g., Grey, "Molecular Motions," 37–38.
35 256 U.S. 506 (1921).
36 256 U.S. at 507 (citation omitted).
37 This is a form of the more general question "When should a rational individual 'stop considering the pros and cons of an issue and reach a decision'?" James M. Buchanan and Gordon Tollock, *The Calculus of Consent* (Ann Arbor: University of Michigan Press, 1962), 97.
38 See *Pokora v. Wabash Ry.,* 292 U.S. 98 (1934); Holmes, *Common Law,* 97–99.
39 Holmes, *Common Law,* 97–99.
40 Wasserstrom, *Judicial Decision,* 43.
41 See ibid., 76 ("There is no reason to suppose – certainly none has ever been suggested – that the court which is first forced to decide a question of a certain kind will inevitably formulate the best rule for that kind of case").
42 See Frederick Schauer, "Precedent," *Stanford Law Review* 39 (1987):571, 575–76; Kenneth J. Kress, "Legal Reasoning and Coherence Theories: Dworkin's Rights Thesis, Retroactivity, and the Linear Order of Decisions," *California Law Review* 72 (1984):369, 400–1. It may be that even on this understanding an economizing explanation could justify precedent. If we believe not only that prior decisions were likely to be correct, and that conditions that would warrant changing the justification for similar cases evolve slowly, then a decision reached today about a case similar to one decided yesterday is likely to be similarly decided. Following the prior decision without investigating the current applicability of its underlying justification, therefore, may simply be a rough but cost-saving surrogate for fuller examination of the current case.
43 One may, of course, create a weaker form of precedent in which prior decisions are presumptively correct but subject to review. For defenses of weaker forms of precedent, see Kornhauser, "Economic Perspective," 78–92; Macey, "Costs and Benefits," 93–113.
44 These are the traditional justifications for the doctrine. See Frank H. Easterbrook, "Stability and Reliability in Judicial Decisions," *Cornell Law Review* 73 (1988):422; Wasserstrom, *Judicial Decision,* 56–83; Schauer, "Precedent," 595–605; Kronman, "Precedent and Tradition," 1036–47; Kornhauser, "Economic Perspective," 71–78.
45 For discussions that rely exclusively on the retrospective nature of precedent, see Kronman, "Economic Perspective"; Gerald J. Postema, "On the Moral Presence of the Past," *McGill Law Journal* 36 (1991):1153. For exceptions that confront both assumptions, see Schauer, "Precedent"; Kenneth I. Winston, "On Treating Like Cases Alike," *California Law Review* 62 (1974):1, 4.
46 See Bruce Chapman, "The Rational and the Reasonable: Social Choice Theory and Adjudication," *University of Chicago Law Review* 61 (1994):41, 78–79.
47 The hypothetical example is drawn from the facts of *Dixon, Iramos & Cia v. Chase National Bank,* 144 F2d 759 (2d Cir. 1944), cert. denied 324 U.S. 850 (1945).
48 See Frederick Schauer, "Slippery Slopes," *Harvard Law Review* 99 (1985):361, 370–73.

49 See "The Rule of Precedent," by Theodore M. Benditt, in *Precedent in Law,* ed. Laurence Goldstein (New York: Oxford University Press, 1987), 104–6; A. W. B. Simpson, "The *Ration Decidendi* of a Case and the Doctrine of Binding Precedent," in *Oxford Essays in Jurisprudence,* ed. A. G. Guest (London: Oxford University Press, 1961), 148.

50 *Schad v. Borough of Mount Ephraim,* 452 U.S. 61 (1981) (Burger dissenting).

51 As Edward H. Levi wrote,

[T]he judge in the present case may find irrelevant the existence or absence of facts which prior judges thought important. It is not what the prior judge intended that is of any importance; rather it is what the present judge, attempting to see the law as a fairly consistent whole, thinks should be the determining classification.

Edward H. Levi, *An Introduction to Legal Reasoning* (Chicago: University of Chicago Press, 1968), 2–3.

52 See, e.g., the statement by Wasserstrom of the doctrine of *stare decisis:* "The rule of stare decisis requires that cases which are similar to earlier cases be decided in the same way in which those earlier cases were adjudicated," *Judicial Decision,* 54.

53 See, e.g., Ronald A. Cass, "Judging: Norms and Incentives of Retrospective Decision-Making," *Boston University Law Review* 41 (1995):75.

54 See Paul Rubin, "Common Law and Statute Law," *Journal of Legal Studies* 11 (1982):205.

55 See Saul Levmore, "Rethinking Comparative Law: Variety and Uniformity in Ancient and Modern Tort Law," *Tulane Law Review* 61 (1986):235.

56 See, e.g., Stan J. Liebowitz and Stephen E. Margolis, "Path Dependence, Lock-Ins, and History," *Journal of Law, Economics, and Organizations* 11 (1995):205–7; Paul A. David, "Why Are Institutions the 'Carriers of History'?: Path Dependence and the Evolution of Conventions, Organizations and Institutions," *Structural Change and Economic Dynamics* 5 (1994):205–20.

57 See, e.g., W. Brian Arthur, "Competing Technologies, Increasing Returns, and Lock-In by Historical Events," *Economics Journal* 99 (1989):116.

58 See Marcel Kahan and Michael Klausner, "Path Dependence in Corporate Contracting: Increasing Returns, Herd Behavior and Cognitive Biases," *Washington University Law Quarterly* 74 (1996):347; Michael Klausner, "Corporations, Corporate Law, and Networks of Contracts," *Virginia Law Review* 81 (1995):757. See also Mark Roe, "Chaos and Evolution in Law Economics," *Harvard Law Review* 109 (1996):641.

59 I discuss the problem at greater length in Clayton P. Gillette, "Rules, Standards, and Precautions in Payment Systems," *Virginia Law Review* 82 (1996):181, 214–16.

60 See Louis Kaplow, "An Economic Analysis of Legal Transitions," *Harvard Law Review* 99 (1986):509.

61 This set of path-dependent examples may come closest to what Liebowitz and Margolis term "second-degree path dependence." In that set of cases, a standard that was previously selected on the basis of the best information then available turns out to be inferior to a rule that would have been selected had all of the relevant information been known. Once investment is made in the standard adopted under the information then available, it may make sense to stay with that standard. Given that imperfect information is simply part of the human condition, decisions made with proper use of the then-best available information cannot be said to be inefficient. Liebowitz and Margolis, "Path Dependence," 206–7.

62 Explored by Frank H. Easterbrook, "Ways of Criticizing the Court," *Harvard Law Review* 95 (1982):802, 818; Maxwell L. Stearns, "Standing Back from the Forest: Justiciability and Social Choice," *California Law Review* 83 (1995):1309, 1356–59.

11.2 Aspect 2: Situation Type Aspect

Thus, in imperfective and optative viewpoints (the latter not illustrated here), there is usually no distinction between durative verbs with natural and arbitrary endpoints: duratives are morphologically unmarked and generally undifferentiated in these viewpoints.

A few preverbs require overt marking of accomplishment situation aspect in imperfective and optative viewpoints. One such preverb is *dah* 'up onto horizontal surface, up to a position of rest'. This form is also used as a noun, meaning 'surface, top'. Some examples are given in (57).

(57) a. dah-**th**-į-t*ł*a
 preverb-accomplishment situation aspect-2sg Subject-stem
 'You sg. get onto it.'
 b. O da-**wh**e-h-téh
 preverb-accomplishment situation aspect-1sg Subject/valence-stem
 'I am putting animate O up.'

Inherent in this preverb is a goal, namely a state of rest. It is thus inherently both durative and telic, and telicity must therefore be indicated in all viewpoints. In general, preverbs requiring accomplishment situation aspect in imperfective and optative viewpoints as well as in the perfective viewpoint are resultative in meaning. The presence of *s* situation aspect is therefore not surprising since resultatives have a telic component.

11.2.1.9 Summary

I have argued for the system in (58).

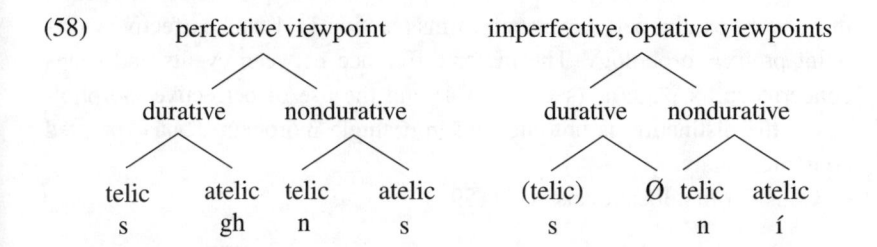

(58)   perfective viewpoint   imperfective, optative viewpoints
           ╱‾‾‾‾‾‾╲   ╱‾‾‾‾‾‾╲
      durative   nondurative   durative   nondurative
      ╱‾‾╲   ╱‾‾╲   ╱‾‾╲   ╱‾‾╲
   telic atelic telic atelic   (telic) Ø   telic atelic
     s   gh   n   s   s   n   í

Achievements involve transitions alone, activities involve processes alone, accomplishments consist of a process followed by a transition, and semelfactives involve neither component. In the perfective viewpoint, both durativity, or process, and telicity, or transition, are important and overtly expressed, while in imperfective and optative viewpoints, processes are not usually further subdivided. Different situation aspects are characterized in other ways as well. As discussed here, different classes are compatible with different preverbs and subsituation aspect markers. For further discussion, see Axelrod 1993, Kari 1979, and Rice 1989. Thus, verbs of different classes show morphosyntactic as well as semantic differences.

11.2.2 States

So far I have focused on the situation aspect of events. States form a second major situation type in Slave and other Athapaskan languages. As Smith 1997:32 points out, states are stable events that may hold for a moment or an interval; they are not divisible into stages. Given that states have duration as an intrinsic property (see (9)), no matter how brief that duration is, and given that they cannot be internally differentiated, one might expect that in languages with overt marking of situation aspect, the same situation aspect marking would be found for all states. But this is not the case – like events, Slave states divide into subgroups with different situation aspect marking. Slave has two familiar kinds of states: locationals, which express position, location, and possession (this latter through causativization; see chapter 7), and descriptives, which express information about mental states and properties of people, things, and concepts. In addition, there is a third type of state, called extension in the Athapaskan literature, which focuses on the linear extension of objects in space. In this section I describe each of these types of states, beginning with the imperfective viewpoint. The use of the term 'imperfective viewpoint' is misleading, for in both imperfective and perfective viewpoints these verbs exhibit perfective stem forms (section 11.4) and perfective viewpoint prefix morphology. The major difference between events and states concerns suffix patterns (section 11.4) and the use of perfective morphology – the distinction is not encoded in a single morpheme, but expressed constructionally.

Consider first locationals, as in (59).

(59) a. **we**-da   'S/he sits.'
     b. **the**-la   'Pl. O are located'
     c. **the**-'ǫ   'Three-dimensional O is located.'
     d. **whi**-h-'ǫ   'I have three-dimensional object.'

11.2 Aspect 2: Situation Type Aspect

Imperfective viewpoint locationals require accomplishment situation aspect. These verbs mean something like attaining a state of being in a position and remaining in that state. The state is attained through a process followed by a transition; it is a type of resultative.

In the Athapaskan literature, extension statives are treated as stative counterparts of achievement verbs on the grounds that they require *n* situation aspect marking and can occur with many of the preverbs found with achievements. Extension statives refer to something extended in a linear way, including streams, trails, rays of sunshine, and gusts of wind (Axelrod 1993:134). Examples are given in (60).

(60) a. **n-i̲-'á**   'It (e.g., road, sticklike object) extends.'
     b. **n-i̲-li̲**   'Water flows.'
     c. ké-**n-i̲** -di   'It shines, it is light.'
     d. **n-i̲**-h-ts'i 'Wind blows.'

Finally, the larger category of states represents descriptions, attributes, mental states, and the like.

(61) a. de-gay
        qualifier-stem
        'It is white.'
     b. de-zhí
        qualifier-stem
        'It is hard.'
     c. ne-da
        qualifier-stem
        'She/he/it is heavy.'
     d. h-i̲-kone
        epenthetic-perfective viewpoint-stem
        'It is clear, shiny, bright.'
     e. h-i̲-ɬǫ
        epenthetic-perfective viewpoint-stem
        'It is many.'
     f. h-i̲-li̲
        epenthetic-perfective viewpoint-stem
        'She/he/it exists, is in a state denoted by complement.'
     g. 'ǫ-t'e
        preverb/perfective viewpoint-stem
        'She/he/it is.' (existential)

h. gǫ-zhǫ
      area/perfective viewpoint-stem
      'S/he is wise.'
   i. k-o-d-į-h-shǫ
      area-area-qualifier-perfective viewpoint-valence-stem
      'S/he knows.'

This interesting category is the prototypical state, representing pure existence and involving inherent properties, either stable or transitory over time. Like most event verbs in imperfective and optative viewpoints, descriptive states are not overtly marked for situation type – it is existence rather than duration or boundedness that is expressed by descriptive verbs.

Assuming that states are inherently durative and unbounded in Slave, as they are in other languages, why do locational states occur with a situation aspect marker indicating boundedness, and why do extension states occur with one indicating boundedness and punctuality? The use of these situation aspect markers is mysterious given the inherent properties of states.

I offer the following speculation in response to this question. Stativity itself is marked by verb suffixation patterns; see section 11.4. In imperfective stative situations, the situation aspect markers, I suggest, do not mark the situation type, as they do with events, but rather tell how the state came about, indicating whether the state is inherent or resultative. This choice is not directly available in languages with covert situation aspect. Consider first descriptive states. These represent pure existence, indicating intrinsic properties of an individual or of a stage in time, and they are structurally simple in that the state is not attained, but inherent. Locational and extension states, on the other hand, are structurally more complex, indicating not inherent properties but rather ones that are attained. For instance, if a boat is located somewhere, this is not an inherent property of the boat, but rather the boat came to occupy that location. Likewise, if the wind is in a state of blowing, it came to this state.

Assuming that in states the situation aspect marker contributes information about whether the state is inherent or the result of a transition, a second question arises. Why are locational states parallel to accomplishments, involving a process and a transition, while extension states are parallel to achievements, involving a transition, but no process?

The major differences between locational states and extension states concern how the state is achieved and the type of space involved in the resultant state. An intimate relationship between space and time is common in Athapaskan languages. For instance, the same postpositions/adverbs are used in

11.2 Aspect 2: Situation Type Aspect

reference to time and space, and the areal refers to both time and space; see, for example, Axelrod 1996, Leer 1995, and Rice 1989 for discussion. It would not be surprising to find that locations in time involve similar parameters to locations in space, with a focus on the type of object involved. In the following I examine the difference between locational and extension states by considering both the way that the transitions are met in the two types of states and the type of space that they occupy.

Consider first extension states. These are reached in an instant in time – the wind goes from not blowing to blowing, a string is suddenly taut. In terms of occupation of space, extension states are unidimensional. For instance, the verb 'stream flows, current flows' refers to water contained within stream banks and not for water flowing outside the banks (see Kari 1990:277 on Ahtna). The verb 'linear object extends' is used if the patient argument of the verb is perceived as having extension without dimension (e.g., Slave extension *nį-'á* 'linear, elongated object extends' vs. location *whe-tǫ*'elongated object is located, is in position'). Linear extension is an important feature of Athapaskan languages and is indicated by verb stems and prefixes both. Extension states are concerned only with an object's linear extension; any other dimensions of that object are irrelevant.

While extension states are reached instantaneously and occupy a single dimension in space, locational states need not be reached instantaneously and occupy two or three dimensions in space. For instance, a state of being seated may result from a process of sitting and may occupy more than a moment, and an object that is in a seated position takes up two- or three-dimensional space.

Suppose that unidimensionality in space equates with instantaneity in time and higher dimensionality with duration. The parallel between states and events is then clear: extension states resemble achievement events in involving a transition and occupying an instant in time or space, and locational states resemble accomplishment events in involving a transition and occupying more than an instant in time or space. The states differ from the events in requiring the state resulting from the transition to continue. Further, descriptive states resemble activity events in occupying time or space but without a transition. Semelfactive events have no parallel state as states obligatorily involve duration, whether for a moment or a period of time, or a transition into a state, both of which are lacking in semelfactives. Thus, the situation aspect markers have core meanings, with different interpretations depending upon whether the particular situation is an event or a state.

The relationship between events and states is summarized in the table in (62).

(62) | **Event type** | **Aspectual composition** | **State type** | **Aspectual composition** |
|---|---|---|---|
| achievement | transition | extension | transition + state |
| accomplishment | duration + transition | location | duration + transition + state |
| activity | duration | description | duration |
| semelfactive | | – | |

States, like events, can be modified by material in the predicate, both purely aspectual material and lexical material with intrinsic aspectual content. Transitionals and inchoatives, marked by the subsituation aspect marker *í*, indicate the change of a state into an event (as marked through stem morphology; see section 11.4) and the abrupt or punctual beginning of a state. The inceptive can occur with states, creating an event, but indicating a more gradual beginning than the transitional/inchoative. The inchoative subsituation aspect marker is used when the focus is on the transition rather than on the state, while situation aspect is used in stative situation types to indicate how the state was attained – when it is the state rather than the transition that is the focus. Various aspectual lexical preverbs also are found with states; as with events, these play a role in the situation type system. See Rice 1989 on Slave; see also Axelrod 1993 and Kari 1979 for discussion of morphosyntactic properties of the different types of stative situations.

So far I have only considered the imperfective viewpoint of states. Stative verbs also are found in perfective and optative viewpoints. Perfective viewpoint statives can be interpreted in one of two ways, depending on context. First, they can indicate that the state existed in the past, but no longer exists with respect to the reference point. Second, they can indicate a present state. In this latter case, the type of transition is not indicated through situation aspect marking, but only duration. This seems to be a marked meaning for perfective statives.

The perfective viewpoint of all stative subtypes is marked by *gh* situation aspect. This is expected of a prototypical stative – states are durative and atelic in nature (Smith 1997). In the perfective viewpoint, it is simply the duration that is focused, without reference to the manner in which the state was achieved.

Events and states differ with respect to viewpoint aspect in an interesting way: in events, the perfective viewpoint shows the most aspectual detail, differentiating telic from atelic events and durative from nondurative ones. The imperfective viewpoint is somewhat more impoverished, distinguishing only durative and nondurative. In states, on the other hand, it is the imperfective viewpoint that shows the most aspectual detail, in contrast to the perfective viewpoints.

11.2.3 Looking Ahead

I have spent a considerable time outlining the situation aspect system in Slave (although, at the same time, I have barely scratched the surface complexities of situation aspect). I have argued that the so-called conjugation markers have content – they are overt markers of situation aspect. I have outlined semantic and morphosyntactic criteria for establishing these classes; see Axelrod 1993, Kari 1979, and Rice 1989 for considerably more detail on characteristics of the classes. This discussion may appear to have taken us far from the major topic, the ordering of morphemes in verbs. However, this excursus was required in order to talk about ordering – it is necessary to know just what it is that is being ordered. If the morphemes in question are conjugation markers that specify arbitrary verb classes, they are perhaps in a surprising position – conjugation markers often attach directly to verb stems (see, for instance, Beard 1995:129). However, I have argued that these morphemes are overt markers of situation aspect. Assuming this now, I am ready to return to the major theme, ordering.

11.3 Ordering within Aspect

I have argued that the basic Slave aspectual system consists of two major components, viewpoint aspect and situation type aspect. Situation types in turn can be subdivided into two major subtypes, events and states, which again subdivide into further categories. It is also possible to focus on a piece of an event or a state by using subsituation aspect markers that indicate beginnings, endings, transitions, attempts, and the like.

Every sentence is marked for viewpoint aspect and for situation type aspect, although in some cases the marking is phonologically null. In Slave, these components of aspect occur in the following order (see chapter 12 for more discussion of subsituation aspect).

(63) subsituation aspect – situation type aspect – viewpoint aspect

The important question is whether this ordering is predictable. Recall my proposal that in Slave in particular and in Athapaskan languages in general, ordering is determined by scope and generality: morphemes of greater scope or generality follow those within their scope or with more specificity. So far, we have seen various ways of looking at scope: a more general form may take scope over a more specific form, an entailing item over the entailed item, a quantifier over the element that it quantifies. Here I consider another way of thinking about scope, one involving co-occurrence restrictions. For instance, we have seen that the presence of semelfactive situation aspect depends on viewpoint aspect, appearing only in nonperfective viewpoints. The relation between viewpoint aspect and situation aspect is thus parallel to the relation between a more general and a more restrictive form: the viewpoint restricts the possible situation types. Aikenvald and Dixon 1998 discuss similar examples of dependency between grammatical systems. They propose that "if the choices in system Y depend on that made from system X ... we shall say that there is a dependency relation between X and Y, i.e., X > Y. For instance, if there are fewer case distinctions in plural than in singular number, we shall say that the number of choices available in the case system depends on the choice that is made in the number system, i.e., number > case" (Aikenvald and Dixon 1998:62). While Aikenvald and Dixon define dependencies in terms of numbers of distinctions, one can think of this in a slightly different way: if a particular choice in system Y is available only under certain conditions in system X, then system Y depends on system X. An alternative way to state this is that system X has scope over system Y.

Consider the relationship between situation aspect and viewpoint aspect in Slave. I have argued that situation aspect choices are limited by viewpoint. The restrictions on semelfactives in certain viewpoints are one illustration of this. Further, it is generally the case that telicity is overtly marked on events in durative situation types in the perfective viewpoint, while only durativity is important in the imperfective and optative viewpoints. Thus, the viewpoint aspect determines the situation aspect possibilities, suggesting that viewpoint aspect has situation aspect within its scope. The viewpoint and situation aspect systems are independent, as Smith 1997 argues, but choices in one of them, viewpoint, restrict the choices available in the other, situation.

Another argument for considering the ordering of viewpoint aspect and situation aspect to be predictable is based on Bybee's 1985a work on relevance. Bybee argues that information that is relevant to the verb correlates with its position with respect to the verb. Relevance is determined by a variety of factors, including whether the category can be expressed intrinsically in the verb, and whether the category functions inflectionally, derivationally, or both.

Bybee argues that situation aspect can be lexical or derivational, while viewpoint aspect is only inflectional (1985a:102). Based partially on this finding, she proposes the following degrees of relevance to the verb. (Note

11.4 On the Role of the Suffixes

that Bybee does not use the terms 'situation aspect' and 'viewpoint aspect', but 'telic/atelic' and 'perfective/imperfective'.)

(64) most relevant   least relevant
     situation aspect > viewpoint aspect > mood

This is exactly the order in which these categories are found in the Slave verb: situation aspect, which is most relevant to the verb in Bybee's schema, is closer to the verb than is viewpoint aspect, which is less relevant to the verb. (Recall from chapter 5 that I am assuming that the verb stem originates within the verb phrase, making a functional category to the left closer to the verb than one to the right.)

To summarize, viewpoint aspect represents a more general category than situation aspect. This claim is supported both in Slave, where situation aspect is determined by viewpoint aspect, and crosslinguistically, by the universal tendency for situation aspect to be realized derivationally, or closer to the verb, and viewpoint aspect to be realized inflectionally, or further from the verb (Bybee 1985a). The ordering of situation aspect and viewpoint aspect thus appears to be predictable from general principles.

Now consider the ordering of subsituation aspect and situation aspect. According to Bybee, both of these are marked either lexically or derivationally, yielding no predictions if both are overt. However, the semantics of subsituation aspects indicates that they are less general than the situation aspect markers themselves. Subsituation aspect markers focus on a particular part of the time line that is partly defined by the situation type aspect and thus further differentiate the situation aspects.

I draw the following conclusion. The ordering of viewpoint aspect and situation aspect is predictable and need not be stipulated by a template – it follows rather from the inherent semantics of the items involved and the relationship between them. The same is true of subsituation aspect and situation aspect. While one can use a template to describe the ordering of these elements, the arbitrariness of the template does not capture the semantic relationships among the elements involved; a template could equally be used to describe any conceivable ordering of these three types of elements.

11.4 On the Role of the Suffixes

I have so far ignored a piece of verb morphology that enters into the aspect system in an important way, namely the suffixes. The suffixes in Slave indicate both viewpoint aspect and situation aspect. However, they do not define these aspects in exactly the same way as the prefixes do. Where situation aspect and viewpoint aspect are marked by distinct prefixes, these two aspect types are collapsed in the suffixes, which express two distinct functions in a single portmanteau-like form. In addition, suffixes mark two distinctions not made in the prefixes. First, the prefixes define two types of processes, activities and accomplishments. The suffixes further delineate these processes, indicating, for instance, whether the process is directed or undirected. Second, suffixes combine with the situation types to produce complex situation types with an internal structure that includes another situation type. These are called derived situation types by Smith 1991:36, superaspects by Kari 1979 and Axelrod 1993, and compounding aspects by Rice 1989. Three such derived aspects are found in Slave: progressive, customary, and distributive.

I begin by describing the aspectual categories defined by the suffix system. I then address the question of why these morphemes are suffixes rather than prefixes.

11.4.1 Suffixes and Events

As discussed in section 11.2, the basic situation types in Slave are overtly marked by situation aspect prefixes. In addition, each situation type has its own set of suffixes in the different viewpoints. The basic suffixation patterns in Slave are summarized in (65). It should be pointed out here that neutralization in Slave renders the suffix system opaque, and I do not attempt to show the internal morphology of stems here; see Rice 1989 for detail.

(65)
Situation type	Imperfective	Perfective	Optative
Achievement	h	N	h or high tone
Activity	Ø	high tone	high tone
Accomplishment	h or Ø	N	h or high tone
Semelfactive	Ø	Ø	Ø

In the discussion in section 11.2, I showed that each situation type aspect class occurs with its own situation aspect marker. The situation aspect classes also differ in the preverbs and subsituation aspect markers that they co-occur with. The chart in (65) illustrates yet another morphosyntactic property that differentiates situation aspect classes: within each viewpoint each has its own suffix pattern.[9] Thus, achievements have a suffix *h* in the imperfective viewpoint, *N* (nasalization) in the perfective viewpoint, and *h* or high tone in the optative viewpoint (depending on verb, with some variation). Activities,

11.4 On the Role of the Suffixes

on the other hand, have no suffix in the imperfective viewpoint and a high tone suffix in the perfective and optative viewpoints. None of the viewpoints or situation types has a unique suffix; rather the suffixes carry information about both viewpoint and situation type.

The suffixes do not divide up the world in the same way that the prefixes do. We earlier saw that imperfective, perfective, and optative are each signaled by distinct prefixes. In the suffixes, on the other hand, imperfective and optative viewpoints may have the same suffix, as in the achievement verbs, and perfective and optative may share a suffix, as in activity verbs.

Suffixes thus differ from prefixes in allowing an overlap in function not found among prefixes. Conversely, suffixes differ from prefixes in making a contrast within a class that has a single marking in the prefixes. This is clear in the perfective viewpoint: activities are marked by a high tone suffix, which simply indicates nonimperfective, while accomplishments and achievements are marked by a nasal suffix. Each suffix thus combines information about viewpoint and situation type, information that is expressed uniquely by the prefixes.

Further investigation of the suffix system confirms that it partitions time differently than the prefixes do. As well as the basic activity, accomplishment, achievement, and semelfactive classes, several additional aspectual classes are found in Slave as defined by the suffixation patterns in combination with other verbal properties. These further suffixation sets function to create derived situation types, either creating a process from a nonprocess or combining with the basic aspect types to create the derived types customary, distributive, and progressive.

I first consider the aspects that create processes. In the following discussion, I illustrate each of these derived situation type aspects with its definition, situation aspect, suffixation pattern, and specific preverbs, and I show that these aspects are only available to certain situation types. It is worth noting that derived situation aspect types are common across languages. According to Smith 1997:24, three major classes of activities exist. One class is unlimited in principle (sleep, laugh), a second has indefinitely many internal stages (eat cherries), and a third class is derived, shifted activities (including iterations of semelfactives and activities derived from achievements). Thus, activities can have different internal structures; in addition, they can be derived from other situation types. The Slave derived situation types are largely of the latter type; for instance, nonprocesses can be made into processes. I look later at the richer suffixation patterns of Ahtna and Koyukon, where suffixes, generally combined with particular preverbs, not only create derived situation types, but also indicate specific types of processes.

One derivation creates repetitive derived activities from semelfactive and achievement situation type verbs, making them into processes, specifically a type of activity.

(66) Aspect name: repetitive activity
    occurrence: with achievement and semelfactive situation types
    definition: prolonged, undirected, segmented activity
    situation aspect marker in perfective: *gh*
    suffixation pattern: *h* imperfective *h* perfective *h* optative
    other aspectual material: preverb *k'ína/k'e* 'around'

Repetitive activities are repeated events with no natural endpoint; typical English translations are 'V around, go around V-ing' in the imperfective viewpoint and 'V-ed around, went around V-ing' in the perfective viewpoint. Repetitives share a suffixation set with customaries (section 11.4.2), and co-occur with the preverb *k'ína/k'e* 'around'. Given that the repetitive derived activity type is semantically durative and atelic, it is not surprising that it occurs with the activity situation aspect marker. Thus, duration is marked in three ways – by situation aspect marker, stem pattern, and preverb. Some examples are given in (67) and (68). In imperfective and optative viewpoints, only durativity is indicated, and situation aspect is not overtly marked.

(67) Achievement
    k'ína-ye-dah
    preverb-activity situation aspect-voice/stem
    'S/he walked around.'
    k'e-ni-e-d-dhe
    preverb-incorporate-activity situation aspect-voice-stem
    'S/he wandered off the subject (in thinking).'

(68) Semelfactive
    k'ína-y-i̧-h-t'uh
    preverb-activity situation aspect-perfective viewpoint-valence-stem
    'S/he swung arms around, pushed things around.'
    O k'e-táh
        preverb-stem
    'S/he is kicking O around.'

The repetitive allows achievement and semelfactive verbs to be viewed as repetitive situation types, or a kind of activity. To my knowledge, activities and accomplishments do not allow for this derived situation type in Slave.

11.4 On the Role of the Suffixes

Another way of creating a process is through the continuative derived situation type.

(69) Aspect name: continuative
occurrence: with achievement situation types
definition: prolonged, bounded event
situation aspect marker in perfective: *s*
suffixation pattern   Ø imperfective *N* perfective   ´ optative
other aspectual material: preverbs *ná* 'continuative', *tah* 'distribute, go among', *ts'á* 'make a return trip'

The continuative occurs only with achievement situation type verbs in Slave. Its contribution is to derive accomplishments, differing from achievements in terms of durativity. The durativity and telicity are seen most clearly in the perfective viewpoint, exemplified in (70).

(70) ná-whe-h-tła
preverb-accomplishment situation aspect-1sg Subject-stem
'I went and returned, made a return trip.'
ná-the-h-gé
preverb-accomplishment situation aspect/perfective viewpoint-valence-stem
'S/he poked, felt around with stick.'

The derived repetitive and continuative situation types both create processes from achievement situation types, but they differ in telicity: the event has a natural endpoint in the continuative derived situation type, but not in the repetitive. For instance, the continuative indicates a return trip, while the repetitive involves going around without a natural endpoint. In the imperfective and optative viewpoints, it is difficult to distinguish repetitive, continuative, and progressive events. As we have seen, in imperfective and optative viewpoints, process but not telicity is normally expressed, and both repetitives and continuatives involve only duration in these viewpoints. Both can be translated 'V here and there, V around, be V-ing around'.

Semelfactive events can be made into processes, activities, in another way.

(71) Aspect name: activity
occurrence: with semelfactive situation type verbs
definition: series or repetition of punctual events
situation aspect marker in perfective: *gh*
suffixation pattern: Ø imperfective   ´ perfective   ´ optative

As we have seen, semelfactive situation type verbs indicate an event isolated from a repetitive process or series of events. Not surprisingly, then, semelfactives can be made into an activity type, namely a multiple event activity that is inherently segmentable or countable. These activities are marked by the activity situation aspect marker and take the activity suffixation set. Some examples of semelfactives compared with activities are given in (72). The semelfactives can mean 'V-ed sg. O, V-ed sg. O once,' and the activities 'V-ed pl. O, V-ed more than once'. In these verbs, the glosses are: disjoint anaphor-situation aspect/viewpoint aspect-valence-stem. The final example has no disjoint anaphor.

(72) **Semelfactive situation type**   **Activity situation type**

y-é-h-thį́	'S/he shot sg. with arrow.'	yį-į-h-thį́	'S/he shot pl. with arrow.'
y-é-h-dzoh	'S/he trapped sg.'	yį-į-h-dzoh	'S/he trapped pl.'
y-é-h-jíh	'S/he caught sg. fish.'	yį-į-h-jíh	'S/he caught pl. fish.'
y-é-h-k'éh	'S/he shot sg. (gun).'	yį-į-h-k'é	'S/he shot pl.'
y-é-lúh	'S/he snared, netted, shot sg. with slingshot.'	yį-į-lú	'S/he snared, netted, shot pl. with slingshot.'
y-é-tsé	'S/he speared sg.'	yį-į-tse	'S/he speared pl.'
yé-h-tsa	'S/he buried sg.'	yį-į-h-tsa	'S/he buried pl.'
whe-h-belí	'S/he gave a swing.'	į-h-belí	'S/he pushed.'

From the perfective viewpoint alone, the semelfactives might be confused with accomplishments: both occur with *s* situation aspect. But despite this neutralization, three facts suggest that they remain distinct from accomplishments. First, the semelfactive stem suffixation patterns differ from those of accomplishments. The details are complex, and I will not address this issue fully. Suffice it to say that in roots that end in a consonant, accomplishment and semelfactive situation type stems (root plus suffix) differ in the perfective viewpoint. Second, semelfactives and accomplishments differ strikingly in other viewpoints. Most obviously, in imperfective and optative viewpoints, semelfactives require the overt situation aspect marker *í*, which is not found with accomplishments.

(73) Semelfactive
    O h-í-h-k'é
    'S/he shoots sg. O.' (semelfactive situation type, imperfective viewpoint)
    O whe-h-k'é
    'S/he shot sg. O.' (semelfactive situation type, perfective viewpoint)

11.4 On the Role of the Suffixes

(74) Accomplishment
O he-h-t'éh
'S/he cooks, is cooking O.' (accomplishment situation type, imperfective viewpoint)
O whe-h-t'é
'S/he cooked O.' (accomplishment situation type, perfective viewpoint)

Third, semelfactives are rare in the imperfective viewpoint. Like achievements, they occur in imperative form and with a following future particle, but not generally on their own. Accomplishments, on the other hand, occur freely in the imperfective.

Semelfactives are marked by suffixation and, in imperfective and optative viewpoints, by a unique situation aspect marker. In the perfective viewpoint, the *s* situation aspect marker combined with the stem form is sufficient to identify the verb as semelfactive.

Some activities can be refocused as accomplishments.

(75)

Accomplishment	**Activity**
whe-ze	y-i̧-ze
accomplishment situation aspect/perfective viewpoint-stem	activity situation aspect-perfective viewpoint-stem
'S/he gave a shout.'	'S/he shouted.'
whe-h-belí	y-i̧-h-belí
accomplishment situation aspect/perfective viewpoint-valence-stem	activity situation aspect-perfective viewpoint-valence-stem
'S/he gave a push on swing.'	'S/he pushed.'
the-h-tsi̧h	i̧-h-tsę
accomplishment situation aspect/perfective viewpoint-valence-stem	activity situation aspect/perfective viewpoint-valence-stem
'S/he got a whiff, sniffed.'	'S/he smelled.'

The accomplishments have *s* situation aspect marking and accomplishment suffixes; the activities have *gh* situation aspect marking and activity suffixes.

Finally, the aspect known in the Athapaskan literature as momentaneous deserves attention. I have used the term achievement where momentaneous is used in the Athapaskan literature, identifying *n* situation aspect as marking achievements. We saw in sections 11.2.1.3 and 11.2.1.4 that material in the predicate can shift the basic situation type. For instance, the preverb *ní* 'finish, end' occurs with achievement situation aspect, *xa* 'completely, up' with accomplishment situation aspect, and so on. Whenever a basic situation type is shifted through a preverb, we no longer find the specific situation types marked in the stem, nor do we find the aspectual pattern associated with the situation aspect marker; instead achievement suffixes are used. Subsituation aspect markers pattern with preverbs: inceptive, egressive, conative, and seriative use achievement stems regardless of the situation aspect indicated by the verb. Thus, when a verb contains either preverbs or subsituation aspect markers, situation type distinctions are neutralized in the stem, which takes achievement class suffixes despite the overt indication of different situations marked by prefixes. In a sense, the category of momentaneous is a formal one, without meaning: it can be thought of as a default pattern.

(76) Aspect name: achievement (momentaneous)
occurrence: with all event situation types
definition: indicates location, direction, manner
situation aspect marker in perfective: *n, s, gh,* Ø
suffixation pattern: *h* imperfective   *N* perfective   *h* or ´ optative
other aspectual material: many preverbs and subsituation aspect markers

11.4.2   Derived Situation/Viewpoint Types: Progressive, Customary, Distributive

In addition to suffixation patterns indicating the derived situation types discussed in section 11.4.1, Slave exhibits another way of modifying aspect. First, a derived or compound viewpoint/situation type is found, the progressive. Second, two further derived situation types exist, the customary and the distributive.

The progressive defines an event that is ongoing or in progress at the reference time. It refers to reference time, making it a type of viewpoint, but also to the internal states of that time, making it a kind of situation type. In Slave, the progressive is found largely with verbs of the achievement class.

(77) Aspect name: progressive
occurrence: with achievement situation types, descriptive states
definition: activity in progress
situation aspect marker in perfective: *gh*
suffixation pattern: *h* imperfective   *h* perfective   *h* optative

Some examples of progressive imperfectives are given in (78).

11.4 On the Role of the Suffixes

(78) a. ye-tɬeh
   activity situation aspect-stem
   'S/he is walking along.'
   b. O ye-leh
   activity situation aspect-stem
   'S/he is carrying along pl. O.'
   c. O da-e-leh
   preverb-activity situation aspect-stem
   'S/he is holding up pl. O.'
   d. tá-k-a-de
   preverb-human plural Subject-activity situation aspect-stem
   'They pl. are going down.'
   e. 'eji-go-k-a-h-we
   preverb-plural number-human plural Subject-activity situation aspect-valence-stem
   'They pl. are running.'
   f. ne-ɬ-a-tɬeh
   preverb-dual number-activity situation aspect-stem
   'They two are coming across.'

Progressives are also possible in the perfective viewpoint, stressing a completed duration.

(79) a. O da-de-į-lá
   preverb-qualifier-activity situation aspect/perfective viewpoint-stem
   'S/he was holding up pl. O.'
   b. na-ɬa-į-h-'óh
   preverb-incorporate-activity situation aspect/perfective viewpoint-valence-stem
   'S/he was pulling with rope, paddling.'
   c. tá-ke-y-į-deh
   preverb-human plural Subject-activity situation aspect-imperfective viewpoint-stem
   'They pl. were going down.'

Progressives are doubly marked. First, the activity situation marker is used in imperfective and perfective viewpoints, overtly marking durativity and atelicity. Second, a suffix marks that the viewpoint is progressive.

Another derived situation type in Slave is the customary. The customary represents a situation that is repeated on a regular, habitual, or customary basis, and is a kind of activity. It is often marked with the optional quantificational adverb *na* (see chapter 4).

(80) Aspect name: customary
   occurrence: with achievement situation types
   definition: habitual, customary
   situation aspect marker in perfective: *gh*
   suffixation pattern: *h* imperfective   *h* perfective   *h* optative
   other aspectual material: quantificational adverb *na* (optional)

Some examples of customary verbs are provided in (81).

(81) a. ní-(na-)yeh
      preverb-(iterative-) stem
      'It arrives regularly.'
   b. t'áhsį se-gha (ra-)de-wee
      thing 1sg-for (iterative-) inceptive-stem
      'S/he carries things for me regularly.'
   c. (na-)d-a-t-'áh
      (iterative-) inceptive-activity situation aspect-voice-stem
      'They two started out customarily.'
   d. ts'elí-(na-)t-'óh
      preverb-(iterative-) voice-stem
      'S/he gets lost by boat.'
   e. se-ghá-(na-)ne-'áh
      1sg-preverb-(iterative-) 2sg Subject-stem
      'You sg. give me default O regularly.'

The customary is marked in stem form. Like the repetitive, it takes the suffix *h* regardless of viewpoint, and as in the repetitive, the suffix has a purely situational role, marking a repeated activity. However, the repetitive differs from the customary in deriving a type of activity. In addition to its stem suffixation pattern, it occurs only in combination with a particular preverb. The customary parallels the repetitive in its suffixation set, but differs in being able to combine with achievement type verbs with or without preverbs. For instance, the customary examples in (81a,d,e) include preverbs; (81b,c) include inceptive subsituation aspect. In the Athapaskan literature, the repetitive is called an aspect, while the customary (and distributive, see further discussion) is termed a superaspect (Axelrod 1993 on Koyukon, Kari 1979 on Ahtna) or a compounding aspect (Rice 1989 on Slave) since the latter forms compound

11.4 On the Role of the Suffixes

with a full predicate. The effect of the customary on situation aspect is fixed in the perfective viewpoint – the customary is a type of activity and has activity situation aspect marking. Some additional examples are given in (82).

(82) a. na-na-n-a-déh
  preverb-iterative-qualifier-activity situation aspect-stem
  'They pl. landed regularly.'
 b. 'e-ghá-na-łé-g-a-tthe
  unspecified Object-for-iterative-dual number-human plural Subject-activity situation aspect-stem
  'They went for meat customarily.'

It is not surprising that the customary is a type of activity – a customary involves duration with no inherent endpoint. In Slave, the customary normally combines only with achievement situation type verbs; customaries of the other categories are formed periphrastically. Other languages allow a richer set of bases for the customary.

The final derived situation type in Slave is the distributive. The distributive combines with any basic situation type to indicate that an event is carried out by more than one individual, each acting separately, is performed separately on each of a number of patients, is performed in a number of distinct locations, or takes place at separate times. See chapter 4 for further discussion.

(83) Aspect name: distributive
  occurrence: with all situation types
  definition: individuation
  situation aspect marker in perfective: s (generally)
  stem pattern: h imperfective N perfective h or $'$ optative
  other aspectual material: quantifier $yá$ (optional)

Several examples of distributives are given in (84).

(84) Semelfactive: sáwé   yá-h-į-h-be
      beaver skin distributive-epenthetic-semelf-
         active situation aspect/perfective
         viewpoint-valence-stem
    'S/he stretched each beaver skin.'

	O yá-the-h-k'e
	distributive-accomplishment situation
	aspect/perfective viewpoint-valence-stem
	'S/he punched each O.'
Achievement:	ní-yá-nǫ-ke-h-t-'e
	preverb-distributive-iterative-human plural
	Subject-accomplishment situation aspect-stem
	'They each returned by boat.'
Activity:	O yá-y-į-'á
	distributive-activity situation aspect-
	perfective viewpoint-stem
	'S/he ate each O.'
Accomplishment:	yá-h-í-h-sį
	distributive-epenthetic-semelfactive situation
	aspect/perfective viewpoint/1sg Subject-
	valence-stem
	'I made each one.'

The s (accomplishment) or $í$ (semelfactive) situation aspect marker is often found in the perfective viewpoint, but which situation aspect marker occurs depends on many factors including the lexical aspectual category of the verb and the other material present in the predicate. In general, when the predicate includes lexical material, the situation aspect marker is s. This has to do with the nature of the distributive. It involves plurality, but each event on its own is bounded, and it involves a number of separate individuals, so telicity is involved. While telicity might seem to be incompatible with the plurality of the distributive, this is not so given the individuation implied by the distributive quantifier. I do not pursue this topic here; see Rice 1989, chapter 24.12 for detailed description of the effect of the distributive on situation aspect in Slave. In addition to simple customary and distributive forms, the customary and distributive can combine; in this case, activity situation aspect marking occurs, denoting a distributed event done customarily.

11.4.3 Summary

The topic of this section has been the suffix system, which reveals a greater richness of aspectual categories than shown by the prefixes alone. The suffixes indicate both situation and viewpoint aspect. They, together with preverbs, allow for a shift of one situation type to another; in particular they allow nonprocesses to be made into activities or accomplishments. In addition the suffixes allow for the creation of super or compound viewpoints and situation types by containing one event inside of another.

We thus see that aspect, in the broadest of senses, is marked in the Slave verb in a number of ways. In the functional system, both viewpoint aspect and situation aspect are signaled overtly. Suffixes carry information about viewpoint and situation aspect both. In addition, further material in the predicate, preverbs, subsituation aspect markers, and quantifiers, play a role in the complex aspect system. These can shift the situation aspect, with the situation aspect supplied by the added predicate material winning out over that of the verb stem. Finally, verbs can combine with other aspectual categories, customary and distributive, in which case we find an event contained within a larger event. The progressive is used to shift an achievement to an activity.

I have examined suffixes relevant to events; statives also enter into a larger aspect system. Stative verbs can be viewed in two ways. They can indicate pure existence, condition, or location, as discussed in section 11.2.2. They can also be viewed as changing in state or entering into a state. As with the inceptive, the transitional or inchoative focuses on the early part of a state. Unlike the inceptive, the transitional aspect with states is a separate aspect that introduces a unique suffix pattern that is typical of events. While a detailed treatment of stative situations is of interest, it is beyond the scope of this book.

11.5 On the Position of the Suffixes

I now return to the main topic of discussion, the positioning of the suffixes. Their positioning following the root is, at first glance, surprising for given that they mark properties of situation and viewpoint aspect, one might expect them to occur as prefixes alongside these categories. In this section, I will look at properties of the aspectual suffixes that suggest that they are best treated as derivational suffixes that are lexically attached to the root rather than as functional elements, as I have argued the prefixes are.

Some preliminaries are required before turning to the discussion of suffixes. Much has been written about inflection and derivation; in (85) I list some of the properties that are often used to distinguish these two types of morphology. The criteria are culled from work by Anderson 1982, Beard 1995, Bybee 1985a, Kibrik 1995, Stump 1998, and others.

(85)
Criterion	Derivation	Inflection
1. Category-changing	can be	no
2. Obligatory (within category to which it applies)	no	yes
3. Generality of meaning	may be idiosyncratic	general

4. Range of applicability	may be narrow	wide
5. Arbitrariness	may be arbitrary	not arbitrary
6. Possibility of fusion	great	weak
7. Produces new lexeme	yes	no
8. Relevant to syntax	no	yes
9. Position	appears close to base	outside of derivation when syntactically relevant

In the following discussion, I consider several of these criteria.[10] As is often discussed in the literature, the distinction between derivation and inflection is murky. These criteria do not necessarily yield clearcut answers for a particular form (see, for instance, work by Bybee 1985a). It is for these reasons, among others, that I have steered away from using the terms inflection and derivation, using instead functional and lexical and assuming that the structure of the verb is basically syntactic. However, these criteria are useful in investigating why the suffixes, unlike the aspect prefixes, should be treated as lexical rather than as functional elements. In this section, I present arguments based on both Slave and other languages that these suffixes are neither inflectional nor syntactic.

11.5.1 Category-Changing Status

It is generally acknowledged in the Athapaskan literature that the basic lexical unit is the root rather than the stem. One piece of evidence for this claim is that a particular root can, in many cases, be used to form either a noun or a verb. Some examples from Sekani, Ahtna, and Navajo are provided in (86), (87), and (88), respectively.

(86) Sekani (Hargus 1988)
    bət/bət   'stomach/be hungry' (198)
    dəl/dəl   'blood/be red, raw' (198)
    t'as/h-t'as   'arrow/shoot O with bow and arrow' (199)
(87) Ahtna (Kari 1990)
    caan/ł-caan   'rain/be raining' (110)
    dzaex/dzaek'   'gum, resin/caulk, smear O with gum, resin, pitch, glue' (169)
    xae/ghae   'grease/be greasy' (214)
    ten/ten   'ice/freeze' (332)

11.5 On the Position of the Suffixes

    tsiis/tsiic   'ochre, minerals used as paint, pigment, yellowish object/be yellow-orange in color' (388)
    sae/zaek'   'spit, saliva, spittle/spit' (453)
(88) Navajo (Young, Morgan, and Midgette 1992)
    dlo/dloh   'laugh (noun, verb)' (156)
    -yih/yih   'breath/breathe' (702)
    łid/łid   'smoke/burn' (370)
    tin/tin   'ice/freeze' (509)
    séí/zéí   'sand/crumble' (739)
    zhǫ'/zhǫǫd   'levity, fun thing/be(come) nice, smooth, tame, happy, gentle' (795, 797)

While noun stems are often formed directly from roots, with no overt suffix, some overt nominalizing suffixes are found. For instance, the suffix -ł indicates an instrumental, as in the Ahtna examples in (89) from Kari 1990 (his glosses).

(89) tl'uu-ł   'rope' from *tl'uu* 'bind' + ł 'instrument for binding' (262)
    xae-ł   'pack' from *ghae* 'pack O' + ł 'instrument for packing' (262)

Now consider the formation of verbs. The following internal structure of the verb stem is usually posited (e.g., Axelrod 1993, Cook 1984, Hargus 1988, Kari 1990):

(90) [root + aspectual suffix]$_{stem}$

The aspectual suffixes attach directly to the root. This suggests that these suffixes have two functions. First, as their name indicates, they provide aspectual information. Second, they provide the root with a category, marking it as a verb – the suffixes are an overt morphological marking that could be the source of the category of verb.

It is often argued that category-changing affixes are derivational. I assume that the same claim can be made for category-determining affixes – they are added in the lexicon. This criterion suggests that the suffixes are part of word formation.

Consider now the seventh point in (85) – that derivation produces a new lexeme while inflection does not. The creation of a lexeme has to do with listing in a dictionary – new lexemes are listed, while new forms of existing ones are not. Category-determining affixes can be thought of as creating new lexemes as for each root it must be listed just what categories can be formed from it. If the Athapaskan suffixes are category-determining, this suggests that they are derivational, being added to the root in the lexicon. The structure of the verb stem is thus as in (91).[11]

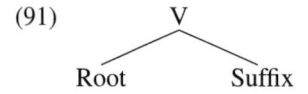

(91)
```
           V
          / \
       Root  Suffix
```

One of the advantages of assuming that the suffixes are added to the root in the lexicon and are lexically part of the verb stem is that they are c-commanded by the situation and viewpoint aspect markers (see chapter 5 on the position of the verb stem). Since the suffixes provide further delineations of the general situation aspects, one would expect under the scopal theory that the suffixes would be within the scope of the situation aspect markers. Under the proposal offered here, this is the case.

11.5.2 Fusion

Next I turn to evidence from fusion with the root. Bybee 1985a:4 hypothesizes that "the degree of morpho-phonological fusion of an affix to a stem correlates with the degree of semantic *relevance* of the affix to the stem" (emphasis in original – KR). In general, derivational and lexical expression is considered by Bybee to have a higher degree of relevance than does inflectional expression; thus degree of fusion can serve as a diagnostic of expression type. There is a high degree of morphological fusion of the suffixes with the root compared with that of prefixes. The complex nature of the Athapaskan verb prefix system has long been recognized and studied; the complex nature of the stem came to light much later (see Leer 1979 for discussion). The suffixes often have a templatic realization – for instance, a suffix pattern may be expressed as vowel lengthening or shortening. In many languages, suffixation patterns are abstract and difficult to ascertain, as in Slave. In many ways, then, suffixes show a high degree of fusion with the root. This contrasts with prefixes. Although prefixes may fuse, they do not generally, with the exception of voice/valence, fuse with the stem. (We saw in chapter 7 that voice/valence require a somewhat different treatment than do the functional items.) Following Bybee's line of reasoning, derivational affixes, being more relevant to the stem than inflectional affixes, are more likely to fuse with the stem. Thus, the fusion of the stem with suffixes in the Athapaskan family is consistent with the hypothesis that the suffixes are derivational.

While this test is consistent with the claim that the suffixes under discussion are derivational rather than inflectional, it must be used with caution as it is highly dependent upon a particular theory of lexical insertion. It could be that a phonological factor like degree of fusion is not relevant; see, for instance,

11.5 On the Position of the Suffixes

Beard 1995 and Halle and Marantz 1993 for theories in which phonological spellout is differentiated from word formation.

11.5.3 Obligatoriness, Range of Applicability, Generality of Meaning, Arbitrariness

In this section I consider four criteria: obligatoriness, range of applicability, generality of meaning, and arbitrariness. The first two are closely related. According to Bybee 1985a:11, "an inflectional category must be combinable with any stem with the proper syntactic and semantic features, yielding a predictable meaning." Derivation, on the other hand, may be restricted in applicability and idiosyncratic in formation or meaning.

I begin with the criterion of range of applicability. Recall that situation aspect prefixes delineate four major situation types (activities, achievements, accomplishments, and semelfactives) and are fully applicable and obligatory within their class. The suffixes, on the other hand, differ in their range of applicability, even within a class. For instance, in a discussion of Koyukon, Axelrod 1993:63,66,73 notes that 27% of the verb roots in her corpus permit activity (her durative) forms; 12% have semelfactive forms, and only 8.5% have consecutive forms. The consecutive derives activities from semelfactive class verbs and indicates repetition. These different distributions suggest that some of the suffix sets do not have a great range of applicability, as some occur with a restricted set of roots, even within their lexical class. Within the verbs that allow the situation aspect, however, the suffixes are obligatory.

While many of the suffixes are not general, appearing with a restricted set of roots, four suffix patterns are usually considered to be quite general. These are the super or compounding aspects of customary, progressive, distributive, and multiple (see chapter 4 on the multiple). Interestingly, however, not every verb stem has a suffix marking these aspects. Axelrod 1993:90,94,97 gives the following percentages for Koyukon: 17% of the verbs in the corpus take distributive stem sets, 15% allow multiple stem sets, and 49% admit customary stem sets. The progressive stem set, Axelrod points out, is quite productive, but does admit cases of ablaut and suppletion. It is important to note that Axelrod refers not to aspects but to stem sets in her discussion: a far greater number of verbs can appear with distributive prefix morphology, say, than can take the distributive stem set. This suggests that, with the possible exception of the progressive, the superaspectual suffixes, like the aspectual suffixes, lack generality: they are not always found when they are expected. In the absence of the suffixes, these aspects are indicated through the situation aspect prefix and by relevant lexical items.

I have so far considered the suffixes basically from the point of view of their situation aspect content. In addition to signaling situation aspect, suffixes also indicate viewpoint aspect. Considering the suffixes from the perspective of viewpoint allows the notions of generality of applicability to be looked at in a slightly different way. Consider the chart in (92), from Kari 1990:663–664, which shows stem suffixation patterns for roots of the shape CVV in Ahtna. I have substituted some terminology: I use accomplishment, activity, and achievement for Kari's conclusive, durative, and momentaneous, respectively. The symbol E stands for expanded vowel, or a vowel that is lengthened and shows umlaut, and L stands for lengthened vowel.

(92)

Aspect	Imperfective	Perfective	Future	Optative	Customary
Accomplishment	Ø	n	ł	ł	s
Continuative	'	n	'	'	E
Distributive	'	n	'	n	E
Activity	L	'	ł	'	x
Achievement	s	n	ł	ł/'	s
Perambulative	ł	n	ł	'	s

The relationship between meaning and form is not unique. For instance, the glottal stop suffix marks nonperfective viewpoints in the continuative but imperfective and future, though not optative, in the distributive. Moreover, no viewpoint is associated wth a unique suffix. For instance, the customary suffix has no single general form, but specific ones depending upon the situation aspectual form that it combines with. The perfective suffix n is quite specific, basically marking telic perfective viewpoint verbs, but notice that this suffix is also sometimes used in the optative. The use of a particular form is quite idiosyncratic in the suffix system. This idiosyncrasy is quite distinct from the generality of form found in the prefix system and is characteristic of derivation.

Another criterion that Bybee argues is useful for distinguishing derivation from inflection has to do with generality of meaning. Inflection is very general in meaning, having minimal specific content, whereas derivation may be quite specific in meaning. Several of the aspectual suffixes have very specific meanings. Consider the following aspects in Koyukon. Axelrod 1993 identifies a consecutive stem set that may differ from the activity stem set. Consecutives, like repetitives, involve repeated actions, but the consecutive conveys a sense of abruptness (Axelrod 1993:69). Axelrod further identifies a bisective aspect by its stem set. The bisective is a type of accomplishment formed from semelfactive verbs; it refers "to single actions in which contact

11.5 On the Position of the Suffixes

is made, resulting in a division of the object-recipient into two (usually equal) parts" (Axelrod 1993:76). These aspects thus have very specific meanings.

Specificity of meaning is difficult to evaluate, as the larger a system is, the more specific the meanings of each member of the system will be. For instance, in a language with five tense markers, each of these must be more specific in meaning than the tense markers in a language with only two of them. Another closely related criterion, idiosyncrasy or arbitrariness of meaning, is thus useful to consider. Based on form (see (92)), the suffixes must have very idiosyncratic meanings, again an indication of their derivational status.

The examples in (93)–(97) are culled from Kari 1990. In each case, a root is shown on the first line and stems formed on that root through suffixation on the next lines. For each stem, its suffix in the imperfective, perfective, and optative viewpoints is given. See Kari 1979:1990 on stem phonology. Although the form of the suffixes is not obvious here, what we can see is that one root can have a range of meanings depending upon the situation aspect in which it occurs. This idiosyncrasy of meaning is related to the lexical class of the stem and could be a property of the suffix. In the following examples, G stands for gender.

(93) Root: *zel* (Kari 1990:454–455)
    Stem: Ø-*zel* 'yell, shout, holler' (activity)
        suffix set: Ø imperfective, *n* perfective, Ø optative
    Stem: *d-l-zeł* 'be creaking sound of footsteps on soft snow' (state)
        suffix set: *n* imperfective, perfective, optative

(94) Root: *ts'etl'* (Kari 1990:409)
    Stem: *gh-l-ts'etl'* 'shrink' (achievement)
        suffix set: lengthening in imperfective and optative, *n* perfective
    Stem: G-*l-ts'etl'* 'be bent, warped, curved' (stative)
        suffix set: *n* imperfective, perfective, optative

(95) Root: *tsiic* (Kari 1990:388–389)
    Stem: G-Ø/*l-tsiic* 'be yellow-orange in color' (stative)
        suffix set: *n* imperfective, perfective, optative
    Stem: O G-Ø-*tsiic* 'make mark on O, write O' (activity)
        suffix set: Ø imperfective, *n* perfective, Ø optative

(96) Root: *dogh* (Kari 1990:156)
    Stem: G-*l-dogh* 'burst, crack, boom, be bursting/booming noise, gun fires' (semelfactive)
        suffix set: obstruent suffix in imperfective, perfective, optative
    Stem: G-*l-dogh* 'be cracked, fissured, chapped' (state)
        suffix set: *n* imperfective, perfective, optative

           Stem: G-*l*-*dogh* 'amorphous substance (fog, smoke, breath, scent,
                         flavor) moves' (achievement)
                    suffix set: lengthening in imperfective and optative, *n* perfective
(97) Root: gaac (Kari 1990:178)
           Stem: G-*l*-*gaac* 'glide, slide, slip, skate, ski on surface, multiple
                         objects (snow, leaves) drift in air' (achievement)
                    suffix set: Ø imperfective and optative, *n* perfective
           Stem: *d*-*g*-*l*-*gaac* 'become impaled (on elongated object)'
                         (semelfactive)
                    suffix set: obstruent suffix in imperfective, perfective, optative

In these examples, the primary difference among the verbs is in stem suffixation patterns rather than in prefixes, suggesting that the meaning differences are attributable to the suffixes.

The chart in (98) compares the aspect prefixes and suffixes on a range of criteria. In choosing any particular suffix, one may find that it is more toward the derivational end (e.g., consecutive, semelfactive suffixes) or more toward the inflectional end (e.g., progressive). However, in comparison with the prefixes, the suffixes all show more derivational criteria.

(98)
Criterion	Suffixes	Prefixes
1. Category-changing	yes	no
2. Obligatory (within category to which it is applicable)	no (except perhaps progressive)	yes
3. Generality of meaning	may be idiosyncratic	general
4. Range of applicability	may be narrow	wide
5. Possibility of fusion with root	great	none

I conclude on the basis of this range of criteria that the aspect suffixes are best treated as derivational, or as being added to the root in the lexicon.

11.5.4 Syntactic Expression

I have argued that the aspect suffixes are added to the root in the lexicon, but another possibility remains – the suffixes could parallel the lexical prefixes and enter into syntactic expression with the verb. Bybee 1985a argues that a major criterion to distinguish syntactic expression is boundness. Syntactic expressions are not bound and may occur as independent words, while derivational

11.6 Beyond Slave

and inflectional expressions are bound and must be attached to a base. It is certainly the case that the Athapaskan aspect affixes are bound, or phonologically part of the verb, suggesting that syntactic expression is not a reasonable way to treat them. I use this criterion with caution – since the structure that I have proposed for the verb is an abstract one that is removed from actual surface forms, it is difficult to dismiss syntactic expression on the grounds of fusion alone. However, given that the suffixes show so many other characteristics of derivation, I will assume that they are derivational, added in the lexicon.

11.5.5 Summary

Based on the criteria of ability to determine category, lack of obligatoriness, restricted range of applicability, and idiosyncrasy of meaning, I have argued that aspect suffixes in Athapaskan languages are derivational, or added to the root in the lexicon. This analysis has the positive result that suffixes are within the scope of prefixally marked aspect, as expected given their meanings. In this way, it provides further support for the scope hypothesis: on the surface, the suffixes follow situation and viewpoint aspect as expressed by the prefixes, but at the level at which scopal relations are determined, they are within the scope of the prefixes.

11.5.6 Further Suffixes

I end this section with a brief note on some other suffixes. In addition to the stem-forming aspect suffixes considered so far, other suffixes have been identified in the Athapaskan verb. These include negative suffixes and enclitics. Hargus 1988:75 lists such forms under the rubric of syntactic affixation, as does Kari 1990. These suffixes are added to stems rather than to roots and are phonologically clitics that are part of syntactic word formation; this assumption is implicit in Hargus's analysis and in Leer's 1979 historical reconstructions and is consistent with the meanings of these items – they indicate negation and complementation. There are also a number of tense/mode/aspect clitics. While the ordering properties of these clitics are worthy of study, they are beyond the scope of this book; see Potter 1997 for discussion.

11.6 Beyond Slave

Up until now, I have provided an analysis of Slave aspect and argued that subsituation aspect, situation aspect, and viewpoint aspect are overtly expressed in the verb in order of generality. In this section, I look beyond Slave, providing short sketches of Ahtna, Navajo, and Hupa to show that the facts of these languages appear to be largely similar to those of Slave. I consider only the event verb system, although, as in Slave, the stative system is of interest as well. I continue to use the terms achievement, accomplishment, activity, and semelfactive rather than motion, conversive, operative, and successive, respectively.

11.6.1 Ahtna

Kari 1979, 1989, 1990, 1992 identifies imperfective, perfective, optative, and future as viewpoints in Ahtna (he calls these modes). The imperfective, perfective, and optative viewpoints pattern similarly to those in Slave, and I therefore identify them as viewpoint aspect or mood. The future in Ahtna, as in Slave, is compositional, consisting of the inceptive followed by the activity situation aspect marker *gh*. As in Slave, the progressive, customary, and distributive function as derived aspects.

Ahtna also has situation aspect. The basic event types that Kari 1979 proposes are given in (99).[12] The terms that he uses in place of achievement, activity, accomplishment, and semelfactive are given in parentheses. As in Slave, each category is identified with a particular situation marker.

(99) Achievement (motion)   *n*
    Accomplishment (conversive)   *s*
    Activity (operative)   *gh*
    Semelfactive (successive)   *i*

In addition, Ahtna has a number of other aspectual categories that are indicated by a combination of verb suffix pattern and situation aspect marker. The examples in what follows include the major derived situation types for each lexical class, as defined by Kari 1979, omitting achievements derived through the presence of preverbs. I have oversimplified the system; see Kari 1979 for full details.

Achievement category verbs can be made into processes in a number of different ways in Ahtna.

(100) Achievement (motion) verb aspects
    a. Perambulative
        definition: motion carried out in wandering or elliptical path, motion carried out to cover an area
        situation aspect marker (perfective): *s*
        predicate preverbs: *łu* 'here and there, about'

11.6 Beyond Slave

  b. Continuative
     definition: smooth, back and forth movement with natural endpoint
     situation aspect marker (perfective): *s*
     predicate preverb: *n*
  c. Persistive
     definition: back and forth motion, done repeatedly, against resistance
     situation aspect marker (perfective): *gh*
     predicate preverb: *niłk'e* 'back and forth, zigzag'
  d. Reversative
     definition: turning over, reversing motion
     situation aspect marker (perfective): some with *s*, some with *gh*
     predicate preverb: *tgge'* 'get up, life O up,' *neke* 'turn back, turn O over,' O-*neke* 'encircling O,' *niłna* 'making round trip'

Verbs of the other situation aspect categories are similar to Slave in the kinds of aspectual derivation found. Both semelfactives and accomplishments can be refocused as activities.

(101) Activity verb aspects
  a. Activity (durative)
     definition: activity carried out over extended time period, as general means of employment
     situation aspect marker (perfective): *gh*

(102) Semelfactive verb aspects
  a. Semelfactive
     definition: abrupt single instance of activity
     situation aspect marker (perfective): *s*
  b. Activity (durative)
     definition: activity carried out over extended time period, as general means of employment
     situation aspect marker (perfective): *gh*

(103) Accomplishment verb aspects
  a. Accomplishment (conclusive)
     definition: completion of activity, attainment of objective
     situation aspect marker (perfective): *s*
  b. Activity (durative)

The definitions of aspect for Slave and Ahtna are similar; see also Axelrod 1993 on Koyukon. Koyukon has an additional way of creating activities from semelfactives: a so-called consecutive that involves a repetition. Semelfactives can also be made into accomplishments, called bisectives, indicating an action resulting in a division of an object into two, usually equal, parts. Ahtna and Koyukon thus offer a richer array of overt aspects than does Slave. As in Slave, process predicates involving a natural goal require the *s* situation aspect marker, while those without such a goal take *gh*. This is one indication that situation aspect functions in a similar way across the family.

11.6.2 Navajo

The aspect system in Navajo has been treated differently from that of Ahtna, Koyukon, and Slave in the literature, although, as discussed in section 11.2, Young and Morgan 1987 suggest that the morphemes that I call situation aspect markers are meaningful. I do not attempt a full analysis of Navajo, but suggest that it is more similar to the languages examined so far than the literature might lead one to believe.

Navajo viewpoint aspect has been studied by Smith 1991, 1996a, 1997. She argues that Navajo contrasts perfective and imperfective viewpoints. In addition, she proposes that progressive viewpoint is available for some verbs, and that a neutral viewpoint is possible. Young and Morgan 1987 identify additional viewpoints. One, the usitative, denotes repetitive verbal action performed customarily. Another viewpoint, the iterative, is similar semantically to the usitative. These are both marked by the same stem set; they differ primarily in that the iterative appears with the quantificational adverb *ná* 'repetitive', while the usitative does not. These represent one and the same entity, with the quantificational adverb being optional; see chapter 4. While Young and Morgan treat the usitative and the iterative as viewpoints, they are cognate with the customary derived situation type in other languages, and they are perhaps better treated as derived situation types, parallel to the Slave customary. I leave this question open.

Situation aspect seems to be represented in Navajo by the situation aspect markers, just as it is elsewhere. Smith 1991:396–397, 1996 argues that it is not possible to assign meanings to these elements, but I suggest that their meanings are systematic. While in the literature, the lexical aspect, or verb theme category system, of many Athapaskan languages has been reduced to four basic event situation types, termed here achievement, activity, accomplishment, and semelfactive, I am not aware of work that looks at Navajo in this way. What is found for Navajo is a rich list of aspects, as distinguished by stem shape, a special prefix, or a combination of the two. These aspects, as in the other languages, distinguish the kind of action or state expressed by

11.6 Beyond Slave

the verb – punctual, continuing, repetitive, occurring a single time, reversing direction, shifting from one state to another, or attempted (Young 1995:34). Each of these aspects has a diagnostic situation aspect marker. The aspects, with the names I use here and definitions taken from Young and Morgan 1987, are listed in (104)–(114).

(104) Achievement (momentaneous)
    definition: punctual
    situation aspect marker (perfective): *s, n, gh,* Ø
(105) Continuative accomplishment type (continuative)
    definition: verbal action that occupies an indefinite span of time and that moves around without specified direction; occurs with verbs of motion and certain processes; in perfective, this aspect is goal-oriented
    situation aspect marker (perfective): *s*
    predicates: *na* 'around, about, here and there'
(106) Activity (durative)
    definition: verbal action that occupies an indefinite span of time; occurs with processes in which the action forms an uninterrupted continuum or has internal repetition
    situation aspect marker (perfective): *gh*
(107) Repetitive activity type (repetitive)
    definition: verbal action that involves continuum of repetitive acts
    situation aspect marker (perfective): *gh*
(108) Accomplishment (conclusive)
    definition: action that terminates with a static sequel
    situation aspect marker (perfective): *s*
(109) Semelfactive (semelfactive)[13]
    definition: isolates a single act from a repetitive act
    situation aspect marker (perfective): *s*
(110) Distributive (distributive)
    definition: distributive placement of objects in space, distribution of objects to recipients, distributive performance of verbal actions
    situation aspect marker (perfective): *s*
(111) Activity, accomplishment (diversative)
    definition: movement that is distributed among things or takes place here and there
    situation aspect marker (perfective): *s* (first type); *gh* (second type)

Type 1 diversatives, with *s* situation aspect in the perfective, indicate a directed process with an endpoint (e.g., visit); type 2 diversatives, with *gh* situation aspect, indicate an undirected process (e.g., go around here and there, roam).

(112) Accomplishment (reversative)
    definition: action resulting in directional change
    situation aspect marker (perfective): *s*
    predicate adverbs: *ná* 'around encircling, around making a turn,'
    náhidi
    'turn over'
(113) conative (conative) (vestigial in Navajo; Young and Morgan 1987:183)
    definition: attempted verbal action
    situation aspect marker (perfective): *s*
(114) transitional (transitional)
    definition: action that involves shift from one state of being, form, condition, or position to another
    situation aspect marker (perfective): Ø
    subsituation aspect: *i* transitional

As in other languages, I set the distributive aside; its morphology is complex. When the other aspects are examined, regular patterns emerge. In particular, *s* appears in the perfective viewpoint with aspects involving telicity and duration (accomplishment, continuative, type 1 diversative), while *gh* occurs with durative aspects without a logical or inherent endpoint (activity, repetitive, type 2 diversative, progressive). It is therefore reasonable to treat the Navajo aspect system as being organized in a similar way to that of Slave. I will not go into detail, but suggest that it would be worthwhile to re-examine Navajo with the situation aspect hypothesis in mind: it may well turn out that the lexicon consists of verbs in four major event categories, with a variety of kinds of processes being identified through the suffix and preverb systems.

11.6.3 Hupa

Hupa is the most distinctive of the languages examined here in terms of its aspect system, and I will not be able to do it justice. Golla 1970 identifies imperfective, perfective, optative, progressive, and potential viewpoints, as well as a customary form. The three situation aspect markers *n*, *s*, *gh* (*w* in Hupa) are found, although Golla states that they occur only in the perfective viewpoint. In the imperfective viewpoint, many verbs with *n* situation aspect in the perfective have a qualifier of the form *n* in a different position, and some verbs with *s* situation aspect in the perfective have *s* in the imperfective

11.6 Beyond Slave

in a different position. It is possible that the system could be reanalyzed as more parallel to that of the other languages discussed so far.

Hupa and some of the other Pacific Coast languages show a fascinating and unusual property – two situation aspect markers co-occur under certain conditions. Consider the following Hupa and Mattole forms, called 'assumption of state' by Golla (personal communication, 1997). In the perfective viewpoints forms in (115) and (116), both the activity situation aspect marker (*w* in Hupa, *gh* in Mattole) and the accomplishment situation aspect (*s* in both languages) occur, in that order.

(115) Hupa *w – s* (Golla 1970)
    a. no-ni-**w**eh-**s**-te:n   'You come to be put down.' (182)
    b. 'a-ni-**w**eh-**s**-t'e'   'It became so.' (66)
    c. dah-ch'i-**w**eh-**s**-Gehc   'He held the boat still.' (66)

(116) Mattole *gh – s* (Li 1930)
    a. di-c-dí-bi:n   'I am sharp.' (67)
        di-**ghe**:-**si**:-dí-bi:n   'I have been sharp.' (67)
    b. **ghi**-n-tɬ'é'ts   'He is hard.'
        ghe:-**si**:-tɬ'é'ts   'I have become hard.'
    c. nixwoŋgw ya:-**ghi**-c-t'cí: 'I smell good (*nixwoŋgw*).'
        nixwoŋgw ya:-**ghe**:-**si**:-t'cí'   'I smelled good.'

To my knowledge, verbs with both activity (*gh*) and accomplishment (*s*) situation aspect marking are found only in some Pacific Coast languages. Consider the meaning of these forms: they indicate that a state was achieved (*s*) and is maintained (*gh*). The meaning is compositional: these are resultatives, consisting of a transition followed by an unbounded duration. The transition, indicated by the situation aspect marker to the right, must precede the duration, indicated by the situation aspect marker on the left. Given that elements to the right have scope over those to their left, this ordering is expected.

The Hupa system differs in many ways from that of the other languages – for instance, stem variation is reduced, and situation aspect is productive only in the perfective viewpoint – and I have not begun to do it justice. Reflections of the existence of situation aspect in the other viewpoints are found, but the system is reduced.

11.6.4 Summary

The Athapaskan languages exhibit a rich aspect system, with overt functional prefixes marking both viewpoint and situation aspect. The basic situation aspect type associated with a verb can be shifted by various types of predicate material (preverbs, quantifiers, subsituation aspect within the verb word). Suffixes indicate properties of situation aspect/viewpoint aspect. Each major situation aspect type (achievement, accomplishment, activity, semelfactive, stative) is associated with a suffixation pattern. In addition, further subtypes of situations can be delineated and are marked by suffixes. Finally, two situation aspect types, customary and distributive, occur together with the other situation types. This core system seems to be common to the family. Ahtna, Koyukon, and Navajo appear to be describable in similar terms to Slave; Hupa is more distinctive, but it too seems to contain the same core elements. Tsuut'ina also seems similar: Cook 1984 divides event verbs into categories that parallel my achievement, semelfactive, and activity situation types. While this topic needs further study, I will assume that the facts are similar across the family.

In the following discussion, I focus on two issues of ordering. The first concerns differences among the languages in the combinatorial properties of elements, which sometimes lead to the positing of different templates. The second concerns some idiosyncrasies of ordering in Ahtna involving negatives and transitionals.

11.7 Ordering and Combinatorics

Recall that I argued that the aspectual elements in Slave discussed in this chapter are ordered as in (117).

(117) **Subsituation aspect** **Situation aspect** **Viewpoint aspect**
　　　inceptive, egressive,　　activity (gh),　　imperfective,
　　　conative, inchoative, etc.　accomplishment (s),　perfective,
　　　　　　　　　　　　　　achievement (n),　　optative
　　　　　　　　　　　　　　semelfactive ($í$),
　　　　　　　　　　　　　　process ($\emptyset$)

11.7.1 Combinatorics

In Slave, situation aspect and viewpoint aspect combine overtly as follows:

(118) $\emptyset$ + imperfective　　$\emptyset$ + perfective　　$\emptyset$ + optative
　　　gh + imperfective　　gh + perfective　　gh + optative (rare)
　　　n + imperfective　　n + perfective　　n + optative
　　　s + imperfective　　s + perfective　　s + optative
　　　í + imperfective　　í + perfective　　í + optative

11.7 Ordering and Combinatorics

The combinatorics are free – all possible combinations of situation aspect and viewpoint aspect are found, although some are more common than others.

For Ahtna, Kari 1990:40–41 proposes the ordering in (119). He labels the second column *s* perfective/negative; I return to the negative.

(119) i transitional   +   s perfective   +   mode   +   perfective
                                                          Ø, n, gh, optative

This schema differs from that given for Slave in (118) in two major respects. First, Kari places optative together with Ø, *n*, and *gh*, elements that I have argued represent situation aspect. Second, he separates the *s* situation aspect marker from the others, placing it in a column of its own.

Kari gives no reason for his treatment of the optative morpheme. The template in (119) predicts that optative and perfective viewpoints should co-occur, but this prediction is not borne out. The template further predicts that the optative should occur together with *s* situation aspect, but again this combination is not found in Ahtna (see section 11.7.2.2). A third incorrect prediction is that *s* situation aspect should occur together with the other situation aspect markers (although these themselves should not co-occur); see section 11.7.2.2. Kari's template does make the correct prediction that the situation aspect markers *n* and *gh* do not occur with the optative. The following combinations are found in Ahtna event verbs (Kari 1990:56).

(120) Ø + imperfective   Ø + perfective   Ø + optative
      gh + imperfective   gh + perfective
      n + imperfective   n + perfective
      s + imperfective   s + perfective
      i + imperfective   i + perfective   i + optative

Suppose that the template in (119) were reanalyzed as in (121).

(121) **Situation aspect**   **Viewpoint aspect**
      Ø, s, n, gh, i   imperfective, perfective, optative

Viewed in this way, the primary difference between Slave and Ahtna concerns their combinatorial properties: in Ahtna only two of the situation aspect markers are found in the optative viewpoint, while Slave allows the full range of situation aspect markers in this viewpoint.

Based on discussion in Golla 1970, 1996, Hupa appears to be even more limited in its combinatorial properties, as shown in (122). The full range of situation aspects is overtly marked only in the perfective viewpoint. I have no information on semelfactives.

(122) Ø + imperfective   Ø + perfective   Ø + optative
     gh + imperfective   gh + perfective
                         n + perfective
                         s + perfective

The optative is further restricted in Hupa in that the overt optative viewpoint prefix appears only in first and third person forms.

Combinatorial restrictions differ across the languages in other ways. According to Kari 1979:98, the Ahtna progressive occurs only with achievement verbs, and only in the absence of additional lexical material in the predicate. In Koyukon and Dena'ina, on the other hand, additional combinations involving the progressive are permissible (Kari 1979). Combinatorial possibilities concerning the distributive and customary aspects with other situation aspects also differ from language to language. Further comparative work in these areas is in order. However, it appears plausible to treat the languages as differing in combinatorial properties rather than in ordering facts. The basic scopal claim then receives support not just within Slave, but across the family: viewpoint aspect has situation aspect to its scope, and thus the former follows the latter. The dependency of situation aspect on viewpoint is particularly striking in the optative in Ahtna and Hupa: this viewpoint combines with only a restricted range of situation aspect types.

11.7.2 Some Idiosyncrasies of Ordering

A second issue concerning ordering involves *i* transitional and *s* perfective-negative (Kari 1990). I use Ahtna as the data are very rich. The transitional is variable in its placement with respect to the inceptive, and the negative also exhibits variable ordering.

11.7.2.1 Future Semelfactive

Consider first the item that Kari labels *i* transitional, which is identical in form and phonological patterning to the semelfactive. It occurs in the following circumstances. First, it is used to form a transitional aspect of stative verbs, creating an event.

(123)   Ahtna (Kari 1990)
    a. descriptive   l-baa   'It is gray.' (97)
    b. transitional   '-**i**-tba'   'It turned gray.' (97)

11.7 Ordering and Combinatorics

According to Kari 1979:178, the transitional aspect is punctual; in Koyukon it marks a sudden transition rather than the gradual transition of the inceptive (Axelrod 1993:107).

Second, *i* marks the semelfactive situation aspect in nonperfective viewpoints, as discussed earlier.[14] Though a semelfactive suffix is typically present, the prefix can also sometimes appear in nonperfective viewpoints without the suffix. Kari 1990:67 gives the two examples 'find' and 'fall down'. These verbs are semantically punctual and atelic, so the presence of the semelfactive morpheme is not surprising.

The form *i* also appears in the perfective negative of event verbs and in the imperfective negative paradigm of state verbs. An example of an event verb is given in (124).

(124) 'ele y-**i**-ł-tsii-l-e
 '*ele* negative + *y* disjoint anaphor + **i** + *łtsii* 'make' + *l* suffix
 + *e* negative enclitic
 'He didn't make it.' (Kari 1990:276)

I postpone discussion of this use until section 11.7.2.2.

Is it possible to conflate the transitional and the semelfactive into a single lexical entry? Recall from chapter 7 that conflation is possible when the different readings can be derived from an underspecified lexical representation through contextual features. Transitionals share with semelfactives punctuality or instantaneity. The second feature that marks semelfactives is atelicity. Transitionals share an atelic sense as a transition does not imply an endpoint – an item changing color, for instance, may not ultimately turn completely gray but it may simply have grayed. If this interpretation is correct, then the semelfactive and the transitional can be considered one and the same morpheme with a core meaning of punctuality. The specific reading can be derived by the combination of this morpheme with a state or an event and by the distinct suffixation patterns found with semelfactive and transitional readings. As with the other conflations of items generally thought to be two morphemes that are proposed in this book (see chapter 14), it is necessary to work out a featural system that will allow for this underspecification.

Consider now the ordering of aspectual information proposed so far: subsituation aspect precedes situation aspect, which in turn precedes viewpoint aspect. Kari 1990:41 remarks on an unexpected ordering found in semelfactive forms of future verbs in Ahtna. Recall that the future is formed from the inceptive and activity situation aspect marking. Kari proposes the ordering inceptive + *i* + *gh*. Two points must be made. First, the future is morphologically complex, consisting of two morphemes. The future is the one clear tense found in Athapaskan languages – it locates the situation after the time of the utterance. What we find, then, in future semelfactives is situation aspect (semelfactive) in the scope of the future: a semelfactive situation will exist at a future time. I return to this point after reviewing Kari's account of the future semelfactives. Second, the hypothesized ordering inceptive-*i*-*gh* is not the actual ordering; instead the order is *i* semelfactive + inceptive + *gh* situation aspect. Kari introduces a metathesis rule that gives the surface order. This metathesis is not restricted to Ahtna. Leer 1996 reports the Ahtna surface order in all the languages he investigated; see Young and Morgan 1987 for discussion of Navajo. The ordering in question is shown in the table in (125), which shows prefix complexes without stems. The inceptive has the form *t* (Ahtna, Koyukon, Carrier), *h* (Gwich'in), or *d* (Navajo); the semelfactive has the form *i* (or *ì* in Navajo). The vowels following the inceptive provide evidence for the inclusion of *gh* situation aspect. The segmentation is rough, but it is evident that the semelfactive consistently precedes the inceptive.

(125)	**1singular**	**2singular**	**3**	**2plural**
Carrier	i-t-a-s-	i-t-a-n-	i-t-a-	i-t-a-h-
Gwich'in	i:-h-ì-h-	i:-h-ì-n-	i:-h-è:-	i:-h-ò-h-
Ahtna	i-t-aa-s-	i-ti-gh-i-	i-t-a-	i-t-u-'uh-
Koyukon	i-tæ-gh ə-s-	i-t ə-gh-i-	i-t-O-	i-t-a-x-
Navajo	ì-d-èè-sh	ì-d-í-í-	ì-d-òò-	ì-d-òò-(h)-

Why might the same metathesis occur throughout the family? A template account has little to offer. First, the very notion of morphologically based metathesis is troublesome for a template, which is designed to ensure strict morpheme order. Second, the template account provides no insight into why this ordering is stable across the family. A scopal account is attractive: in the future a semelfactive event exists. The future is a tense, and thus would be expected to occur to the right of the semelfactive situation aspect marking (see chapter 13, Bybee 1985a).[15] There is no particular reason to posit metathesis: other orderings are simply not interpretable. In the future, *gh* functions not as a situation aspect marker, but as part of the complex future tense marking.

11.7.2.2 Negatives

Some northern Athapaskan languages mark negation in the verb word. Negative morphology is complex and relevant to questions of ordering. It includes prefix and suffix components; as discussed in section 11.5.7 the enclitic is syntactic rather than lexical.

11.7 Ordering and Combinatorics

The form of the negative prefix depends upon viewpoint. In nonperfective viewpoints (imperfective, progressive, future, optative), the negative is marked by *s*. Kari 1979, 1990 conflates this *s* and the situation aspect marker *s*, and labels it *s*-perfective/negative. In the perfective viewpoint, the morpheme that Kari calls *i* transitional and that I have labeled semelfactive is found instead of *s*.

I address three questions. First, is the *i* that occurs in the perfective viewpoint of negative verbs identical to the one that I have called semelfactive? Second, is the *s* that appears in nonperfective viewpoints the same morpheme as *s* situation aspect? Third, I examine cases of variability in ordering involving the negative.

I begin by addressing the question of whether the *i* found in the negative of perfective viewpoint forms is only homophonous with the semelfactive, or the same morpheme, with the apparently different readings determined by context. Kari 1979, 1990 treats all meanings under a single lexical entry, while Leer 1996 appears to treat the negative as a distinct item from the semelfactive. Recall that negation is marked elsewhere in the verb (by the syntactic enclitic *e* in (124)). The element *i* itself therefore need not have negative content as negation is contributed through the enclitic. What would the effect of negation be on the situation type of a perfective viewpoint event? There would be no process and no inherent endpoint. Thus, the semelfactive, marking absence of process and atelicity, is not unexpected in negative perfectives. I thus assume that there is a single element *i*, which marks atelicity and absence of process. In negative paradigms, the negative enclitic, which c-commands the verb word, provides the negative meaning, co-occurring with semelfactive situation aspect in the perfective viewpoint. In answer to the first question, then, it appears that there is a single *i* in Ahtna, with a general meaning semelfactive and the specific meaning determined by context. This is an occasion in which the semelfactive appears regularly in the perfective viewpoint.

I now turn to the nonperfective viewpoints, where the semelfactive is not found in the negative paradigm; rather *s* occurs. The chart in (126), from Kari 1990:55, shows his analysis of the distribution of *i* and *s* in the different viewpoints of events.[16]

(126) **Transitional (my   s-perfective/   Mode   Perfective
      semelfactive)   negative**
         i   perfective-
                                                        negative
                              s, z   imperfective-
                                                        negative

	s, z	gh	progressive-negative
	s, z	gho	optative

This chart makes clear why Kari places *s* situation aspect in a different column from *n* and *gh* (see (119)): under the assumption that a single morpheme marks *s* situation aspect and *s* negative, this element can co-occur with *gh* in the progressive (and future) and with *gho* in the optative and thus must be in a different position from these.

In non-negative verbs, *s* marks a durative telic situation type. Is the *s* in the negative a distinct homophonous item marking negation, or is it the same item? To answer this question, I examine the phonology of these forms.

The phonology of *s* situation aspect marker and *s* negative is distinct in Ahtna (Kari 1979:46) and in other languages with negative paradigm (Hargus, personal communication on Babine-Witsuwit'en; Poser, personal communication on Carrier). This is illustrated by the Ahtna verb 'caulk, smear O with pitch, resin, glue' (Kari 1990:678). The first column shows the verb in the *s* situation aspect perfective viewpoint and the second column in the imperfective viewpoint negative. In the left column, the segments in boldface represent situation aspect; in the right column, they indicate the negative.

(127)   *s* **situation aspect perfective**   **Imperfective negative**
  a. **z**-i-dzae'   z-i-**s**-dzaegh-e
      situation aspect-2sg Subject   **negative**-2sg Subject-**negative**
      'You sg. caulked it.'   'You sg. don't caulk it.'
  b. yi-**z**-dzae'   i-**s**-dzaegh-e
      disjoint anaphor-**situation aspect**   epenthetic-**negative**
      'S/he caulked it '   'S/he doesn't caulk it.'
  c. ts'e-**z**-dzae'   ts'e-**s**-dzaegh-e
      HSubject-**situation aspect**   HSubject-**negative**
      'We caulked it.'   'We don't caulk it.'

In the second person singular perfective viewpoint form, *s* situation aspect, in the form [z], precedes *i* second person singular subject. In the imperfective negative, on the other hand, the negative occurs in two places, with [z] preceding the second person singular subject *i* while [s] follows it. In number forms, the situation aspect marker surfaces as [z] directly before the stem, *dzae*'; the situation aspect marker is regularly voiced when there is null voice/valence marking. In the imperfective negative, on the other hand, the consonant is in the same position, but voiceless. This difference in phonological patterning

11.7 Ordering and Combinatorics

suggests that situation aspect and the negative are two morphemes, and I will therefore treat them as distinct. Since the negative is not telic semantically, on semantic grounds, too, the conflation of the negative and situation aspect is not expected.

The negative exhibits odd ordering properties, as can be seen in the imperfective negative form just given in (127) – in the second person singular, the negative occurs in two places in the verb, both preceding and following the subject marker. The location of the negative in the optative and the future is likewise odd, as in (128) and (129).

(128) Negative optative
   a. z-gho-s-dzaegh-e
      negative-optative-1sg Subject-stem-negative enclitic
      'I should not caulk it.'
   b. z-ghu-s-dzaegh-e
      negative-optative/2sg Subject-**negative**-stem-negative enclitic
      'You sg. should not caulk it.'
   c. y-u-s-dzaegh-e
      disjoint anaphor-optative-**negative**-stem-negative enclitic
      'S/he should not caulk it.'

(129) Negative future
   a. d-z-gha-s-dzaegh-e
      inceptive-**negative**-activity situation aspect-1sg Subject-stem-negative enclitic
      'I will not caulk it.'
   b. d-z-gh-i-s-dzaegh-e
      inceptive-**negative**-activity situation aspect-2sg Subject-**negative**-stem-negative enclitic
      'You sg. will not caulk it.'
   c. i-t-a-s-dzaegh-e
      disjoint anaphor-inceptive-activity situation aspect-**negative**-stem-negative enclitic
      'S/he will not caulk it.'

In first person singular forms, the negative prefix [z] precedes the optative viewpoint aspect marker, as in (128a), but it follows the inceptive and precedes the *gh* situation aspect marker in the future, as in (129a). In second person singular forms, the negative [z] appears twice, once preceding the optative or the situation aspect marker, as in (128b) and (129b), respectively, and once after the subject. Finally, in the number forms it follows the optative ([u] in (128c)) and the situation aspect marker ([a] in (129c)) and directly precedes the verb stem.

The negative prefix is thus variable in position with respect to situation aspect, viewpoint, or tense; its positioning is determined by other factors. Hargus and Tuttle 1997 argue that phonological factors determine the placement of the negative; see their work for justification.

We will see in chapter 12 that when comparative Athapaskan evidence is considered, the negative prefix shows two further interesting properties. First, when the negative precedes situation aspect, its exact position is variable across the family. Second, in all languages it directly precedes the stem in third person forms. Why might the negative prefix exhibit this variation in ordering? The variable position of the negative is allowed by the scope hypothesis: negation is always expressed by a syntactic suffix that has scope over the entire verb word. Thus, the position of the negative marker under consideration here is not regulated by scope and can be determined by phonological factors instead.

A template account of the positioning of the negative is necessarily complex – it is not found in a single position, as required by the template, but rather its position is determined by morphological and phonological factors. The scope hypothesis does not predict exactly where it will go, but it does predict where it cannot go, and that it might be subject to a certain degree of variability.

If s negative and s situation aspect are distinct functional items, then s, n, and gh situation aspect occupy the same basic position in the verb, as discussed in section 11.7.1. I now return to the positioning of i semelfactive. Recall the ordering of morphemes proposed by Kari 1990 for Ahtna, slightly revised in (130) to put the situation aspect markers together and the optative with the perfective.

(130) $i + s$ negative $+ s, n, gh$ situation aspect $+$ perfective, optative viewpoint aspect

The i semelfactive situation aspect marker precedes the negative, as can be seen in second person singular imperfective forms.

(131) a. na-'-**i-z**-i-ł-taeg-e
preverb-epenthetic-**semelfactive-negative**-2sg Subject-valence-stem-negative enclitic
'You sg. are not finding it.'(Kari 1990:676)

b. '-**i**-**z**-i-**s**-t'as-e
epenthetic-**semelfactive**-**negative**-2sg Subject-**negative**-stem- enclitic
'You sg. are not cutting it once.' (Kari 1990:687)

In other forms, the negative also follows the semelfactive.

(132) ts'-**i**-**s**-t'as-e
HSubject-**semelfactive**-**negative**-stem-negative enclitic
'We are not cutting it once.' (Kari 1990:687)

In progressive forms with activity situation aspect, the negative can either precede (first person singular) or follow (third person) the situation aspect marker.

(133) a. **z**-gha-s-kael-e
negative-activity situation aspect-1sg Subject-stem-negative suffix
'I am not going by boat, paddling.' (Kari 1990:671)
b. a-**s**-kael-e
activity situation aspect-**negative**-stem-negative suffix
'S/he is not going by boat, paddling.'

The ordering of situation aspect and the negative is not fixed, but depends on the situation aspect marker and person. The most salient difference between semelfactive and progressive negatives concerns the phonological form of the situation aspect marker: the semelfactive is a vowel and the progressive a consonant. Phonological factors appear to determine details of ordering (see Hargus and Tuttle 1997). Once again, the scope hypothesis, while not predicting the exact ordering in the different persons, allows variability. Since the negative enclitic has scope over the verb word, the position of the negative prefix can be variable.

11.7.3 Summary

While I have given a more detailed analysis of Slave than of any other language, the languages appear to be similar in two ways. First, the situation aspect markers in all of the languages are meaningful, overt expressions of situation type. Second, ordering among subsituation aspect, situation aspect, and viewpoint aspect is stable across the family, as expected under the scope hypothesis. The major differences between languages concerns not ordering, but combinatorial restrictions on situation aspect and viewpoint aspect on the one hand and the distribution of the semelfactive on the other. Assume that the languages exhibit the order in (134). I oversimplify the position of the semelfactive; see section 11.7.1 and chapter 12.

(134) **Subsituation aspect   Situation aspect   Viewpoint aspect   Mood**
      s, n, gh, i, Ø   imperfective,   optative
                              perfective

The following combinatorial possibilities of viewpoint and situation aspect are observed.

(135) Combinatorics of situation aspect and viewpoint:
   a. Situation and viewpoint and mood combine freely (Slave).
   b. Situation aspect and viewpoint combine freely; mood (optative) limited to Ø situation aspect (Ahtna, Koyukon, Navajo).
   c. Situation aspect and perfective viewpoint combine freely; only Ø situation aspect in imperfective generally; only Ø in optative (Hupa).

Additional statements are required to account for the distribution of the semelfactive.

In addition, the languages differ in their ability to combine situation aspect markers.

(136) activity + accomplishment: Hupa, Mattole
      semelfactive + activity: all (?), in future only

Though the languages differ, it appears that semantically well-formed combinations exist in at least some of the languages.

11.8 Summary

The goal of this chapter has been to examine systematically the part of the verb that has variously been called aspect (e.g., Cook 1984, Li 1946), mode (e.g., Golla 1970, Hoijer 1946b), and conjugation mode (e.g., Hargus and Rice 1989, Rice 1989). I have argued that conjugation is better identified as situation aspect and mode as viewpoint aspect and mood. Both categories are overtly marked rather than covert. In addition, there is a future tense. The languages differ primarily, I have argued, not in content but rather in combinatorial possibilities. These combinatorial possibilities deserve more study than I have given them. However, for my purposes, I have shown what the content of this span of the verb is, and that, given this content, the ordering

11.9 Appendix

among morphemes is largely predictable based on their scopal relationships. The template approach has problems with certain orderings – for instance, *s* negative is variable in its placement, and the semelfactive appears in an unexpected position in the future. The scope hypothesis, on the other hand, is consistent with these phenomena. In particular, variable orderings are not ruled out if the elements in question do not interact with each other, as with the negative, or if scopal relations can differ, as with the semelfactive. But variable orderings are not found when the scopal relations are fixed. The basic orderings of material within the aspectual complex are determined by scope, and variation arises in the absence of scopal relationships.

11.9 Appendix: A Comparative Look: Situation Aspect and Aspectually Determining Morphemes

In discussions of individual languages in this chapter, I examined the major situation aspect categories and showed that they are defined by features of durativity and telicity, which are indicated by situation aspect markers. The strongest evidence for the situation aspect markers is semantic content, which comes from the minimal predicates (ones without preverbs). When preverbs enter in, the combinations of preverb with situation aspect marker may well seem arbitrary, as Axelrod 1993, quoted in the text, observes. In this appendix I compare purely aspectual material and lexical aspectual material across the languages to show that they impose similar requirements across the family. Consider first the purely aspectual material.

(1)   **Prefix**   **Situation aspect (perfective)**
   a. Inceptive   *s*   (Dogrib, Navajo, Tsuut'ina, Sekani, Slave *d*; Ahtna, Babine-Witsuwit'en, Chilcotin, Hupa, Koyukon, Tututni *t*; Chipewyan *t/h*)
   b. Egressive   *s*   (Ahtna, Chipewyan, Dogrib, Koyukon, Navajo, Tsuut'ina, Slave, Tututni *n*)
   c. Conative   *n*   (Ahtna, Chilcotin, Chipewyan, Koyukon, Slave)
                   s   (Navajo; rare in perfective)

Across the language family, for a particular subsituation aspect, the situation aspect marker is either identical or differs only in telicity (as in the Navajo conative).

I have compiled a number of preverbs that interact with the situation aspect system to show the similarities in co-occurrence with situation markers found across the family. Several examples of preverbs along with the situation aspect marker that they occur with and the form in a number of languages are given in (2).

(2) Lexical aspect
    a. to a point, ending   *n* (Ahtna, Hupa, Navajo *ni*, Chipewyan, Slave *ní*, Dogrib *nì*, Galice *doo/noo*, Koyukon *nee*, Tsuut'ina *nà*, Tututni *no*)
    b. through O   *n* (Ahtna, Slave, Tututni *gha*, Hupa *wa*, Navajo *ghá*, *níká*)
    c. out of, off of (it)   *n* (Tututni O-*k'e*, Hupa O-*k'ya*)
    d. out of enclosure   *n* (Hupa *ch'e*, Koyukon *ts'aa*, Navajo *ch'í*, Tututni *cr'e*, Ahtna *ts'i*)
    e. up onto surface   *s* (Ahtna, Koyukon, Navajo *da*, Slave *dah*)
    f. reversative   *s* (Ahtna, Hupa, Navajo, Sekani, Slave *na*, Koyukon *no*)
    g. out of (water, fire)   *s* (Hupa *tah*, Slave *ta*, Ahtna *ta*)
    h. up to top, reaching top, completing climb   *s* (Hupa *xa*, Koyukon *ho*, Navajo *ha*, Ahtna *ka*, Babine-Witsuwit'en *ha*)
    i. across (river)   *n* (Ahtna, Hupa, Navajo *na*, Koyukon *no*, Chipewyan *ną́*, Babine-Witsuwit'en *ne*   *s* (Slave *ná/nee*)
    j. up and out, ascending   *gh* (Koyukon, Navajo *ha*, Hupa, Tututni *xa*, Slave *ká/xá*, Tsuut'ina *xá*, Ahtna *ka*, Chipewyan *xá*, Dogrib *kà/xà*, Babine-Witsuwit'en *ha*)
    k. into enclosure   *gh* (Hupa *yeh*, Tututni *e*, Tsuut'ina *kú*, Koyukon *yee*, Ahtna *ku*, Slave *yî*)
    l. into fire   *gh* (Hupa, Tututni *de#di*, Slave *di#d*, *tthí#d*, Navajo *di#d*, Ahtna *s#d*)
    m. upward   *gh* (Ahtna, Hupa, Slave, Tututni *ya*)
    n. down from above   *gh* (Ahtna, Hupa, Navajo *na*, Koyukon *no*, Slave *ná*, Galice *da*, Babine-Witsuwit'en *ne*)
    o. into water   *gh* (Ahtna, Hupa, Slave, Tututni *ta*)
    p. suffering, harm, injury   *gh* (Ahtna *ti#da*, Navajo *'atí*)
    q. in recess, pocket, covered space   *gh* (Ahtna *t'a*, Navajo, Slave *t'áh*)
    r. into mouth   *gh* (Ahtna, Navajo *za*)

11.9 Appendix

The similarity in a particular preverb's choice of situation aspect marker across the languages is very strong. Kari 1979:7 remarks "the most convincing proof of the ancient basis of verb theme categorization is the degree to which grammatical selections of mode and aspect are cognate among different languages in theme after theme." This seems to extend to the interaction of situation aspect and other elements of the verbal system, suggesting that a reason exists for the particular choice of situation aspect marker with a particular subsituation aspect or preverb.

One final point is worth noting. Preverbs having to do with movement out of or upwards occur with the situation aspect marker *s*, while those having to do with movement in or downwards occur with the situation aspect marker *gh*, as noted by Axelrod 1993 in her discussion of Koyukon. I do not understand the semantics here, but it is consistent both within a single language and across the family.

12

Qualifiers and Their Ordering

I have so far examined the lexical, pronominal, and aspectual complexes of the verb. A remarkable stability exists across the family in ordering within these complexes; differences between languages can be largely attributed to the noninteraction of systems and to the different importance assigned to contradictory universals. In this chapter I investigate ordering inside the qualifier complex. It is here that the greatest variation in morpheme ordering is found both across languages and within a particular language.

12.1 The Qualifiers: Content

Unlike the argument and aspect systems discussed in the previous two chapters, the qualifiers do not form a functionally homogeneous class. As discussed in chapter 9, qualifiers are of several types. Some are aspectual – inceptive, conative, egressive, inchoative, negative.[1] Others are noun class markers that index properties of patient/theme arguments. A third set marks noun class qualities, but does not share all properties with noun class markers. Others mark classes of descriptive stative verbs in some languages. Another one interacts with the middle voice system in marking reflexive and self-benefactive. A final set is difficult to assign meanings to; they might be historical noun class markers that are now frozen in use with particular verbs. This last set is generally called thematic in the Athapaskan literature.

12.1.1 The Noun Class System

Many Athapaskan languages show some productive use of noun class markers, usually called gender in the Athapaskan literature, although the system is more productive in some languages than others. I begin by arguing that these qualifiers are best considered classifiers rather than gender markers (see

12.1 The Qualifiers: Content

Corbett 1991 on this distinction; see also Aikenvald 1997). Because of the use of the term 'classifier' in the Athapaskan literature to refer to the voice/valence morphemes, I call these items noun class markers rather than classifiers when discussing Athapaskan languages.

12.1.1.1 Background – Gender versus Classification

Noun classifiers and gender are easily confused, as discussed by Corbett 1991. In this section I summarize the properties of classifiers as opposed to gender, following Corbett.

Gender is usually considered to be a type of agreement. Thus, it is useful to begin with a definition of agreement. Corbett 1991:105, after Steele 1978:610, states that "the term agreement commonly refers to some systematic covariance between a semantic or formal property of one element and a formal property of another. For example, adjectives may take some formal indication of the number and gender of the noun they modify."

Classifiers (noun class markers in this book) are distinct from gender in several ways, as Corbett discusses (136–137). One difference has to do with distribution. Corbett points out that classifiers often do not co-occur with certain nouns. They may be obligatory with other nouns, or their use may vary according to speech style. Different noun class markers may be possible with the same noun, with the choice depending on meaning. Further, more than one classifier may be found with a particular noun; Corbett points out that in Yidin^y (Australia), for instance, two classifiers may be found on a single noun. Gender, on the other hand, is obligatory and invariant.

Noun classifiers fail to show agreement as a defining characteristic in the way that gender does. Gender shows variation of a formal property (e.g., an adjective marks agreement in gender), while noun classifiers select one marker as opposed to others. Noun classifiers are independent items, selected largely according to semantic criteria, while gender markers typically appear attached to agreement targets.

Corbett concludes that noun classifiers differ from gender markers in various ways. The question that I address in the next section concerns the status of the items in the Athapaskan verb that have been identified as marking gender.

12.1.1.2 Gender or Noun Classifiers in Athapaskan Languages?

Noun class markers in Athapaskan languages are part of the argument system, indexing theme/patient arguments. I begin discussion of these elements with some examples from Ahtna (Kari 1990) and Carrier (Poser 1996) to illustrate the phenomenon under discussion.

Kari 1990 identifies three overt gender prefixes and one null prefix in Ahtna. These are shown in (1), where they index the subject of an intransitive. The noun class markers are in boldface.

(1) a. Ø: tsic'uuts'   z-'aan
       hat   accomplishment situation aspect-stem
       'A hat is there.' (53)
    b. *d*: c'ecene' **de**-z-'aan
       stump   **noun class marker**-accomplishment situation aspect-stem
       'A stump is there.' (53)
    c. *n*: gig   **ne**-z-'aan
       berry   **noun class marker**-accomplishment situation aspect-stem
       'A berry is there.' (53)
    d. *ko*: hwnax   **ku**-z-'aan
       house   **area**-accomplishment situation aspect-stem
       'A house is there.' (54)

The marker in (1d) is the areal. It is part of the number system (chapter 10), but is similar semantically to noun class markers, so I include it here.

Kari identifies the following groups of entities for each noun class marker:

(2) *d* (Kari 1990:131)
     stick, tree, leaf, plant, bark, pitch
     dish, cup, basket
     feather, hair, fur
     enclosed liquids, lake, puddle, pus, afterbirth, breast, egg
     word, song, story, news, name
     day, day's journey, units of time
     fire, smoke, star
(3) *n* (Kari 1990:285)
     round objects (e.g., head, eye, face, nose, cheek, bead, berry, fish egg, hailstone, mountain, hill)
     rope or stringlike object (rope, thread, chain, sinew, foot strap, intestine, umbilical cord)
     liquids (water, blood)
(4) *ko* (Kari 1990:243)
     area in space or time

12.1 The Qualifiers: Content

Kari's information on noun class markers (his gender) comes primarily from one speaker of each Ahtna dialect, and Kari remarks that there may be undocumented dialect differences (1990:34). This statement suggests that the system is not a gender system, but rather a noun class marker system; as Corbett argues, gender systems do not exhibit variability, while noun class marker systems do. Kari 1990:34 further points out that some nouns have two or more distinct meanings with distinct noun class markers.

Further support for the claim that the relevant system is one of noun class marking comes from Carrier. The following examples of noun class markers in Carrier are taken from Poser 1996. Noun class markers are in boldface in the examples and glosses.

(5) *d*: a. nak'albən ta-**di**-n-tel
Stuart Lake water-**sticklike**-perfective viewpoint-be wide
'Stuart Lake is wide.'
b. dzihtel **di**-n-tel
board **sticklike**-perfective viewpoint-be wide
'The board is wide.'
c. s-kechən b-əɬ-'ə-**də**-ts'əɬ
1sg-leg 3 Object-with-unspecified Object-**sticklike**-pains
'My leg aches.'

(6) *n*: u-<u>tsi</u> b-əɬ-'ə-**nə**-l-ts'əɬ
3-head 3 Object-with-unspecified Object-**round**-voice/valence-pains
'My head aches.'

(7) Ø: s-gwət b-əɬ-'ə-l-tsəɬ'
1sg-knee 3 Object-with-unspecified Object-voice/valence-pains
'My knee aches.'

Support for the position that the elements under discussion are noun class rather than gender markers comes from the fact that a particular noun does not always appear with a particular marker. For example, the noun 'rope' often takes the sticklike noun class marker *d* (8a). However, with some verbs it does not appear with this marker (8b), despite the fact that the verb does appear with noun class markers (8c).

(8) a. *d*: tl'uɬ **di**-n-cha
rope **sticklike**-perfective viewpoint-be big
'The rope is thick.'

b. Ø: tl'uɫ   n-yi<u>z</u>
       rope   perfective viewpoint-belong
       'The rope is long.'
   c. *d*: shən   **di**-n-yi<u>z</u>
       song   **sticklike**-perfective viewpoint-be long
       'The song is long.'

These morphemes do not mark agreement in the way that gender does, suggesting that they are best considered a type of noun class marker rather than gender.

Some Slave facts show the nonobligatory nature of noun class markers. The areal is perhaps the best candidate for a gender marker – it is often said to mark agreement with an areal noun (a reasonably well-defined class of nouns which, in some sense, occupy space). One noun that is usually areal is *kóę́* 'house.' With this noun, the areal *go* may or may not be present, with semantic interpretation depending on its presence.

(9)   a. Areal present
       kóę́   **gó**-'ǫ
       house   **area**/accomplishment situation aspect-default object is located
       'The house is located.'
   b. Areal absent
       kóę́   the'ǫ
       house   accomplishment situation aspect-default object is located
       'The house (e.g., toy made of lego) is located.'

In a gender system, the noun determines the agreement; agreement is not variable.

A further fact argues for the categorization of the items in question as noun class markers: two can co-occur. For instance, Leer 1995 shows that in Koyukon and Carrier (based on Morice 1932) *d-n* is a compound noun class marker, *d* plus *n*. With the stem 'handle object (default)' it identifies the object as round and heavy (rock, head, large fruit); with just *d* the object is sticklike (stick, log, tree, box, table, chair, bed); with just *n* the object is small and round (berry, bead, ring, coil of rope). In Carrier, the compound *d-n* is used with the handle default object verb to identify a loop, snare, or meshes of a net. The *d* occurs when a rock is the object, and the *n* when a ball, head, or berry is the object.

12.1 The Qualifiers: Content

Poser 1996 gives several examples of Carrier verbs with two noun class markers.

(10) d + areal
 nedo ts'eke u-ts'itoh **x^{w}ə-di-n-dot** həkwadatni
 white person woman 3-waist **area-sticklike**-perfective crave
 viewpoint-be narrow
 'White women are frantic for narrow waists.'

In (10), both d, marking a sticklike object, and the areal, x^w, marking an area (the waist is an area of the body) occur, and the meaning is compositional.

(11) $d + n$
 ndi łembił **də-ni-n-t'əm**
 this fishnet **noun class marker-noun class marker**-perfective
 viewpoint-be small
 'This fishnet has a fine mesh.'

As Poser points out, when d and n co-occur, the meaning is not compositional.

To conclude, three facts suggest that the morphemes in question are noun class markers rather than gender: they are not obligatory, a particular noun can appear with more than one with different interpretations, and they can be compounded.

12.1.2 Middle Voice

A qualifier may be used productively in the voice system. In particular, a qualifier of the form d enters into the argument and voice system, as the following Ahtna examples from Kari 1990 illustrate. The middle voice forms contain the qualifier d.

(12) Reflexive
 d-ze-l-ghaen
 middle-qualifier/accomplishment situation aspect-voice/valence-stem
 'He killed himself.' (131)
 cf. i-ze-ł-ghaen
  disjoint anaphor-qualifier/accomplishment situation aspect-valence-stem
  'He killed it.' (131)

(13) Benefactive
i-**d**-ze-l-ghen
disjoint anaphor-**middle**-qualifier/accomplishment situation aspect-voice/valence-stem
'He killed it for his own benefit.' (131)

12.1.3 Lexicalized Qualifiers

In addition to productive uses, qualifiers can be lexicalized with a particular verb stem. These, known as thematic prefixes in the Athapaskan literature, have no obvious meaning. A few Ahtna examples are given in (14) and (15). The abbreviation 'O' indicates that the verb is transitive and takes an object; 'D' and 'G' are Kari's 1990 abbreviations for 'middle voice' and 'gender,' respectively.

(14) **d**-ɬ-tiy   'be strong' (131)
     d-D-tsets   'plant, tree dies' (130)
(15) O **n**-'ii   'steal O' (285)
     G-**n**-yaa   'grow' (285)
     O **n**-ts'etl' 'wink at O' (285)

12.1.4 Verb Class Markers

In some Athapaskan languages, qualifiers are also markers of descriptive verb classes. Hupa and Slave are good exemplars of such languages. In Hupa and Slave, three classes of descriptive verbs, or verbs marking adjectival classes, are found. One is marked by the class marker *n*, a second by the class marker ɬ, and a third by the marker *d*.

(16) *n*
   a. Hupa (Golla 1970:137)
      ni-nes   'be long, tall'
      ni-das   'be heavy'
   b. Slave
      ne-déh   'He, she, it is long, tall.'
      ne-dah   'He, she, it is heavy.'
(17) ɬ
   a. Hupa (Golla 1970:139)
      ɬi-xan   'be sweet, good-tasting'
      ɬi-q'ah   'be fat'

12.1 The Qualifiers: Content

    b. Slave
        ɬe-kǫ   'It is sweet, good-tasting.'
        ɬek'á   'He, she, it is fat.'

(18) *d*
    a. Hupa (Golla 1970:140)
        di-l-Gay   'be whitish'
        di-l-Win   'be blackish'
    b. Slave
        de-gai   'be white'
        de-zene   'be black'

Krauss 1969 argues that the first of these, *n*, derives historically from the perfective marker, and the second two from voice/valence markers. He suggests that all of these slipped leftwards to their current positions. In at least some languages, these must be regarded as verb class markers rather than as voice/valence and perfective markers because they co-occur with voice/valence, and because the reflex of the perfective marker can be found in imperfective and perfective viewpoints.

12.1.5 Others

There remains a group of qualifiers that do not fall into the categories identified so far. They are not aspectual, they do not classify theme/patient arguments, they are not an obligatory part of the verbal lexical entry, they are not part of the voice/valence system, and they do not mark verb classes. In Navajo, for example, Young and Morgan 1987 list a number of *d*'s. Ignoring *d* inceptive and noun class marker, *d*'s also occur in many verbs involving movement of the arms or legs; opening or closing; refuge, relief, or succor; fire or light; the mouth, stomach, throat, oral action, food, smell, noise, speech; pain, hurt; holiness; tilting, slanting, dangling, leaning; and sound, hearing. The *d* relating to noise, speech, and sound is illustrated for Ahtna in (19).

(19) a. da-y-**de**-ɬ-tsiin
        mouth-disjoint anaphor-**qualifier**-valence-stem
        'He made it (song, name).' (Kari 1990:131)
      cf. yi-ɬ-tsiin
        disjoint anaphor-valence-stem
        'He made it.' (386)
    b. ti-seɬ-**d**-ghe-l-ggaac
       preverb-shout-**qualifier**-activity situation aspect-voice/valence-stem
       'He ran out shouting.' (455)

cf. ti-na-'i-l-ggaac
preverb-iterative-epenthetic-voice/valence-stem
'He went back out.' (189)

The effect of the qualifier *d* 'noise, sound' can be seen by comparing the examples in (19). In the first form of each set, the verb has to do with sound, and *d* occurs; in the second form *d* is absent. These examples show that this *d* is not identical in patterning to a noun class marker: the noun class markers refer to themes/patients, while the *d* referring to sound can reference an argument (14a), but it can also refer to an event (14b).

Ignoring *n* noun class marker and egressive, Young and Morgan recognize several *n*'s in Navajo – *n* occurs with verbs relating to the mind and mental processes; sight and vision; and subjects that are weak or incapacitated. The *gh* qualifier (*y* in Navajo) occurs with verbs that describe the passage of night and the coming of dawn and in several verbs where the meaning is uncertain. Tenenbaum 1978 identifies similar categories in Dena'ina, Golla 1970 in Hupa, Hargus 1988 in Sekani, and Rice 1989 in Slave. Kari 1990 groups all of these *n*'s (plus the noun class marker) under a single lexical entry in the Ahtna dictionary. I group these qualifiers with noun class markers functionally in the following discussion.

12.2 The Ordering of Qualifiers

12.2.1 Introduction

Qualifiers can be divided into five major types: noun class markers, aspectual, verb class markers, other productive qualifiers (including middle voice), and lexicalized qualifiers (this last group is called thematic in the Athapaskan literature). I now turn to the internal ordering of the qualifiers. Although numerous functions can be assigned to the qualifiers, formally, there are only a few forms – the most frequent of these are *d*, *n*, *gh*, and *i*, and I focus my discussion on the ordering of these elements.

A chart showing the ordering of some qualifiers with respect to each other in a number of languages is given in (20). The Ahtna scheme is from Kari 1990, Koyukon from Axelrod 1993, Babine-Witsuwit'en (B-W) from Hargus 1995a, Sekani from Hargus 1988, Navajo from Kari 1989, Slave from Rice 1989, and the others from Kari 1993. Three Dena'ina dialects are distinguished:Inland, Iliamna and Upper, and Outer. This chart does not include verb class markers. Note that apart from aspectual conative, inceptive, and

12.2 The Ordering of Qualifiers

negative, all qualifier functions are grouped together under *d*, *n*, and *gh* (and cognates).

(20) Ahtna **conative inceptive** *d-qualifier n-qualifier* z-neg gh-qualifier
Lower Tanana **conative inceptive** *d-qualifier n-qualifier* dh-neg gh-qualifier
Koyukon **conative** gh-qualifier *d-qualifier* **inceptive** *n-qualifier* l-neg
Upper Tanana **conative inceptive** *d-qualifier n-qualifier*
Dena'ina
  Inland **conative inceptive** *d-qualifier n-qualifier* z-neg gh-qualifier
  Iliamna, **conative** z,y-neg **inceptive** *d-qualifier n-qualifier*
  Upper gh-qualifier
  Outer z-neg gh-qualifier **conative** *d-qualifier n-qualifier* **inceptive**
B-W **conative** *d-qualifier n-qualifier* **inceptive**
Slave **conative** gh-qualifier *d-qualifier/***inceptive** *n-qualifier*
Sekani **conative** *d-qualifier/***inceptive** *n-qualifier*
Navajo y-qualifier **conative** *d-qualifier/***inceptive** *n-qualifier*

I call the subsituation aspect morphemes discussed in chapter 11 (e.g., inceptive, conative) aspectual qualifiers. I consider the negative to be aspectual also. The remaining productive qualifiers I refer to as nonaspectual qualifiers; the nonproductive ones I call lexicalized qualifiers. Recall that aspectual and nonaspectual qualifiers have the same phonological forms and patterning. However, they can be differentiated by their morphosyntactic patterning. Aspectual qualifiers are not related to the argument structure of the verb in any way, but rather provide part of its event structure. Noun class markers, on the other hand, are part of the argument system. Verb class markers are not part of either of these systems. Other productive qualifiers are adverbial in nature. I look first at the ordering within a group of qualifiers, and then at the interaction across different groups.

12.2.2 Ordering within Aspectual Qualifiers

First consider ordering within the aspectual qualifiers. Given the scope hypothesis, one might expect that subsituation aspect markers would appear in a fixed order inasmuch as the aspects interact with each other.

12.2.2.1 Conative and Inceptive

The ordering of the conative and the inceptive suggests that this is the case: the table in (20) illustrates that the conative is always to the left of the inceptive (boldfaced items), although they are not always adjacent to each other. Turning to the semantics of these forms, recall that the conative marks a situation that is attempted, referring to an endpoint, while the inceptive spans the early part of an event or state, referring to initiation. In order to attempt a situation, it must begin. Therefore if both the conative and inceptive are present, the scope hypothesis predicts that the conative will be to the left of the inceptive, within the scope of the inceptive – initiations logically precede outcomes. This fixed ordering thus can be attributed to scopal relations. I have found no examples of the conative and the egressive co-occurring; their combination is semantically infelicitous as the conative implies lack of completion, while the egressive refers to the endpoint.

12.2.2.2 Navajo Inchoative

The Navajo inchoative, not included in (20), presents a similar case. The inchoative "mark[s] the inception of verbal action for non-motion themes, placing the focus on the point in time at which the verbal action begins" (Young and Morgan 1987:187). Two qualifiers are involved, identified tentatively by Young and Morgan 1987:187 as n egressive (their terminal) and y transitional (my semelfactive; see chapter 11). The transitional (which may actually mark situation aspect rather than subsituation aspect; see chapter 11) focuses on a change of state or condition, without an endpoint implied, while the egressive provides an endpoint. Thus, such a form involves a transition and an endpoint. The ordering is compatible with this. Alternatively, the inchoative may be noncompositional in meaning, as in the prolongative, discussed in section 12.2.2.4.

12.2.2.3 Navajo Seriative and Inceptive

The ordering of the Navajo seriative and inceptive is also of interest. Navajo exhibits several cases of metathesis (Kari 1973). One involves an element of the form h/y, which marks seriative and segmented situations and arguments. Young and Morgan indicate that this element can appear in two places, their position VIa or their position VIc. These two positions are separated by their position VIb. This element exhibits allomorphy depending on its location: in position VIa it has the form h, but in position VIc it has the alternate form y.[2]

12.2 The Ordering of Qualifiers

The conditions which determine the position of the seriative are largely morphological. Consider the singular forms of the verb 'break it up, future' (Kari 1973:233), where the seriative occurs together with *d* inceptive.

(21) a. seriative *h* + inceptive *d*
  ni-**hi**-**de**-e-sh-tih
  preverb-**seriative**-**inceptive**-activity situation aspect-1sg Subject-stem
  'I will break it up.'
  ni-**hi**-**d**-í-í-tih
  preverb-**seriative**-**inceptive**-activity situation aspect-2sg Subject-stem
  'You sg. will break it up.'
 b. inceptive *d* + seriative *y*
  ni-i-**di**-**y**-oo-tih
  preverb-disjoint anaphor-**inceptive**-**seriative**-optative-stem
  'S/he will break it up.'

In (21a), *h* seriative precedes *d* inceptive, while in (21b) the seriative, in the form *y*, follows *d* inceptive. Kari 1973:233 treats this as a metathesis that reorders the morphemes from seriative followed by inceptive to the reverse when a functional prefix precedes; in (21b) the disjoint anaphor, in a reduced form *i*, is present, while in the forms in (21a) a lexical item precedes. Metathesis is not restricted to the number subject environment, as (22) shows.

(22) inceptive *d* + seriative *y*
  na-ho-**di**-**y**-ii-dlał
  preverb-area-**inceptive**-**seriative**-1pl Subject-stem
  'We will plow it.' (Kari 1973:234)

In (22) the functional *ho* 'areal' is present, and metathesis is found. Some forms allow a double occurrence of the seriative, separated by the inceptive.

(23) seriative + inceptive + seriative (Kari 1973)
  yi-**di**-**y**-oo-tih ~ **hi**-**di**-**y**-oo-tih
  'break off, snap off one after another, future' (277)
  dah **y**i-**di**-**y**-ii-ł-tį́ ~ dah **hi**-**di**-**y**-ii-ł-tį́
  'hang an animate object up, future' (275, 277)

Three variants exist: inceptive-seriative, seriative-inceptive, and seriative-inceptive-seriative, as shown by the following forms with the unspecified human subject *j/zh* (Young and Morgan's fourth person subject).

(24) a. ji-**di**-**y**-oo-tih
　　 b. **h**i-zh-**d**-oo-tih
　　 c. **h**i-zh-**di**-**y**-oo-tih
　　　　 'break off, snap off one after another, future' (Kari 1973:277)

The conditions governing metathesis are morphophonological, depending on the presence of functional material before the seriative and on the presence of the unspecified subject, discussed later. The seriative thus can appear on either side of other qualifiers, depending upon morphophonological conditions. Does metathesis of the seriative and inceptive destroy scopal relations? In order to answer this question, it is necessary to look more closely at the semantics of the seriative. Young and Morgan 1987:166 define the seriative as follows: "occurs with verbs of motion, intransitive and transitive, where it (1) describes the plural (3+) subjects of an intransitive verb as performing the verbal action in sequence – seriatim (one after another), (2) describes the plural (3+) objects of a transitive verb as being moved in sequence (one after another), (3) describes the sgl or dpl subject(s) of an intransitive or a transitive verb as performing the verbal action in sequential form (as one time after another), and (4) describes verbal action as segmented in form (as hop, skip, hobble, wriggle)." An example of each function is given in (25) (from Young and Morgan 1987:166). The seriative is in boldface.

(25) a. Plural subject of intransitive
　　　　 hastóí　　 hooghan　　 góne'　　 yah　　 'a-da-**h**-aa-s-kai
　　　　 men　　　 hogan　　　 inside　　 into　　 they entered one
　　　　　　　　　　　　　　 enclosed　 enclosed　 after another
　　　　　　　　　　　　　　 space　　　 space
　　　　 'The men entered the hogan one after another.'
　　 b. Plural objects of transitive
　　　　 naaltsoos　　 hooghan-déé'　　 ch'é-**h**-é-jaa'
　　　　 book　　　　 hogan-from　　　 I carried out one after the other
　　　　 'I carried the books out of the hogan one after the other.'
　　 c. Plural times
　　　　 'ashkii　　 'ólta'-déé'　　 yóó'　　 'a-ná-**h**-á-l-yeed
　　　　 boy　　　 school-from　　　　　　　 he runs away repeatedly one
　　　　　　　　　　　　　　　　　　　　　 time after another
　　　　 'The boy runs away from school repeatedly one time after another.'

12.2 The Ordering of Qualifiers

    d. Segmented action
       gah   **h**-oo-t'eeł
       rabbit   it is hopping along
       'The rabbit is hopping along.'

The examples in (25a–c) show events involving three or more subjects (25a), objects (25b), or times (25c); (25d) illustrates the use of the seriative to indicate an inherently segmented action. The seriative has two major functions. One, involving activity situations, informs about individuation rather than collectivity of entities, and contributes to the interpretation of entities. Inasmuch as the seriative has to do with arguments, its ordering with respect to subsituation aspectual material is not fixed, and it can either precede or follow the inceptive d.[3] In (24), the following orders occur: unspecified human subject-inceptive-seriative (24a), seriative-unspecified human subject-inceptive (24b), seriative-unspecified human subject-inceptive-seriative (24c). The second major-function of the seriative is to mark an inherently segmented activity, as in (25d). Here, it divides the event into a number of identical subparts: the larger event is composed of a series of smaller events.[4] As an element that affects the interpretation of an event, the interaction of this reading of the seriative with other event-oriented markers is of interest. Inceptive seriatives are possible, as in (26).

(26)   seriative h + inceptive d
       hi-di-sh-t'e
       seriative-inceptive-1sg Subject-stem
       'I start to hop or skip along.' (YMM 543)

The event begins only once, and the action that began is then inherently segmented. The inceptive singles out the start of the event. Following the reasoning used for the order of the conative and the inceptive, the expectation is that, with inherently segmented events, the inceptive should follow the seriative because the beginning point is necessary for the segmentation. Interestingly, inherently segmented actions marked by the seriative are intransitive. Therefore, the seriative cannot be preceded by an object, and thus an object can never create the conditions for metathesis of the seriative with a following inceptive. The seriative can, however, be preceded by an unspecified human subject. One might expect to find cases, then, where the seriative and following inceptive metathesize similar to those in (21)–(24). However, it is the seriative and unspecified subject that metathesize instead (see chapter 13). I have not found examples in which the morphophonological conditions for metathesis of the seriative and inceptive are met in intransitive aspectual seriatives. It is possible that in forms where the seriative contributes to the aspect system, the expected seriative-inceptive order is always found.

12.2.2.4 Navajo Prolongative

One further aspectual form is worthy of mention. Young and Morgan 1987 propose a subsituation aspect for Navajo that they call prolongative. The prolongative "marks the verbal action as a type in which subject or object remain in a state (terminal) of having begun to perform the action denoted by the verb. 'Cry and cry', 'enter and stay', 'get stranded', 'get stuck or trapped', 'over-do' are expressed as Prolongatives" (Young and Morgan 1987:166). The prolongative is similar in function to the errative, found in many northern languages including Ahtna, Carrier, Koyukon, and Slave; see chapter 7 for brief discussion. Young and Morgan suggest that the Navajo prolongative is compositional, consisting of inceptive d and egressive (Young and Morgan's terminal) n in that order. (The errative in the northern languages involves only n.) Following the reasoning for conative inceptives, one might have expected the reverse ordering – the event must begin to remain or continue in a state. If the compositional analysis is correct, the scope hypothesis fails; the ordering is arbitrary, and a stipulation of ordering is required. However, no arguments are provided for treating the prolongative as compositional; Young and Morgan 1980 suggest that it may be compositional, while Young and Morgan 1987 simply state that it is. Any argument from the prolongative against the scope hypothesis is thus weak at best, as its compositional nature is far from proven.

12.2.3 The Ordering of Noun Class Markers

Consider next the ordering of noun class markers when more than one is present. The noun class markers do not interact with each other. Given that noninteracting systems may show variation in ordering, the prediction can be made that the noun class markers might exhibit variable order across the family. This is indeed the case. First, the noun class markers d and n can appear in the following orders (see (20)).

(27) $d - n$ $n - d$

The former is by far the more common order across the family, but the latter occurs in some cases in Babine-Witsuwit'en and Carrier.

12.2 The Ordering of Qualifiers

When the *gh* qualifier is taken into account, it too can be seen to occur in variable positions with respect to the other qualifiers, and it is absent in some languages.

(28) *d – n – gh*   *gh – d – n*

The ordering of the aspectual qualifiers, which indicate subsituation aspect, is fixed within and across languages, while ordering of the noun class markers is variable across languages. This is exactly the patterning predicted by the scope hypothesis. The template hypothesis, though capable of producing these patterns, makes no particular prediction.

12.2.4 The Ordering of Nonaspectual and Aspectual Qualifiers

I next turn to the order of aspectual and nonaspectual qualifiers with respect to each other. The scope hypothesis makes no prediction in this case, as the aspectual and nonaspectual qualifiers are part of different systems. This prediction is borne out. Both between languages and within a language, variation in the ordering of aspectual and nonaspectual qualifiers is found.

Consider first Slave, where the *gh* qualifier may vary in order with *d*. The examples in (29) show verbs with a *gh* qualifier (realized as *y*) and the aspectual qualifier *d* inceptive.

(29) a. *y-d* order
'e-ghá-la-**ye**-**de**-da
unspecified Object-preverb-work-**qualifier-inceptive**-stem
'S/he starts to work.'
'óné-**yé**-**de**-h-shu
preverb-**qualifier-inceptive**/accomplishment situation aspect/1sg Subject-valence-stem
'I threw out sg. object.'
b. *d-y* order
le-ke-**de**-**y**-éh-ła
dual-human plural Subject-**inceptive-qualifier**-accomplishment situation aspect-stem
'They two started out.'

Consider more generally the interaction of noun class markers and aspectual qualifiers. The ordering of the conative and inceptive with the noun class markers is variable, as the chart in (20) shows. To repeat, the following orders occur.

(30) conative – inceptive – noun class markers
conative – noun class markers – inceptive
conative – *gh, d* noun class markers – inceptive – *n* noun class marker
conative – *d* noun class marker/inceptive – *n* noun class marker
gh noun class marker – conative – *d, n* noun class markers – inceptive

Noun class markers can follow the aspectual qualifiers, they can intervene between them, and they can precede them. Though not all conceivable orders are found, a range of them are. The scope hypothesis has nothing to contribute unless the elements in question enter into a scopal relationship. Given the absence of such a relationship, the variability between noun class markers and subsituation aspect in ordering is expected.

Just as noun class markers and aspectual qualifiers are relatively free in their order, ordering between verb class markers and aspectual qualifiers is not fixed. The following example from Sekani (Hargus 1988) shows that the verb class marker *ł* can vary in its ordering with *d* inceptive.

(31) a. verb class + inceptive
łə-d-a-jìhe
verb class-inceptive-activity situation aspect-stem
'S/he will be sweet.' (111)
b. inceptive + verb class
də-ł-a-jìhe
inceptive-verb class-activity situation aspect-stem
'S/he will be sweet.' (111)

Verb class markers indicate classes of descriptive verbs; the inceptive is part of the aspect system. Since these are non-interacting systems, scope has nothing to say about ordering.[5]

A similar explanation is available for other variable orderings. The qualifier that enters into the voice/valence system, those that are lexically frozen with a particular item, and the adverbial types do not enter into the argument system nor do they interact with the subsituation aspect system. Thus the lack of systematicity in ordering is not surprising.

The negative qualifier, boldfaced in (32), too appears in different places in the languages in which it occurs. This is shown in (20) and repeated in (32).

(32) conative – inceptive – *d, n* qualifiers – **negative** – *gh* qualifiers
conative – *gh, d* qualifier, inceptive – *n* qualifier – **negative**
conative – **negative** – inceptive – *d, n, gh* qualifiers
negative – *gh* qualifier – conative – *d, n* qualifiers – inceptive

Recall in addition from the discussion in chapter 11 that the placement of the negative is more complex within an individual language than the table in (25) leads one to believe. In Ahtna, for instance, the placement of the negative depends on whether the verb has a first/second person subject. Tenenbaum 1978:112–113 reports a similar situation in Dena'ina, where the negative appears within the qualifiers when a phonologically overt first or second person subject is present, but adjacent to the verb stem in the absence of such a subject. Why is such variability in the placement of the negative allowed?

The negative has received little attention beyond its existence and its location. Axelrod 1993:109 comments on its content: "The negative in Koyukon has the meaning typically associated with the negative in most languages (i.e. a negation of the affirmative assertion)." Others make no comments on its use. Based on Axelrod's statement and on the examples given for languages that mark it, the negative indicates propositional negation. As discussed in chapter 11, the presence of a sentential negative enclitic removes constraints from the prefix and allows it to be ordered according to nonscopal considerations.

12.3 Summary

In this chapter I have examined some of the variation in ordering within the qualifier complex across the family and within individual languages. The results of the survey are striking: morphemes that appear in variable order (whatever it is that conditions this) have no scopal relationship to each other, whereas those that appear in fixed order often have a scopal relationship, although they need not. Only aspectual qualifiers relate to each other; it is precisely these that we find in a fixed order across the family. The locus of variation thus lends support to the scope hypothesis. Under the template hypothesis, many facts can be accounted for, but similarities across the family become accidental, as does the fact that some orderings are never found or are dispreferred. The template hypothesis allows for a far greater range of orderings than actually occurs. The scope hypothesis offers an account of the fact that not all orderings are possible. It too, however, allows a greater range of orderings than is found either within a language or between languages when nonrelated elements are involved.

The qualifier complex illustrates the role of scope – it is involved in ordering the aspectual qualifiers – coupled with the need for some other device to order the remainder of the morphemes. This device is probably not a template since variable orderings are found within a language, but rather something that can fix the order, while allowing a degree of flexibility. Just what this is is beyond the scope of this book, though it clearly needs to be understood to have a full knowledge of morpheme ordering within the family.

13

On the Ordering of Functional Items

In this chapter I examine the ordering of material within the functional complex. In all of the Athapaskan languages except Hupa and Kato (see chapter 10), object pronominals systematically precede number subjects and aspectual material, be it subsituation aspect, situation aspect, or viewpoint aspect. Qualifiers are generally sandwiched between number subjects and aspect. Finally, first and second person subjects appear at the right edge, to the right of aspect. The basic schema is shown in (1).

(1) object – number subject – qualifiers – aspect – 1/2 subject

This schema is simplified, with much omitted. Recall that in chapter 10 I argued that the ordering of subjects and objects in general is not surprising. I am concerned in this chapter with ordering among positions; see chapters 10–12 for discussion of ordering within each position.

In this chapter I argue that the overall ordering in (1) is consistent with the scope hypothesis. Scope predicts some fixed orderings, such as objects appearing to the left of situation aspect, and also allows for some variable orderings.

13.1 The Ordering of Objects and Situation Aspect

13.1.1 Background

One striking fixed ordering across the languages involves objects and situation aspect – this is the only possible ordering across the family. Objects are consistently at the left edge of the functional complex (with the exception of Hupa and Kato; see chapter 10). Recall from chapter 11 that situation

13.1 The Ordering of Objects and Situation Aspect

aspect markers indicate whether an event is an activity, accomplishment, achievement, or semelfactive. These classes differ with respect to features of durativity and telicity. We also saw in chapter 11 that objects play an important role in determining the situation aspect of a predicate. For instance, in English in 'he played a sonata,' with a singular object, the predicate is an accomplishment, while in 'he played sonatas,' with a plural object, the predicate is an activity, without an inherent goal. In this section I argue that situation type plays an important role in assigning readings to objects in Athapaskan languages. Objects of accomplishment verbs delimit the event, while objects of activity verbs do not. In my discussion, I focus on activities and accomplishments.

I frame my discussion in the terms used by Tenny 1994. Tenny focuses on the interface between arguments and aspect, arguing that verbs fall into two major classes with respect to the interpretation of direct internal arguments. One class of verbs 'measures out' its internal argument; a second class does not. Arguments that are measured out have two characteristics, only one of which is relevant here. First, they are delimited. This can be put in other ways – they are objects of telic verbs, have a distinct definite, inherent endpoint, or are temporally bound (Tenny 1994:4). Second, arguments that are measured out are associated with a measuring scale. I ignore the measuring scale here as it is relevant to indirect arguments, and I consider only direct arguments. I thus examine how situation aspect interacts with temporal boundedness in interpreting objects. I use the terms object and direct internal argument interchangeably.

Delimiting verbs are, basically, accomplishments. Some English examples are given in (2) (Tenny 1994:14).

(2)   a. Mary built a house.
       b. The lake froze.

With these verbs, the internal argument measures out the event, which progresses through its various stages, with the final stage involving completion. Tenny 1994:95 argues that MEASURE is an aspectual role that "is assigned to an argument of the verb, which (in the event as described by the verb) either undergoes some internal change or motion, along a single parameter, or provides a scale or parameter without undergoing change or motion; that measures out or defines the temporal extent of the event." Tenny thus proposes that a verb may take an aspectual grid, or be subcategorized for particular types of aspectual roles in addition to thematic roles; a typical accomplishment verb would be subcategorized for a MEASURE aspectual role.

Nondelimiting verbs, on the other hand, are activities. Examples are shown in (3) (Tenny 1994:13).

(3) a. Dan pounded the wall.
    b. Susan shook the tree.

With these verbs, the object is not measured out. These verbs would not allow the MEASURE role as part of their lexical entry.

The tests for delimitedness of verbs, or the type of aspectual role that they allow or require, are numerous in English. For example, delimiting verbs (accomplishments) can occur with prepositional phrases that mark a point in time, such as 'in an hour.' Nondelimiting verbs (activities), on the other hand, occur with prepositional phrases that indicate a time span, such as 'for an hour.' In addition, the conative may occur with nonmeasuring verbs (e.g., hit) or with verbs that are ambiguous with respect to measuring events (e.g., eat), but not with verbs that require measuring arguments (e.g., break, splinter). Tenny argues that the conative removes the measuring properties of the verb's internal argument, if it has any; thus, it is not felicitous with verbs that require a measuring argument (Tenny 1994:47).

In general then, with certain classes of verbs, objects prototypically have a measuring out role, while with other classes of verbs they do not.

13.1.2 The Relationship between Objects and Aspect in Athapaskan Languages

In chapter 11 I showed that accomplishment verbs in Athapaskan languages appear with the *s* situation aspect marker and activity verbs with the *gh* situation aspect marker, and I argued that these elements are grammatical indicators of situation aspect. In Tenny's terms, verbs with *s* situation aspect measure out their objects, while those with *gh* situation aspect do not. In this section I argue that the situation aspect of the verb imposes readings on its object.

13.1.2.1 Object Number

We saw in chapters 10 and 11 that singular/plural number is not a strong category in the nominal system of Athapaskan languages. Number is not distinguished at all in nonhuman nouns, although it is in human pronouns and nouns (optionally in the latter). In chapter 11, I showed that an intimate

13.1 The Ordering of Objects and Situation Aspect

relationship exists between situation aspect and object in one verb class: in durative verbs with inherent number specified in the root, the situation aspect marker varies with the intrinsic number of the object. Specifically, the *s* situation aspect marker, indicating durativity and telicity (see chapter 11), is found with inherently singular objects, while the *gh* situation aspect marker, indicating durativity and atelicity, is found with inherently plural objects. Examples from several languages are given in (4)–(8).

(4) Slave (Rice 1989) situation aspect
we-h-xį̀ 'I killed singular O.' s
ku-y-i-ghǫ 'I killed plural O.' gh

(5) Tsuut'ina (Cook 1984)
zì-sī-s-yí 'I killed singular O.' (223) s
yī-s-ɣó 'I killed plural O.' (223) gh

(6) Ahtna (Kari 1990)
O ze-ł-ghen 'S/he killed singular O.' (213) s
O ghi-ghaan 'S/he killed plural O.' (204) gh

(7) Navajo (Young and Morgan 1987)
'á-di-yé-sh-yį́ 'I killed myself.' (32) s
y-í-gháá' 'I killed them.' (782) gh

(8) Koyukon (Axelrod 1993)
hʉtl e-tl-tseenh 'S/he made a (single) sled (hʉtl).' (139) s
hʉtl ghee-ghonh 'S/he made (series or number of) gh
sleds, was a sledmaker.' (139)

In the singular form, the object is obligatorily delimited, or measured out, while the inherently plural stems do not allow this interpretation of their objects. The situation aspect markers reinforce this, correlating with the interpretation imposed on the object.

It should be noted that inherent number in verb stems is not common in Athapaskan languages – only a few verb stems that are suppletive based on number of the direct internal argument exist in any language.

13.1.2.2 Situation Aspect and the Interpretation of Object Number

In verbs without intrinsic number marking on the stem, the object can often be interpreted as singular or plural. However, there are situations in which the situation aspect marker provides the number interpretation of the object.[1]

In particular, there is a class of verbs in which the object is interpreted as singular in the presence of the *s* situation aspect marker and as plural in the presence of the *gh* situation marker. An example from Ahtna is given in (9); see chapter 11 for Slave examples.

(9)   a. *s* situation aspect
         i-ne-ł-tl'uul
         disjoint anaphor-qualifier/accomplishment situation aspect-valence-stem
         'He braided it (rope).' (Kari 1990:366)
      b. *gh* situation aspect
         i-ng-i-ł-tl'uul
         disjoint anaphor-qualifier-activity situation aspect-valence-stem
         'He braided them.' (Kari 1990:366)

The existence of such pairs provides further evidence for the claim that situation aspect has scope over objects: it is the situation aspect marker that distinguishes whether the object is singular or plural rather than some kind of marking on the nominal itself or in the pronominal system. Situation aspect thus provides an interpretation for the object.[2]

13.1.3 Summary

I have argued that situation aspect plays a role in interpreting object number: objects are delimited or measured in accomplishments, which have *s* situation aspect marking, but not in activities, which have *gh* situation aspect marking. It is possible to impose a delimited reading on nondelimited verbs through the situation aspect system (see chapter 11). These facts provide evidence both for the verb classes and for the claim that situation aspect is relevant to the interpretation of objects. In other words, situation aspect can be said to have scope over objects; thus, the ordering of object to the left of situation aspect is predicted.

13.2 The Ordering of First/Second Person Subjects and Aspect

The ordering of first/second person subjects and aspectual material differs from that of objects. This ordering too is fixed across the family: first/second person singular, second person plural, and, in some cases, first person dual/plural subjects, follow situation aspect and viewpoint aspect; see chapter 10 for details.

13.2 The Ordering of First/Second Person Subjects and Aspect

It has often been observed that aspect does not interact with external subjects. In versions of syntactic theory without functional categories, subjects of transitives and agentive subjects of intransitives are assigned an external argument position, outside the maximal projection of the verb, while objects of transitives and nonagentive subjects of intransitives are assigned an internal argument position, within the verb phrase (see Rice, forthcoming a, for the Athapaskan languages). Assuming that aspectual material is part of the verb phrase, an asymmetry between subject and object is apparent: aspect and subject do not share the relationship that aspect and object do.

Tenny 1994:164 gets at this point in a different way. She cites Kenny 1963:180–181, who points out that subjects do not change as result of an action, but objects do. As discussed in section 13.1, Tenny argues that subjects are nondelimited or nonmeasured, having no choice of aspectual role, while objects can be either delimited or not. Again, objects, but not subjects, interact with aspect.

Bybee 1985a expresses the special status of subjects in another way. She argues that morphological categories that are more relevant to the verb tend to be ordered more closely to it: they tend to be derivational. Of interest in her survey of the ordering of various categories with respect to the verb stem is the fact that person agreement is expressed by inflection crosslinguistically, while aspect can be either inflectional or derivational. Person agreement is not of particular relevance to the verb and thus is ordered further from the stem. (Note the assumption that inflection is outside of derivation.) Bybee 1985a does not distinguish subject and object in her discussion of person. However, we have seen that objects interact with aspect in a way that subjects do not. This suggests that objects are more relevant to the verb than subjects are, and thus the ordering of subjects to the right of objects in Athapaskan languages is not surprising.

Smith 1991, 1997 conceptualizes the relationships of subjects as opposed to objects of the verb in still another way. She makes use of the notion of a causal chain, a chain of circumstances and participants in events that include cause, agent, instrument, and action, and she assumes that cause is primary, functioning to define events. The causal chain that she proposes, following Croft 1987:120, is shown in (10) (Smith 1997:21).

(10) CAUSE – SUBJECT – ACTION – INSTRUMENT – OBJECT – RESULT

Smith 1997:21 argues that the "scheme is roughly iconic from left to right." The leftmost parts of the chain are earlier in time than those on the right, and prior to them in clausal terms. What is interesting is that the subject precedes the action while the object follows it, again suggesting the relevance of aspect to the object but not to the subject.

There is thus general agreement that subjects are in some way irrelevant to aspect: they are outside the verb phrase, they are not relevant to the verb in the same way that objects are, and they bear a different relationship to actions than objects do. Since aspect cannot have scope over them, the scope principle correctly predicts that in Athapaskan languages, where morpheme order is largely semantically based, subjects should follow aspectual material.

13.3 The Ordering of Subject Number and Aspect

In section 13.2 I examined the ordering of aspectual material and first/second person subjects, but ignored number subjects. I argued in chapter 10 that number subjects, unlike first/second person subjects, are a reflection of number/gender and do not contain a feature for person in their lexical entry. As discussed in chapter 10, these elements in Athapaskan languages precede aspectual material. The goal of this section is to examine why first/second person singular subjects follow aspectual material, while number subjects precede it.[3]

Recall from chapter 10 that first/second persons are presupposed, inherently referential, or local arguments, and that such arguments must be structurally higher at the level of logical form than number, or nonpresupposed, inherently nonreferential, or nonlocal arguments (e.g., Diesing and Jelinek 1995, Jelinek 1993). This pattern, I suggested, is represented in Athapaskan languages not just at logical form, but in the syntax, placing first/second person subjects higher, or to the right of, number subjects. The effect of the referential hierarchy can be seen in Athapaskan languages precisely because subject number and subject agreement are separated by aspectual (and qualifier) material. As also discussed in chapter 10, while the scope hypothesis accounts for why subject agreement c-commands subject number, it as yet gives no insight into why subject number occurs where it does: the referential hierarchy simply sandwiches subject number somewhere between objects and first/second person subjects, but does not locate it exactly. I would now like to examine if there is a reason why number subjects are below aspect, or if this must simply be stipulated. In order to do this, I examine some parallels between tense/aspect systems and nondiscourse participant/discourse participant pronominal systems.

Aspect is often distinguished from tense, which, other than future, is not thought to be overtly morphologically expressed in Athapaskan languages; however, see Hargus and Tuttle 1997 for an analysis positing tense

13.3 The Ordering of Subject Number and Aspect

between viewpoint aspect and agreement subjects, except in some cases where phonological constraints intervene. Strikingly, aspect and tense are often discussed in terms similar to those used to distinguish the pronominal types. Aspect is internal, indicating how a situation obtains throughout the reference time; tense is external, locating the situation with respect to the time of speaking (e.g., Comrie 1976, Michaelis 1998, Smith 1997). Aspect gives direct information about the situation; tense does not, requiring reference to the speech time in order to locate the situation by specifying its relation to an orientation point. Smith 1997:101 points out that tense has a consistent relational value calculated relative to an anchor. Terms such as anaphoric, deictic, and referential are used of tense, but not of aspect. Finally, according to Michaelis 1998:260, aspect expresses a speaker's categorization of a situation; tense locates the situation with respect to speech time.

Consider the parallels between participant/nonparticipant and aspect/tense. Like first/second persons, aspect provides an insider view. It is internally defined rather than relational. Tense parallels number, with an external view. Both tense and number subjects are defined relative to an anchor; they are anaphoric, deictic, or noninherently referential. It thus appears that there are strong parallels in the functions of participant subjects and aspect and of nonparticipant subjects and tense.[4]

Assuming that it is feasible to group together participant subjects and aspect in terms of their essential semantics, I return to ordering relationships. I use the terms local/nonlocal in the following discussion. As discussed in chapter 10, Diesing and Jelinek 1995 and Jelinek 1993 argue that a hierarchical ranking of local above nonlocal arguments is universal at logical form and parametrized in the syntax. Suppose that this condition can be extended to local and nonlocal material more generally, and that it requires structural superiority of local over nonlocal material (see Georgi and Pianesi 1997 for discussion). In a verb with a first/second person subject, the subject is local and can be the highest functional category, but in a verb with a number subject, it is aspect rather than person that is local. If nonlocal material must be in the scope of local material, the ordering properties in the Athapaskan family follow: aspect follows number subjects, having scope over these subjects, to satisfy the requirement that nonlocal material be within the scope of local material. Aspect provides the inherent referentiality that number subjects lack by giving a c-commanding inherently local or presupposed referent.

Before leaving this section, a brief return to objects is in order. One might expect first/second person objects to be structurally higher than number subjects, since local, inherently referential material has scope over nonlocal, noninherently referential material. As we have seen, this is not the case. Instead, in Athapaskan languages a syntactic ranking of subjects as structurally superior to objects takes precedence over the semantic ranking of inherently referential or local material over nonlocal material. This yields the actual ordering: objects precede subjects for syntactic and semantic reasons, number subjects precede aspect on semantic grounds, and aspect precedes first/second person subjects, again for semantic reasons.

13.4 The Ordering of Subject Number and Qualifiers

While objects are consistently at the left edge of the functional complex, number subjects are simply required to precede situation aspect and to follow objects. With qualifiers, no such requirement is found, and one might therefore expect variable ordering between the number subject and qualifiers. In some languages, qualifiers may indeed precede number subjects. I examine the possible ordering of number subjects with some of the qualifiers in Sekani, the variable ordering of verb class markers with number subjects in Slave, and the variable ordering of the human number marker with a meaningless qualifier in Babine-Witsuwit'en. Dogrib shows similar orderings of qualifiers with respect to the number subjects (Saxon, personal communication, 1998); see also note 3 on Navajo.

First consider Sekani. The pronominal *ts'* unspecified human subject exhibits variable order with respect to some qualifiers – it can appear to the left or right of the qualifiers *u* and *įd* (the latter is not a single morpheme as it is separable, see (12b)). The qualifiers cannot be assigned any particular meaning in these verbs (*u* is historically conative).

(11) a. *ts'* unspecified human number – *u* qualifier
     'ə-**ts'**-**u**-h-ch'às
     unspecified Object-**HSubject-conative**-valence-stem
     'We go fishing.'(Hargus 1988:112)
  b. *u* qualifier – *ts'* unspecified human number
     '-**u-ts'**a-h-ch'às
     unspecified Object-**conative-HSubject**-valence-stem
     'We go fishing.'(Hargus 1988:112)
(12) a. *ts'* unspecified human number – *į* qualifier
     ts'-į-d-èh-'į
     HSubject-qualifier-qualifier-accomplishment situation aspect/
     perfective viewpoint-stem
     'We hide O.' (Hargus 1988:112)

13.4 The Ordering of Subject Number and Qualifiers

    b. i̧ qualifier – *ts'* unspecified human number
       i̧-ts'-ə-d-èh-'i̧
       qualifier-HSubject-qualifier-accomplishment situation aspect/ perfective viewpoint-stem
       'We hide O.' (Hargus 1988:113)

Free ordering of human number, translated as first person plural (see chapter 10), with qualifiers is not surprising – scope does not control order, as these classes do not interact.

In Sekani, the first person dual subject is discontinuous – *i* first person plural agreement appears at the right edge of the functional items, and *s* dual number follows the direct objects; see chapter 10. Like the unspecified human plural subject *ts'*, the *s* portion of the first person dual subject is not fixed with respect to qualifiers.

(13) a. *s* dual number – *z* qualifier (Hargus 1988:113)
       sə-z-ì-ghi̧
       dual number-qualifier-1pl Subject-stem
       'We 2 killed O.'
   b. *z* qualifier – *s* dual number
       zə-s-ì-ghi̧
       qualifier-dual number-1pl Subject-stem
       'We 2 killed O.'

(14) a. *s* dual number – *d* qualifier (Hargus 1988:113)
       ni-sə-d-ì-t-'àh
       preverb-**dual number-qualifier**-1pl Subject-voice-stem
       'We 2 lift compact O.'
   b. *d* qualifier – *s* dual number
       ni-də-s-ì-t-'àh
       preverb-**qualifier-dual number**-1pl Subject-voice-stem
       'We 2 lift compact O.'

(15) a. *s* dual number – *n* qualifier (Hargus 1988:113)
       u-sə-n-ì-be
       qualifier-**dual number-qualifier**-1pl Subject-stem
       'We 2 pick berries.'
   b. *n* qualifier – *s* dual number
       u-nə-s-ì-be
       qualifier-**qualifier-dual number**-1pl Subject-stem
       'We 2 pick berries.'

The examples in (11)–(15) show a number pronominal and a qualifier that is not productive; ordering is variable. The scope hypothesis makes no predictions about these noninteracting elements; variability is thus not unexpected.

The verb class marker qualifier ɬ also is found to the left of *s* dual number in Sekani.

(16) ɬə-s-ì-jìh
verb class marker-dual number-1pl Subject-stem
'We 2 are sweet.' (Hargus 1988:113)

Other qualifiers with nontransparent meanings precede the unspecified human plural subject *ts'*, the number plural human subject *gh*, and the dual number *s* (Hargus 1988:114).

(17) a. *gh* qualifier – *ts'* subject
   da-**ghə-ts'**-a-tlah
   preverb-**qualifier-HSubject**-activity situation aspect-stem
   'We grabbed O.'
  b. *ts'* qualifier – *gh* subject
   wə-**ts'ə-gh**ə-də-h-dəne
   preverb-**qualifier-plural Subject**-qualifier-valence-stem
   'They are lonesome.'
  c. *gh* qualifier – *s* dual number
   dah-na-**ghə-s**-ì-tl'ụ
   preverb-reversative-**qualifier-dual number**-1pl Subject-stem
   'We 2 tied up O.'

The variability in the placement of the Sekani number subjects with respect to the qualifiers is consistent with the scope hypothesis. Under the template hypothesis, it is necessary to posit various metathesis rules (see Hargus 1988) to capture the variation. Such metathesis rules go against the spirit of a template, which stipulates fixed ordering. Under the scope hypothesis, when morphemes bear a scopal relationship to each other, their ordering is predictable, with the morpheme of greater scope appearing to the right. But when the ordering is not predictable due to the absence of a scopal relation, it must be determined in some other way, and variability is not unexpected.

Slave shows some similar properties to Sekani. The examples in (18) involve verb class markers (ɬ, *n*) and subject number (*k* human plural subject).

(18) verb class   number + verb
   marker + number   class marker
   ɬe-ke-k'á   ke-**ɬe**-k'á   'They are fat.'
   ne-ke-zǫ   ke-**ne**-zǫ   'They are good.'

13.5 The Ordering of Noun Class Markers

The pronouns and qualifiers are part of the argument and verb class systems, respectively; no interaction is expected, and variability is not surprising.

Another similar example is found in Babine-Witsuwit'en (Hargus 1997).

(19) a. **tsʼ**ə-**y**ə-t-a-ɬ-ʼəs
HSubject-qualifier-inceptive-activity situation aspect-valence-stem
'We'll sneeze.'
b. yə-z-t-a-ɬ-ʼəs
qualifier-HSubject-inceptive-activity situation aspect-valence-stem
'We'll sneeze.'

There are two variants. In (20a), the first person plural *tsʼ* precedes *y*, a nonmeaningful item that is part of the basic lexical entry. In (20b), these morphemes are metathesized, with the meaningless *y* preceding the first person plural, here reduced to *z*. Hargus 1995a argues that a principle of syllable economy is important: the first form has two schwa vowels, an epenthetic segment, while the second has only one. Variable ordering can occur because the scope principle is not at play here, and the principle of syllable economy is free to specify what the surface ordering is.

13.5 The Ordering of Noun Class Markers

The ordering of pronouns, noun class markers, and situation aspect is close to invariant across the family – noun class markers normally precede situation aspect and follow pronouns other than first/second person subjects. In this section I examine scopal relations involving noun class markers.

13.5.1 The Ordering of Noun Class Markers and Objects

There is a clear relationship between noun class markers and objects. This relationship can be thought of as one in which the noun class marker plays a role in delimiting the interpretation of the noun with which the object pronoun is associated. As discussed in chapter 12, some nouns can take more than one noun class marker, with the noun class marker assigning an interpretation to the noun. For instance, in Ahtna, the noun *dingi* 'money' appears with the *n* noun class marker when referring to a coin, but without an overt noun class marker when referring to paper money (Kari 1990:34, 155). The noun 'property,' Kari 1990:34 notes, also allows more than one noun class marker. We see then that the noun class marker imposes a particular reading on a noun. With pronominal arguments, this is even more dramatic – the noun class marker provides all of the information about the class of the argument. Thus, just as the situation aspect marker defines the role of the object aspectually, the noun class marker defines the role of the object classificatorily. Since the noun class markers are important in defining the objects, they can be said to have scope over them, and thus they follow them.

13.5.2   The Ordering of Noun Class Markers and Situation Aspect

I argued in section 13.2 and chapter 11 that situation aspect plays a role in interpreting objects, determining an object's delimitedness. Situation aspect has a similar role with respect to noun class markers. As discussed in section 13.5.1, noun class markers do not classify all verbal arguments, but only internal ones. This suggests that they are involved with the situation aspect system, given its close connection with objects.

13.5.3   The Ordering of Noun Class Markers and Subjects

Noun class markers generally follow subject number but precede subject agreement. Recall from chapter 12 that noun class markers refer to direct objects of transitives, oblique objects of postpositions, and nonagentive, nonhuman arguments of intransitives, but not to subjects of transitives, agentive subjects of intransitives, or human subjects of intransitives.

Agreement and overt number subjects do not take an overt noun class marker, and thus nothing can be said about ordering with respect to such subjects. As discussed in chapter 10, nonhuman subjects may be internal subjects, with object marking. These subjects are involved in the noun class system, and the noun class markers, not surprisingly, follow them since they classify these subjects. It is exactly this class of subjects that the noun class markers delimit.

The position of noun class markers to the right of subject number is a surprise, however. These subjects (chapter 10) are not classified by noun class markers any more than first/second person subjects are, and one might therefore expect the noun class markers to fall between number subjects and objects, since they relate only to objects. As discussed in section 13.4, qualifiers are variable in ordering with number subjects. It is not obvious why noun class markers frequently follow number subjects as they could precede them without affecting scopal relations, and the scope hypothesis appears to have nothing to offer; a phonological account may be of value here.

13.6 The Ordering of Pronouns and the Middle Voice Qualifier: Semipassives in Navajo

In Navajo, the morpheme *d* found in semipassives (see chapter 10) is variable in positioning with respect to an unspecified pronominal. The following examples are taken from Young and Morgan 1987:70–71.

(20) a. unspecified argument ' + *d*
   táá-bí-**'-d**i-s-d-giz
   water-3-**unspecified-middle**-situation aspect-voice-wash
   'He was washed.'
   b. *d* + unspecified argument'
   bi-**d**i-**'**-ní-l-'į́
   3-**middle-unspecified**-situation aspect-voice/valence-see
   'He is looked at.'

These examples contain *'a* unspecified (or its reduced form *'*) and *d*, which Young and Morgan identify as reflexive, and which Kibrik 1995 calls a marker of transitivity decrease; it can be identified with middle voice (chapter 12). In addition, a pronominal object is present (*b* here). Kibrik 1995 argues that the unspecified pronominal is linked to the subject argument, and *b* to the object. The object-subject ordering is fixed, as seen in chapter 10. The morphemes that vary in ordering are middle voice and the unspecified subject. Kibrik argues that the ordering is phonologically predictable: the underlying order is subject-middle voice, and these metathesize when a qualifier follows. Until the nature of the *d* is better understood, it is difficult to know whether scopal relationships are involved; however, the morphemes are likely not to interact.

A second set of examples illustrates a similar phenomenon. These are also from Young and Morgan 1987:70–71.

(21) a. unspecified human subject *zh* + middle *d*
   'á-**zh-d**í-l-zhééh
   unspecified-**HSubject-middle**-voice/valence-shave
   'He shaves himself.'
   b. middle *d* + unspecified human subject *zh*
   ná-'á-**di-zh**-ni-l-ts'in
   preverb-reflexive-**middle-HSubject**-qualifier-voice/valence-punch
   'He punches himself.'

Young and Morgan treat the reflexive as discontinuous, *'a-d*, and *zh* is the reduced form of the unspecified human subject. If *d* here is simply a marker of middle voice, the problem reduces to the same one as with the semipassives: a subject and a morpheme from the voice system can appear in either order.

13.7 Situation Aspect and *d/n* Qualifiers in Navajo

We have seen that qualifiers generally precede situation aspect. The scope hypothesis offers a reason for this with aspectual qualifiers (chapter 11) and with productive noun class markers (section 13.5.2). There are, however, conditions under which the ordering of a qualifier and situation aspect is variable in Navajo. This variation occurs in first/second person dual forms of verbs with a qualifier *n* or *d* and the *s* situation aspect marker. The expected order is qualifier–situation aspect–1/2 subject. Kari 1973:262 quotes Hoijer as reporting the following variants for these duals ('C,' for consonant, represents the qualifier). The first person dual can be *Cee* or *Cisii*, and the second dual can be *Coo(h)*, less often *Cisoo(h)*, or, rarely *siCoo(h)* (Sapir and Hoijer 1967:37). Similar variation is reported in Young and Morgan 1943:92–94 and Reichard 1951:181 and by Kari 1973:263 in a dialect survey. The unexpected form is *siCoo(h)*, where the qualifier (C) follows the *s* situation aspect marker. According to Kari 1973:264, a "less frequent, and for many speakers an unacceptable variant for these verbs, is a form with metathesized aspect and mode prefixes, *sidiibaa'*, *sidoobaa'*" ('we two went to war', 'you two went to war'). Kari further remarks that one speaker consistently preferred the metathesized version, *sidi*, where the situation aspect marker precedes the qualifier, to its nonmetathesized variant *disi* (though deletion of *s* still yielded the best alternant). With the morpheme *n* Kari 1973:264 reports that the dual form with the deleted *s* was best, but that the only acceptable alternant involved metathesis, with situation aspect preceding the qualifier (*siniit'į́į́'* 'we two stole it', *sinoo'į́į́'* 'you two stole it'). Nonmetathesized forms, where the qualifier precedes situation aspect, were unacceptable.

Young 1995 shows a similar kind of metathesis. He does not note metathesis with either *d* or *n* in first person dual forms, but he notes regular metathesis with *n* in second person dual forms with middle voice/valence (chapter 7).

(22) a. *n* qualifier + *s* situation aspect
 ni–s–oo–ł–tsiz
 'You pl. extinguished fire.' (Young 1995:178 (ł valence))
 b. *s* situation aspect + *n* qualifier
 si–n–oo–líį́d
 'You 2 squatted down.' (Young 1995:179 (l voice/valence))

13.8 A Navajo 'Floating' Qualifier

c. *s* situation aspect + *n* qualifier (noun class marker)
dí-sí-n-óoh-t-'ą́
'You 2 hung your heads.' (Young 1995:180 (d voice))

To summarize, with a *d* qualifier, the *d* generally precedes *s* situation aspect if both are present, while with *n*, the metathesized form, with *n* before *s*, is preferred, if not required. Kari 1973 indicates that the form without *s* is preferred with *n*, while Young 1995 gives both forms. This is perhaps an indication of language change. Because of the variability in the reported facts, it is difficult to know just how to interpret this phenomenon. However, it is interesting that there is a difference between the patterning of *d* and *n*. The qualifier *d* is productive as an inceptive, as a noun class marker, and as an indicator of middle voice. On the other hand, *n* is largely lexicalized in its aspectual use, while remaining somewhat productive as a noun class marker; although it can be identified as an egressive, it is not used productively as such (Midgette, personal communication,1996). In the examples with both *n* and *s*, *n* is part of the lexical entry of the verb, without any particular individual contribution to the meaning, as in (50a,b), or it is a noun class marker, as in (50c). No ordering relationship between the qualifier and *s* situation aspect is predicted when it is meaningless, although ordering is expected when it functions as a noun class marker; see section 13.5.2. The *d* in some of the examples has a clear meaning since it is identifiable as the inceptive, an obligatory component of the future paradigm. Interestingly, it is precisely in this case that Young and Morgan report no metathesis, and that Kari reports metathesis as dispreferred.

This metathesis, while at first appearing to contradict my claim, may in fact then support it. When the meaning of the qualifier is transparent and interacts with the situation aspect system, the ordering qualifier–situation aspect is fixed or at least highly preferred. But when the meaning of the qualifier is opaque, then the order situation aspect–qualifier is possible or even preferred. The template hypothesis is silent with respect to this type of metathesis, which contradicts the basic claim of fixed ordering inherent in the template.

13.8 A Navajo 'Floating' Qualifier

Kari 1973 reports a case of unstable morpheme ordering in the Navajo verb 'scold'. He remarks that this verb contains an unusual prefix, *sh*, that is found in no other verb (1973:283). According to Young and Morgan 1987:86, *sh* is "a thematic prefix that appears in a set of verb themes with the meaning 'scold, be mean or fierce'." This prefix 'floats' between qualifier and voice/valence positions. It is illustrated in (23), where it appears in boldface (Kari 1973:284).

(23) a. ho-**shí**-**sh**-kééh   'I scold him.' (sh - sh subject)
b. ho-**sh**-**í**-kééh   'You sg. scold him.' (sh - í subject)
c. ha-**sh**-kééh   'S/he scolds her/him.' (no obvious ordering)
d. ho-de-e-**sh**-keeł   'I will scold him.' (single occurrence of sh subject)
e. ho-d-**í**-**í**-**sh**-keeł   'You sg. will scold him.' (í subject + sh)
f. ho-d-oo-**sh**-keeł   'S/he will scold him.' (oo + sh)
g. ho-d-ii-keeł   'We 2 will scold him.' (absence of sh)
h. ho-d-o-oh-keeł   'You 2 will scold him.' (absence of sh)
i. ho-**shí**-í-sh-keed   'I scolded him.' (sh + sh subject)
j. hóó-**sh**-keed   'He scolded him.' (no obvious ordering)

This prefix has the form *sh*, either preceding or following the subject, or it is absent. Kari found variability in its position. While no variation was found in (23a,b,c,j), other cases exhibited variation. Alternative forms to those in (23) are given in (24).

(24) d. ho-**shi**-dee-**sh**-keł (sh + sh subject)
    e. ho-**shi**-d-oo-keeł ~ ho-d-íí-keeł (sh present ~ sh absent)
    f. ho-**shi**-d-oo-keeł ~ ho-d-oo-keł (sh present ~ sh absent)
    h. ho-**shi**-d-oo-keeł (sh present)
    i. ho-**shíí**-keed (sh present)

Kari suggests that there is no single underlying form for this morpheme, given its variable patterning. Young and Morgan 1987:86 do not report variation, but rather irregularity: "shi- (~sh-): a thematic prefix that appears in a set of verb themes with the meaning 'scold, be mean or fierce,' as in: bich'a ho**shi**shké/bich'a ho**shíí**shkeeł, I scold/scolded him; yich'a hodoo**sh**keeł, he will scold him; shich'a hojó**shke**', that he might scold me; bich'a ho**shó**shke', that I might scold him; ha**sh**ké, he's mean, fierce. (Shi-is highly irregular, dropping its vowel when positioned immediately before the classifier/stem.)" The positioning of this morpheme is clearly interesting and is reminiscent of the placement of the negative in northern languages like Ahtna (chapter 12), with which it may be cognate. However, for my purposes the variation found with this element can be accounted for by the scope hypothesis. The morpheme is rare and not productive, suggesting that it is part of the lexical entry of the verb with which it occurs. Since it interacts in no way whatsoever with anything else in the verb, its rather free positioning is perhaps not so unusual. The template hypothesis has nothing to contribute in the case of a morpheme that is unstable in its position.

13.9 Interacting Systems

13.9.1 Scope and the Functional Items

In this chapter I have examined interactions between the pronominal system, the aspect system, and the qualifier system. Assuming that material of greater scope follows material within its scope, the global uniformity in the ordering of elements that bear a relationship to each other is predictable by the scope hypothesis. For instance, the ordering of objects and situation aspect is predictable from the importance of situation aspect for the interpretation of object number. Likewise, situation aspect is important in delimiting readings of noun class markers, and noun class markers are important in delimiting objects. Thus, the hypothesis that elements that enter into a scopal relationship are ordered in a particular way receives support from the interface of the pronominal and aspectual systems. I have argued that scope predicts the following hierarchy: 1/2 subject > aspect (viewpoint, situation) > number subject > object.

There is also local variability in the ordering of the functional items. I have argued that such variation is possible in the absence of scopal relations. One might ask why there is not more variation, especially among qualifiers and number subjects and among idiosyncratic qualifiers and objects. I have no answer for this; perhaps the limited phonological possibilities available to qualifiers keep them together, and perhaps more languages exhibit the types of variation reported in Sekani, Slave, Babine-Witsuwit'en, Dogrib, and Navajo. In any case, with the qualifiers that make no individual contribution to the meaning, no semantic principles can play a role in assigning them a position. An understanding of their ordering must await further work.

The scope hypothesis offers a systematic account for some cases of morphological metathesis, a process that weakens the restrictiveness of the template model. As discussed in chapter 12, future tense is marked by a bipartite form, and the pieces are often separated by material that does not interact with the future semantically, such as the negative. The first part of the future is a qualifier that generally precedes situation aspect. However, when this qualifier is part of the future tense, the semelfactive situation aspect precedes the entire unit that makes up the future. This odd placement of situation aspect before the qualifier is a consequence, I suggest, of the scopal relationship between the future and the semelfactive – tense has scope over situation aspect, and thus the entire tense marker must follow it.

I began this part of the book with the question of whether the types of principles argued to play a role in ordering lexical items are also important in the functional component of the Athapaskan verb. I have argued for an affirmative answer to this question: scopal principles predict when ordering of two types of items is fixed and when it is, potentially, subject to variability. This result is important, as it shows that ordering of morphemes within the verb is not accomplished by simply slotting them into a template. Rather ordering relates to semantic principles. As the languages have changed, orderings that are determined by these principles have remained globally uniform. It is only those elements that do not enter into a scopal relationship with each other that have been, and continue to be, subject to reordering, or local variability.

13.9.2 Origin of Different Language-Particular Patterns

I would like to close this chapter with a more general question. I have argued that the ordering of functional elements in the Athapaskan family is to a large degree a consequence of universal scopal principles. Why, one might ask, if these principles are universal, do languages differ in their ordering of functional categories? Doesn't this negate the claim of universality? There are several factors that interact that allow the claim of universality to be maintained, and I detail these here.

13.9.2.1 Scope Controls Ordering Only With Interacting Items

First, I have argued that scope controls the ordering of functional categories only when they interact with each other. The lexicalized qualifiers in Athapaskan languages do not interact with any other system and therefore show some freedom of distribution. The noun class system and subsituation aspect systems do not interact, and they are intermingled in different ways in different languages and can vary in order within a language. Elements not related by scope can switch positions easily. The systems that interact, on the other hand, show very little variation in ordering.

13.9.2.2 Scope is Not a Single Principle

A second factor that creates differences in ordering is that scope is not a single, global principle, although much is subsumed under the terms general > specific. Rather it breaks down into several subprinciples that may give contradictory results. For instance, subjects take objects in their scope, and definites take indefinites in their scope. In cases of indefinite subjects and definite objects, either one of these principles may take priority, yielding two possible orderings, both consistent with the scope hypothesis. This case

13.9 Interacting Systems

involves a syntactic principle (subject > object) and a semantic one (definite > indefinite). As another example, it might be possible to place all inherently referential material, subject and object both, above noninherently referential material, resulting in a language with first/second persons, subject or object, above third persons.

13.9.2.3 Syntactic and Semantic Factors May Interact

Third, syntactic factors may disrupt the ordering predicted by scope alone, as in the examples in 13.9.2.2. For instance, I suggested that aspect has scope over number subjects. However, a syntactic requirement that subjects occur together may result in subjects occurring in a single position. More generally, syntactic and semantic requirements may differ, leading to differences between languages (e.g., Diesing and Jelinek 1995).

13.9.2.4 Morphological Requirements May Mask Semantic Requirements

A fourth factor that may mask semantic requirements concerns morphological requirements. For instance, if a language has prefixes and suffixes, ordering is difficult to discern. In addition, languages may differ in whether a form with a particular meaning is an affix, a clitic, or an independent word, requiring different positions for semantically similar forms (see Baker 1992:104–105). In a similar vein, languages differ in the semantic categories that are overtly marked. For instance, we have seen that in Athapaskan languages situation aspect is morphologically marked while third person object number generally is not (see section 13.1), and that situation aspect has number in its scope. A language that marks object number overtly and situation aspect covertly might show a different scope relationship if number selects a particular reading for situation aspect.

13.9.2.5 Phonological Requirements May Mask Semantic Requirements

Fifth, phonological requirements may obscure semantic ones. For instance, in Slave, a suffix marking a possessed noun precedes diminutive and augmentative suffixes, an unpredicted order. I have argued that the inflectional suffix is subject to two conditions. The first is morphosyntactic – it attaches to an inflected noun. The second is prosodic – it attaches to a minimal word. Since the diminutive and augmentative suffixes are not part of the minimal word, they follow the possessive suffix, contrary to semantic expectations; see Rice

1998 for recent discussion. Language-particular phonological requirements thus may obscure the scopal basis of ordering.

Phonological requirements can obscure semantic relationships in other ways as well. For instance, a phonological principle in some Athapaskan languages guards against the co-occurrence of homophonous functional items, obscuring ordering. Kari 1989, 1990, in discussion of Ahtna, proposes that homophonous qualifiers (noun class markers and subsituation aspect) be considered simply as qualifiers lexically, with the particular meaning derived from the verb base that they occur in. In support of this proposal he adduces the fact that, in general, only a single qualifier of a particular phonological shape can occur in a word. As he points out in a discussion of principles for establishing what should count as a single lexical entry, "I have tried to set a consistent policy regarding cumulative morphs and homophony. For example, the notorious n- and d-qualifier prefixes in positions 4B and 4C are each treated as single lexical entries, rather than as a series of homophonous prefixes in the same positions ... My reasoning here is that in a verb where two or more conjunct prefixes of the shape d- or i-, for example, are present as cumulative morphs (lexically, derivationally, and inflectionally) only a single d- or i- appears in an actual phonetic form. I prefer to think of a prefix such as the d-qualifier in pos. 4C as a single morpheme that is extremely multifunctional and abstract (or even neutral) in meaning" (Kari 1989:441). I agree with Kari's general strategy of reducing the number of morphemes through the use of underspecification in the lexicon; see chapter 14. However, it is probably not the case that all qualifiers of the same shape reduce to a single lexical entry (see chapter 14 for some discussion). The observation that repetition of morphemes of identical form is avoided finds much support in the phonological and morphological literature; see, for example, Brentari 1998, Matthews 1991, and Yip 1998 for discussion.

Hargus 1995a shows this pattern in Babine-Witsuwit'en qualifiers. In (25) the verb 'kill' has a qualifier /z/; when combined with a verb with /z/ negative, a single [z] occurs.

(25) a. yə-tə-z-i-ł-ɣił
disjoint anaphor-inceptive-**qualifier**-aspect-valence-stem
z = noun class marker
'He/she will kill him/her/it.'
b. we-yə-tə-z-i-ł-ɣitl
negative-disjoint anaphor-inceptive-**qualifier/negative**-aspect-valence-stem
we = negative, z = qualifier/negative
'He/she won't kill him/her/it.'

13.9 Interacting Systems

It is unlikely that the qualifier and the negative share a lexical entry as they do not appear to have any common conceptual content. However, a phonological constraint against repetition allows the meanings of both to be present even though only a single form appears on the surface.

As another example, /d/ can be a reflexive or lexicalized qualifier; these do not co-occur. The reflexive is shown in (26). In the verb 'ask', /d/ qualifier is present, as in (27a). In the reflexive form, /d/ reflexive is also expected, but only a single [d] appears, as shown in (27b).

(26) a. ts'ə-z-c'ey
HSubject-accomplishment situation aspect-stem
'We shot him/her/it.'
b. ne-'ə-z-**d**i-s-tc'ey
preverb-preverb-HSubject-**reflexive**-accomplishment situation aspect-stem
d = reflexive
'We shot ourselves.'

(27) a. so-**d**i-ɬ-qət
preverb-**qualifier**-valence-stem
d = qualifier
'S/he he asks me.'
b. ne-'o-**d**ə-l-qət
preverb-preverb-**reflexive/qualifier**-voice/valence-stem
d = reflexive/qualifier
'S/he asks her/him.'

Qualifiers have few forms, show the same phonological patterning, enter into blocking, and occupy the same positions independent of their functions. Semantically, verbs like those in (25b) and (27b) contain the information content of each of the components. However, a phonological constraint against co-occurrence of homophonous material takes precedence over the phonological realization of both items, resulting in a haplology effect. For a language with this type of constraint, the phonological principle disallows two phonological occurrences, at the cost of obscuring content; in other languages the phonetic specification of morphological content has priority. This phonological condition on homophony does not interfere with ordering, and thus does not interact with the semantic principles, but rather competes with a principle requiring phonetic realization of semantic material. The domain differs from language to language, as does the set of segments subject to the haplology effect; see Hargus 1995a for discussion.

Phonological principles are required in other ways. As we have seen, in some cases items do not interact semantically. One can then appeal to phonological principles to order the items. For instance, in languages including Sekani and Slave, any functional item of the shape [d] must precede a functional item of the shape [n] (Hargus 1998, Rice 1989). Interestingly, no semantic relationships between these items exist.

Another case where we see the importance of phonological principles is in the placement of accomplishment situation aspect and the negative. These sometimes appear in onsets and sometimes in codas; see Randoja 1990 on situation aspect and Hargus and Tuttle 1997 on both. Hargus and Tuttle argue that s situation aspect appears in a coda unless an ill-formed consonant cluster is created. The different positions in which it can appear are prosodically defined. Notice that no other morphological elements are involved; the different positions of s do not interact with the semantically determined ordering. The negative in languages such as Ahtna and Babine-Witsuwit'en is amenable to a similar analysis.

A problem related to phonology concerns the phonological realization of functional items. In Athapaskan languages, functional items interact phonologically in many ways (see, for instance, Hargus 1988 on Sekani and Kari 1973 on Navajo). In addition to phonological interactions between morphemes, two distinct meanings may be realized in portmanteau form. This is common in the perfective viewpoint of verbs with a causative or null voice/valence marker. The spelling out of inflectional items may obscure scopal relations by collapsing two or more distinct concepts (e.g., first person singular, perfective viewpoint) into one phonological form. See Hargus and Tuttle 1997, McDonough 1990, and Rice 1993 for discussion.

Although phonology may obscure scopal relations, it does not disrupt them in general. However, it is possible for phonological principles to take precedence over semantic principles, yielding an order not predicted by the scope principle. In particular, under certain phonological conditions, unspecified objects may follow number subjects in Navajo and Ahtna (chapter 10). This is the one case that I have found of a phonological principle overriding a prediction of the scope hypothesis; elsewhere the phonology does not disrupt basic scopal relations.

13.9.2.6 Terminology May Mask Semantic Differences

Finally, it is difficult to simply take terminology proposed in descriptions and compare languages. For instance, in the Athapaskan literature the terms mode and aspect are used by different linguists to describe different things – some

13.9 Interacting Systems

use one for what I have called subsituation aspect and the other for what I have called situation and viewpoint aspect, and others use the terms in the converse way. Tense and aspect are easily confused (see, for instance, Comrie 1976), and these terms are not always used consistently across language descriptions. Baker 1992:104 points out that one language may have a preposition where another has case, with superficially similar properties. If the analysis of the Hupa/Kato third person subject prefixes in chapter 10 is correct, this is a case in point – these have been described in the same terms as number subjects in other Athapaskan languages, but are very different in patterning. The terminology alone therefore might give us the mistaken notion that their properties are similar to those in the other languages. Likewise, the term distributive has been used for any D-quantifier, even in the absence of distributive force (see Kari 1989:450). Thus, caution is in order when comparing languages: it is necessary to ensure that apples are being compared with apples rather than with oranges.

13.9.2.7 Conclusion

One cannot expect the scope principles alone to predict all surface ordering of morphemes in all languages even though such principles are universal. The principles do not make unique predictions because they themselves may lead to contradictory orderings, because only categories that interact can be regulated by scope, and because other principles from other domains (syntax, morphology, phonology) may play a role. My claim is that in the Athapaskan family, scope plays an extremely important role in regulating the order of functional elements. Variation among languages of the family arises largely from different priorities of different scopal subprinciples, from different patterning of noninteracting functional items, from different phonological properties, and finally, from the different status of related morphemes in the lexicon. To return to the question posed in chapter 9, the same types of principles that govern the ordering of lexical items govern the ordering of the functional items as well.

PART IV

A VIEW OF THE LEXICON

14

The Scope Hypothesis and Simplifying the Lexicon

I have argued that the verb in Athapaskan languages illustrates a close mirroring between function and structure, with the largest disruption in this functionally determined ordering coming in the surface position of the verb stem and voice/valence. In this chapter I review the types of cases that argue for the scope principle and consider consequences of this principle for the lexicon.

Recall the predictions of the scope hypothesis from Part I.

(1) a. The ordering of elements is fixed when the scopal relationship between them is fixed.
 b. The ordering of elements may be variable when there is no scopal relationship between those elements.
 c. The ordering of elements is variable when the scopal relationship between them is not fixed.

First consider the claim that ordering is fixed when the scopal relation between elements is fixed. This has been shown in several ways. For example, the relationship among participant subject, viewpoint aspect, situation aspect, and object agreement/number is fixed across the family, and I have argued that this ordering is predicted by the scope hypothesis. As another example, preverbs occur in a fixed position with respect to quantifiers and incorporates, again as predicted by the scopal ordering hypothesis.

The second claim is that ordering may be variable when no scopal relationship exists between elements. We have seen several cases of variable ordering. Noun class markers do not interact and occur in variable order across the family. Non-contentful qualifiers vary in order with accomplishment situation aspect in Navajo and with number subjects in Sekani. Verb class qualifiers and number subjects exhibit variable ordering in Slave. Some preverbs occur in either order, with no meaning difference – this is found when they bear no semantic relation to each other. The iterative and distributive are variable in order; as parts of different systems, they have no scopal relationship to each other.

Finally, I have claimed that ordering is variable when the scopal relationship between elements is not fixed. This claim has been supported in several ways. First, the forms known as reversionary and iterative in Navajo have the same basic content, and the particular interpretation depends upon the form's order with respect to other morphemes; see chapter 6. We also saw variable ordering of voice/valence morphemes (chapter 7), with distinct surface forms for middles inside causatives and causatives inside middles.

The case of the reversionary and iterative is particularly interesting. Young and Morgan 1987 posit lexical entries for two items of the same form on the grounds that the meanings of the two items are distinct, and that they can be separated from each other by the semeliterative. I have been assuming that identical phonological material shares a single lexical representation if the meanings can be unified through underspecification of the entry, with contextual determination of meaning. This assumption eliminates the first argument for two lexical entries for the reversionary and iterative because the readings are predictable from the context in which the lexical item occurs; see chapter 6. The second argument, separation, is relevant if morphemes are ordered by a template. But if scope regulates morpheme ordering to the extent possible, then two orders exist because two interpretations are possible, depending on whether the reversionary/iterative precedes or follows the semeliterative.

Given the few phonological shapes available to them, one might extend this reasoning to functional items – two functional items of the same phonological form might reduce to one, with the exact meaning depending on the construction and the position that the functional item occurs in. Recall from chapters 7 and 13 that phonological form on its own is not sufficient grounds for reducing the number of lexical entries; two or more lexical entries can be reduced to one only if a representation is available from which all of the meanings can be derived. The following cases look like potential instances of this.

The conative and optative functional items present a likely case for consolidating two lexical entries. I have identified the conative as a subsituation aspect qualifier and the optative as viewpoint aspect/mode; these are ordered differently with respect to situation aspect. In many Athapaskan languages, the phonological form of the conative is identical or very similar to that of the optative. The core meaning of the two forms is similar – both denote irrealis, or something not realized. It is therefore plausible to posit a single lexical entry for what is sometimes assigned a conative reading and sometimes an optative reading. The position of the item and the construction that it occurs in determine the interpretation: in viewpoint aspect position, following situation aspect, it is interpreted as optative, and in subsituation aspect position, preceding situation aspect, as conative. Moreover, stem suffixation patterns differentiate the two interpretations. This analysis requires a rethinking of the inventory of morphemes in Athapaskan languages. The optative and conative are generally considered to be two morphemes; for instance, Kari 1990 lists the optative as having the form *gho* in Ahtna, with a positional allomorph *u*, and the conative as having the form *u*. The difference in phonological patterning is taken as diagnostic for two morphemes. However, an alternative interpretation is possible: the forms might be associated with a single entry in the lexicon, with differences in phonological realization reflecting the position of the morpheme with respect to other elements. (The optative and the conative are reconstructed as distinct, but they are synchronically identical in some languages. For instance, in Tolowa (Givón 1997) and Babine-Witsuwit'en (Hargus, personal communication, 1996) they are identical in form, differing by position. Givón 1997 assumes the single morpheme hypothesis.)

Another similar example of an item receiving different interpretations depending upon position is *n* subsituation aspect and *n* situation aspect. Ahtna *n* is translated by Kari 1990 as 'assume a position' when it marks subsituation aspect; it also marks an achievement situation type. Telicity is inherent in both uses; with subsituation aspect, durativity is contributed by the co-occurrence with *s* situation aspect. Both uses could be associated with a single lexical entry indicating telicity, with the construction determining the specific reading. I have assumed that *n* noun class marker is not associated with the same lexical entry despite its common phonological form; this assumption follows from the fact that the aspectual meaning involving telicity and the meanings of the noun class marker (round object, rope or stringlike object, liquid in Ahtna; see Kari 1990:285) do not appear to have anything in common, and thus the lexical entries must be distinct.

Pronominal forms for first/second person subject, direct object, and oblique object are often identical, as are, in many cases, third person direct and oblique objects. Spencer 1991:211 comments on this type of affixal homophony, stating that the position determines the grammatical role. Here again we see an example of the scope hypothesis at work: the interpretation of the pronominal affix depends upon its position with respect to other items.

The human plural marking may also be a case in point. Recall from chapter 10 that in languages with a human plural subject reflex of Proto-Athapaskan **q*, this element appears as part of a plural disjoint anaphor, reflecting **q-y*, and as part of other complex number expressions. If there is a lexical entry 'human plural', it can be realized as a subject or as a specifier. Again, underspecifying the lexicon and allowing scope to assign a reading creates the appropriate readings and simplifies the lexicon.

The distribution of the middle voice marker also is rather free. It can be a functor predicate, as discussed in chapter 7, where it indicates middle voice; the specific reading is determined by material in the predicate. A morpheme of the same form can appear as a reflexive object. While it is generally labeled reflexive in this case, it might simply indicate middle voice; the reflexive reading would simply follow from its occupying an argument position. While the *d* noun class marker has the same phonological form, a reduction of lexical entries again seems unlikely because of the strong differences in meaning.

All of these cases require careful formal investigation to see if appropriate feature systems can be devised that allow the unity of meanings to be captured lexically and the variation to be captured contextually. I do not attempt this here, but offer these as suggestive cases of the importance of the role of scope in determining readings.

The scope hypothesis, then, receives support from the ordering of affixes in the Athapaskan family. Global uniformity is attributable to semantic and syntactic principles, and local variability to the absence of a semantic relationship between items. The scope hypothesis may well effect a simplification of the lexicon: if two or more entries of identical phonological form share core semantics, then they may be reducible to a single lexical entry even if they appear in different positions. Scope relations and construction both determine the exact readings and the possible positions of an item.

15

Evidence from the Lexicon

So far, I have made the following observations: morphemes that enter into a scopal relationship with each other exhibit fixed order if their semantic relationship is fixed, if their semantic relationship is variable, their ordering varies according to this relationship, and if there is no semantic relationship between morphemes, their ordering with respect to each other may also vary. Based on these observations, I concluded that morpheme order in the verb of Athapaskan languages is regulated by scope. In this chapter, I would like to examine the morpheme stock of Athapaskan languages to provide further evidence for the claim that morpheme order is regulated not by an arbitrary template but rather by principles of universal grammar.[1]

15.1 Predictions

In chapter 3, I laid out two hypotheses that might account for morpheme order in the verb of Athapaskan languages. Under the template hypothesis, morphemes are marked for the position that they appear in, and linear order need not reflect word formation. Thus, the ordering in a template is arbitrary, and, as discussed by Spencer 1991, in many ways quite unconstrained as compared with layered morphology.

Consider the consequences of the template hypothesis for language change. According to this hypothesis, the similarities in morpheme order across the language family are a consequence of common origins: at an early stage of the family, only a single template was available. While the protolanguage has diverged into many daughter languages, one might propose that little change has taken place in the ordering of morphemes because the time depth is not great enough to have allowed major changes. The fact that certain areas have changed and others have not is simply an accident of history. Over a longer time period, more changes are to be expected, with some making verbs across the languages more alike and others making them more different.

The second view, the one that I have espoused, states that the global uniformity found across the family results from a constraint of universal grammar, namely scope, while the local variability is accounted for by the fact that not all morphemes enter into a semantic relationship with each other.

My argument for the second hypothesis has come from one major source – while Athapaskan languages have diverged in many ways, including changes in the ordering of morphemes within the verb, major orderings have remained constant. I argued that it is the principle of scopal ordering that has regulated what is able to change.

Another possible way of deciding between the two hypotheses involves an examination of changes in the lexical inventory of morphemes with similar functions and changes in the functioning of morphemes. In this section, I outline some of the different predictions made by the two theories with respect to lexical change.

15.1.1 One Morpheme Disappears and Another with the Same Meaning Replaces It

There are cases in the Athapaskan family where a morpheme with a particular phonological form is lost, yet its function is expressed by another phonological form. In the following examples, we see that an identical semantic concept can have a number of different phonological realizations.

Consider first the element that Kari 1990 and Axelrod 1993 call perambulative, and that is called repetitive by Rice 1989.

(1) Ahtna ɬu
    Koyukon kk'o
    Slave k'e, k'ína/k'éna
    Dogrib k'e
    Sekani k'è
    Chipewyan dzéré 'around' (Li 1946:418)

In all languages, a single function is involved; however, the form is different.

Consider how this is to be accounted for under the template hypothesis, which requires that a morpheme's position be coded as part of its lexical entry. One could imagine different ways of encoding position. Spencer 1991:208 points out that in languages that are characterized as templatic "each affix has its position in the string and optional affixes are slotted into this string,

15.1 Predictions

at the appropriate point in the sequence, as required." He further states, in a discussion of Navajo, that "the precise meaning of the grammatical terminology used for labeling the prefixes is irrelevant for our present concerns (and in any case it is fairly arbitrary)" (1991:208). Kari 1989:435 argues that functional or semantic similarity of a group of prefixes is not alone justification for the creation of a prefix category; some positions contain prefixes with more than one function, and some prefixes that do not occupy the same position are functionally similar. Thus, function cannot be used to predict position, which must be indicated in some other way. Kari, in the Athapaskan tradition, indicates this through the use of numbers. Essentially, each morpheme has as part of its lexical entry a number that indicates its position class, or slot in the template. Kari also uses names for the positions; some names are vague (e.g., derivational/thematic; qualifier), while others are very specific (e.g., iterative, conative).

Consider now the loss of a morpheme from a language. Presumably when a morpheme is lost, information about its position is lost as well. But while a morpheme may be lost, often another item takes over the function of the original morpheme, as indicated in the examples of the perambulative/repetitive in (1). Under the template hypothesis, when a new morpheme enters the language or an old morpheme takes over a new function, it brings with it its own restrictions, including restrictions on its position class. It may end up in the same position as the lost morpheme, but, since function is not a general regulator of position, it may occur in a different position. Thus, loss and replacement of morphemes could easily lead to evolution and change of the template.

Under the scope hypothesis, on the other hand, one would expect that when one morpheme is lost and replaced by another, the new morpheme should appear in the same position as the old one since position is related to function and semantic relationship with other morphemes. In other words, there is no reason to expect reorganization of the 'template.' Since it is largely function that regulates morpheme order, a change in morpheme form alone is not enough to disrupt order.

The example of the perambulative in (1) is compatible with the template hypothesis: it is possible that the form with this meaning could occupy the same position regardless of its phonological form. However, this situation is not predicted in any way; it is merely compatible with the hypothesis. By contrast, the crosslinguistic similarity in this morpheme's position is predicted by the scope hypothesis. Particular phonological forms come and go, but morphemes with the same function occupy the same position because order is regulated by scopal relations.

Other items lead to the same conclusion. The distributive quantifier (see chapter 4) varies in form, as illustrated in (2). I include only forms with distributive semantics.

(2) Distributive quantifier forms
    n   Ahtna, Dena'ina
    n   Koyukon
    n   Gwich'in
    yá   Slave
    yà, dà   Sekani
    n   Carrier
    da   Tsuut'ina
    da   Navajo
    n   Babine-Witsuwit'en

While the distributive quantifier is not identical in form across the family, it has the same general function of distributively quantifying entities. The positions that it appears in differ little across the family (chapter 6) and are related to scope.

A preverb with a particular meaning may have different forms in different languages. For instance, even within Slave, more than one preverb is found for 'into, towards fire', as illustrated in (3), and a greater range exists when more languages are examined.

(3)   di# d
       tthi# d

Each piece of this bipartite form is stable in its position – the first part is always a preverb, the second part a qualifier indicating fire.

The examples that I have given so far involve lexical items. One might argue that these do not provide a true test between the two hypotheses since with these items each position class has reasonably well-defined semantic content. Kari 1989:450, for instance, in a discussion of lexical items, points out that "there is something functionally similar in this region of the verb complex in perhaps all the languages, but the prefixes attested here are only partially cognate."

It is more difficult to find analogous examples with functional items as here there often appears to be loss without replacement. Functions of the qualifiers are similar across languages, and there do not appear to be cases where a particular qualifier has been lost and replaced by a different form. One might think that the inceptive is an exception to this claim: it has the

15.1 Predictions

form /t/ in some languages, /d/ in others, and /h/ in still others. However, this is a case of phonological change rather than of loss and replacement. A case in point may be the first person dual/plural subject agreement, which exhibits a variety of phonological forms across the family. According to Krauss 1969:82, this morpheme is not reconstructable for Proto-Athapaskan, and Story 1989 hypothesizes that it originated as a second person singular reflexive. In any event, however, the first person dual/plural agreement, despite its varying phonological form, occupies the same position within the verb. (I am not referring here to the languages which mark first person plural subjects with a cognate of Slave *ts'*; see chapter 10.)

First person plural objects are likewise quite varied in form across the family. In some languages, they are distinct in form from second person plural objects, while in others the two forms are identical. Various languages are illustrated in (4).

(4) Object pronouns

	first person plural	second person plural
Koyukon	dinaa	yʉh
Ahtna	ne	nhw
Dena'ina	dna	nh/h
Hupa	noh	noh
Slave	naxe	naxe
Navajo	nihi	nihi
Tsuut'ina	nihi/naa	nihi/naa
Sekani	naxə (dual)	naxə (dual/plural)
	xo (plural)	
Babine-Witsuwit'en	niy (dual)	nəxw (dual/plural)
	nəxw (plural)	

All the object pronominals appear together across the family. It would have been possible for these to occupy different positions, but in fact this has not occurred.

15.1.2 The Development of New Morphemes

Navajo presents an unusual situation in having innovated what is elsewhere a single morpheme, the semeliterative. As discussed in chapters 4 and 6, Navajo has two forms, *ná* reversionary/iterative and *náá* semeliterative, where other languages have only one form. Kari 1989 and Young and Morgan 1987 give the ordering reversionary–semeliterative–iterative. This group of forms precedes the distributive and follows the preverbs.

Consider first the placement of the group of morphemes as a whole. Under the template approach, it is equally possible for the new morpheme to occupy the position of the original morpheme or a different one. The scope hypothesis, on the other hand, predicts that the position of the morphemes in question will be similar because of their similar scopal properties.

Consider second the ordering of the morphemes within the group. The template hypothesis simply stipulates that they appear in the order that they do, and it is compatible with the existence of a Navajo', where, for example, the semeliterative is placed first, or a Navajo'', where the semeliterative is final. The scope hypothesis rules out such languages since the positioning is regulated by scope. In fact, as discussed in chapters 6 and 14, the scope hypothesis allows for a simpler view of the lexicon as it requires only two morphemes, *náá* semeliterative and a single item *ná*, whose interpretation as reversionary or iterative is a consequence of what it combines with. The Navajo development of the iterative may thus provide evidence for the scope hypothesis.

Another Navajo innovation is a qualifier *dzi*, which Young and Morgan 1987:38 assign the meaning 'away into space or time'. According to Kari 1989:449, this prefix is not attested in any northern language, suggesting that it is an innovation. *Dzi* is the leftmost qualifier. It does not interact semantically with noun class markers, but has aspectual content involving duration in time or space. An example is given in (5).

(5) **dzí**-gai
 qualifier-stem
 'There is a white streak (extension of land or valley).' (YM 82)

This morpheme can occur with the semelfactive (transitional reading; see chapter 11); note the different stem form.

(6) bi-k'i **dzi-i**-gááh
 3 Object-on **qualifier-semelfactive**-stem
 'Something white comes into view.' (YM 107)

Here it precedes the semelfactive, which is not unexpected semantically, since its position on the left edge position of the qualifiers allows for scopal relations to be maintained.

Hupa too provides evidence for the scope hypothesis. Hupa exhibits a viewpoint/situation type, customary, that is overtly marked by a functional item. The marking consists of a morpheme *'i*, found along with the other aspectual material in the verb; in some cases a special stem form is found. The customary is illustrated in (7).

15.1 Predictions

(7) a. ch'e'ilij
   ch' 'third person human Subject'+ 'i 'customary' + lij 'urinate'
   'He urinates.' (Golla 1970:67)
   b. 'e'iWlij
   'e peg + 'i 'customary' + W 'first person singular Subject' + lij 'urinate.'
   'I urinate.' (Golla 1970:67)

No cognate appears in other languages, and the form appears to be a Hupa innovation (Golla, personal communication, 1996; Leer, personal communication, 1996). As a result, the template hypothesis makes no prediction about where it will be positioned. It is thus notable that this functional item occupies the same position as aspect, precisely the position predicted by the scope hypothesis.

Jung reports a collective quantifier in Jicarilla Apache (personal communication, 1998). When the distributive functions as a plain plural, the collective can occur with it to further identify the actors as a group rather than as individuals. The collective precedes the distributive/plural, as expected given that it elaborates the plural.

15.1.3 The Shifting of Functions of Morphemes

Another class of phenomena that supports the scope hypothesis concerns functional shifts. Under the scope hypothesis, one might expect morphemes that change in function to change position. Under the template hypothesis, any function should be compatible with any position since position and function are unrelated.

As discussed in chapter 10, the Hupa/Kato pronoun *ch'i* is a third person pronoun that marks discourse topic. Its cognate in other languages marks a human proximate subject; see chapter 10. While one can imagine the Hupa/Kato function developing out of the general Athapaskan function, Hupa/Kato is unique in limiting this pronoun to a third person interpretation and to discourse topics. Further, the Hupa/Kato pronoun appears to be a lexical item while in the other languages the form appears to be functional, indicating number and gender; see chapter 10. One might therefore expect the difference in position that is found: in Hupa/Kato the phonology suggests that the pronoun is at the right edge of the lexical items, while in other languages it follows object inflection. The scope hypothesis predicts exactly the positional change that has occurred.

Another instance of a functional shift concerns the development of the Navajo seriative form, which has the form *hi*. Thompson 1989a:225 suggests that this morpheme is cognate with the third person human number prefix (**q*) found in many Athapaskan languages (chapter 10). The seriative, as discussed in chapter 11, modifies the argument or aspect system, serving to mark an argument or event as individualized and segmented rather than collective. Thompson 1989a argues that Proto-Athapaskan **q* marked individualized third person plural arguments. If Thompson is correct, we see a pronominal element developing into an element that modifies the aspectual and argument systems. Under the template hypothesis, there is no particular reason for the position of this element to change. The scope hypothesis, on the other hand, correctly predicts that once the element comes to mark subsituation aspect, as it does when it modifies the event system, its position changes.

15.1.4 The Development of Semantic Opacity

Another way in which one might differentiate the hypotheses concerns the development of semantic opacity. Suppose that a morpheme becomes opaque in meaning so that its primary function can no longer be discerned. Under the template hypothesis, such a morpheme should retain its position since its position is independent of its function. But under the scope hypothesis, a morpheme that loses its meaning no longer interacts with other morphemes in terms of scope and might therefore be expected to become mobile.

There is some evidence from Navajo in favor of the scope hypothesis. The two subsituation aspect markers of inceptive and egressive differ in Navajo in terms of their placement in the verb. Both present analytical problems, but for very different reasons. First consider the inceptive, *d*. This morpheme is problematic only in that the form /d/ can mark subsituation aspect mark, noun class, or be part of the lexical entry. The order of these with respect to each other is indeterminate, and more than one can occur. The problem with *n* is different. Three types of /n/ can be recognized as well, egressive subsituation aspect, noun class marker, and lexicalized. The *n* subsituation aspect occurs with only a very few verbs, unlike the inceptive, which is highly productive. Interestingly, as discussed in chapter 13, *n* subsituation aspect is variable in position with respect to *s* situation aspect, while variation in the ordering of *d* inceptive and *s* situation aspect is much rarer. Under the scope hypothesis, the ordering of a productive *n* subsituation aspect to the right of *s* situation aspect would be surprising. However, given its unproductive character, *n* subsituation aspect can simply be included in the lexical

15.1 Predictions

representation of the verb as a meaningless element, in which case no ordering relationship between it and *s* situation aspect is predicted. As an obligatory component of the future paradigm, *d* has a clearer aspectual meaning. Significantly, Young and Morgan report no metathesis with *d*, and Kari reports that metathesis is highly dispreferred. In this case, then, opacity of meaning correlates with greater variability and constancy of meaning with less variability.

15.1.5 Expansion/Extension of Functions of Existing Morphemes

Another possible way of deciding between the template and the scope hypotheses concerns cases where the function of an existing morpheme changes. Under the template hypothesis, there is no reason to expect a concomitant change of position; the scope hypothesis does predict possible changes in position if a meaning shifts.

Slave has an interesting case of what appears to be expansion of meaning. Subject number is marked as described in chapter 10 – first/second person subjects are agreement markers and follow aspectual items, whereas number subjects precede aspectual items. In a few intransitive verbs in Slave, an additional marking for number is found, *łéh* (or a variant depending on dialect) indicating dual and *go* indicating plural.

(8) a. be-yí-**le**-y-ah-ła
3 Object-into-**dual**-qualifier-2pl Subject-stem
'You two bump into him/her.' (Rice 1989:641)
b. -ts'á-**łé**-ge-h-tthe
preverb-**dual**-human plural Subject-accomplishment situation aspect-stem
'They two made a return trip.' (641)
c. ná-**łe**-k-a-gwe
preverb-**dual**-human plural Subject-activity situation aspect-stem
'They two stood.' (643)
d. 'ele-k'e-rá-**le**-k-a-gwe
reciprocal-preverb-preverb-**dual**-human plural Subject-activity situation aspect-stem
'They two fought each other.' (643)
(9) a. se-ch'a ra-**go**-ke-h-we
1sg Object-away preverb-**plural**-human plural Subject-valence-stem
'They pl. got away from me.' (643)

b. ká-**go**-d-ah-whi
preverb-**plural**-inceptive-2pl Subject-stem
'You pl. go out.' (643)

c. nóǫ-**gó**-thí-dhe
preverb/iterative-**plural**-1pl Subject-stem
'We pl. came back across.' (643)

While the first of these marks a reciprocal object and the second a plural object when the subject is third person, the verbs in (8) and (9) are intransitive, and these items are not arguments. Rather they modify the subject, specifying subject number. Their position to the left of plural subjects is expected under the scope hypothesis since they modify and delimit them. There is no model that I know of for this structure in intransitive verbs. Thus, we see a case where expanded use of an item has led to the creation of a position for the new use; the scope hypothesis predicts the location of these number modifiers to the left of all subjects.

A similar phenomenon is found in Tolowa. Givón 1997 reports a distinction between first/second person dual and plural subjects, marked by an immediately preceding prefix. This may be an innovation, since other languages that distinguish dual and plural subjects use other devices: Apachean languages and Chipewyan use the distributive quantifier to mark plural subjects of all persons, and some languages use a subject agreement pronoun to mark dual first persons and the human number prefix to mark plural first persons (see chapter 10). To my knowledge, other languages do not distinguish dual and plural participant subjects in the way that Tolowa does. The position of the plural participant marker is striking – immediately preceding the participant subjects, where it is in the scope of participant subjects, but not of nonparticipant subjects. Again, the order is consistent with the template hypothesis, but it is predicted by the scope hypothesis.

15.1.6 Frequency and Learnability

Issues of transparency of meaning and frequency provide another possible way of deciding between the two hypotheses. Under the template hypothesis, a learner's input concerning the position of a morpheme comes from exposure. Thus, morphemes of low frequency should be relatively hard to learn and might be expected to be quite variable in their position. The position of higher-frequency morphemes, on the other hand, should be easier to learn because of frequency of exposure. Transparency or opacity of meaning should play little role.

Under the scope hypothesis, on the other hand, frequency should not be as strong a factor in determining position as transparency of meaning. Regardless of frequency, semantically transparent morphemes should be fixed in position, while semantically opaque ones should be more variable.

I do not have the acquisition data that are necessary to decide between the hypotheses. In addition, it is difficult to sort out frequency and transparency as the meaning of low-frequency morphemes is often hard to determine. However, when one considers a language like Slave, where noun class markers have some uses, but are not strongly productive, it is noteworthy that they are not variable in position. Other forces might keep them where they are (e.g., phonological identity), but they do not move around. The one with the least clear meaning, y, tends to be unstable in position, even though it is found in quite a few common verbs. If the common verbs formed a model, as under the template hypothesis, the position of y would not be expected to be variable.

15.2 Summary

I have argued in this chapter that as new morphemes enter a language, their position is functionally determined to the degree possible; as morphemes shift in function, they may move to a new position that is compatible with their new function. Evidence from both stability and change support the scope hypothesis. While the template hypothesis allows the kinds of stability and changes found, it also allows for many other kinds of changes that do not seem to occur. The scope hypothesis restricts the kinds of changes that can be found as the morpheme stock evolves, and those changes that actually have occurred are compatible with its limited predictions.

PART V

THE END OF THE JOURNEY

16

Looking Back, Looking Ahead

The Athapaskan verb is often regarded by linguists as an object of some wonder, and I have frequently been asked how anyone could ever acquire an Athapaskan language, given the extreme complexities of the verb system. In this book, I have tried to come to an understanding of some of the mysteries of the verb, arguing that scope is an important factor in regulating morpheme order in the verb. I hope the reader has enjoyed this journey through the verb, received some satisfactory answers, and, most important, been stimulated and engaged.

In this final chapter, I turn away from ordering and briefly examine several issues that arise from the claims that I have made related to the lexicon and word formation. These include the nature of the lexical entry, models of word formation, the distinction between inflection and derivation, and the nature of morphological change. I do not provide answers to any questions, but intend instead to demonstrate more of the fascination of the Athapaskan verb and the important issues that it raises for the study of morphology.

16.1 On the Nature of the Lexical Entry

In this section, I examine the nature of the lexical entry. What is listed in the lexical entry of a typical verb in an Athapaskan language? I pose this question from a theoretical rather than a lexicographic perspective.

16.1.1 Lexical Entries 1: Stems and Lexical Items

I begin with the lexical entry of a morpheme. The basic lexical entry of a verb is a root, which includes necessary information about its event structure, argument structure, and qualia structure. Like roots (chapters 5 and 11), lexical items (chapter 4) also have lexical entries which include information about argument structure, event structure, and qualia structure, as required. These two types are prototypical lexical items and have the types of lexical properties normally associated with lexical items in other languages.

16.1.2 Lexical Entries 2: Functional Items

The status of functional items in the lexicon is a point of controversy in the morphology literature; see Borer 1998 and Stump 1998 for recent discussion and overviews of the issues. Different positions have been taken on the phonological nature of inflection in the lexicon and on the position of inflection in the grammar. With respect to the phonological issue, some argue that functional items have representations of the same type as lexical items, with an entry that indicates phonological form, semantic content, subcategorization restrictions, and morphosyntactic properties (see Stump 1998:35). Others argue for a nonisomorphic relation between word structure and phonological representation, proposing that functional items are introduced by inflectional rules that give a phonological representation to an abstract entity (e.g., Anderson 1992, Beard 1995) or map syntactic amalgams to phonology on the basis of paradigmatic representations (Borer 1998:173–174). Still others propose that inflectional items consist of bundles of morphosyntactic features without phonological features, and that phonological forms are spelled out at a late stage (e.g., Halle and Marantz 1993). I have not taken a stand on the representations of functional items. Athapaskan languages offer a rich testing ground for hypotheses on the relationship between morphology and phonology, given the existence of haplology, metathesis, portmanteau realizations, and the like (see chapters 9–13) and their rich functional systems. Resolution of this issue would take several books in itself, and I do not attempt to deal with it here.

16.1.3 The Semantic Content of Morphemes: Underspecification and Construction

I turn now to the semantic content of lexical entries, including both lexical and functional items, regardless of the outcome on the status of functional items. I have used the term 'semantic' in a liberal way to refer to both meaning and to grammatical function, or morphosyntactic features such as person, number, and aspect. Following a long Athapaskan tradition, I argued that the semantic content of particular items listed in the lexicon is minimally specified, with specific interpretations contributed by context. For instance, the iterative has a number of readings depending on context; see chapters 4,

16.1 On the Nature of the Lexical Entry

6, and 14. The productive voice/valence elements are similar, with different readings depending on the particular construction in which they occur; see chapter 7. Functional items too can be underspecified. For instance, first and second person singular markers tend to be identical in phonological form regardless of grammatical relation and can have a single entry, leaving their syntactic function to be determined by their context. The conative and optative may be associated with a single entry indicating irrealis; see chapter 14. The elements identified as transitional, semelfactive, and negative too may reduce to a single lexical entry (chapter 11).

Functional items present interesting problems in that few phonological forms are available to them. Underspecification of lexical entries, with constructionally defined meaning, thus returns us to the issue of phonological form. A theory admitting underspecification and constructionally defined meaning tempts one to attempt to collapse all items of a single phonological form into a single entry. This is often possible, but form alone is not the only indicator of the appropriate number of entries, as discussed in chapter 14. Kari 1990:285, for instance, lists several subentries under the Ahtna entry for *n* qualifier, including use as a noun class marker (roundish objects, ropelike objects) and a subsituation aspect marker (egressive) as well as unidentifiable functions. One of Kari's reasons, discussed in chapter 13, is that only a single *n* appears phonologically in an Ahtna verb, but that the content of both the noun class marker and the subsituation aspect marker may be present. In addition, the noun class marker and the subsituation aspect marker are disparate in features – they belong to different systems (the noun class marker is part of the argument system, while the subsituation aspect marker is part of the aspect system), and the meanings cannot be captured with the same features (see chapter 7). Thus, while entries may be underspecified, with a specific interpretation arising from the construction, homophony may remain, and similarity of form serves as a guideline, but not as an absolute criterion, for collapsing lexical entries.

16.1.4 Lexical Entries 3: The Lexicon and Word Formation

So far I have focused on the lexical entries of individual morphemes. As discussed in chapters 7 and 13, various lexical and functional elements can be lexicalized along with a root, so that a lexical entry of a particular verb word may be complex, including information in addition to the root.[1] For instance, a basic verbal entry may include a lexicalized voice/valence marker (chapter 7). The following Ahtna examples from Kari 1990 show a productive causativizer in (1) and the same form as part of a lexical entry in (2).

(1) a. tsagh
   'He is crying.' (374)
   b. se-ł-tsagh
   'He is making me cry.' (374)
(2) ghi-ł-caax
   'He, it is big.' (109)

Lexicalized voice/valence markers, as in (2), do not contribute an independent meaning. Nonlexicalized ones, on the other hand, make a regular, systematic contribution to the meaning of the verb word as a whole, as in (1b), where causativity is added, and are introduced through word formation.

Qualifiers are often lexicalized, with no independent meaning to contribute; nonlexicalized qualifiers add to the meaning. Ahtna examples from Kari (1990) are given in (3) (productive) and (4) (lexicalized).

(3) a. yi-ł-tl'es
   'He hit it once (semelfactive).' (361)
   b. i-**n**-e-ł-tl'es
   'He hit him in the face (semelfactive).' (361)
(4) i-**n**-ez-'iin
   'He stole it.' (92)

In (3), *n* contributes to the meaning by indicating that the object (face) is small and round; in (4), *n* is obligatory, and makes no identifiable individual contribution to the meaning.

Preverbs may also be lexicalized. Such preverbs either have no independent meaning as in (5), or do not contribute their usual meaning, as shown by the semantic contrast between (6) and (7). In (5) and (7) the meaning of the whole is noncompositional. In (5), it is impossible to assign an independent meaning to the preverb; it and the stem must be taken as a lexical unit with a single meaning.

(5) Babine-Witsuwit'en lexicalized preverbs (Hargus 1997)
   a. preverb tə
      tə-l-ɣəs
      'S/he is bathing.' (394)
   b. preverb də
      cas **du**-t'ɛn
      cas 'grizzly'
      'It looks like a grizzly.' (394)

c. preverb ne
ne-yə-z-dzeɣ
'S/he caulked it.' (396)

In (6), the preverb *'a* 'away out of sight' and the stem combine to yield a regular, compositional meaning. The same preverb is present in (7), but the meaning is idiomatic, and this preverb-stem combination must be listed in the lexicon.

(6) Navajo productive preverb *'a* 'away out of sight' (from Smith 1996b)
 a. **'i**-ish-yeed
  'I run away out of sight.'
 b. **'i**-is-ts'ǫǫd
  'I stretch away out of sight.'
 c. **'i**-ish-tįįh
  'I carry O away out of sight.'
(7) Navajo lexicalized preverb *'a* (from Smith 1996b)
 'i-ish-dlóóh
 'I laugh and laugh, laugh myself to death.'

Lexical entries of verbs may be simple, consisting of just a root. They generally contain more information than this, however, including voice/valence elements, lexical items, and functional items. The same type of material then, is available at different levels – in the lexicon and in word formation (be it morphology or syntax; see section 16.3) – with meaning depending on the level at which it is introduced. Material that is part of a basic lexical entry either has no independent meaning or does not contribute its usual meaning, whereas material introduced through productive word formation makes a systematic contribution to the meaning of the verb word as a whole. I continue discussion of word formation in section 16.3.

16.2 On the Distinction between Inflection and Derivation

In discussions of morphology, it is difficult to avoid the terms 'inflection' and 'derivation,' terms that I have largely shied away from, referring instead to functional and lexical items. The terms inflection and derivation are standardly used in Athapaskan linguistics as well as in linguistics in general. In this section, I briefly justify why I have avoided this terminology.

The distinction between inflection and derivation is particularly complicated in the Athapaskan verb, where inflectional and derivational morphemes are intermingled; see Kibrik 1995 for a recent overview. Kibrik gives the following schema for the prototypical Athapaskan verb.

(8) proclitic   quasi-inflectional, derivational
     oblique (postpositional object) +   inflectional
     preverb (postposition)   quasi-inflectional, derivational
     various derivational   derivational
     reflexive accusative (direct object)   inflectional
        pronoun
     iterative   quasi-inflectional
     distributive   quasi-inflectional
     incorporate   derivational
     number   quasi-inflectional
     accusative (direct object) pronoun   inflectional
     3 person nominative (deictic subject)   inflectional
     transitivity decrease   quasi-inflectional
     qualifier   derivational
     inceptive   quasi-derivational,
                                                    derivational
     qualifier   derivational
     conjugation   inflectional
     mode   inflectional
     1/2 person nominative pronoun   inflection
     transitivity indicator   inflectional/derivational
     root
     mode/aspect suffix   inflection + derivation (?)

In addition to the categories of inflection and derivation, Kibrik adds categories of quasi-inflection and quasi-derivation for morphemes with mixed properties. The iterative and distributive fall in the quasi-inflectional category; these, Kibrik suggests, are largely inflectional but have properties of derivation as well. For instance, the Navajo distributive marks the derivational category of distributivity in addition to the inflectional category of plurality. Suppose that the iterative and distributive are quantifiers that are introduced syntactically, as I have argued. Part of the definitional problem then disappears as the status of quantifiers as inflectional or derivational is not an issue. For the functional items as well, the terms derivation and inflection do not seem to pick out important properties. So it is probably better to think of a morpheme as making a productive or compositional semantic contribution, in which case it is added syntactically, or not, in which case it is part of the basic lexical entry. Thus, moving away from the terms inflection and derivation frees one to examine different properties of the lexical items without trying to pigeonhole them in inappropriate ways.

16.3 On the Domain of Word Formation

While I have talked extensively about word formation in this book, much remains unsaid. In this section, I consider the component in which word formation occurs and then return briefly to the nature of the lexical entry.

What is the domain of word formation? One could imagine word formation being done all in the morphology, all in the syntax, or some in the morphology and some in the syntax. If word formation is morphological, the traditional assumption in the Athapaskan literature (chapter 2), then the verb word is the output of the morphology and is a word on both morphological and phonological grounds. Alternatively, if word formation is syntactic, the verb word is the output of the syntax and is a word on phonological grounds alone; see Rice 1992, 1993, 1998 and Speas 1990. Finally, if word formation takes place in both the morphology and the syntax, as I have claimed, then a piece of the word is a morphological unit and the rest is a word on phonological grounds. I have located aspectual suffixation in the morphology and assumed that other active word formation is syntactic for the following reasons. For one thing, assuming largely syntactic word formation allows me to sidestep the problematic terms inflection and derivation, discussed in section 16.2. Other theoretical reasons exist for reconsidering the placement of word formation. For instance, discontinuous dependencies between morphemes, discussed throughout the book, and variable morpheme order within a language that is not a consequence of scope or phonological principles are not typical of morphological systems. In a typical morphological system, dependencies are strictly local (see references in chapter 1), and variability in morpheme ordering is attributable to different scopal relationships or to phonological principles. On the other hand, nonlocal dependencies and variable order are typical of syntax, where they may be attributable to factors beyond scope and phonological principles.

I continue this line of thinking by returning to the form of the basic lexical entry. Recall from section 1 of this chapter and from other chapters that a lexical entry includes a root and possibly other nonpredictable, idiosyncratic information. As shown by the examples in section 16.1, many lexical entries include a lexicalized voice/valence marker that contributes no independent meaning, a lexicalized qualifier, or a lexicalized preverb. The assumption that word formation is syntactic has the consequence that the lexical entry of a typical verb consists of more than one word, or is a phrasal idiom, similar to English expressions such as *kick the bucket, paint the town red, hit the road*, and *take advantage of*. These idioms pattern as single lexical items with respect to meaning but consist of more than one word. They can be broken up on the surface by inflection (e.g., *kicked the bucket*), by other material (e.g., *take* tremendous *advantage of*), or by appearing in some other order (e.g., *advantage was taken of* ...). The Athapaskan complex lexical entries are similar in forming discontinuous strings within the verb word; for instance, functional items must be present, and productive lexical items may also occur within the verb word. This is not a question of word formation, but rather of the lexicon: lexical entries can be complex. Word formation is regular and systematic, and governed, when possible, by scope.

While I have assumed that word formation is largely syntactic and that Athapaskan verb entries resemble syntactic idioms in other languages, I do not believe that anything that I have said rests crucially on this assumption. This assumption has allowed me to ask somewhat different questions than if I had assumed that word formation is morphological. My primary goal, however, has been to better understand the content of the different morphemes that make up the verb and to account for morpheme ordering; the assumption that the verb word is actually syntactic requires far deeper study. What is quite clear in the Athapaskan family is that it is necessary to distinguish lexicalized elements, with unpredictable and idiomatic meanings, from word formation, which is characterized by semantic predictability and consistency. The question of whether active word formation is purely morphological, purely syntactic, or a combination of the two will continue to be with us for some time to come. Just what a word is is another question with a long history, and again Athapaskan languages offer fertile testing grounds.

16.4 On the Role of Scope in Determining Morpheme Order

My goal in this book has been to show that scope is important in the ordering of morphemes in the Athapaskan verb. I have not been explicit, however, about just how scope functions in a formal way in word formation, and in this section I briefly lay out two models. According to the one that I have been assuming implicitly, scope regulates word formation. The alternative is that word formation is free, and scope evaluates the acceptability of a word, filtering out illicit items.

In the first model, word formation would be governed by scope, which would allow only certain orderings. This would order all interacting items, subject to language-particular parametrization of the types discussed in chapter 14. The scope hypothesis has nothing to say about the ordering of non-interacting items, as we have seen. For such items, language-particular statements would be required to order them relative to one another (e.g., distributive and iterative, noun class markers) and to allow for nonphonologically controlled variability.

In the second model, word formation generates all possible orderings of morphemes, and scope filters out verb with inappropriate or uninterpretable scopal relations. In addition, language-particular filters come into play to remove variation that is possible in principle, but that is not found in the language.

The first type of grammar, where scope controls the generation of verb words, is consistent with derivational theories; the second, where scope functions as a filter, is consistent with constraint-based theories. Tension between these models is ongoing in linguistics, and I cannot hope to resolve this problem here (see, for instance, Archangeli and Langendoen 1997 for recent discussion).

In general, I have not formalized the mechanisms that I have proposed. Any model must account for several things: the scopal principle is an overarching principle that consists of interacting subprinciples. Syntactic, morphological, and phonological principles also play a role in determining morpheme order. In addition, mechanisms are required to situate noninteracting material and to account for the variability associated with it. The best model for capturing all of this is the topic of another piece of work. Here I hope to have made clear the range of facts.

16.5 On Consequences for a Template Model

The template has long been used in the Athapaskan literature. I have argued that it is not an appropriate device to account for word formation, and I believe that it may have prevented linguists working on Athapaskan languages from noting both the crosslinguistic uniformity and the degree of variability that actually appear to exist. I am not the first to express this view – Kari 1989:434 remarks that "In Krauss's view, the purely linear charts are an artifact of the Hoijer era that may even be counterproductive to documentary and explanatory endeavors."

What becomes of the template under the scenario that I have proposed? It reduces to a descriptive device that provides a readable outline of the order of elements within the verb, and that allows us to examine similarities and differences between languages at a glance. However, it has no theoretical status. On the one hand, it lacks restrictiveness and predictive power for any ordering of morphemes that one finds can be described by a template, and there is no particular reason why an element appears in one position rather than another. On the other hand, the template is too restrictive: it requires language-particular metathesis rules that are not phonologically motivated. Such rules undermine the template, as the rigid ordering that it demands is not in fact found.

Nevertheless, under the scopal ordering hypothesis, pockets exist that might yield to a template analysis. Although the ordering of morphemes within the verb is largely controlled by scope, an additional device is required to order elements about which scope makes no prediction. A template is one such device. However, as discussed throughout the book, such a template cannot demand rigid ordering except under phonological conditions. Since nonphonological variation in ordering may exist even for a single speaker, this suggests that the template, or any other device demanding fixed ordering, is inadequate. A notion of transportability (chapter 6) is required, suggesting that a rigid template is not appropriate even for the non–scope based orderings.

16.6 On Consequences for Historical Change

In chapter 3, I posed the question of why, given the number of phonological, morphosyntactic, syntactic, semantic, and lexical ways that Athapaskan languages have changed, the order of morphemes has been largely stable. My goal in this book has been to argue that the scope principle plays a critical synchronic role in the ordering of morphemes in Athapaskan languages, and that, moreover, it serves as a regulator of linguistic change – items that bear a scopal relationship are reluctant to move around (to speak anthropomorphically), while those that do not are relatively free.

There are many other factors that I have not considered that are important in language change, such as language contact. It could well be that the rather dramatic differences between Hupa and the other Athapaskan languages studied here are partially due to language contact. My study has concentrated on the structural factors that regulate morpheme order; I have not looked beyond these at other factors.

Another reason that morpheme order remains quite constant across the family might be that morpheme order is simply less vulnerable to change than are other areas of language. This view has been expressed by some; Thomason 1980 cites Hymes 1956:634–635, who in turn attributes this view to Meillet, Sapir, Hoijer, and Swadesh. Thomason herself, however, in a discussion of what can change in a language, argues that morpheme order is as subject to change as anything else is in language. She examines Hymes's work on morpheme ordering in Na-Dene (Athapaskan, Eyak, and Tlingit), according to which morpheme order within the verb is quite stable across Na-Dene. Thomason claims that this stability cannot be a result of common ancestry as morpheme order would have been subject to change along with

16.6 On Consequences for Historical Change

everything else. She argues that the convergence must therefore be due to contact with other, unrelated languages, and that the similarities in morpheme ordering are accidental. In particular, she suggests that it is "reasonable to assume that the Na-Déné languages had typologically similar structures to begin with; and that, in some former long-term situation of intensive contact, with either one-way interference or a Sprachbund-like convergence through mutual bilingualism, the Na-Déné languages evolved to a state of exact correspondence in categories and in their order within the verb complex.... the extensive current morphological similarities in the Na-Déné languages are most likely to be due to contact-induced changes in systems that started out with a high level of agreement in morphological categories, and least likely to be due to direct genetic inheritance of the morphological categories in their present ordering relations" (Thomason 1980:369).

I agree with Thomason that there are no a priori reasons to believe that morpheme order is less vulnerable to change than other areas of language. But we disagree on why there might be an appearance of invulnerability. Thomason argues that the lack of change is in fact only apparent, and that the external factor of contact created convergent orderings. I have argued instead that morpheme order is preserved because of an internal factor, namely scope.

I have shown that what obtains across the family is not identity of morpheme order. The languages differ to some degree in categories that are overtly expressed. For instance, the multiple (chapter 4) is limited to few languages, and the number of aspect classes marked by suffixation differs in different languages (chapter 11). The languages also vary in several ways in their ordering (chapters 6, 10, 11, 12, and 13), and they differ in the use of various morphemes like the distributive (chapter 5) and qualifiers. My proposal is that the languages did undergo changes – they lost and gained morphemes, and morphemes shifted in meaning. In addition, morpheme order was vulnerable to change. However, changes in order were largely regulated by scope, which prohibited reordering leading to the destruction of semantically based relations between items. Thus the global uniformity discussed in chapter 1 results from the linguistic factor of scope; the local variability is a consequence of the absence of scope, the different interactions of scopal principles, syntactic principles, and phonological principles. The language contact hypothesis, like the template hypothesis, makes both convergences and the restriction of divergences from shared ordering to areas without semantic interaction between morphemes an accident of fate; by contrast, the scope hypothesis provides an explanation for where convergences and divergences might lie.

16.7 For the Future

In this work, I hope to have opened up some new lines of inquiry regarding morpheme order in the Athapaskan languages and possible factors that might constrain linguistic change. The scope hypothesis relies on an understanding of semantic properties of morphemes, and I have barely scratched the surface in coming to an understanding of these. In addition, there are many traditional problems in morphology that I have not addressed in any depth, as the discussion in this chapter shows, but I have merely touched upon some very major issues.

The language survey that I have undertaken is inadequate in many ways. No single language receives full study, and many languages of the family are addressed only cursorily, or not at all, even though each language is likely to exhibit its own set of interesting ordering properties. In addition, the materials are uneven in depth, and even with the languages covered here, they do not necessarily provide a complete picture.

I have tended to treat as similar patterns that appear constant across languages, and I have assumed that an analysis based on one or two languages extends to the others. I have tried to take into account both similarities and differences, but have likely erred in overestimating similarities and in not considering enough details of meaning in the individual languages. I hope nevertheless to have stimulated the reader to think about the Athapaskan verb in a very different way.

I would like to end with a question. In chapter 3 I showed that Athapaskan languages have diverged in many ways, and I asked why the verb complex has remained remarkably stable. I answered this question by proposing the scope principle, which prevents changes that would obscure the structural representation of scopal relations. We must ask why the scope principle is so strong across the family. Why haven't other principles taken over? One could easily imagine syntactic and phonological principles overriding semantic principles more often than they do. For instance, why is it that participant and nonparticipant subjects have not fallen together in position in any language? Why do phonological principles function, overall, to maintain the scope hypothesis? Does adherence to scopal relationships in morpheme ordering perhaps represent some kind of unmarked state, all other things being equal? I leave this book with an important question in my mind: Why is the scope principle such a strong regulator of morpheme order and change throughout the Athapaskan family?

PART VI

APPENDIXES

APPENDIX 1

Templates and Affix Ordering

In this appendix, I provide templates for a number of Athapaskan languages and present attempts to provide a template for what Kibrik 1995 labels Standard Average Athabaskan.

1.1 The Template

1.1.1 Macrolevel Organization

Kari 1989 argues that the verb word in an Athapaskan language is best thought of as consisting of a number of groupings of morphemes, which he refers to as zones. The zones are largely phonologically defined – morphemes within each zone pattern similarly phonologically; morphemes in different zones show different phonological patterning. Here I am largely concerned with the ordering of the zones as a whole with respect to each other and of the morphemes within each zone; see the sources for information on the phonology. While I have not used the term zone in this book, the major zones, which are constant across the family, are easily identified and are given in (1). (1a) gives the traditional Athapaskan terminology that Kari uses; where the terms used in this book differ, I give them in (1b).

(1) a. disjunct pronominal conjunct classifier-stem
    b. lexical   functional voice/valence-stem

The disjunct zone, or my lexical items, as defined in chapters 2 and 4, includes morphemes indicating oblique relations, manner, quantificational concepts, and, in some languages, incorporates. The pronominals include both those that are typically labeled direct objects and non-first/second person subjects (chapter 10). The conjunct morphemes, functional items in my terms, include qualifiers, aspect, and first/second person subjects (chapters 9–13).

1.1.2 A Finer Look at Ordering

In this section I give the overall structure of the verb complex for a large number of Athapaskan languages as given by the source, with no reinterpretation. The first line of each set gives the language, any alternate names for it, its location, and the data source. The next lines show the template proposed in the source. I follow the terminology of the source, so rather variable terms are used in these templates. I include boundary symbols where they are part of the template in the source. The symbol # indicates the disjunct boundary, or the boundary between the disjunct (lexical) and conjunct (functional) prefixes.

(2) Ahtna (United States, Alaska; Kari 1990)
postpositional object + derivational/thematic + iterative + distributive + incorporate + thematic # third person plural plus y + direct object + first person plural + indefinite object-subject + y-thematic + third person plural subject = areal-qualifier + conative + inceptive + d qualifier + n qualifier + z + gh qualifier % transitional + s perfective-negative + mode + perfective + subject [classifier + root + suffixes

(3) Babine-Witsuwit'en (Canada, British Columbia; Hargus 1997:388)
preverb + iterative + multiple + negative + incorporate + inceptive + distributive # pronominal + qualifier + conjugation/negative + tense + subject + classifier + stem

(4) Beaver (Canada, British Columbia, Alberta; Randoja 1990)
incorporated postpositional phrase + adverb + incorporated stem + customary/reversative + distributive # object + deictic subject + derivational/aspectual/thematic + conjugation + mode + subject + classifier + stem

(5) Chilcotin (Canada, British Columbia; Cook 1989)
(disjunct) # (pronominal) + secondary mode (conative) + secondary aspect (inceptive) + conjugation + primary aspect/mode + subject + classifier + root

(6) Chipewyan (Canada, Manitoba, Saskatchewan, Alberta, Northwest Territories; Li 1946; Richardson 1968)
incorporated postposition with pronominal object + local/adverbial prefixes + plural + iterative + incorporated stem # pronominal

Templates and Affix Ordering 403

  objects + third person pronominal subjects % modal + aspectival + pronominal subjects + classifiers = stem
- (7) Chiricahua Apache (United States, Southwest; Hoijer 1946b)
  proclitic + adverbial + indirect object pronoun + adverbial + iterative + distributive + direct object pronoun + deictic + adverbial + tense/modal + subject + classifier + stem
- (8) Dena'ina (Tanaina; United States, Alaska; Tenenbaum 1978)
  object of postposition + postposition + adverbial/derivational + iterative + incorporate + distributive plural # object pronouns + deictic pronouns + thematic + conative/semitransitive + inceptive + gender + negative + thematic + semelfactive + mode + perfective + subject pronoun + classifier + stem
- (9) Dogrib (Canada, Northwest Territories; Davidson 1963)
  indirect object + postposition + adverbial prefixes + iterative mode + theme prefix + included noun + number prefix + direct object + deictic and 3 plural + aspect prefix + modal prefix + subject pronoun + classifier + stem
- (10) Galice (United States, Oregon; Hoijer 1966)
  pronoun + postposition + derivation + 3 pl. subject + object pronoun/areal subject + derivation + aspectival + subject + classifier + stem
- (11) Hupa (United States, California; Golla 1970)
  adverbial + iterative + plural + deictic subject + object + thematic + adverbial + distributive + mode + subject + classifier + stem
- (12) Koyukon (United States, Alaska; Axelrod 1993)
  postpositional object + postposition + derivational/thematic + iterative + distributive + incorporate # 3y + direct object + indefinite + 3plural + 1plural + 3singular = areal/qualifier + conative + qualifier (d) + inceptive + qualifier (n) + transitional + s perfective/negative + mode + perfective + subject [classifier + root + suffixes
- (13) Mattole (United States, California; Li 1930)
  adverbial/local + pronominal objects + third person subjects + modal + aspectival + pronominal subject + classifier + stem
- (14) Navajo (United States, Southwest, Young, Morgan, and Midgette 1992)
  pronominal + null postposition + postpositional/adverbial-thematic/nominal + reflexive + reversionary + semeliterative + iterative + distributive plural # object + subject + thematic-adverbial + modal-conjugation + subject pronoun + classifier + stem
- (15) Sekani (Canada, British Columbia; Hargus 1988)
  postposition + adverbial + incorporated stem + distributive +

reversative, customary + inceptive # object + subject % derivational + conjugation + mode + subject [classifier + stem

(16) Slave (Canada, Northwest Territories, Alberta, British Columbia; Rice 1989, Howard 1990)
adverb # distributive plural # iterative # incorporate+ object + deictic + theme/derivation + aspect + conjugation + mode + subject [classifier + stem

(17) Tsuut'ina (Sarcee; Canada, Alberta; Cook 1984)
incorporated postposition + adverbial + iterative + incorporated stem + distributive # (direct) object + 3p subject + thematic + aspect 2 + aspect 1 (mode) + 1/2 subject + classifier + stem

(18) Tolowa (United States, Oregon; Givón 1997)
plural 3 person + object pronoun + adverb + plural 3 person + adverbial/locative + reversative + plural 3 person + transitivity + thematic prefix + desiderative/conative + perfective + plural 1/2 + 1/2 subject + d classifier + ł classifier + stem

(19) Tututni (United States, Oregon; Golla 1976)
outer (disjunct) adverb or postposition + object, deictic subject, and plural markers + inner (conjunct) adverb, aspect markers + first and second person subject markers + classifier + stem

While the terminology used for the position classes differs from language to language, a constant pattern is evident: in all the languages the macrolevel overall ordering is that in (1).

1.2 Pan-Athapaskan Templates

Hoijer 1971 provides a generalized verb template for Athapaskan family, given in (20).

(20) adverbial(s) + iterative + pluralizing + object + deictic subject + adverbial + mode/tense/aspect + subject pronoun + classifier + stem

I have used the term D-quantifier rather than pluralizing, qualifier rather than adverbial for the prefixes following the deictic subjects, and subsituation aspect, situation aspect, and viewpoint aspect rather than mode/tense/aspect.

Kibrik 1995, in an attempt to provide a template for what he calls Standard Average Athabaskan, gives the following, based on Navajo, Hupa, Slave, and Tsuut'ina.

(21) proclitic
 oblique pronoun + preverb
 various derivational
 reflexive accusative (direct object) pronoun (Navajo, Hupa)
 iterative
 distributive
 incorporate
 number (Hupa, Slave)
 accusative (direct object) pronoun
 3 person nominative (deictic subject) pronoun
 transitivity decrease
 qualifier
 inceptive
 qualifier
 conjugation
 mode
 1/2 person nominative (subject) pronoun
 transitivity indicator (classifier)
 root
 mode/aspect suffix
 enclitic

Parenthesized material indicates traditional terminology and language names if the position in question is restricted in occurrence. The lines at the right indicate positions that are transposed in some languages.

The two templates in (1) and (21) capture the overall global uniformity, but miss much of the local variability discussed in this book.

APPENDIX 2

The Languages

In this appendix I list the Athapaskan languages, divided into major groupings, and when appropriate, into subgroupings within the larger groupings. It should be noted that it has been argued that the subclassification assigned to the northern group is inappropriate on the grounds that overlapping distribution of diagnostic features precludes subclassification; see Krauss and Golla 1981 for discussion.

The languages discussed in this book are in boldface. Following the list of languages, I discuss briefly why this particular set was chosen.

2.1 Language Classification

The following classification is based on Goddard 1996:5. I supplement it only by including in square brackets names that are now used (and are used in this book) for several of the languages.

Family: Athapaskan
Southern Alaska
   Ahtna (Lower, Central, Western, Mentasta)
   Tanaina [Dena'ina] (Upper Inlet, Lower Inlet, Outer Inlet, Lake Iliamna, Inland)
Central Alaska-Yukon
   Koyukon-Ingalik
      Ingalik [Deg Hit'an] (Yukon, Kuskokwin)
      Holikachuk (Upper Innoko)
      Koyukon (Lower, Central, Upper)
   Tanana-Tutchone
      Upper Kuskokwin (Kolchan)
      Tanana

The Languages

      Lower Tanana (Minto-Nenana, Chena, Salcha-Goodpaster)
      Tanacross (Healy Lake-Mansfield Lake, Tetlin)
      Upper Tanana
    Tutchone
      Northern Tutchone
      Southern Tutchone
  Kutchin-Han
    Kutchin [Gwich'in] (Eastern, Western)
    Han (Eagle, Dawson)
Northwestern Canada
  Cordillera
    Central Cordillera
      Tagish
      Tahltan
      Kaska
    Southeastern Cordillera
      Sekani
      Beaver
  Mackenzie
      Slavey-Hare
        Slavey (Slave)
        Mountain
        Bearlake
        Hare
      Dogrib
    Chipewyan
Central British Columbia
  Babine-Carrier
    Babine (Bulkley River [**Witsuwit'en**], Babine)
    Carrier (Central, Stoney Creek-Prince George, Southern)
  Chilcotin
    Nicola (?)
Tsetsaut
Sarcee [Tsuut'ina]
Pacific Coast Athapaskan
    Kwalhioqua-Clatskanie (Kwalhioqua [Willapa, Suwal], Clatskanie)
    Oregon Athapaskan
      Upper Umpqua
      Tututni (Tututni-Chasta Costa, Coquille)
      Galice-Applegate

Tolowa (Chetco, Tolowa)
California Athapaskan
　　Hupa (Hupa, Chilula-Whilkut)
　　Mattole (Mattole, Bear River)
　　Eel River (Nongatl, Lassik, Sinkyone, Wailaki)
　　Cahto (formerly Kato)
Apachean
　　Western Apachean
　　　Navajo
　　　Western Apache (Tonto, Cibecue, San Carlos, White Mountain)
　　　Mescalero-Chiracahua
　　Eastern Apachean
　　　Jicarilla
　　　Lipan
　　　Kiowa Apache

2.2 Why These Languages?

I highlighted the languages that I discuss in this book in section 2.1. The sample draws on languages from each of the major geographical locations (northern, Pacific Coast, American Southwest) where the languages are spoken. In addition, in most cases a language from each subgroup is included. Only certain languages met the criteria for inclusion in terms of documentation: material of a fair degree of depth is required in order to do the kind of work that I undertook in this book. The languages that are best represented throughout the entire book are Ahtna, Dena'ina, Koyukon, Sekani, Beaver, Slave (including Hare), Dogrib, Chipewyan, Babine-Witsuwit'en, Chilcotin, Tsuut'ina, Tututni, Galice, Hupa, Mattole, and Navajo; among these Ahtna, Koyukon, Sekani, Slave, Babine-Witsuwit'en, Tsuut'ina, Hupa, and Navajo stand out, simply because of the extent of documentation on these languages. I have examined material from a number of other languages (Ingalik, Upper Kuskokwim, Tanana, Northern and Southern Tutchone, Tahltan, Kaska, Kwalhioqua-Clatskanie, Tolowa, Chiracahua Apache, and Jicarilla Apache). These seem largely consistent with the claims that I have made here, but deeper knowledge of these languages might reveal more differences.

APPENDIX 3

Summary of Constraints and Language Differences

In this appendix I summarize the major principles proposed in the book and some of the differences among the languages discussed in it.

3.1 Ordering Principles

3.1.1 Ordering the Lexical Items

In the lexical items, the following fixed ordering obtains (chapters 4–8).

(1)   preverb – quantifiers
                incorporates

    First consider ordering within the preverbs, where the scopal ordering principles in (2) yield fixed ordering (chapter 6). The 'greater than' sign indicates structural superiority; the actual linear ordering is the reverse.

(2)   Ordering within preverbs
        more general > more specific
        modified > modifying
        entailing > entailed

The last two cases can be seen as specific instances of the first.
    The ordering of the quantifiers and the preverbs is also a consequence of a scopal principle (chapter 6).

(3)   Ordering of preverbs and quantifiers
        quantifying > quantified

The ordering of incorporates and preverbs is a consequence of object types often selecting for particular stems (chapter 6).

(4) Ordering of preverbs and incorporates
    selector > selected

These principles impose ordering within the preverbs when they are related and places quantifiers and incorporates in a c-commanding position with respect to the preverbs. They do not affect the ordering of the noninteracting quantifiers and the incorporates with respect to each other.

3.1.2 Ordering the Functional Items

Within the functional items, the following orderings are largely fixed (chapters 9–13).

(5) objects – number subjects – subsituation aspect – situation aspect – viewpoint aspect – 1/2 subjects

Several factors determine this ordering. The ordering of first/second person subjects and number subjects follows from the principle in (6) (chapter 10).

(6) Ordering of first/second person subjects and number subjects
    inherently referential > noninherently referential

The relationship between first/second person subjects, situation and viewpoint aspect, and number subjects is a consequence of this hierarchy as well: situation and viewpoint aspect and first/second person subjects share inherent referentiality, and thus both c-command the third person subjects (chapter 13).

The relationship between viewpoint aspect and situation aspect follows from the dependence of situation aspect on viewpoint (chapter 11).

(7) Ordering of situation aspect and viewpoint
    selector > selected

The relationship between situation aspect and object is similar – here the situation aspect marker defines or limits the reading assigned to the object (chapter 13).

(8) Ordering of object and situation aspect
    limiter > limited

Subsituation aspects are defined within situation aspects and more finely delineate how the situation is to be viewed. Their ordering therefore follows from the principles given so far (chapter 11).

Constraints and Language Differences 411

Within subsituation aspect, fixed orderings basically follow from principles of iconicity – subsituation aspects that focus on beginnings have those related to ends in their scope (chapter 12).

(9) Ordering within subsituation aspect
    beginnings > endings

Subsituation aspect is generally considered to be a type of qualifier, a grabbag class semantically. Beyond the fixed ordering of subsituation aspects due to their scopal relationship, the qualifiers are relatively free in their ordering. In the languages with future semelfactives, the interaction between tense and situation aspect yields the hierarchy in (10) (chapter 11).

(10) tense > aspect

The principles presented so far are all semantic. A syntactic principle is also important (chapter 10).

(11) subject > object

This interacts with a semantic principle that sometimes overrides the normal ordering of grammatical roles (chapter 10).

(12) definite > indefinite

In addition, the thematic hierarchy plays a role in ordering entity-related information (chapter 6).

(13) agents > themes > obliques

The scope principles make no predictions about certain orderings. These include the ordering of qualifiers with respect to each other beyond the aspectually interacting ones and the order of qualifiers generally with respect to number subjects. These orderings exhibit much variation.

3.1.3 Summary

The semantic principles summarized in sections 3.1.1 and 3.1.2 are, with the exception of (11), of a similar cast, involving semantic compositionality, with layering motivated by a well-defined semantic concept.

3.2 Interfaces

The semantic principles identified in section 3.1 form the scope principle and interact in limited ways with syntactic principles. The syntactic principle subject > object overrides the semantic principle inherently referential material > inherently nonreferential material, dividing pronominals along grammatical rather than semantic lines. The semantic principle plays a role, however, in ordering subjects by placing number subjects lower than participant subjects (chapter 10).

In Ahtna a semantic distinction emerges in one pocket of the language, when the subject is indefinite and the object is definite. The semantic principle takes precedence over the syntactic one, yielding the linear order indefinite subject – number object. In other languages, the syntactic principle is always more important (chapter 10).

In Navajo, all themes follow preverbs, as predicted by the principle selector > selected. In Slave, a syntactic principle takes precedence with obliquely marked themes, ordering these to the left of other preverbs, along with other obliquely marked roles (chapter 6).

Phonological principles may enter in to order noninteracting items. For instance, phonology conditions the exact placement of the accomplishment situation aspect marker, but does not locate it to the right of viewpoint aspect. Phonological principles override syntactic/semantic principles in one case that I know of, where human subjects appear to the left of indefinite objects in Ahtna and Navajo, under phonological conditions. The syntactic hierarchy subject > object predicts the reverse ordering, as does the semantic hierarchy inherently definite > indefinite. Otherwise, the complex phonology does not destroy scopal (or syntactic) relationships (chapter 10).

3.3 Differences Not Related to Scope

Differences in morpheme order across the languages come from two major sources:

(14) a. different interactions between principles in different languages (part III)
 b. different choices in the ordering of noninteracting systems

Many further differences exist between the languages. Many concern the lexicon, both the stock of lexical items and their semantics and combinatorics. Some are listed below.

Constraints and Language Differences   413

(15) Quantifiers
Semantics: Some languages have a distributive, some a collective, some a general plural, and some a multiple. More than one can exist in a language. Navajo is unusual in having two A-quantifiers.
Combinatorics: The range of thematic relations that the D-quantifier can quantify differs (chapter 4).

(16) Human plural
Semantics: It can be a dual (Galice; Hoijer 1966) or plural. In many languages it marks only human plurals; in others it can accommodate other animate beings as well (dogs in Slave; animates in general for some Babine-Witsuwit'en speakers).
Distribution: It is missing in some languages (Apachean, Hupa, Mattole) (chapter 10).

(17) Semelfactive
It is missing in the imperfective and optative paradigms in some languages as well as in the perfective (Babine-Witsuwit'en) (chapter 10).

(18) First person plurals
Some languages use a subject agreement marker for all nonsingular first persons, some a reflex of Proto-Athapaskan *chr'* for all nonsingular first persons, and some the former as a dual and the latter as a plural (chapter 10).

(19) Optative
Languages differ in the distribution of the optative according to person. They also differ in the readings of the optative; in some, like Slave, it can include a future reading (chapter 11).

(20) Future
Semantics: In some languages the future tense marker marks any future, in others only immediate futures (Slave). In some languages the future can combine with verbs from any aspectual class; in some it is limited in combination (Slave) (chapter 11).

(21) Negative
Languages differ in whether negation is marked in the verb by a functional item, lexical item, and an enclitic, by a functional item and an enclitic, by a lexical item and an enclitic, or not at all. The position of the functional item and the lexical item differs across languages (chapters 11 and 12).

(22) Subject pronominals
Pronominals are generally functional; in Hupa/Kato third person subjects are lexical (chapter 10).

(23) Aspect
Languages differ in combinatorial properties of situation and viewpoint aspect (chapter 11).

3.4 Idiosyncrasies

The greatest idiosyncrasy in the verb is the position of the verb stem and the markers of voice/valence (chapters 5 and 7). Given the scope hypothesis, one expects these to occur within the verb phrase. I have treated their actual placement as a quirk of the Athapaskan verb, achieved through the raising of verbs.

Notes

Chapter 2. Introducing the Problem

1. I draw examples from a wide range of Athapaskan languages. See appendix 2 for a list of the names of the languages and their locations.

    A few notes on transcription are in order. An acute accent over a vowel represents a high-toned vowel; a grave accent represents a low-toned vowel. A vowel with no tonal mark is realized as low-toned in a high-marked language and as high-toned in a low-marked language. A hook under a vowel represents nasalization. C' is an ejective consonant. A glottal stop is consistently represented with a raised comma except in Carrier data from Morice 1932, where I follow the source. The following symbols require comment: *gh* is a voiced velar fricative, *sh* is a voiceless alveopalatal fricative, *dh* is a voiced labiodental fricative, *c* is a front velar stop. Following Athapaskan tradition, *d*, *dz*, etc., represent voiceless unaspirated stops, *t*, *ts*, etc., voiceless aspirated stops and *t'*, *ts'*, etc. glottalized stops. In general, phonological detail is not important to this study. I follow the transcription from the source, but substitute the terminology used in this book in the glosses. Translations are from the source.
2. See chapter 10 on this terminology.

Chapter 3. Global Uniformity and Local Variability: A Possible Account

1. Athapaskan languages are head-final on the surface. Given the analysis that I propose for verbs, it is possible that nouns and postpositions require a different analysis than that normally assumed. The pronominal element in a possessed noun and the complement of a postposition would be treated as a functional category that c-commands the noun or postposition and is to its right; the noun or postposition would then have to move to follow this element.
2. See Jelinek and Willie 1996 for an alternative conception within the same basic set of assumptions. Rather than having the subject at the top of the tree, they treat Navajo as having the subject very low in the tree, dominated by Aspect Phrase, etc., making Navajo an ergative language. I will not comment further on this analysis.

Chapter 4. First Stop: Introducing the Lexical Items

1. Preverbs also make a contribution to event structure by interacting with situation aspect; see chapter 11 for discussion. They may take arguments as well.
2. See Jones and Jetté forthcoming, Kari 1990, Rice 1989, and Young and Morgan 1987 for lists of preverbs and meanings in Koyukon, Ahtna, Slave, and Navajo respectively.
3. The status of pronominals as arguments or agreement is a topic of dispute in Athapaskan studies. Their status is irrelevant at this point; I return to this issue in chapter 10.
4. An implication of this statement is that these morphemes form separate words syntactically. See Cook 1984 and Rice 1990 for discussion.
5. Alternations between voiced and voiceless fricatives are found in many Athapaskan languages. In Slave, a stem-initial fricative of a noun or postposition is voiceless when word-initial and voiced after another morpheme. See Rice 1989 for details.
6. Since the requirement for an object is built into the lexical entry of the preverb, the position 'object of postposition' is not necessary within the verb complex.
7. In Hupa, the form cognate to the distributive in other languages, *ya*, indicates a collective total rather than an individuated plural, as in the following examples from Golla 1970:117.

   (i) Subject
   na:-**ya**:-y-dil
   preverb-**plural**-1pl Subject-stem
   'We all are on our way back.'

   (ii) Subject, direct object, subject and direct object
   ya-'-wi-we:l
   plural-3 human Subject-situation aspect-stem
   'They are packing it along, he is packing them along, they are packing them along.'

   (iii) Oblique object
   xo-ł-**ya**:-te:-se:-ya:-te
   3pl Oblique-with-**plural**-qualifier-situation aspect/1sg Subject-stem-future
   'I will go with them.'

In Tututni also, the translation of the cognate form is the collective 'all' (Golla 1976:223).

   (i) Subject
   ya-'-ghi-'a'ł
   plural-unspecified Object-situation aspect/perfective viewpoint-stem
   'They all have chewed something.'

   (ii) Object
   na-**gha**-si-sh-ł-'a'
   preverb-**plural**-situation aspect-1sg Subject-valence-stem
   'I carried (the babies) around.'

Distributivity is marked in Hupa by a functional item, *t*, with a similar translation to the distributive elsewhere. I have nothing more to say about the Hupa distributive.

8. The Carrier distributive *ne* (Morice 1932) can combine with a form that Morice calls numerositive (1932:383). He notes that the distributive (his pluralative) represents plurality and the numerositive combines plurality and numerousness. The numerositive is *yane* or *yanê*.

   (i) nes-tɬes
   'to tread, trample on (e.g., grass)' (II:383)
   yane-nes-tɬes
   'to tread, trample in many places' (II:383)
   yanepes-qĕh
   'I irritate them (all, that is many).' (II:384)

   It is difficult to tell, but the distributive may indicate an individuated plural and the numerositive simply numerousness, without individuation.

9. The Hupa and Tututni forms discussed in note 7 mark plurality and totality, like the distributive, and collectivity, like the multiple.

10. The most frequent translations that Cook 1984 provides for the iterative in Tsuut'ina are 'now and then' and 'keep'.

    (i) **ná**-dí-yī-c-ɬ-'ātc
    iterative-qualifier-situation aspect-1sg Subject-valence-stem, customary
    'I ran every now and then.' (220)
    (ii) tā-**ná**-yi-c-'ótc
    preverb-**iterative**-situation aspect-1sg Subject-stem, customary
    'I kept putting it up.' (220)

    These are customary forms, with customary stems; see chapter 11.

Chapter 6. Ordering of the Lexical Items

1. An incorporated noun can serve as the complement of a preverb; I ignore such cases here.
2. This display is overgeneralized as incorporates can intervene between quantifiers; see later sections of this chapter for discussion.
3. As will become clear in this chapter, the higher 'preverbs' in this structure are often verbal in nature, representing events, or nominal, representing theme arguments. Thus the term preverb is not really appropriate for this item.
4. The notion of general-specific is not absolute, but relative to the preverbs compared.
5. Thompson 1991 provides some interesting examples from Koyukon that appear to parallel these Navajo forms with two themes. Consider the following examples (his glosses).

   (i) lit-ɬ-tuɬ
   perfective-1sg Subject-shoot
   'I shot it.'
   (ii) bi-yiɬ   k'i-l-tɬtuɬ
   3 Object-with   k'i-perfective-1sg Subject:shoot
   'I shot it.'

(i) and (ii) are transitive verbs. In (ii), an unspecified object, *k'i*, is present. Thompson 1991:65 argues that *bi*, the complement of the comitative postposition *yił*, and *k'i*, the unspecified object, are coreferential, both referring to the thing being shot. Thompson suggests that this construction is used to infer that the hunter and hunted both participated in the shooting, as animals are held to allow themselves to be trapped or killed. While the semantics of the Navajo verbs does not suggest a cultural need for this type of indirect statement, the structure may be grammaticized – the Koyukon facts suggest that a direct and an oblique complement may have the same referent.

6. For the sake of completeness, I mention here some other complications of the Navajo pronoun system. Navajo has a complex causative construction (see chapter 7 for comment). In this construction, the verb has a required object, boldfaced in (i).

(i) a. **b**i-dii-sééh
'I'm burping it (baby).' (YM 184)
b. **b**ii-sh-chxééh
'I'm honking it (car horn).' (YM D:65)

The iterative may follow this object, as in (ii).

(ii) a. **b**i-'-iis-są́
'I feed him, make him eat (baby).' (YM D:215)
bi-**ná**-'-iis-sį́įh
'I customarily feed him.'
b. **b**i-'-iish-háásh
'I put him to sleep.' (YM D:215)
bi-**ná**-'-iish-hosh
'I customarily put him to sleep.'

The iterative may also precede the pronoun, as in (iiib) and (ivb). This appears to be the more common order.

(iii) a. **b**i-**ná**-'-ii-sh-dlį́įh
'I feed him (liquid), water him, get him to drink customarily.' (YM D:215)
b. **ná**-**b**i-'-ii-sh-dlį́įh
same gloss as (iii.a)
(iv) a. 'a-**b**-ii-shį́įł
'I cause him to gasp for breath.' (YM D:76)
b. 'a-**ná**-**b**-ii-shił
'I cause him to gasp for breath customarily.'

The pronoun in question, *b*, is the subject of the noncausative verb (see chapter 7) and is morphologically an oblique object; in (ii) and (iii) an unspecified object, ', is also present. These examples show variability in the placement of the iterative similar to that found in some other languages; see section 6.7.4. The iterative, which quantifies over events (see chapter 4) can precede or follow the pronoun without affecting its scope.

Finally, the inchoative construction in Navajo is complex and worthy of brief comment; see Young and Morgan 1987G:187–188 and Hale 1997 for discussion. In the following examples the inchoative is marked by the presence of ' 'unspecified object' and the prefixes *n* and *i*; Young and Morgan 1987G:187 identify the former as perhaps a terminative and the latter as the transitional. The thematic argument of the verb is in boldface.

(v) a. **bi**-'-n-ii-sh-ghal
'I started to eat it (meat).' (187)
b. **bi**-náá-da-'-n-ii-l-ghal
'We 3+ started to eat some more of it.'
(vi) a. ha-**ho**-'-n-ii-geed
'I started to dig a hole (*ho*).' (187)
b. ha-ná-**ho**-'-n-ii-sh-go'
'I repeatedly start to dig a hole.'

Note two aspects of this construction. First, an unspecified object ' is present. It has the same referent as the oblique object (in boldface), reminiscent of the Navajo constructions discussed in this section. Second, the adverbial quantifiers (*náá* in (v), *ná* in (vi)) can follow the oblique object (vb) or precede it (vib).

In general, the inchoative construction introduces an unspecified argument; note the following intransitive.

(vii) ha-**shi**-'-n-ii-tih
'I started to get old.' (YM G:187)

This verb literally means 'it (') started to get old of me (*sh*).' The unspecified pronoun is an internal subject (chapter 10), but it does not have the same referent as the other pronoun. The position of A-quantifiers with respect to the oblique pronoun is unstable. It precedes in (viii), but follows in (ix) and (x).

(viii) 'a-**náá-ho**-'-n-ii-ł-tą́
'It (') again started to rain (*ho*).' (YM G:187)
(ix) 'i-**náá**-'-n-ii-hai
'Another winter started.'
(x) 'i-**náá**-'-n-ii-chííl
'It (') again started to snow (').'

This construction is worthy of investigation. In any event, however, since the iterative relates to events and exhibits variable ordering with an argument, these examples pose no problem for the scope hypothesis.

7. I have not found examples with two transitive preverbs in Slave and Ahtna parallel to the Navajo examples in (38) and (39).
8. The morphophonemics of these forms is complex, and they often do not show up as *ná* and *náá*. Variant forms for *ná* include *ní*, *´n*, and *né*; it may also contract with the preceding prefix, losing the initial nasal. Young and Morgan 1980, 1987 suggest that the variant forms are phonologically conditioned. I ignore the phonological variation here, assuming that Young and Morgan are correct.
9. Young and Morgan 1987:156 suggest that the iterative may be "cognate with or identical with *ná*-^{5} Position Ib, also denoting repetition, although both may co-occur in the same verb, as in **nánístsxis** (Imperfective), I'm giving him a whipping (= I'm hitting him a connected series of blows with a whip) (ní- = ná-^{5} / ná- = ná-II)." They suggest that "the Iterative Mode is simply the Usitative + ná-^{5}"

(Young and Morgan 1987:53). It seems likely that these *ná*'s with similar meaning have a single lexical entry. This preverb *ná* is translated as repetition; it co-occurs with a thematic *ni* to give the meaning 'repetition in the form of a chain of linked but separate acts: e.g. a series of blows or slaps' (Young and Morgan 1987:53). The different meanings depend on what it co-occurs with. As a preverb, it provides the meaning of repeated but separate acts. As a quantificational adverb, it expresses return to a state (one complete cycle) with most stem forms, but with the repetitive stem form it reinforces that repetition, though still involving a return.

10. VP adverbs, or adverbs that are strictly subcategorized under VP, do not show the same privileges of occurrence. This is comparable to the situation in Athapaskan languages where the preverbs are adjacent to the verb stem underlyingly; these can be thought of as constituents of V or V′ while the quantificational adverbs are constituents of VP.

11. I have ignored one other reading assigned to the iterative, the reversative (see chapter 4). This item is categorized as a preverb when it is part of the basic lexical entry. This follows from the scope hypothesis: it would appear to the left, in a c-commanded position.

12. When a disjunct morpheme ending in the vowel /a/ is followed by the iterative *na*, the vowel [ǫ] results by regular phonological process.

13. According to Kari 1989, 1990:40, distributive *n* precedes incorporates in Ahtna. I have found one counterexample.

(i) Ahtna (Kari 1990)
da-n-h-t-n-es-t-ga'
mouth-distributive-areal-qualifier-qualifier-situation aspect-voice-stem
'Their mouths are dirty.' (it is dirty in their mouths) (179)

The distributive follows the incorporate *da*, contrary to the ordering specified by Kari 1989, 1990. The template account has little to say here; I argue that the scopal account allows for the ordering in (i) as well as the more common opposite order.

Chapter 7. Voice/Valence

1. An alternative analysis is that voice/valence elements are functional projections higher than the subject. The phonology militates against this because voice/valence markers and the verb stem form a constituent phonologically; this is accounted for by the raising analysis because the verb stem and the voice/valence element combine. A second analysis, according to which voice/valence elements attach to the stem lexically, is problematic because the voice/valence elements would not c-command elements within their scope.

2. The causativizer can also change an experiencer subject to an agentive subject (Kibrik 1993), as can be seen in the following Navajo examples.

i. Ø: yoo-'į́
'S/he seems him/her.' (Young and Morgan 1980:420)
ł: yini-ł-'į́
'S/he looks at, examines him/her.'

Notes to pp. 140–198 421

    ii. Ø: disíní-ts'ą́ą́'
           'You sg. heard it.' (Young and Morgan 1980:344, 767)
     ł: yíní-ł-ts'ą́ą́'
          'You sg. listened to it.'

3. The causativizer never appears as an independent verb, but merges with the verb in its complement.
4. The standard analysis of the first person plural is that it is a single morpheme, *Vd*, with *d* included. I assume that it is a complex lexical entry, *V* 'first person plural' + *d* 'middle voice'.
5. The errative occurs in at least a few Slave verbs also: *'enéhdǫ* 's/he overate, got drunk'.
6. See Thompson 1996a for arguments about the historical source of middle voice in Athapaskan languages.

Chapter 9. An Introduction to the Functional Elements

1. Kari 1989:433 quotes Jetté 1906 as saying, "There are seven qualifiers, which, being ranked in order of proximity to the pronoun in simultaneous prefixation are L [thematic 'kill, listen'], N, D, Ra [ghe], U, Ro [xa 'area'], Y."

Chapter 10. Pronominals

1. The details of lexical entries of these inflectional elements are beyond the scope of study here. I assume that a feature is present (feature in (1) without valence) or absent (feature in (1) with ±); in the case of features that are absent, a reading is determinable from the context or by default. The details are, I believe, irrelevant for the discussion at hand.
2. The human plural subject can also be used with dogs in Slave.
3. I include AgrS and NumS in a single structure, contrary to Rice and Saxon 1994. This raises the question of why AgrS and NumS fail to co-occur within a verb. I assume that this is a result of feature interaction. For instance, agreement is definite and specific, while number is not marked for definiteness; agreement is marked for person, while number is not. Number thus adds no information to that given by agreement. In addition, there may be featural incompatibilities. For example, some agreement elements are marked as singular; these could not co-occur with an element that is marked for plurality.
4. I am not aware of discussion of coordination for languages other than Slave and Dogrib. In Navajo, Willie 1991 shows that noun phrases can co-occur with third persons, but not with first and second persons.
5. Young and Morgan 1987:76 point out that this form is also used to represent the main character in a narrative and can disambiguate between two third persons.
6. Hargus (personal communication, 1998) reports that some speakers of Babine-Witsuwit'en can use the plural *h* for animate beings in general, not just for humans.

7. The first person nonsingular subject form is complex to reconstruct (Story 1989). For my purposes, what is important is that first person nonsingular subjects can be marked in two different positions; phonological details are irrelevant. First, the first person nonsingular subject can be at the right edge of the functional complex (Slave, Navajo, Apache, Pacific Coast languages, Babine, Carrier, some Gwich'in). Second, in many languages, a cognate prefix to Slave *í-d* is absent (Upper Tanana, Tanacross, Upper Kuskokwim, Koyukon, Holikachuk, Ingalik, Dena'ina, Ahtna; see Story 1989:497 for discussion), and the cognate of Slave *ts'*, appearing to the right of the object, is used to mark first person nonsingular subjects. A third pattern is discussed later on.
8. See Story 1989 for detailed discussion. As Story discusses, there are differences among the languages in the uses of the cognates of *í-d*. According to her, cognates of *ts'* are "found universally, or almost universally, in Athapaskan, with an indefinite first or third person meaning," while the cognate of *í-d* "may be a first person duoplural or first dual subject prefix" (Story 1989:512).
9. The *s* element is not present in all of Hargus's examples of first person duals. The examples below are translated by Hargus as duals but do not include the *s*; she does not comment on the absence of *s* in these forms.

   (i) a. chu ghù-dǫ-azią́
       'We dual have a little drink.' (optative) (Hargus 1988:79)
   b. k'è-də-də-d-ì-ghit's
       'We dual will step on O.' (103)
   c. gh-ù-tsəgh
       'We dual cry.' optative (108)

See Story 1989 for detailed discussion of the development of these forms in Sekani and in Doig Beaver, which has a similar pattern. The cognate of Sekani *s* surfaces in other languages also (Slave, Dogrib, Tsuut'ina, Tagish, Tahltan, Kaska; see Story 1989:504), but is always adjacent to the cognate of *í-d*. Story hypothesizes that *s* in these forms originated as a situation aspect marker (chapter 11). I follow Hargus in assuming that it is a number marker in Sekani synchronically. In Rice 1989 I suggested that the *s* cognate marked situation aspect; here I follow Hargus in making it part of the first person duoplural subject.
10. Hargus 1988 does not report second person plurals with the number morpheme *s*.
11. The forms identified as anaphors exhibit other properties associated with anaphors. As seen in the text, their distribution is determined by their relationship to the subject. They do not occur as subjects (but see section 10.3.5), nor can their possessive counterparts be found as possessors of subjects. The disjoint anaphor patterns with the reflexive and reciprocal. In general, the disjoint anaphor must be licensed by a Number subject; it is not licensed by first/second person subjects in AgrS. But it is not licensed by all material in Number – *ts'* and its cognates do not license it. This can be seen in the following examples, with *ts'* cognates as subjects (in boldface) and no overt direct object.

   (i) a. Navajo ($j = zh$ = unspecified human subject)
       yisdá-**zh**-d-oo-ł-téét
       'Someone will rescue him.' (Young and Morgan 1987:773)

b. Dogrib (*ts'*)
k'e-**ts'**e-te
'Someone is carrying him around.' (Willie and Saxon 1995)
c. Slave (*ts'*)
k'ína-**ts'**e-teh
'Someone is carrying him/her around.' (Rice 1989)
d. Koyukon (*ts'*)
ts'i-nee-ł-'aanh
'We/someone/she/he is looking at him/her/it.' (Thompson 1989b:11)

Thompson 1989b:11 comments for Koyukon that "Morphologically, ts'i- is treated as a non-third-person prefix in that it does not cooccur with a yi-object prefix; rather, it takes Ø or, when the object is topical, bi-."

(ii) Koyukon
bi-**ts'**i-nee-ł-'aanh
'We/someone/she/he is looking at him/her.' (Thompson 1989b:11)

12. I only consider the plural disjoint anaphor, although there are two other forms *go* in Slave, both of which are third person, or number, types. It is the nonsubject counterpart of *ts'*. Another homophonous form is *go* areal. I leave open the question as to how many morphemes are involved; see Saxon 1986 for detailed discussion.
13. *Raxe* and its cognates collapse first and second persons. This is consistent with the claim that first/second person form a natural class to the exclusion of third person.
14. I ignore (58c), which illustrates a topical oblique object and nontopical subject and direct object. It suggests that the placement of objects is more complex than I am assuming; in particular, it is likely that topical objects occupy a different position from nontopical objects (see (45), Rice 1999). I am concerned only with cases of topical object and nontopical subject; examples with nontopical object and nontopical subject are realized as *y-y* as in (58c), and the ordering cannot be determined on empirical grounds. To fill out the paradigm, cases involving nontopical object and topical subject have external subjects, as in (58a,d). The fourth possibility is topical object and topical subject; I have not found such cases and suspect that they do not exist.
15. Many Athapaskan languages have impersonal, or nonpromotional, passives, where logical themes of any person are in the object form, and no external subject is present.
16. The order reflects grammatical relations and not topic and focus, since both focus-topic and topic-focus ordering is possible.
17. Thompson 1989b:11 points out that the object form has the same range of meanings as the subject form.
    (i) **dinaa**-nee-ł-'aanh
    'He, she, it is looking at **us/someone/him/her**.'
    (ii) dinaa-**ts'**i-nee-ł-'aanh
    '**We/she/he** is looking at us/someone/him/her.'
18. Note that *ts'* and its cognates often have an unspecified, indefinite reading, suggesting that it is an internal rather than an external subject. However, *ts'* with its cognates is obligatorily human, and human subjects tend to be external. I assume

that the human property is sufficient to license it externally. Its value for specificity is not lexically marked, but is rather contextually determined. It is also possible that this position is simply grammaticized. Thompson 1989a argues that this morpheme was historically a proximate argument, and it is likely that such an argument would be external.

19. In section 10.3.5, I argued that the disjoint anaphor occurs as a subject in some of northern languages. Could the plural disjoint anaphor show parallel patterning? I have no data, but the conditions are clear: the human plural subject would have to be less salient than the object, which would be the topic of the clause.

20. In this note I summarize the distribution of the pronouns y and b. The conditions under which each occurs are much discussed in the Athapaskan literature; for recent work see Rice 1999, Rice and Saxon 1991, Thompson 1996b, and Willie and Jelinek 1996. Thompson and Willie and Jelinek propose that both pronouns have a semantic component, with b marking an object as discourse topic and y marking the object as discourse focus. The analysis I have proposed is slightly different: y must meet licensing conditions for the language. It is licensed by a third person c-commanding argument; in some of the languages any c-commanding third person is a licenser (e.g., Ahtna, Koyukon, Tsuut'ina), whereas in others only a third person external argument is a licenser. Third person licensers include the elements in NumS other than the unspecified human subject. In languages like Ahtna, NumO elements can also license y, while in languages like Slave, they never do, and b appears instead as the elsewhere form. Consider the simplified structures in (i). NP_i is a subject; NP_j a direct or oblique object.

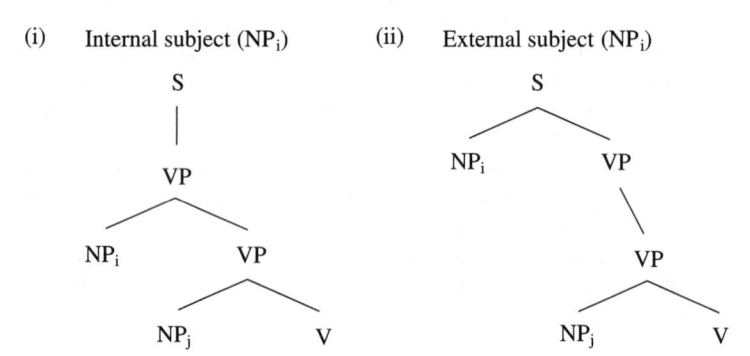

(i) Internal subject (NP_i) (ii) External subject (NP_i)

The chart in (iii) shows the possible combinations of third person subject and object pronouns in Ahtna, Slave, and Navajo; the forms depend upon the position of the subject, as in (i) and (ii).

(iii)
	Subject	**Object**	**Subject**	**Object**
Ahtna	Ø	b	Ø	y
	y	b		
Slave	Ø	b	Ø	y
Navajo	Ø	b	Ø	y

Slave and Navajo differ largely in requirements on the appearance of Number objects. To put it simply, they are normally found in Slave only when no nominal object occurs; in Navajo they are generally found regardless of whether an overt noun

Notes to pp. 235–251

is present. The unspecified pronoun' does not generally occur with a noun, although there are examples (see chapter 5) where it has the same referent as an oblique object.

21. Kari 1990 assumes that the basic ordering is subject-object, but this is not a necessary assumption.
22. The transcription of Kato (Goddard 1912) is inadequate, leading to a perception that third person forms serve as both subjects and objects. Both Sapir and Harrington differentiate forms that Goddard collapses (Golla, personal communication, 1996).
23. For completeness, I describe another case where Hupa exhibits odd ordering involving pronouns. In forms with the conative (Golla's 1970:111 semitransitive postposition), the object pronouns appear in their expected position to the left of the conative. The ordering is subject-object when the object is first person singular and the subject is third person.

(i) ch'i-**W-o-ł**-kyis
3 Subject-**1 sg Object-conative**-valence-stem
'He strikes at me.'

When the subject is third person and the object is unspecified, the order object-conative-subject is found.

(ii) **k'y-o:-'**-o-ł-kyis
Unspecified Object-conative-ch'i Subject
'He strikes at something.'

(iii) **k'yid-o:-y**-oh-ł-kyis
Unspecified Object-conative-y Subject
'Let it be struck at by something.'

The plural lexical item *ya* (chapter 4) is ordered strangely in this construction, following the conative rather than preceding it, as expected given the patterning in other languages. This is shown in Kato forms from Goddard 1905:114–115 and confirmed by Golla (personal communication).

(iv) a. ch'-o-xai
third person subject-conative-stem
'He buys it.'

b. y-o-xai
y subject-conative-stem
'He (*y*) buys it.'

c. ch'-o-**ya**-xai
third person subject-conative-**plural**-stem
'They buy it.'

d. y-o-**ya**-xai
y subject-conative-**plural**-stem
'They (*y*) buy it.'

Chapter 11. The Aspect System

1. It is misleading in Athapaskan languages, as in English, to speak of a verb being of a particular situation type – situation type is determined at the level of the sentence, or predicate; see, for example, Smith 1997, Tenny 1994, van Valin 1993, and Verkuyl 1972, 1993. However, it is convenient to talk about verbs on their own in Athapaskan

languages, and I use the situation aspect classes as if they categorized verbs. I thus talk of shifting from one situation type (defined by the lexical class of the verb) to another, one either compatible with the inherent aspect of the verb or determined by material in the predicate.

2. In the following discussion I examine the regular, predictable nature of the situation aspect markers. Like the voice/valence markers discussed in chapter 7, situation aspect markers are lexicalized with particular verbs to some degree, with noncompositional meaning. I abstract away from these cases in my discussion.

3. This class includes prototypical motion verbs (verbs of going, verbs of handling), but it also includes verbs like 'break', 'shatter', and 'crush'. These verbs do not so much involve motion as the absence of duration, suggesting that the Athapaskan label 'motion' is not the most felicitous one for the class.

4. This lexical categorization of roots, while commonly discussed in the Athapaskan literature, is misleading in that it suggests that a particular root belongs to a single situation aspect category. Consider the Ahtna verb *l-dogh* (Kari 1990:156). Kari lists this verb as having an activity (successive) form 'burst, crack, boom; be bursting, booming noise; gun fires; causative: cause O to crack, boom; crack O', a stative form 'be cracked, fissured, chapped', and an achievement form 'amorphous incorporated noun moves; causative: cause amorphous incorporated noun to move'. In addition, *d-l-dogh* is an onomatopoetic form meaning 'be bursting, booming, cracking sound'. This example shows that the verb root itself is not lexically of a particular situation type since it can appear in different situation types. It is probably more reasonable to think in terms of some notion of compatibility of verb meaning in at least some cases. In other cases, the verb root is compatible with only a single situation type; the root *t'aes* 'roast, fry, bake; causative roast, fry, bake O' (Kari 1990:347) can only be an accomplishment. While verb roots cannot all be slotted into a lexically indicated situation type, I will write for convenience as if they could be.

5. As discussed at the end of chapter 7, in middle voice verbs, perfective viewpoint is not expressed by the perfective viewpoint prefix; rather the imperfective prefix is found. However, perfective viewpoint is expressed by a suffix; see section 11.5. In this section, I intend the term 'perfective viewpoint' to encompass perfectivity as expressed by either the prefix or the suffix.

6. Verbs of the semelfactive situation type occur with *s* in the perfective viewpoint and with *i* in nonperfective viewpoints. As we will see in sections 11.2.1.3 and 11.2.1.4, other material in the predicate can express aspectual requirements. Preverbs with semelfactive content occur with *i* in all viewpoints. Primary semelfactive verbs are distinguished in the perfective by their stem type, while derived semelfactives have an achievement stem; see section 11.4.

7. Phonologically, subsituation aspect markers are part of the qualifier system. The qualifier system is not functionally unified in the way that the pronominal and aspectual systems are – it includes material that enters into the argument system, material that enters into the aspect system, and material that adds to a word's qualia structure. See chapter 12 for discussion; I am concerned only with the aspectual qualifiers here.

8. The classificatory verbs of handling do not exhibit the number-dependent type of alternation in (45). This might be because only verbs with inherent duration

participate in the alternation, whereas classificatory verbs are achievements. Alternatively, two types of plurals might be involved, with plurals of verbs with duration being individual plurals, but plurals of classificatory verbs being group or collective plurals, or only incidentally plurals. Further work on the semantics of this class of achievements is in order.

9. This fact is far more striking in other Athapaskan languages. In Slave syllable-final consonants neutralize, with voiceless consonants becoming [h] and voiced consonants other than nasals and glides having no phonetic realization. This massive leveling of stem-final consonants makes the suffix system less transparent than it is in many other languages, though it fails to completely obscure the kinds of patterns contributed by suffixes. In this discussion, I confine myself to the suffixation of open (CV) roots, where the suffixation patterns are clearest. See Rice 1989 for further discussion of suffixation in Slave; see Axelrod 1993, Hardy 1979, Kari 1979, and Leer 1979 for detailed discussion of suffixation in Koyukon, Navajo, Ahtna, and Proto-Athapaskan, respectively.

10. I refrain from discussing relevance to the syntax for the following reason. Aspect (both situation and viewpoint) is relevant to syntax. However, since aspect is represented in both the prefix and suffix systems, it is difficult to pinpoint whether it is the prefixes, the suffixes, or both that have syntactic relevance. I assume here that the prefixes are syntactically relevant, and that the suffixes are not, but I am not sure that this is empirically testable.

11. In the Athapaskan literature, Cook 1984:225 treats suffixes as inflectional. Midgette 1987, 1995 argues that they are basically derivational, but that some, especially the progressive, have inflectional properties as well. Kari 1990, 1992 treats as derivational his aspectual derivation (situation aspect as a verbal diacritic), superaspectual derivation (customary, distributive), and noninflectional derivation (iterative, passive, benefactive, gender, incorporation); he treats as inflectional what he calls mode-negative (particular choice of situation, viewpoint) and pronominals.

12. The overall scheme proposed by Kari differs from the one argued for here; what is important is that the elements s, n, and gh can be identified with aspect of some type.

13. Young 1995 notes two other kinds of semelfactives. One he calls the *ńdi* semelfactive. This co-occurs with achievement stems, and takes gh situation aspect in the perfective viewpoint; it is used only with verbs describing a blow. The second he calls the *yíní* directive semelfactive. This too occurs with the achievement stem set, but takes a null situation aspect marker. The semelfactive morpheme is absent in the simple semelfactive perfective viewpoint, but present in the *yíní* semelfactive perfective.

14. Kari 1979:118 notes that in third person perfective viewpoint forms the semelfactive is present in the absence of a noun class marker, but absent in the presence of such a marker.

15. I have found one Ahtna example with the order inceptive-semelfactive, the future transitional of a stative verb in (i).

   (i) **t-i**-n-a-l-k'uuts
       t inceptive + i semelfactive + n qualifier + a gh situation aspect + $k'uuts$
       'fat, transitional'
       'S/he will become fat.' (Kari 1990:687)

This ordering is not predicted by Kari's template, in which the *n* qualifier follows the inceptive but precedes the semelfactive (Kari 1990:41). The morphology and semantics of this construction require further work.

16. See Cook 1989 on problems of ordering in Chilcotin. He adopts a slightly different model from Kari, as shown in (i).

    (i) Conjugation   Primary aspect/mode
        Ø, ŝ, gh, n   n perfective, ŵ optative, ghe progressive

    Cook analyzes *ŝ* as marking both situation aspect (his conjugation) and negation. Its co-occurrence with *gh* in the progressive forces him to list *gh* in two columns. Kari instead moves *ŝ* out of the conjugation column.

Chapter 12. Qualifiers and Their Ordering

1. The negative may not be aspectual. Kari 1989 introduces the term qualifier to refer to the affixes that are sandwiched between pronominals and situation aspect/viewpoint aspect. As discussed in chapter 11, the negative may appear in this position, but can also be found to the right of viewpoint aspect.
2. Young and Morgan (1987:38) structure their position VI in Navajo as follows:

Position VIa	Position VIb	Position VIc
i thematic	*ni* thematic	*yi* transitional
di inceptive		*yi* semelfactive
di thematic		*yi* seriative (alternate form)
dzi		*hi* hang suspended (alternate form)
hi seriative		*yi* (alternate form of *si* thematic)
hi hang suspended		
ji thematic		
łi adjectival		
si thematic		
yi thematic		

3. Thompson 1989a hypothesizes that the source of the Navajo seriative is human plural number. If this is correct, the association of the seriative with arguments is not surprising.
4. The seriative has the same phonological form as the semelfactive, discussed in chapter 11, but the semelfactive does not show variation in position as the seriative does (see note 2). The seriative and the semelfactive differ in meaning: the semelfactive indicates a single punctual, atelic event and is purely aspectual, while the seriative involves a seriation and refers to the argument system or the event system, depending on characteristics of the verb.
5. I have focused on variable orderings within qualifiers in Sekani, but many orderings are fixed as well. As in other Athapaskan languages, more than one qualifier can occur in a verb. Hargus 1988 points out that certain orderings are fixed. The qualifier *gh* always precedes the qualifiers *d* and *n*, as in (i).

    (i) a. k'è-**ghə-nə**-dah
           'S/he staggers around.' (111)
        b. **ghə-d**-ès-ts'èt
           'S/he ate up [O].'

In these examples, the qualifiers do not appear to have a productive function.
The qualifier *u* precedes the qualifiers *z* and *d*.

(ii) a. **u-z**-èh-ts'ǫ
'S/he listens to [O].'
b. jìje **u-d**ə-n-a-bèł
berry
'S/he will pick berries.'

Here *d* represents the inceptive, while *u*, a frozen conative, and *z* are unproductive. The qualifier *d* inceptive also precedes the *n* and *z* qualifiers.

(iii) a. 'ədənəghįts'įe
'You sg. will get sick from eating too much fat.'
b. dəzahxeł
'S/he will kill [sg O].'

The qualifiers *n* and *d* precede *ì*. In (ivb), the *d* qualifier is a verb class marker; *ì* is aspectual, with an inchoative force.

(iv) a. whè-**n-ì**-tsègh
'S/he started to cry.'
b. **d-ì**-gày
'It turned white, light.'

Chapter 13. On the Ordering of Functional Items

1. Translating objects as singular or plural is not the only way to express the meaning differences associated with different situation aspect markers. Other readings can occur – do something once (*s*) as opposed to do repeatedly (*gh*), meet a goal as opposed to leave a goal unmet (e.g., boiled vs. had been boiling; beat up vs. used to beat up). See Axelrod 1993 on Koyukon for discussion.
2. Recall from chapter 12 that Navajo has a seriative morpheme that can relate to either the event or the entity system depending on the verb that it is in construction with. The seriative always precedes situation aspect. When it is part of the event system, this is understandable – it marks a subtype of a situation type. But one might ask why, when it individuates an entity, it must still precede situation aspect. The answer is that on this reading, the seriative can occur only with an accomplishment situation type. Thus situation aspect defines the conditions under which an entity can receive a seriative reading.
3. I know of one counterexample to the claim that number subjects must precede aspectual material, and this involves subsituation aspect rather than situation aspect and viewpoint aspect. In Navajo inherently segmented events marked by a seriative subsituation aspect marker (chapter 12), the unspecified human subject and the seriative may appear in either order, as in (i). (See chapter 12 for discussion of the seriative.)

(i) a. seriative *hi* + unspecified human subject *j*
hijeeghał 'He arrives wriggling.' (Kari 1973:237)
b. unspecified human subject *j* + seriative *y*
jiyeeghał 'He arrives wriggling.'

The aspectual seriative marks that an activity is segmented or an achievement repeated.

4. One might ask why, under this account, tense often appears in a higher position than aspect (see Demirdache and Uriba-Extebarria 1998 for recent discussion). Davis 1998 examines this question, focusing on why there is a crosslinguistic connection between tense and subject agreement. He argues that first/second person subject features are associated with tense, and number features with aspect. A local and a nonlocal item are thus paired, with the local one above the nonlocal one, at least for number subjects, where it is possible to discern this in the Athapaskan family. Smith 1997:105 argues that tense is independently required to appear above aspect since temporal location is predicated externally of a situation. The role of tense is not obvious in Athapaskan languages since it is not overtly expressed in the verb except in the future, where tense has scope over all interacting material but first/second person subject. We can generally see only that local material appears above nonlocal material. Once tense is excluded, and assuming that in general subjects appear above objects, the hierarchy inherently referential > inherently nonreferential yields the order first/second person subject > aspect > number subject > object.

Chapter 15. Evidence from the Lexicon

1. Thanks to a reviewer for suggesting this line of inquiry to me. I would like to express a note of caution before beginning this chapter. I speak in this chapter of morphemes being innovated, being replaced, shifting in function, and the like. Such statements imply an understanding of what the morpheme stock once was – this is a prerequisite for knowing, for instance, if a morpheme is innovative, or if two forms once existed with some languages retaining one and some another. The presentation in this chapter is thus simplistic in the absence of deeper knowledge about historical stages.

Chapter 16. Looking Back, Looking Ahead

1. Nonroot material that is part of a lexical entry is also found in nouns built on that entry; see Hargus and Tuttle 1997 for general discussion and Rice 1989 for discussion of Slave.

References

Aikenvald, Alexandra Y. 1997. Classifiers. A typology of noun classification devices. Manuscript, Research Centre for Linguistic Typology, Australia National University.
Aikenvald, Alexandra Y. and R.M.W. Dixon. 1998. Dependencies between grammatical systems. *Language* 74:56–80.
Allen, Margaret. 1978. Morphological investigations. Doctoral dissertation, University of Connecticut.
Anderson, Stephen R. 1982. Where's morphology? *Linguistic Inquiry* 13:571–612.
Anderson, Stephen R. 1988. Morphological theory. In Frederick J. Newmeyer (ed.), *Linguistics: The Cambridge series*, vol. 1. Cambridge: Cambridge University Press. 146–191.
Anderson, Stephen R. 1992. *A-morphous morphology*. Cambridge: Cambridge University Press.
Anderson, Stephen R. 1996. How to put your clitics in their place. *The Linguistic Review* 13:165–191.
Arce-Arenales, Manuel, Melissa Axelrod, and Barbara Fox. 1994. Active voice and middle diathesis: A cross-linguistic perspective. In Barbara Fox and Paul Hopper (eds.), *Voice: Form and function*. Amsterdam: Benjamins. 1–21.
Archangeli, Diana and D. Terence Langendoen. 1997. *Optimality Theory: An introduction*. Oxford: Blackwell.
Aronoff, Mark. 1994. *Morphology by itself*. Cambridge, Mass.: MIT Press.
Auger, Julie. 1994. Pronominal clitics in Québec colloquial French: a morphological analysis. Doctoral dissertation, University of Pennsylvania.
Axelrod, Melissa. 1990. Incorporation in Koyukon Athapaskan. *International Journal of American Linguistics* 56:179–195.
Axelrod, Melissa. 1993. *The semantics of time. Aspectual categorization in Koyukon Athabaskan*. Lincoln, Nebraska: University of Nebraska Press.
Axelrod, Melissa. 1996. The semantics of classification in Koyukon Athabaskan. Paper presented at the Athabaskan Conference on Syntax and Semantics, Swarthmore College.
Axelrod, Melissa. 1998. Lexis, grammar, and grammatical change: The Koyukon classifier prefixes. In M. Darnell, E. Moravscik, M. Noonan, F. Newmeyer, and K. Wheatly (eds.), *Functionalism and formalism in linguistics*. vol. 2: Case studies in language companion series. Amsterdam: John Benjamins. 39–58.

References

Baker, Mark. 1985. The Mirror Principle and morphosyntactic explanation. *Linguistic Inquiry* 16:373–415.

Baker, Mark C. 1988. *Incorporation: A theory of grammatical function changing.* Chicago: University of Chicago Press.

Baker, Mark C. 1992. Morphological classes and grammatical organization. In Geert Booij and Jaap van Marle (eds.), *Yearbook of morphology*. Dordrecht:Kluwer. 89–106.

Baker, Mark C. 1996. *The polysynthesis parameter.* Oxford: Oxford University Press.

Beard, Robert. 1995. *Lexeme-morpheme base morphology*. Albany, N.Y.: SUNY Press.

Benveniste, Emile. 1971. *Problems in general linguistics* (Translated by Mary Elizabeth Meek). Coral Gables, Fla.: University of Miami Press.

Binnick, Robert. 1991. *Time and the verb.* New York and Oxford: Oxford University Press.

Bonet, Eulàlia. 1991. Morphology after syntax: Pronominal clitics in Romance. Doctoral dissertation, MIT.

Bonet, Eulàlia. 1995. Feature structure of Romance clitics. *Natural Language and Linguistic Theory* 13:607–647.

Borer, Hagit. 1998. Morphology and syntax. In Andrew Spencer and Arnold Zwicky (eds.), *The handbook of morphology*. Oxford: Blackwell. 141–190.

Bouchard, Denis. 1995. *The semantics of syntax.* Chicago: University of Chicago Press.

Brentari, Diane K. 1998. Comments on the paper by Yip. In Steven G. Lapointe, Diane K. Brentari, and Patrick M. Farrell (eds.), *Morphology and its relation to phonology and syntax.* Stanford: CSLI. 247–258.

Brunson, Barbara. 1989. Thematic dependencies and government. In *Proceedings of the Eastern States Conference on Linguistics* 6:26–36.

Brunson, Barbara. 1992. Thematic discontinuity. Doctoral dissertation, University of Toronto.

Bybee, Joan. 1985a. *Morphology: A study of the relation between meaning and form.* Amsterdam: Benjamins.

Bybee, Joan. 1985b. Diagrammatic iconicity in stem inflection relations. In John Haiman (ed.), *Iconicity in syntax.* Amsterdam: Benjamins.11–47.

Bybee, Joan, William Pagliuca, and Revere Perkins. 1994. *The evolution of grammar: Tense, aspect, and modality in the languages of the world.* Chicago: University of Chicago Press.

Carrier-Duncan, Jill. 1985. Linking of thematic roles in derivational word formation. *Linguistic Inquiry* 16:1–34.

Carter, Richard. 1988. On linking: Papers by Richard Carter. Lexicon Project Working Papers no. 23. Cambridge, Mass.: Center for Cognitive Science, MIT.

Chierchia, Gennaro and Sally McConnell-Ginet. 1990. *Meaning and grammar: An introduction to semantics.* Cambridge, Mass.: MIT Press.

Comrie, Bernard. 1976. *Aspect.* Cambridge: Cambridge University Press.

Cook, Eung-Do. 1984. *A Sarcee grammar.* Vancouver: University of British Columbia Press.

Cook, Eung-Do. 1989. Chilcotin tone and verb paradigms. In Eung-Do Cook and Keren Rice (eds.), *Athapaskan linguistics. Current perspectives on a language family*. Berlin: Mouton de Gruyter. 145–198.

Cook, Eung-Do. 1996. Third-person plural subject prefix in Northern Athapaskan. *International Journal of American Linguistics* 62:86–110.

References

Corbett, Greville. 1991. *Gender*. Cambridge: Cambridge University Press.
Cowper, Elizabeth. 1995. A minimalist account of English participle constructions. *Canadian Journal of Linguistics* 40:1–38.
Craig, Colette and Kenneth Hale. 1988. Relational preverbs in some languages of the Americas. *Language* 64:312–344.
Croft, William. 1987. Categories and relations in syntax: The clause-level organization of information. Doctoral dissertation, Stanford University.
Croft, William. 1990. *Typology and universals*. Cambridge: Cambridge University Press.
Cummins, Sarah. 1996. Meaning and mapping. Doctoral dissertation, University of Toronto.
Cummins, Sarah and Yves Roberge. 1994. Romance inflectional morphology in and out of syntax. In Heidi Harley and Colin Phillips (eds.), *The morphology-syntax connection. MIT Working Papers in Linguistics* 22:53–70.
Dahl, Östen. 1985. *Tense and aspect systems*. Oxford: Blackwell.
Davidson, William. 1963. A preliminary analysis of active verbs in Dogrib. In Harry Hoijer (ed.), *Studies in the Athapaskan languages*. University of California Publications in Linguistics 29. Berkeley and Los Angeles: University of California Press. 48–56.
Davis, Henry. 1998. Person splits, Φ-features and temporal architecture. Paper presented at GLOW Syntax Workshop, KUB Tilburg.
Davis, Philip and Ross Saunders. 1975. Bella Coola deictic usage. *Rice University Studies* 61:13–35.
Demirdache, Hamida and Myriam Uribe-Exterbarria. 1998. On the projection of temporal structure in natural language. *GLOW newsletter* 40:28–29.
Denham, Kristin E. 1995. Wh-question formation in Athabaskan languages. Talk presented at the Athabaskan Languages Conference, University of New Mexico, Albuquerque.
Denham, Kristin E. 1997. A minimalist account of optional wh-movement. Doctoral dissertation, University of Washington.
Denny, Peter. 1975. Locating the universals of space in lexical systems for spatial deixis. Proceedings of the Chicago Linguistic Society, Papers from the parasession on the lexicon, 71–84.
Diesing, Molly. 1992. *Indefinites*. Cambridge, Mass.: MIT Press.
Diesing, Molly and Eloise Jelinek. 1995. Distributing arguments. *Natural Language Semantics* 3:123–176.
Dowty, David. 1979. *Word meaning and Montague Grammar*. Dordrecht: Reidel.
Embick, David. 1996. Causativization in Hupa. In *Proceedings of the Berkeley Linguistic Society* 22:88–94.
Ernst, Thomas. 1997. Scope-based adjunct licensing. Talk presented at NELS, University of Toronto.
Evans, Nick. 1995. A-quantifiers and scope in Mayali. In Emmon Bach, Eloise Jelinek, Angelika Kratzer, and Barbara Partee (eds.), *Quantification in natural languages*, vol. 1. Dordrecht: Kluwer. 21–58.
Faltz, Leonard. 1995. Towards a typology of natural logic. In Emmon Bach, Eloise Jelinek, Angelika Kratzer, and Barbara H. Partee (eds.), *Quantification in natural languages*, vol. 1. Dordrecht: Kluwer. 271–319.

Fillmore, Charles. 1968. The case for case. In Emmon Bach and Robert Harms (eds.), *Universals in linguistic theory*. New York: Holt, Reinhart, and Winston. 1–88.

Foley, William and Robert Van Valin. 1984. *Functional syntax and Universal Grammar*. Cambridge: Cambridge University Press.

Frawley, William. 1992. *Linguistic semantics*. Hillsdale, N.J.: Erlbaum.

Fukui, Naoki and Margaret Speas. 1986. Specifiers and projection. *MIT Working Papers in Linguistics* 8:128–172.

Giorgi, Alessandra and Fabio Pianesi. 1997. *Tense and aspect. From semantics to morphosyntax*. New York: Oxford University Press.

Givón, Talmy. 1984. *Syntax: a functional-typological introduction*. Amsterdam Philadelphia: Benjamins.

Givón, Talmy. 1997. Internal reconstruction: As method, as theory. Institute of Cognitive and Decision Sciences Technical Report No. 98–01. Linguistics Department, University of Oregon.

Goddard, Ives. 1996. Introduction. In Ives Goddard (ed.), *Handbook of North American languages*, vol. 17. Washington, D.C.: Smithsonian Institution. 1–16.

Goddard, Pliny Earle. 1905. The morphology of the Hupa language. *University of California Publications in American Archaeology and Ethnology* vol. 3, 1–344.

Goddard, Pliny Earle. 1912. *Elements of the Kato language. University of California Publications in American Archaeology and Ethnology* 11:1–176.

Golla, Victor. 1970. Hupa grammar. Doctoral dissertation, University of California, Berkeley.

Golla, Victor. 1976. Tututni (Oregon Athapaskan). *International Journal of American Linguistics* 42:217–227.

Golla, Victor. 1985. A short practical grammar of Hupa. Hoopa, Calif.: Hoopa Valley Tribe.

Golla, Victor. 1995. Hupa: 3 versus 4 in disjoint reference. Talk presented at the Workshop on Athapaskan Morphology and Syntax, University of New Mexico, Albuquerque.

Golla, Victor. 1996. Sketch of Hupa, an Athapaskan Language. In Ives Goddard (ed.), *Handbook of North American Indians: Languages*, vol. 17. Washington, D.C.: Smithsonian Institution. 364–389.

Golla, Victor. 1997. The 'indefinite' deictic subject pronoun in California Athabaskan. Talk presented at the Athapaskan Languages Conference, University of Oregon, Eugene.

Greenberg, Joseph. 1966. *Universals of language*. Cambridge, Mass.: MIT Press.

Grimshaw, Jane. 1990. *Argument structure*. Cambridge, Mass.: MIT Press.

Gunlagson, Christine. 1995. Third person object marking in Babine-Witsuwit'en. Talk presented at the Athabaskan Morphosyntax Workshop, University of New Mexico, Albuquerque.

Hale, Kenneth. 1997. Remarks on the syntax of the Navajo verbs. Parts I, II, III. Manuscript, MIT and Navajo Language Academy Linguistics Workshop, Navajo Community College.

Hale, Kenneth. 1998. On endangered languages and the importance of language diversity. In Lenore Grenoble and Lindsay Whaley (eds.), *Endangered languages. Current issues and future prospects*. Cambridge: Cambridge University Press. 192–216.

References

Hale, Kenneth and Samuel J. Keyser. 1993. On argument structure and the lexical expression of syntactic relations. In Kenneth Hale and Samuel J. Keyser (eds.), *The view from Building 20: Essays in linguistics in honor of Sylvain Bromberger.* Cambridge, Mass.: MIT Press. 43–109.

Hale, Kenneth and Paul Platero. 1996. Navajo reflections of a general theory of lexical argument structure. In Eloise Jelinek, Sally Midgette, Keren Rice, and Leslie Saxon (eds.), *Athabaskan language studies. Essays in honor of Robert W. Young.* Albuquerque, N.M.: University of New Mexico Press. 1–14.

Halle, Morris and Alec Marantz. 1993. Distributed morphology and the pieces of inflection. In Kenneth Hale and Samuel Jay Keyser (eds.), *The view from Building 20: Essays in linguistics in honor of Sylvain Bromberger.* Cambridge, Mass.: MIT Press. 111–176.

Halpern, Aaron. 1992. On the placement and morphology of clitics. Doctoral dissertation, Stanford University.

Hardy, Frank. 1979. Navajo aspectual verb stem variation. Doctoral dissertation, University of New Mexico.

Hargus, Sharon. 1988. *The lexical phonology of Sekani.* New York: Garland.

Hargus, Sharon. 1991. The disjunct boundary in Babine-WitsuWit'en. *International Journal of American Linguistics* 57:487–513.

Hargus, Sharon. 1995a. Interactions of phonology and morphology in Athabaskan languages. Paper presented at the Workshop on the Morphology-Syntax Interface in Athapaskan Languages, University of New Mexico, Albuquerque.

Hargus, Sharon. 1995b. The areal prefix in Witsuwit'en. Talk presented at the Athapaskan Conference, University of New Mexico, Albuquerque.

Hargus, Sharon. 1997. The Witsuwit'en disjunct morphemes: clitics or affixes? In Jane Hill, P.J. Mistry, and Lyle Campbell (eds.), *The life of language. Papers in linguistics in honor of William Bright.* Berlin: Mouton de Gruyter. 385–412.

Hargus, Sharon. Forthcoming. *The phonology and morphology of Witsuwit'en.*

Hargus, Sharon and Siri Tuttle. 1997. Augmentation as affixation in Athabaskan languages. *Phonology* 14:177–220.

Hoijer, Harry. 1946a. The Apachean verb, part III: The classifiers. *International Journal of American Linguistics* 12:51–59.

Hoijer, Harry. 1946b. Chiricahua Apache. In Harry Hoijer (ed.), *Linguistic structures of Native America.* New York: Viking Fund. 55–85.

Hoijer, Harry. 1966. Galice Athapaskan: A grammatical sketch. *International Journal of American Linguistics* 32:320–327.

Hoijer, Harry. 1971. Athapaskan morphology. In Jesse Sawyer (ed.), *Studies in American Indian languages.* Berkeley, Calif.: University of California Press. 113–147.

Hopper, Paul J. and Sandra A. Thompson. 1980. Transitivity in grammar and discourse. *Language* 56:251–299.

Howard, Philip. 1990. *A dictionary of the verbs of South Slavey.* Yellowknife, Northwest Territories: Department of Culture and Communication.

Hymes, Dell. 1956. Na-Dene and positional analysis of categories. *American Anthropologist* 58:624–638.

Inkelas, Sharon. 1993. Nimboran position class morphology. *Natural Language and Linguistic Theory* 11:559–624.

Jackendoff, Ray. 1972. *Semantic interpretation in generative grammar*. Cambridge, Mass.: MIT Press.
Jelinek, Eloise. 1993. Ergative 'splits' and argument type. In Jonathan Bobaljik and Colin Phillips (eds.), *Papers on Case and agreement* 1. *MIT Working Papers in Linguistics* 18:15–42.
Jelinek, Eloise 1995. Quantification in Straits Salish. In Emmon Bach, Eloise Jelinek, Angelika Kratzer, and Barbara Partee (eds.), *Quantification in natural languages*, vol. 2. Dordrecht: Kluwer. 487–540.
Jelinek, Eloise and MaryAnn Willie. 1996. 'Psych' verbs in Navajo. In Eloise Jelinek, Sally Midgette, Keren Rice, and Leslie Saxon (eds.), *Athabaskan language studies. Essays in honor of Robert W. Young*. Albuquerque, N.M.: University of New Mexico Press. 15–34.
Jetté, Jules. 1906. On the language of the Ten'a. Manuscript, Crosby Archives, Gonzaga University file 2, drawer 13, microfilm 19:19–234.
Jones, Eliza and Jules Jetté. Forthcoming. *Koyukon Athabaskan dictionary*. Fairbanks, Alaska: Alaska Native Language Center.
Jung, Dagmar. 1995. Distributive in Jicarilla Apache: Between aspect and number. Paper presented at the Athabaskan Language Conference, University of New Mexico, Albuquerque.
Kari, James. 1973. *Navajo verb prefix phonology*. Doctoral dissertation, University of New Mexico.
Kari, James. 1975. The disjunct boundary in the Navajo and Tanaina verb prefix complexes. *International Journal of American Linguistics* 41:330–345.
Kari, James. 1979. *Athabaskan verb theme categories: Ahtna*. Alaska Native Language Center Research Papers no. 2. Fairbanks, Alaska: Alaska Native Language Center.
Kari, James. 1989. Affix positions and zones in the Athapaskan verb complex: Ahtna and Navajo. *International Journal of American Linguistics* 55:424–454.
Kari, James. 1990. *Ahtna Athabaskan dictionary*. Fairbanks, Alaska: Alaska Native Language Center.
Kari, James. 1992. Some concepts in Ahtna Athabaskan word formation. In Mark Aronoff (ed.), *Morphology now*. Albany, N.Y.: SUNY Press. 107–132.
Kari, James. 1993. Diversity in morpheme order in several Athabaskan languages: Notes on the gh-qualifier. In *Proceedings of the Berkeley Linguistic Society* 19, 50–56.
Kemmer, Suzanne. 1993. *The middle voice*. Amsterdam: Benjamins.
Kenny, Anthony. 1963. *Action, emotion, and will*. London: Routledge and Kegan Paul.
Kibrik, Andrej A. 1993. Transitivity increase in Athabaskan languages. In Bernard Comrie and Maria Polinsky (eds.), *Causatives and transitivity*. Amsterdam and Philadelphia: Benjamins. 47–67.
Kibrik, Andrej A. 1995. Inflection versus derivation and the template for Athabaskan verb morphology. Paper presented at the Workshop on the Morphology-Syntax Interface in Athapaskan Languages, University of New Mexico, Albuquerque.
Kibrik, Andrej A. 1996. Transitivity decrease in Navajo and Athabaskan: Actor-affecting propositional derivations. In Eloise Jelinek, Sally Midgette, Keren Rice, and Leslie Saxon (eds.), *Athabaskan language studies. Essays in honor of Robert W. Young*. Albuquerque, N.M.: University of New Mexico Press. 259–303.
Koopman, Hilda and Dominique Sportiche. 1991. The position of subjects. *Lingua* 84: 211–258.

Krauss, Michael. 1964. Proto-Athapaskan-Eyak and the problem of Na-Dene I: The phonology. *International Journal of American Linguistics* 30:118–131.

Krauss, Michael. 1965. Proto-Athapaskan-Eyak and the problem of Na-Dene II: The morphology. *International Journal of American Linguistics* 31:18–28.

Krauss, Michael. 1969. On the classifiers in the Athabaskan, Eyak, and Tlingit verb. Indiana University Publications in Anthropology and Linguistics 23/24. *Supplement to International Journal of American Linguistics* 35:49–83.

Krauss, Michael. 1978. Athabaskan tone. Manuscript, Alaska Native Language Center, University of Alaska, Fairbanks.

Krauss, Michael and Victor Golla. 1981. Northern Athapaskan languages. In June Helm (ed.), *Subarctic*. Washington, D.C.: Smithsonian Institution. 67–85.

Kuroda, S.-Y. 1988. Whether we agree or not: A comparative syntax of English and Japanese. *Lingvisticae Investigationes* 12:1–47.

Langacker, Ronald. 1969. Pronominalization and the chain of command. In David Reibel and Sanford Schane (ed.), *Modern studies in English*. Englewood Cliffs, N.J.: Prentice-Hall. 160–186.

Lapointe, Steven G. 1997. The Navajo deictic subject marker and the generation of inflections. In *Proceedings of the West Coast Conference on Formal Linguistics*. 15:289–303.

Larson, Richard. 1988. On the double object construction. *Linguistic Inquiry* 19:335–391.

Leer, Jeff. 1979. *Proto-Athapaskan verb stem variation I: Phonology*. Alaska Native Language Center Research Papers no. 1. Fairbanks, Alaska; Alaska Native Language Center.

Leer, Jeff. 1990. The Tlingit anaphoric system and the typology of voice systems. Paper presented at the Athapaskan Linguistics Conference, Vancouver, British Columbia.

Leer, Jeff. 1995. Class notes, Comparative phonology of Athabaskan. LSA Linguistic Institute, University of New Mexico.

Leer, Jeff. 1996. The negative-irrealis category in Athabaskan-Eyak-Tlingit. Paper presented at the Swarthmore Conference on Athabaskan Syntax and Semantics. Swarthmore College.

Li, Fang-Kuei. 1930. *Mattole, an Athabaskan language*. Chicago: University of Chicago Press.

Li, Fang-Kuei. 1946. Chipewyan. In Harry Hoijer (ed.), *Linguistic structures of Native America*. New York: Viking Fund. 398–423.

Lieber, Rochelle. 1980. On the organization of the lexicon. Doctoral dissertation, MIT.

Marantz, Alex. 1984. *On the nature of grammatical relations*. Cambridge, Mass.: MIT Press.

Matthews, P.H. 1991. *Morphology* (second edition). Cambridge: Cambridge University Press.

Matthewson, Lisa. 1996. Determiner systems and quantificational strategies: Evidence from Salish. Doctoral dissertation, University of British Columbia.

McCawley, James D. 1988. *The syntactic phenomena of English*, vol. 2. Chicago: University of Chicago Press.

McDonough, Joyce. 1989. Argument structure and the Athabaskan 'classifier' prefix. In *Proceedings of the West Coast Conference on Formal Linguistics* 8, 220–236.

McDonough, Joyce. 1990. Topics in the phonology and morphology of Navajo verbs. Doctoral dissertation, University of Massachusetts, Amherst.
Michaelis, Laura A. 1998. *Aspectual grammar and past-time reference*. London: Routledge.
Midgette, Sally. 1995. *The Navajo progressive in discourse: A study in temporal semantics*. New York: Lang.
Midgette, Sally. 1996. Lexical aspect in Navajo: The telic property. In Eloise Jelinek, Sally Midgette, Keren Rice, and Leslie Saxon (eds.), *Athabaskan language studies. Essays in honor of Robert W. Young*. Albuquerque, N.M.: University of New Mexico Press. 305–330.
Mithun, Marianne. 1986. On the nature of noun incorporation. *Language* 62:32–37.
Moore, Patrick and Angela Wheelock (eds.) 1990. *Wolverine myths and visions: Dene traditions from Northern Alberta*. Lincoln, Nebraska: University of Nebraska Press.
Moravcsik, Edith A. 1978. Agreement. In Joseph H. Greenberg (ed.), *Universals of human language*. Stanford, Calif.: Stanford University Press. 331–374.
Morice, Adrian G. 1932. *The Carrier language*. Collection Internationale de Monographs Linguistiques, Anthropos, vol. 9. Vienna.
Myers, Scott. 1987. Tone and the structure of words in Shona. Doctoral dissertation, University of Massachusetts, Amherst.
Napoli, Donna Jo. 1993. *Syntax. Theory and problems*. New York: Oxford University Press.
Partee, Barbara. 1987. Noun phrase interpretation and type-shifting principles. In J. Groenendijk, D. de Jongh, and M. Stokhof (eds.), *Studies in discourse representation theory and the theory of generalized quantifiers*. Foris: Dordrecht. 115–143.
Partee, Barbara. 1991. Adverbial quantification and event structure. In *Proceedings of the Berkeley Linguistic Society* 17, 439–456.
Partee, Barbara, Emmon Bach, and Angelika Kratzer. 1987. Quantification: a cross-linguistic perspective. NSF proposal. Amherst, Mass.: University of Massachusetts.
Perlmutter, David. 1971. *Deep and surface structure constraints in syntax*. New York: Holt, Reinhart, and Winston.
Platero, Paul. 1978. Missing noun phrases in Navajo. Doctoral dissertation, MIT.
Poser, William J. 1996. Noun classification in Carrier. Paper presented at the Winter Meeting of the Society for the Study of the Indigenous Languages of the Americas, San Diego, Calif.
Potter, Brian. 1996. Minimalism and the Mirror Principle. In *Proceedings of NELS* 26, 289–302.
Potter, Brian. 1997. Wh/indefinites and the structure of the clause in Western Apache. Doctoral dissertation, UCLA.
Prince, Alan and Paul Smolensky. 1993. Optimality Theory: Constraint interaction in generative grammar. Manuscript, Rutgers University and University of Colorado, Boulder.
Pustejovsky, James J. 1991. The syntax of event structure. *Cognition* 41:47–81.
Pustejovsky, James J. 1995. *The generative lexicon*. Cambridge, Mass.: MIT Press.
Randoja, Tiina. 1990. The phonology and morphology of Halfway River Beaver. Doctoral dissertation, University of Ottawa.
Reichard, Gladys. 1951. *Navajo grammar*. Publications of the American Ethnological Society no. 23. New York: J.J. Augustin.

Reichenbach, Hans. 1947. *Elements of symbolic logic*. London: Macmillan.
Reinhart, Tanya. 1976. The syntactic domain of anaphora. Doctoral dissertation, MIT.
Rice, Keren. 1989. *A grammar of Slave*. Berlin: Mouton de Gruyter.
Rice, Keren. 1991a. Intransitives in Slave (Northern Athapaskan): Arguments for unaccusatives. *International Journal of American Linguistics* 57:51–69.
Rice, Keren. 1991b. Predicting the order of the disjunct morphemes in the Athapaskan languages. *Toronto Working Papers in Linguistics* 11:99–121.
Rice, Keren. 1992. On deriving rule domains: The Athapaskan case. In *Proceedings of the West Coast Conference on Formal Linguistics* 10, 417–430.
Rice, Keren. 1993. The structure of the Slave (northern Athapaskan) verb. In Sharon Hargus and Ellen Kaisse (eds.), *Issues in lexical phonology*. San Diego: Academic. 145–171.
Rice, Keren. 1998. Slave (Northern Athapaskan). In Andrew Spencer and Arnold Zwicky (eds.), *The handbook of morphology*. Oxford: Blackwell. 648–689.
Rice, Keren. 1999. Another look at the Athapaskan yi/bi pronouns: Evidence from Slave. Paper presented at the West Coast Conference on Formal Linguistics, University of Arizona, Tucson, Arizona.
Rice, Keren. Forthcoming a. Monadic verbs and argument structure in Ahtna, Navajo, and Slave. In Theodore Fernald and Paul Platero (eds.), *The Athabaskan languages: Perspectives on a Native American language family*. Oxford: Oxford University Press.
Rice, Keren. Forthcoming b. Voice and valence in the Athapaskan family. In Alexandra Aikenvald and R.M.W. Dixon (eds.), *Changing valency: Case studies in transitivity*. Cambridge: Cambridge University Press.
Rice, Keren and Leslie Saxon. 1991. A structural analysis of *y in Athapaskan. Paper presented at the Athapaskan Conference, University of California at Santa Cruz.
Rice, Keren and Leslie Saxon. 1993. Paradigmatic and syntactic mechanisms for syntactic change in Athapaskan. In *Proceedings of the Berkeley Linguistic Society: Special Session on Syntactic Issues in Native American Languages*.148–159.
Rice, Keren and Leslie Saxon. 1994. The subject position in Athapaskan languages. In Heidi Harley and Colin Phillips (eds.), *The morphology-syntax connection. MIT Working Papers in Linguistics* 22:173–195.
Rice, Keren and Leslie Saxon. 1997. Re-examining na-iterative in Slave (Athapaskan). Talk presented at the Canadian Linguistic Association, Memorial University, St. John's, Newfoundland.
Richardson, Murray. 1968. *Chipewyan grammar*. Cold Lake, Alberta: Northern Canada Evangelical Mission.
Ritter, Elizabeth. 1995. On the syntactic category of pronouns and agreement. *Natural Language and Linguistic Theory* 13:405–443.
Ritter, Elizabeth. 1996. Pronouns from the inside out. Talk presented at the University of Toronto.
Ritter, Elizabeth and Sara Thomas Rosen. 1993. Deriving causation. *Natural Language and Linguistic Theory* 11:519–555.
Sandoval, Merton and Eloise Jelinek. 1989. The bi-construction and pronominal arguments in Apachean. In Eung-Do Cook and Keren Rice (eds.), *Athapaskan linguistics: Current perspectives on a language family*. Berlin: Mouton de Gruyter. 335–378.
Sapir, Edward. 1915. The Na-Dene languages, a preliminary report. *American Anthropologist* 17:534–559.

Sapir, Edward. 1929. Central and North American Languages. *Encyclopedia Britannica* (4th edition), vol 5, 138–141.

Sapir, Edward and Harry Hoijer. 1967. *The phonology and morphology of the Navaho language*. University of California Publications in Linguistics 40. Berkeley and Los Angeles: University of California Press.

Saxon, Leslie. 1984. Disjoint anaphora and the binding theory. In *Proceedings of the West Coast Conference on Formal Linguistics* 3, 242–251.

Saxon, Leslie. 1986. The syntax of pronouns in Dogrib (Athapaskan): Some theoretical consequences. Doctoral dissertation, University of California, San Diego.

Saxon, Leslie. 1989a. Agreement in Dogrib: Inflection or cliticization? In Donna Gerdts and Karin Michelson (eds.), *Theoretical perspectives on Native American languages*. Albany, N.Y.: SUNY Press. 149–162.

Saxon, Leslie. 1989b. Lexical versus syntactic projection: The configurationality of Slave. In Eung-Do Cook and Keren Rice (eds.), *Athapaskan linguistics: Current perspectives on a language family*. Berlin: Mouton de Gruyter. 379–406.

Saxon, Leslie. 1993. A personal use of the Athapaskan 'impersonal' ts'e-. *International Journal of American Linguistics* 59:342–354.

Saxon, Leslie. 1995. Complex pronominals, disjoint anaphora, and indexing. Talk presented at the Annual Meeting of the Linguistic Society of America, New Orleans.

Saxon, Leslie. 1998. Complement clauses in Dogrib. In Pamela Munro and Leanne Hinton (eds.), *Studies in American Indian languages: Description and theory*. Berkeley, Calif.: University of California Press.

Saxon, Leslie and Keren Rice. 1993. On subject-verb constituency: Evidence from Athapaskan languages. In *Proceedings of the West Coast Conference on Formal Linguistics* 11, 434–450.

Schauber, Ellen. 1975. Theoretical responses to Navajo questions. Doctoral dissertation, MIT.

Siegel, Dorothy. 1974. Topics in English morphology. Doctoral dissertation, MIT.

Siegel, Dorothy. 1978. The Adjacency Constraint and the theory of morphology. In *Proceedings of NELS* 8, 189–197.

Simpson, Jane and M. Withgott. 1986. Pronominal clitic clusters and templates. In Hagit Borer (ed.), *Syntax and semantics 19: The syntax of pronominal clitics*. New York: Academic. 149–174.

Smith, Carlota. 1991. *The parameter of aspect*. Dordrecht: Kluwer.

Smith, Carlota. 1996a. Aspectual categories of Navajo. *International Journal of American Linguistics* 62:237–263.

Smith, Carlota. 1996b. Lexical semantics of Navajo verb bases. Talk presented at the Athabaskan Conference on Syntax and Semantics, Swarthmore College.

Smith, Carlota. 1997. *The parameter of aspect* (second edition). Dordrecht: Kluwer.

Speas, Margaret. 1984. Navajo prefixes and word structure typology. In *MIT Working Papers in Linguistics* 7:86–109.

Speas, Margaret. 1987. Position classes and morphological universals. In Paul Kroeber and Robert E. Moore (eds.), *Native American languages and grammatical typology*. Bloomington, Ind.: Indiana University Linguistics Club. 199–214.

Speas, Margaret. 1990. *Phrase structure in natural language*. Dordrecht: Kluwer.

Speas, Margaret. 1991a. Functional heads and inflectional morphemes. *The Linguistic Review* 8:233–273.

Speas, Margaret. 1991b. Functional heads and the Mirror Principle. *Lingua* 84:181–214.
Speas, Margaret. 1995. Clause structure in Athapaskan languages. Paper presented at the Workshop on the Morphology-Syntax Interface in Athapaskan Languages, University of New Mexico, Albuquerque.
Speas, Margaret and Evangeline Parsons Yazzie. 1996. Quantifiers and the position of noun phrases in Navajo. In Eloise Jelinek, Sally Midgette, Keren Rice, and Leslie Saxon (eds.), *Athabaskan language studies. Essays in honor of Robert W. Young.* Albuquerque, N.M.: University of New Mexico Press. 35–80.
Spencer, Andrew. 1991. *Morphological theory: An introduction to word structure in generative grammar.* Oxford: Blackwell.
Sportiche, Dominique. 1988. A theory of floating quantifiers and its corollaries for constituent structure. *Linguistic Inquiry* 19:425–449.
Sproat, Richard. 1998. Morphology as component or module: Mapping principle approaches. In Andrew Spencer and Arnold Zwicky (eds.), *The handbook of morphology.* Oxford: Blackwell. 335–348.
Stanley, Richard. 1969. The phonology of the Navaho verb. Doctoral dissertation, MIT.
Steele, Susan. 1978. Word order variation: A typology study. In Joseph H. Greenberg, Charles A. Ferguson, and Edith A. Moravcsik (eds.), *Universals of human language IV: Syntax.* Stanford, Calif.: Stanford University Press. 583–623.
Story, Gillian. 1989. The Athapaskan first duoplural subject prefix. In Eung-Do Cook and Keren Rice (eds.), *Athapaskan linguistics: Current perspectives on a language family.* Berlin: Mouton de Gruyter. 487–531.
Stump, Gregory T. 1998. Inflection. In Andrew Spencer and Arnold Zwicky (eds.), *The handbook of morphology.* Oxford: Blackwell. 13–43.
Talmy, Leonard. 1987. Lexicalization patterns: Semantic structure in lexical forms. In *Typologies and universals.* Cognitive Science Report No. 47. Berkeley, Calif.: University of California at Berkeley.
Tenenbaum, Joan. 1978. Morphology and semantics of the Tanaina verb. Doctoral dissertation, Columbia University.
Tenny, Carol L. 1994. *Aspectual roles and the syntax-semantics interface.* Dordrecht: Kluwer.
Thom, Margaret and Ethel Blondin-Townsend (eds.). 1987. *Nahecho keh/Our elders.* Slavey Research Project, Government of the Northwest Territories.
Thomason, Sarah Grey. 1980. Morphological instability, with and without language contact. In Jacek Fisiak (ed.), *Historical morphology.* Berlin: Mouton de Gruyter. 359–372.
Thompson, Chad. 1977. Koyukon verb prefixes. M.A. thesis, University of Alaska, Fairbanks.
Thompson, Chad. 1989a. Voice and obviation in Athabaskan and other languages. Doctoral dissertation, University of Oregon, Eugene.
Thompson, Chad. 1989b. Pronouns and voice in Koyukon Athabaskan: A text-based study. *International Journal of American Linguistics* 55:1–24.
Thompson, Chad. 1990. The diachrony of the deictics in Athabaskan. Presented at the Athapaskan Conference, University of British Columbia, Vancouver.
Thompson, Chad. 1991. The low topicality prefix *k'i-* in Koyukon. *Studies in Language* 15:59–84.

Thompson, Chad. 1993. The areal prefix *hu-* in Koyukon Athapaskan. *International Journal of American Linguistics* 59:315–333.

Thompson, Chad. 1996a. The Na-Dene middle voice: An impersonal source of the D-element. *International Journal of American Linguistics* 62:351–378.

Thompson, Chad. 1996b. The history and function of the yi-/bi- alternation in Athabaskan. In Eloise Jelinek, Sally Midgette, Keren Rice, and Leslie Saxon (eds.), *Athabaskan language studies: Essays in honor of Robert W. Young.* Albuquerque, N.M.: University of New Mexico Press. 81–100.

Thompson, Chad. 1996c. Iconicity and word order in Koyukon Athabaskan. Talk presented at the Athabaskan Conference on Syntax and Semantics. Swarthmore College.

Travis, Lisa de Mena. 1992. Two quirks of structure: non-projecting heads and the Mirror Image Principle. *Journal of Linguistics* 28:469–484.

Tuttle, Siri. 1996. Direct objects in Salcha Athabaskan. In Eloise Jelinek, Sally Midgette, Keren Rice, and Leslie Saxon (eds.), *Athabaskan language studies. Essays in honor of Robert W. Young.* Albuquerque, N.M.: University of New Mexico Press. 101–121.

Van Valin, Robert D., Jr. 1993. A synopsis of Role and Reference Grammar. In Robert D. Van Valin, Jr. (ed.), *Advances in Role and Reference Grammar.* Amsterdam and Philadelphia: Benjamins. 1–164.

Vendler, Zeno. 1967. *Linguistics in philosophy.* Ithaca, N.Y.: Cornell University Press.

Verkuyl, Henk. 1972. *On the compositional nature of the aspects.* Dordrecht: Reidel.

Verkuyl, Henk. 1993. *A theory of aspectuality: The interaction between temporal and atemporal structure.* Cambridge: Cambridge University Press.

Whorf, Benjamin Lee. 1932. The structure of the Athabascan languages. Manuscript, Sterling Memorial Library, Yale University.

Whorf, Benjamin Lee. 1956. *Language, thought, and reality: Selected writings of Benjamin Lee Whorf* (edited by J. Carroll). Cambridge, Mass.: MIT Press.

Willie, MaryAnn. 1991. Pronouns and obviation in Navajo. Doctoral dissertation, University of Arizona.

Willie, MaryAnn and Eloise Jelinek. 1996. Navajo as a discourse configurational language. Paper presented at the Conference on Athabaskan Syntax and Semantics, Swarthmore College.

Willie, MaryAnn and Leslie Saxon. 1995. Third person forms in Athapaskan languages: An examination of the 'fourth' person. Paper presented at the Workshop on the Morphology-Syntax Interface in Athapaskan Languages, University of New Mexico, Albuquerque.

Yip, Moira. 1998. Identity avoidance in phonology and morphology. In Steven G. Lapointe, Diane K. Brentari, and Patrick M. Farrell (eds.), Morphology and its Relation to Phonology and Syntax. Stanford: CSLI Publications. 216–246.

Young, Robert W. 1995. Navajo Verb Morphology: An Overview. manuscript, University of New Mexico.

Young, Robert W. 1997. The indefinite pronoun in Navajo. manuscript.

Young, Robert W. and William Morgan Sr. 1943. *The Navajo Language, Grammar, and Dictionary.* Phoenix: Bureau of Indian Affairs.

Young, Robert W. and William Morgan Sr. 1987. *The Navajo Language: A Grammar and Colloquial Dictionary.* (Second edition). Albuquerque: University of New Mexico Press.

Young, Robert W. and William Morgan Sr., with Sally Midgette. 1992. *Analytical Lexicon of Navajo.* Albuquerque, New Mexico.

Name Index

Aikenvald, Alexandra, 282
Allen, Margaret, 2
Anderson, Stephen, 2, 18, 74, 175, 295, 388
Arce-Aranales, Manuel, 142
Archangeli, Diana, 17, 395
Aronoff, Mark, 9, 28
Auger, Julie, 3
Axelrod, Melissa, 50, 51, 60, 70, 71, 106, 110, 119, 120, 128, 154, 165, 167, 214, 249, 253, 257, 266, 268, 276, 277, 279, 280, 281, 284, 292, 294, 299, 300, 301, 305, 321, 323, 332, 341, 345, 374, 403, 427, 429

Baker, Mark, 1, 4, 18, 24, 25, 29, 141, 169, 175, 215, 242, 361, 365
Beard, Robert, 2, 28, 281, 295, 299, 388
Benveniste, Emile, 182
Binnick, Robert, 251
Blondin-Townsend, Ethel, 188, 190
Bonet, Eulàlia, 3, 16
Borer, Hagit, 388
Bouchard, Denis, 127
Brentari, Diane, 362
Brunson, Barbara, 24, 83
Bybee, Joan, 2, 4, 24, 75, 78, 175, 250, 282–283, 295, 296, 298, 299, 300, 302, 314, 347

Carrier-Duncan, Jill, 96
Carter, Richard, 27, 127

Cherchia, Gennaro, 4
Comrie, Bernard, 246, 349, 365
Cook, Eung-Do, 22, 34, 46, 51, 66, 79, 148, 180, 184, 194, 195, 198, 218, 224, 225, 227, 228, 229, 257, 297, 310, 320, 345, 402, 404, 416, 417, 427, 428
Corbett, Greville, 325
Cowper, Elizabeth, 27, 127
Craig, Colette, 40
Croft, William, 3, 347
Cummins, Sarah, 3, 16, 27, 127, 143

Dahl, Osten, 246
Davidson, William, 403
Davis, Henry, 430
Davis, Philip, 59
Demirdache, Hamida, 430
Denham, Kristin, 22, 23
Denny, Peter, 59
Diesing, Molly, 193, 231, 348, 349, 361
Dixon, R.M.W., 282
Dowty, David, 251

Embick, David, 140
Ernst, Thomas, 113
Evans, Nick, 65

Faltz, Leonard, 59
Fillmore, Charles, 96
Foley, William, 4, 24, 25, 35, 75, 175
Fox, Barbara, 142

443

Frawley, William, 4, 34, 35, 42, 55, 59, 61
Fukui, Naoki, 211

Georgi, Alessandra, 349
Givón, Talmy, 96, 371, 382, 404
Goddard, Ives, 406
Goddard, Pliny Earle, 128, 240, 425
Golla, Victor, 22, 38, 61–62, 131, 145, 150, 152, 153, 159, 160–161, 163, 203, 225, 236, 237, 238, 239, 240, 241, 242, 253, 308, 309, 311, 320, 330, 331, 332, 379, 403, 404, 416, 424, 425
Greenberg, Joseph, 4
Grimshaw, Jane, 35, 127
Gunlagson, Christine, 22

Hale, Kenneth, 3, 41, 133, 135, 140, 418
Halle, Morris, 175, 299, 388
Halpern, Aaron, 17
Hardy, Frank, 427
Hargus, Sharon, 4, 9, 12, 13, 14, 17, 18, 34, 46, 50, 51, 55, 56, 57, 60, 66, 67, 72, 73, 91, 92, 101, 102, 115–116, 121, 122, 123, 126, 142, 164, 176, 178, 199, 201, 202, 229, 240, 248, 296, 297, 303, 316, 318, 320, 332, 340, 348, 350, 351, 352, 353, 362, 363, 364, 371, 390, 402, 403, 421, 422, 428, 430
Harrington, J.P, 424
Hockett, Charles, 193
Hoijer, Harry, 15, 84, 128, 152, 320, 356, 396, 403, 404
Hopper, Paul, 169
Howard, Philip, 86, 88, 90, 112, 113, 114, 267, 404

Inkelas, Sharon, 10

Jackendoff, Ray, 24, 96, 112
Jelinek, Eloise, 24, 26, 41, 75, 180, 193, 211, 242, 348, 349, 361, 415, 424
Jetté, Jules, 129, 131, 134, 136, 137, 139, 142, 144, 145, 148, 153, 155, 157, 162, 177, 416
Jones, Eliza, 129, 131, 134, 136, 137, 139, 141, 144, 145, 148, 153, 155, 157, 162, 416

Jung, Dagmar, 44, 45, 379

Kari, James, 2, 4, 10, 15, 16, 17, 18, 26, 34, 37, 38, 39, 40, 49, 51, 53, 55, 56, 66, 67, 69, 70, 71, 76, 79, 84, 85, 86, 87, 91, 93, 99, 101, 106, 107, 108, 110–111, 117, 118, 128, 129, 134, 137, 138, 139, 141, 142, 144, 145, 146, 147, 148, 149, 150, 153, 154, 162, 165, 166, 167, 168, 177, 179, 200, 213, 214, 215, 217, 219, 225, 227, 231, 232, 234, 235, 253, 257, 276, 279, 280, 281, 284, 292, 296, 297, 300, 301, 303, 304, 311, 312, 313, 314, 315, 316, 318, 319, 327, 329, 330, 331, 332, 334, 335, 345, 346, 353, 356, 357, 358, 362, 365, 371, 374–375, 376, 377, 378, 389, 390, 395, 401, 402, 415, 420, 421, 425, 426, 427, 428, 429, 434, 436
Kemmer, Suzanne, 143–144
Kenny, Anthony, 347
Kibrik, Andrej, 74, 127, 128, 133, 138, 142, 144, 162, 165, 167, 219, 220, 221, 223, 238, 295, 391–392, 401, 404, 420
Koopman, Hilda, 211
Krauss, Michael, 21, 26, 256, 257, 377, 395
Kuroda S.-Y., 211

Langacker, Ronald, 25, 83
Langendoen, Terry, 18, 395
Lapointe, Steven, 175, 181
Larson, Richard, 77, 96–97, 110
Leer, Jeff, 21, 179, 211, 216, 217, 218, 219, 279, 298, 303, 314, 328, 379, 427
Li, Fang-Kuei, 45, 374, 402, 403
Lieber, Rochelle, 2

Marantz, Alex, 25, 29, 110, 175, 213, 299, 388
Matthews, P. H., 362
Matthewson, Lisa, 41, 59
McCawley, James, 24
McConnell-Ginet, Sally, 4
McDonough, Joyce, 18, 127, 176, 178, 364
Meillet, Andre, 396

Name Index

Michaelis, Laura, 349
Midgette, Sally, 84, 95, 97, 132, 135, 136, 137, 138, 155, 158, 159, 168, 268, 297, 337, 357, 403, 427
Mithun, Marianne, 120
Moore, Patrick, 186, 187, 188, 189, 191
Moravscik, Edith, 182
Morgan, William, 13, 15, 43, 44, 68, 84, 85, 87, 89, 94, 95, 96, 97, 102, 103, 104, 105, 130, 132, 135, 136, 137, 138, 145, 148, 150, 151, 153, 155, 158, 159, 168, 197, 213, 220, 221, 223, 233, 234, 256, 257, 297, 306, 307, 334, 336, 337, 338, 355, 356, 357, 358, 377, 378, 403, 416, 418, 419, 420, 421, 422
Morice, Adrian, 48, 49, 54, 66, 67, 68, 72, 84, 87, 88, 89, 90, 92, 97, 98, 108, 108–109, 111, 116, 117, 119, 133, 135, 137, 138, 145, 147, 151, 154, 155, 163, 328, 417
Myers, Scott, 1

Napoli, Donna Jo, 26

Pagliuca, William, 250
Partee, Barbara, 41, 192, 193
Perkins, Revere, 250
Perlmutter, David, 3
Pianesi, Fabio, 349
Platero, Paul, 3, 22, 133, 135, 140
Poser, William, 199, 316, 326, 327, 329
Potter, Brian, 17, 18, 23, 180, 242, 243, 303
Prince, Alan, 18
Pustejovsky, James, 35, 252

Randoja, Tiina, 4, 15, 34, 47, 51, 54, 56, 66, 69, 71, 76, 116, 117, 118, 402
Reichard, Gladys, 84, 85, 356
Reichenbach, Hans, 246
Reinhart, Tanya, 25, 82
Rice, Keren, 1, 5, 9, 12, 18, 22, 23, 26, 27, 34, 38, 47, 48, 50, 51, 52, 57, 58, 62, 63, 65, 74, 76, 78, 84, 86, 89, 93, 98, 99, 107, 109, 111, 114, 119, 127, 128, 130, 132, 136, 141, 142, 144, 147, 148, 149, 151, 152, 153, 156, 176, 178, 179, 180, 181, 182, 184, 185, 187, 188, 189, 191, 192, 199, 203, 204, 205, 206, 211, 213, 215, 216, 217, 220, 222, 225, 226, 227, 229, 236, 243, 244, 250, 253, 254, 255, 257, 268, 270, 276, 279, 280, 281, 284, 292–294, 320, 332, 345, 347, 361, 374, 381, 393, 404, 416, 421, 422, 423, 424, 427, 430
Richardson, Murray, 402
Ritter, Elizabeth, 126, 127, 139–140, 142, 192, 193
Roberges, Yves, 3, 16
Rosen, Sara, 126, 127, 139–140, 142

Sandoval, Merton, 75, 180, 242
Sapir, Edward, 15, 26, 84, 356, 396, 424
Saunders, Ross, 59
Saxon, Leslie, 22, 27, 62, 65, 109, 156, 180, 181, 182, 184, 187, 189, 191, 192, 198, 199, 200, 201, 203, 204, 205, 211, 213, 216, 217, 220, 225, 226, 227, 228, 230, 236, 242, 243, 244, 350, 421, 422, 423, 424
Schauber, Ellen, 22
Siegel, Dorothy, 2
Simpson, Jane, 10, 11, 14, 19
Smith, Carlota, 35, 146, 247, 251, 252–253, 260, 276, 280, 282, 284, 285, 306, 347, 349, 391, 425, 430
Smolensky, Paul, 18
Speas, Margaret, 1, 5, 9, 18, 24, 26, 27, 74, 75, 76, 78, 175, 180, 211, 242, 393
Spencer, Andrew, 9, 10, 12, 13, 371, 373, 374
Sportiche, Dominique, 211
Sproat, Richard, 24
Stanley, Richard, 142
Story, Gillian, 199, 377, 422
Stump, Gregory, 10, 295, 388

Talmy, Leonard, 35
Tenenbaum, Joan, 47, 51, 53, 66, 67, 196, 197, 218, 219, 225, 227, 229, 332, 341, 403
Tenny, Carol, 35, 127, 343–344, 347, 425
Thom, Margaret, 188, 190

Thomason, Sarah, 396–397
Thompson, Chad, 55, 56, 57, 58, 119, 127, 128, 142, 144, 145, 147, 148, 149, 150, 154, 165, 180, 196, 200, 216, 217, 218, 219, 223, 229, 230, 231, 236, 239, 380, 417–418, 423, 424, 428
Thompson, Sandra, 169
Travis, Lisa, 9
Tuttle, Siri, 17, 18, 130, 176, 178, 180, 248, 318, 348, 364, 430

Uriba-Extebarria, Myriam, 430

Van Valin, Robert, 4, 24, 25, 35, 75, 175, 425
Vendler, Zeno, 251
Verkuyl, Henk, 425

Wheelock, Angela, 186, 187, 188, 189, 191
Whorf, Benjamin Lee, 15
Willie, MaryAnn, 24, 26, 75, 180, 190, 197, 199, 200, 201, 211, 242, 415, 421, 422, 424
Withgott, M., 10, 11, 14, 19

Yazzie, Evangeline Parsons, 242
Yip, Moira, 362
Young, Robert, 13, 15, 43, 44, 57, 58, 68, 84, 85, 87, 89, 94, 95, 96, 97, 102, 103, 104, 105, 130, 132, 135, 136, 137, 138, 145, 148, 150, 151, 153, 155, 158, 159, 168, 197, 213, 220, 221, 223, 233, 234, 256, 257, 297, 306, 307, 334, 336, 337, 338, 355, 356, 357, 358, 370, 377, 378, 403, 416, 418, 419, 420, 421, 422, 427

Languages Index

Ahtna, 10, 21, 22, 37, 38, 40, 45, 49, 51, 53, 54, 56, 66, 67, 69, 70, 71, 76, 80, 81, 84, 85–86, 86, 87, 91, 94, 99–100, 101, 108, 109, 110–111, 117, 118, 119, 124, 128, 129, 133, 134, 137, 138–139, 141, 144, 145, 146, 147, 148, 149, 150, 153, 154, 162, 165–167, 168, 179, 199, 200, 213, 214, 215, 216, 217, 219, 224, 225, 227, 231, 232, 233, 234–235, 253, 285, 293, 296–297, 300, 301, 302, 304–306, 306, 310, 311, 312–314, 315–319, 320, 321, 322, 323, 326–327, 329, 330, 331–333, 338, 341, 345, 346, 353, 358, 362, 364, 371, 374, 376, 377, 389, 390, 402, 412, 416, 419, 420, 424, 426, 427–428
Apache, 22, 23, 81, 422

Babine-Witsuwit'en, 22, 23, 49–50, 55–56, 60, 72, 81, 92, 121–122, 122–124, 125, 199, 229, 240, 243, 316, 332–333, 338, 350, 353, 359, 362–363, 371, 376, 377, 390–391, 402, 412, 422
Beaver, 21, 22, 45, 46–47, 51, 54, 56, 66, 67, 69, 71, 80, 112, 115–116, 117, 118, 119, 402, 422

Carrier, 21, 22, 45, 48–49, 54, 60, 66, 67, 68, 72, 81, 86, 87, 88, 89, 90, 92, 97–98, 100, 108–109, 111, 116, 117–118, 119, 121, 133, 135, 137, 138, 144, 147, 151, 154, 155, 163, 199, 314, 316, 326, 327–328, 329, 338, 376, 417, 421
Chilcotin, 195, 224, 225, 226, 321, 402, 428
Chipewyan, 22, 26, 45, 54, 80, 187, 194–195, 196, 321, 322, 374, 402
Chiracahua Apache, 403

Dena'ina, 22, 47, 51, 53, 54, 66, 67, 80, 119, 196, 197, 198, 199, 218, 219, 224, 225, 229, 312, 332–333, 341, 376, 377, 403
Dogrib, 21, 80, 106, 187, 196, 222, 224, 225, 226, 227, 228, 230, 321, 322, 350, 359, 374, 403, 421, 422, 423

Galice, 21, 152, 322, 403, 413
Gwich'in, 314, 376, 422

Holikachuk, 422
Hupa, 22, 38, 61, 62, 81, 131, 132, 145, 150, 152, 153, 159–161, 163–164, 236–244, 245, 253, 304, 308–309, 310, 311–312, 320, 322, 330–331, 332, 342, 365, 377, 378–379, 403, 404, 405, 416, 417, 425

Ingalik, 422

Jicarilla Apache, 44, 45, 54, 379

Kaska, 422

Kato, 236–244, 245, 342, 365, 379–424, 425
Koyukon, 21, 22, 45, 49–50, 51, 54, 56, 58, 60, 69, 70, 71, 80, 81, 106, 119, 120, 129, 131, 134, 136–137, 138, 139, 141, 144, 145, 146, 147, 148, 149, 150–151, 153, 154, 155, 156, 157, 162, 199, 200, 214, 217, 218–219, 222, 223, 224, 225, 227, 229, 231, 232, 233, 242, 253, 257, 266–267, 268, 285, 293, 299, 300, 305–306, 310, 312, 314, 320, 321, 322, 323, 328, 332–333, 338, 341, 345, 374, 376, 377, 403, 416, 417, 418, 422, 423, 424, 427, 429

Mattole, 320, 403
Minto, 22

Na-Dene, 26, 396–397

Navajo, 13, 21, 22, 43, 54, 57–58, 59, 68, 76, 81, 85, 86, 87, 89, 94–98, 100, 102–105, 106, 111, 124, 130, 132, 133, 135–136, 137–138, 145, 148, 150, 151, 153, 155, 158–159, 162, 168, 172, 197, 213, 220–222, 223, 233–234, 235, 242, 256, 296, 297, 304, 306–308, 310, 314, 320, 321, 322, 323, 332–333, 334–338, 345, 355–358, 359, 364, 370, 375, 376, 377–378, 380–381, 391, 403, 404, 405, 412, 413, 415, 416, 417, 418, 419, 420, 421, 422, 424, 427, 428, 429

Proto-Athapaskan, 4, 34, 220, 230, 371, 377

Salcha, 119

Sekani, 14, 21, 22, 45, 46, 51, 54, 55, 56, 66, 67, 72, 73, 80, 81, 91, 101–102, 112, 115–116, 121, 122, 199, 201–202, 296, 321, 322, 332–333, 340, 350–352, 359, 364, 369, 374, 376, 377, 403, 422, 428–429
Slave, 11–12, 21, 22, 23, 35, 36–37, 39, 40, 45, 47–48, 50, 51, 52, 54, 55, 57, 58, 59, 62–65, 68, 69, 70, 71, 76, 77, 80, 86, 88, 90, 92–93, 94, 98–99, 100, 107, 110, 111, 112–115, 116, 119, 130, 132, 133, 136, 139, 141, 144, 146, 147, 149, 151, 152, 153, 156, 172, 178, 179, 181, 182–191, 194, 195, 196, 197, 198, 199, 203–209, 210, 213, 215, 216, 222, 223, 224, 225, 226, 227, 229, 242, 243, 247–251, 253–295, 305, 306, 310, 319, 320, 321, 322, 323, 328, 331, 332–333, 338, 339, 345, 346, 350, 352, 359, 361, 364, 369, 374, 376, 377, 381–382, 383, 404, 405, 413, 416, 419, 421, 422, 423, 424, 426, 427

Tagish, 422
Tahltan, 422
Tanacross, 422
Tanana, Lower, 333
Tanana, Upper, 33, 422
Tolowa, 371, 382, 404
Tututni, 224, 225, 321, 322, 404, 416, 417
Tsuut'ina, 22, 45, 46, 51, 66, 80, 119, 148, 195, 218, 222, 224, 225, 227, 228, 229, 310, 321, 322, 345, 376, 377, 404, 417, 422, 424

Upper Kuskokwim, 422

Western Apache, 242, 243

Subject Index

accomplishment, 177, 251, 252, 254, 256, 257, 258, 259–260, 261–262, 263–265, 267–268, 269, 270, 272–276, 280, 284, 285, 287, 288–289, 290, 293–294, 300, 304, 305, 306, 307, 308, 343, 345–356
achievement, 177, 251–252, 254–255, 256, 257, 258–259, 260, 261–262, 263–264, 269, 270, 272–276, 280, 284, 285, 286, 287, 290, 292, 300, 304, 305, 307, 347
activity, 177, 251–252, 254, 256, 257–258, 260, 261–262, 263–266, 267–268, 269, 270, 271–276, 280, 284, 285, 287–289, 290, 291, 292, 293, 295, 300, 304, 305, 307, 314, 345–346
adverb, 35–41, 268–270, 420
adverb, transportability, 112–115
anaphor, 204–207, 216–220, 224–230, 231, 422, 423
areal, 55–59, 326, 328
aspect, 1, 16, 42, 59, 75, 84, 176, 177, 179, 246–323, 342–350, 410–411, 414
aspect, combinatorics, 310–320
aspect, derived situation type, 285–290; *see also* bisective; consecutive; continuative; diversative; perambulative; persistive; repetitive; reversative
aspect, derived situation/viewpoint type, 290–294; *see also* customary; distributive; progressive

aspect, ordering, 281–283, 310–320, 333–338, 339–341, 359
aspect, situation, 16, 17, 59, 177, 246, 251–283, 284, 286–290, 299, 304–308, 309, 309–310, 318, 321–323, 342–346, 354, 356–357, 359, 369, 371, 380, 410, 415, 425, 426, 427, 428, 429; *see also* accomplishment; achievement; activity; semelfactive
aspect, situation and preverbs, 262–268, 321–323
aspect, situation and subsituation, 260–262
aspect, situation and viewpoint, 281–283
aspect, situation, and external adverb/postposition, 268–270
aspect, situation, and theme number, 271–272, 344–346
aspect, situation, compound, 309, 312–314, 320, 359
aspect, subsituation, 17, 75, 177, 246, 260–262, 281–283, 290, 310, 321, 371, 380, 410–411, 426, 429; *see also* conative; egressive; inceptive; seriative
aspect, subsituation, ordering, 333–338, 339–341
aspect, viewpoint, 16, 17, 75, 177, 178, 246–251, 256, 281–283, 284–285, 304, 306, 308, 310, 315, 410; *see also* imperfective; optative; perfective

bisective, 300–301, 306

449

Subject Index

causal chain, 347
causative, 16, 22, 128–142, 158–164, 370, 418, 420, 421
causative, position, 140–142
classificatory verb, 110–111, 426–427
collective, 379, 416
conative, 260–262, 290, 308, 324, 334, 370, 425, 429
conjugation markers, 177, 246, 256, 267, 272, 428
conjunct prefixes, 34, 74, 79, 176
conjunction, 189–191, 208–210, 320, 421
consecutive, 299, 300, 306
continuative, 287, 300, 305, 307
customary, 16, 61–62, 114–115, 156, 290, 291–293, 300, 417

dependencies, discontinuous, 9, 11–12, 15, 16, 27
dependencies, local, 2, 11
derivation, 1, 2, 15–16, 18, 74, 75, 295–302, 391–392
dimensionality, 278–279
direct discourse, 22
disjunct prefixes, 34, 73, 74, 79, 420
distributive, 16, 42–60, 61, 68, 81, 101–102, 119–120, 122, 155, 172, 290, 293–294, 300, 307, 370, 376, 392, 417, 420
diversative, 307–308

egressive, 260–262, 290, 324
entity, 34–35, 41–42, 50–60, 68–71, 109–111, 116–117, 118
errative, 16, 154–155, 156, 338, 421
event, 34–35, 41–42, 51–60, 61–68, 71, 92, 107–109, 116, 117–118, 251, 253–276, 279–280, 284–290
event structure, 35, 127

functional items, 26–27, 74, 75, 79, 175–178, 388, 410–411, 416
functor predicate, 126, 140–142, 169, 171
future, 22, 249–250, 300, 312–314, 317, 348, 412, 413, 427
future semelfactive, 312–314

gender, 16, 324–329
global uniformity, 4, 19, 20–21, 24, 80–81, 239, 359, 360, 372, 374, 397

headedness, 25, 84

idiom, lexical, 27, 77, 393–394
idiom, syntactic, 213–214
imperfective, 75, 178, 247, 248, 251, 272–276, 280–281, 300, 315–316
inceptive, 6, 72–73, 81, 91–92, 121, 122–124, 260–262, 280, 290, 292, 324, 334–338, 339–340, 376–377, 427, 429
inchoative, 260, 280, 324, 334, 418, 419
incorporate, 16, 17, 22, 33, 34, 68–71, 75, 80–81, 106, 107–120, 124, 147–148, 156, 214–215, 410, 417, 420
incorporate, body part, 147–148, 156
inflection, 1, 2, 15–16, 18, 74–75, 241–242, 391–392, 421
inflection vs. derivation, 241–242, 295–302, 391–392, 427
information structure (topic, focus), 217–220
iterative, 16, 61–68, 76–77, 81, 101–106, 112–119, 152–154, 156, 172, 306, 370, 377, 392, 417, 418, 419, 420

language change, 374–382, 396–397
lexical entry, 16, 17, 27, 42, 75, 105, 127, 168–169, 176, 253, 369–372, 380–381, 387–391, 430
lexical items, 26–27, 33–73, 74–78, 79–125, 171–172, 387–388, 409–410
lexical phonology, 17
lexicon, 23, 369–372, 373–383, 387–398
local variability, 4, 19, 20–21, 24, 80–81, 359, 397
locality, 2, 11
location, 45, 50–60, 70–71

mediopassive, 148–149
metathesis, 12–14, 16, 233–235, 314, 335, 345–357, 359
middle voice, 142–157, 158–164, 324, 329–330, 340, 355–356, 370, 372, 426
middle voice, position, 157

Subject Index

middle, spontaneous, 149
Mirror Principle, 24
modification, 83–84
momentaneous, 289–290
morpheme, zero, 11
morphology, layered, 10, 11, 19
morphophonemics, 21–22, 129, 143, 176, 419
multiple, 60–61, 299, 417

negative, 16, 22, 72, 121–122, 123–124, 141, 178, 303, 311, 313, 314–319, 324, 340–341, 413, 428
negative, ordering idiosyncrasies, 316–319
noun, 296–297, 361–362, 415
noun class marker, 177, 324–329, 338–339, 353–354, 369
noun class marker, ordering, 338–339
numerositive, 416–417

object, 16, 17, 22, 176, 203, 210, 342–346, 353–354, 355, 377, 423
object, lexicalized, 15
opacity, 380–381
optative, 22, 178, 249–251, 272–276, 280, 300, 311, 317, 370, 413
Optimality Theory, 17–18
ordering principles, 25, 82–92, 96–97, 100, 171–172, 191–194, 210, 220, 222–224, 226, 232, 244–245, 246, 282–283, 348–350, 360–365, 409–411, 412
ordering, between aspect and objects, 342–346
ordering, between aspect and subjects, 346–350
ordering, between preverbs and incorporates, 107–111
ordering, between preverbs and quantifiers, 76–77, 107
ordering, between qualifiers and aspect, 354, 356–358
ordering, between qualifiers and objects, 353–354, 355, 356
ordering, between qualifiers and subjects, 350–353, 355–356
ordering, between quantifiers and incorporates, 111–120
ordering, between subjects and objects, 222–244, 281–283, 310–320, 330–338, 339–341, 359
ordering, pronoun subject and object ordering, 222–244, 349–350
ordering, within aspect, 281–283, 310–320, 330–338, 339–341, 359
ordering, within incorporates, 106
ordering, within preverbs, 84–101, 120–124
ordering, within qualifiers, 332–341
ordering, within quantifiers, 101–105
ordering, within subjects, 192–194
ordering, within voice/valence, 157–164

passive, 16, 150–151, 156, 423
perambulative, 155, 156, 300, 304, 374
perfective, 75, 178, 247–248, 256–260, 272–276, 280, 284, 288, 300, 315, 316, 426
persistive, 305
phonology, 1, 10, 13, 16, 17, 18, 21, 24, 34, 159, 176, 317, 318, 361–364, 412, 420, 426, 427
postposition, 35, 38–41, 268–270, 415
preverb, 16, 33, 34, 35–41, 73, 75–77, 80–81, 84–101, 107–111, 122–123, 124, 253, 262–268, 280, 286, 287, 322–323, 369, 376, 390–391, 409–410, 416, 417, 419, 420, 426
preverb, lexicalized, 390–391
progressive, 290–292, 299
prolongative (Navajo), 155, 338
pronominal argument language, 180, 241–242, 416
pronominal system, 176, 180–245, 371, 413, 424
pronoun, first person plural, 151–152, 156, 198–202, 413, 421, 422, 423
pronoun, human plural, 188–189, 194–195, 197–198, 224–230, 371, 424
pronoun, object, 203–210, 342–346, 353–354, 377
pronoun, object number, 271–272, 344–346

pronoun, object ordering, 209–210
pronoun, object, comparison between persons, 203–209
pronoun, ordering problems, 224–244; *see also*: metathesis; pronoun, object ordering; pronoun, three plural acting on three singular; pronoun, unspecified subject
pronoun, subject, 180–203, 216–220, 230–233, 354
pronoun, subject, comparison between persons, 181–186, 189–191, 194–195
pronoun, subject, first and second person, 181–186, 189–193, 346–348, 410
pronoun, subject, third person, 177, 181–193, 194–198, 348–353, 369, 379, 410
pronoun, subject, third person, semantics of, 186–189
pronoun, three plural subject acting on three singular object, 224–230
pronoun, unspecified human subject, 187–188, 196–197, 413, 421, 422, 423

qualia, 35, 42, 127
qualifier, 15, 17, 176, 177, 324–341, 350–353, 356–358, 369, 378, 390, 411, 421, 428
qualifier, lexicalized, 330, 350–352, 356–358, 390
qualifier, ordering, 332–341
quantifier, 33, 34, 41–68, 73, 75, 76–77, 80–81, 101–105, 107, 112–120, 124, 253, 262–263, 292, 306, 392, 409–410, 413, 417, 420; *see also* collective; distributive; iterative; multiple
quantifier, A-, 41–42, 61–68; *see also* iterative
quantifier, D-, 41–42, 42–61; *see also* distributive, multiple
question, wh, 243–244

reciprocal, 145–147, 156, 204–205
reflexive, 144, 145, 146, 156, 204–205
relations, aspectual, 42, 127, 131, 133, 137, 138, 155, 169
relations, thematic, 35, 42, 94, 101, 127

relative clause, 22
relevance, 24, 175, 282–283, 347
repetitive, 155–156, 286, 292, 300, 307, 374
reversative, 64, 67–68, 305, 420
reversionary, 102–106, 370, 377
root, 15, 16, 17, 179, 296–297, 426

scope hypothesis, 4, 5, 18, 20–21, 24, 23–26, 76–78, 79–125, 164, 170, 171–172, 175, 191–193, 210, 232, 233, 235, 244–245, 283, 312, 314, 319, 321, 341, 342, 349–365, 369–372, 373–375, 378–379, 380, 381, 382, 383, 387, 394–395, 397, 409–411, 420, 430
self-benefactive, 147, 156
semantic compositionality, 76–77
semelfactive, 177, 252, 255–256, 257, 259–260, 261–262, 263–264, 266, 271–272, 272–276, 280, 284, 285, 286, 287–289, 293–294, 299, 305, 306, 307, 312–314, 315, 318–319, 347, 413, 426, 427, 428
semeliterative, 102–106, 377
semipassive, 220–222, 355–356
seriative, 290, 334–338, 380, 428, 429
state, 22, 131, 251, 252, 276–281
state, descriptive, 276, 277–278, 280
state, extension, 276, 277, 278–279
state, locational, 276–277, 278–279
stem, verb, 33, 74–78, 169–170, 171, 179, 283–303, 387–388, 414
subject, clausal position, 2, 16, 17, 75, 210–220, 222, 415
suffix, 16, 17, 27, 179, 278, 283–303, 427
suffix, category determining, 296–298
suffix, fusion, 298–299
suffix, inflection versus derivation, 295–303
suffix, obligatoriness, 299–301
suffix, position, 295–303

template hypothesis, 1–3, 9–19, 20, 23, 26, 33, 79–80, 93–94, 100–101, 104, 105, 106, 109, 113, 125, 164, 170, 172,

233, 235, 245, 283, 318, 321,
341, 352, 358, 373–375, 378–379,
380, 381, 382, 383, 395–396, 401–405,
427
tense, 247, 249, 348–349, 411, 429,
430
thematic hierarchy, 96–97, 411
totalative, 61
transitional, 280, 308, 311–313

underspecification, 27, 127, 313–314,
370–372, 388–389

verb base, 15–16

verb class marker, 324, 330–331, 340,
352
verb raising, 78, 169–170, 171
voice/valence, 15, 16, 17, 33, 74,
126–170, 171, 177, 178, 420
voice/valence, idiosyncratic, 164–167,
390

word formation, 15–19, 26, 75–76,
389–391, 393–394
word formation, syntactic, 4–5, 18, 22,
26–28, 124, 140–142, 156–157,
393–394
word order, 215, 242–243